## Acclaim/Endorsements

Dr. Brij Bhushan Goel, eminent naturopath and yoga exponent, is one such person who has done pioneering work in the field of nature cure. I am sure that this book will be of immense value to society and wish him all the best in his noble endeavour.

**S. B. Mathur**
*Chairman*
Life Insurance Corporation of India

By virtue of the topics conveyed in, this book can easily be termed as a guide to balanced living.
I recommend this book to all those who really believe that "Health is the most precious wealth".

**Rajiv Kumar Raizada**
*President*
Shriram Group of Companies (Madras)

A great comprehensive book. In todays world of sadeltary life style if we follow even part of what is mentioned, I am sure our fitness will improve drestically.

**Gaurav Aggarwal**
Tata Consultancy Services

*Secrets of Naturopathy and Yoga* written by Dr. Brij Bhushan Goel is very useful for every family. Therefore we have distributed this book in large number as a gift on various occasions.

**Subhash Aggarwal**
*M.D. Action Group*

Dr. Brij Bhushan has brought out this valuable book with his untiring efforts and rich experience in the field for the benefit of people in general, particularly students, youth, naturopaths and others interested in the subject.

**Dr. N.S. Adhikari**
*General Secretary*
International Foundation of Natural Health & Yoga
New Delhi

It is a universal fact that by abiding to rule of nature we can be far more healthy. This book has laid stress on the same. It can prove useful in getting rid of medicines by adopting natural way of life.

*Nav Bharat Times*

Any one can go through this book attentively, to be able to treat oneself and ones family against disease successfully. I wish this book should reach every family.

**Teerath Ram**
*Chairman*
Gandhi Smarak Prakritic Chikitsa Samiti

*Secrets of Naturopathy and Yoga* is a wonderful book which is written with such simplicity that everyone can understand and benefit from it. If even one person in a family reads this book, I am sure they will have a better tomorrow.

**Krishan Lal Bansal**
*President*
Maharaja Agrasen Hospital Charitable Trust (Regd.)

Full information regarding being free from diseases and treatment of diseases is provided herein in a very simple way but based on scientific facts.

**Santosh Aggarwal**
*Hyderabad*

This book is a wonderful exposition of the multi-facets of naturopathy.

**Rupa Srikumar**
*Naturopath*

*Secrets of Naturopathy and Yoga* by Dr. Brij Bhushan Goel is comprehensive and complete book in itself which not only takes care of physical and mental well being of mankind but also spiritually elates the human being.
Even being a professional in allopathic system of medicine I congratulate Dr. Goel for this dedicated and sincere effort in the form of this book. I am sure this book will alleviate the sufferings of mankind by adopting natural means.

**Dr. Mahesh Sharma**
*Chairman & Managing Director*
Kailash Hospital & Research Centre Ltd.

This book *Secrets of Naturopathy and Yoga* is a complete guide to physical, mental and spiritual happiness. By reading this book one can become his own doctor. This will also prove beneficial for people related to this field.

*Meri Dilli*

By means of this book Dr. Goel has brought out a good plan for the life of the whole humanity. I firmly believe, that if we adopt natural way of life, not only will we lead disease free lives but will also be physically and mentally meaningful and balanced. I fully believe that this book will be widely welcome.

**Dr. Pritam Gupta**
*Cardiologist*

In today's unnatural life knowledge of Natural health and Yoga has become the most important requirement of people. Experienced author Dr. Brij Bhushan Goel has written a book for this purpose with great effort and research. This book has all details written in a beautiful way.

*Hindustan*

Dr. B.B. Goel's book sheds new light on how to view and improve health. "Health is more than absence of disease". The ultimate responsibility of each one of us is to become responsible for our own health.

**Vijay Batra**
*(Think Inc.)*

"Self dependence in matters of health" has been a motto of naturopathy movement. In the present book Dr. Goel has tried to incorporate all these dictums. that is why this book is different from other books and better than them. I appreciate Dr. Goel and hope that this book will be liked by people in general and also intellectuals.

**Dr. S.N. Pandeya**
*Asst. Research Officer (Naturopathy)*
Central Council for Research in Yoga & Naturopathy
Government of India, New Delhi

This book will prove to be extremely useful for every man. The information regarding living disease free is given in beautiful words in this book.

*Akhil Bhartiya Prakartik Chikitsa Parishad*

The value and benefit that will accrue by a study of this book is indeed considerable and great. This book must come as an eye opener to numerous person.

**Vinod Aggarwal**
*Kolkata*

I have a firm conviction that general public, students and fellow practitioners of nature cure will reap its profits alike. Every family should have a copy of it.

**Dr. K.C. Bhardwaj**
*Registrar and Controller of Examination*
M.D. University, Rohtak.

It is a wonderfully inspiring work which only a simple, gentle and noble person like Dr. Goel could have gifted to the common man, disclosing to him his close affinity with nature the gifts of nature and their utilization for the benefit of mankind.

**Prof. R.K. Bansal**
*Registrar, Vaish College of Engg., Rohtak*

A book that shows that the best medicine exist within our body.

**Narendra Kumar Sharma**
Deen Dayal Upadahya College

*Secrets of Naturopathy and Yoga* is a comprehensive book including Nature Cure, Yoga, Anatomy, Causes, Symptoms and Cure of more than 150 diseases. Its main attraction is the simple language which enables all to understand it.

*Sujeewan, Magazine*

The book *Secrets of Naturopathy and Yoga* will work as a Sanjivani Booti (Herb) in this modern ailing society. Dr. B.B. Goel is absolutely practical who has practised his teaching on himself and his spouse.

We therefore have no doubt that the present publication will have a warm reception and wide circulation.

**Dr. S.R. Goel** *(Eye Surgeon)*
**Dr. (Mrs.) Kaushal Goel** *(Gynaecologist)*

*Secrets of Naturopathy and Yoga* is a result of 17 years of experience in the field of Naturopathy. The book has all aspects related to health. It is useful for patients, doctors and students equally.

*Vaidya Raaj, Magazine*

It is a blessing for the mankind wreathing in the agony of disease and expensive medication with after effects. I hope that people in general read this book widely and benefit from it.

**S.L. Bansal** *(I.A.S.)*
Sr. Commissioner, Delhi

*Secrets of Naturopathy and Yoga* is a very useful book and has become indispensable to me. I am sure those reading this will also feel the same.

**Lalita Goenka**
*Bangalore*

*Secrets of Naturopathy and Yoga* provides various natural solutions including Yoga which give knowledge regarding the beautiful art of living and also simple treatment of various diseases.

**Subhash Mishra**
*President - LIAFI*

*Secrets of Naturopathy and Yoga* not only protect us against the diseases but also saves us from the modern day medicines and their side effects.

This book broadly renders this advice to all people in a simple language through which even a common man without any technical background can understand.

**S.S. Gupta**
*Chief Manager (Law)*
Syndicate Bank (Mumbai)

*Secrets of Naturopathy and Yoga* is an excellent exposition on leading one's life in a perfectly healthy and simple manner.

This book must be read by every one to be able to lead a healthy life.

**Prof. K.K. Aggarwal**
*Vice Chancellor*
G.G. Indraprastha University, Delhi

'Health is Wealth'. People who live by this notion must definitely read this book as it has all the means to stay healthy and lead a tension free life. English edition will be more useful.

**Dr. P.N. Gupta** *(Phys.)*
**Dr. (Mrs.) Shashi Gupta** *(Gynae.)*

By bringing out this book the society has been served in an unforgettable manner. We hope that each family will benefit fully and improve general health to contribute in making the humanity happy and prosperous.

**Dr. Neelam Sharma**
*Gen. Secretary (AINCF)*

# Secrets of
# NATUROPATHY & YOGA

Dr. Brij Bhushan Goel

D.Ph., NDDY, PGDHHC, Ph.D.

ALL INDIA NATURE CURE FEDERATION
BM-7 (WEST) SHALIMAR BAGH, DELHI-110 088
Phone (Office) : 8826574242 - 27482211 - 27481710
Fax : 27477576 • E-mail : bbgoel@lifehappy.org
Mobile : 9810019273 • Website : www.lifehappy.org

STERLING

**STERLING PAPERBACKS**
An imprint of
Sterling Publishers (P) Ltd.
Regd. Office: A1/256 Safdarjung Enclave,
New Delhi-110029. CIN: U22110DL1964PTC211907
Tel: 26387070, 26386209; Fax: 91-11-26383788
E-mail: mail@sterlingpublishers.com
www.sterlingpublishers.com

*Secrets of Naturopathy and Yoga*
Copyright © 2017 by Brij Bhushan Goel
ISBN 978 81 207 7997 6
First Edition 2004
Fifth Reprint 2012
Sixth Revised Edition 2013
Reprint 2015, 2017

All rights are reserved.
No part of this publication may be reproduced, stored in a retrieval system or transmitted, in any form or by any means, mechanical, photocopying, recording or otherwise, without prior written permission of the original publisher.

Printed in India

*Printed and Published by* Sterling Publishers Pvt. Ltd., Plot No. 13, Ecotech-III, Greater Noida - 201306, Uttar Pradesh, India

# Foreword

I have been in contact with Dr. Brij Bhushan Goel for the past two decades. He has understood the importance of naturopathy and yoga and with commitment and faith has practiced it procedurally and regularly, meditated over it which is a commendable step. Thereafter he did not make it a profession but used it for increasing awareness about health among common men.

He is publishing a magazine titled "Happy Life" for free distribution among people. He is an active and humble social worker. He is also secretary of Internatioal Foundation of Natural Health & Yoga and remained executive member of Gandhi Smarak Prakritik Chikitsa Samiti. For the past seventeen years, from time to time many national and international camps, assemblies and seminars were organised for wide propagation and circulation. Thousands of people not only benefited from these camps and seminars but also treated their family members when the need arose. His mission of welfare of the people is still on, and he is well determined to carry it on in future. With this motive only he has opened a *Natural health and yoga* centre right opposite his residence for imparting this creative knowledge to students.

It was increasingly desired that various queries of people should find an answer in one book. Consequently, all the needs of natural health and yoga had to be compiled at one place in a book, and he decided to publish this auspicious work. On that basis only, this saga has been brought out for the readers.

Honourable author has given special importance to virtuous food, proper diet and living. No matter how many new medicines be invented by today's science but as long as due priority will not be given to virtuous food, proper diet and living in human life, newly diseases will keep occuring. Now human society is badly affected by diseases like cancer, aids, etc. If he will not make changes in his diet and mode of living during the due course of time, he should be ready to face its ill effects.

I am impressed that Dr. Brij Bhushan Goel and his wife Usha Bhushan Goel have adopted appropriate natural food (uncooked) for years now and the capacity to work in both of them is enormous. They are physically, mentally and financially healthy, prosperous and content. This is the reason why their speech and writings impress the listener so much.

There are many who profess to others. There are'nt many who practice it themselves.

In the end, I will only request that for happy and healthy life permanently, reading this sacred book is a must and on auspicious occasions gift it to your relatives and friends.

**Dr. Jagdish Chandra Jauhar**
*Specialist in Naturopathy, Yoga, Ayurveda & Herbal Science*
*Ex-Editor Swasth Jeevan (Monthly magazine)*
*Ex- Secreatary Gandhi Smarak Prakritic Chikitsa Samiti*
*Ex- Examination secretary Gandhi National Academy of Natropathy*

# Preface

I have been a student of medical science and I very well understand that it is not possible to cure diseases with medicines. They can only suppress the immediate symptoms and provide instant temporary relief. But suppression of disease leads to accumulation of toxins manifesting in copping up of other diseases, and then again medicine and its reaction, leading to ever new diseases, is a never ending chain for the whole of the life.

The health level of humans is falling day by day due to this. After viewing this situation, the urge to save the humanity from this calamity was strong within me.

With this thought in my mind in the year 1986, I started taking regular training from Dr. Hiralal and got my diploma from International Foundation of Natural Health and Yoga. I got knowledge of treating, acute and chronic diseases without medicines, successfully by naturopathy and yoga. It provided encouragement and belief that this is the only means available for the art of living healthy and raising the falling level of human health.

I decided to adopt uncooked food. My wife Usha Bhushan Goel cooperated with me in this auspicious work with equal zeal. This gave double boost to my resolve.

With great self confidence, I organised within the country and abroad naturopathy and yoga camps, assemblies, seminars along with other social service, giving priority to naturopathy and yoga resolutely. People asked inquisitively many questions on various subjects during these camps, assemblies and seminars. Keeping in mind the increasing inquisitiveness of people I felt the need of a self contained book satisfying these queries to be published.

Thus this book has been brought out and I am extremely happy to present it for the benefit of the mankind. This book will be useful for every family and also specially for students, youngsters, naturopaths and all researchers.

I am fully content to see men and women, young students who attended the camps, assemblies and seminars and learnt art of healthy living and adopted it as their lifestyle, benefit fully from these events.

My sole mission is to educate people and enable them to be their own doctor in order to help them lead a simple, peaceful and healthy life.

I am grateful to Professor R.K.Bansal (Registrar, Vaish College of Engineering, Rohtak), Yogacharya Shri Anil Sharma, Shri Parmod Batra / Shri Vijay Batra (Think Inc.) and my other companion for their inspiration, guidance and co-operation towards this book.

I would be greatful to them who would read this book and forward their suggestions.

**Dr. Brij Bhushan Goel**

# Contents

*Foreword* ................................................................. ix
*Preface* .................................................................. xi

## Part-I
## NATURAL HEALTH

| | |
|---|---|
| **Perfect health** | 2 |
| Indicators of perfect health | 2 |
| Indicators of unhealthy body | 2 |
| Cause of diseases | 3 |
| Cure of all diseases | 4 |
| Naturopathy | 5 |
| Healing crisis | 5 |
| Mud therapy | 6 |
| Hydro therapy | 8 |
| Chromotherapy | 18 |
| Air therapy | 23 |
| Space therapy | 25 |
| Food | 28 |
| Important rules for food | 29 |
| Balanced diet | 31 |
| Balance of alkaline and acidic food | 43 |
| Food combination | 43 |
| Precautions in preparing food | 45 |
| Sprouted food | 46 |
| Uncooked food | 48 |
| Milk | 52 |
| Juices | 55 |
| Wheat grass juice | 56 |
| Less food for better health | 58 |

| | |
|---|---|
| Taste is not in food but in appetite | 59 |
| White sugar a sweet poison | 60 |
| Salt is also poison | 60 |
| Food products causing diseases | 61 |
| Effects of non-vegetarian food | 62 |
| Food of special quality | 62 |
| Indications of pure honey | 68 |
| Intoxicating products—enemy of health | 68 |
| For healthy life what to leave and what to adopt | 71 |
| Sound sleep | 72 |
| Power of silence | 74 |
| Anger—a dangerous disease | 75 |
| Mental tension | 76 |
| Positive thinking | 81 |
| Creative thinking | 84 |
| Memory power | 85 |
| Power of desire and aim | 86 |
| Character formation | 87 |
| Laughing for health | 87 |
| For attractive beauty | 88 |
| Motherhood and child care | 91 |
| Questionnaire on child problems | 98 |

## Part-II
## YOGA—THE SCIENCE OF HAND POSTURES AND ACUPRESSURE

| | |
|---|---|
| **Yoga** | **106** |
| (1) Yama (behaviour) | 106 |
| (2) Niyama (regulations) | 107 |
| (3) Asana (postures) | 107 |
| *Yogic Exercises* | |
|   1. Yogic exercise for improving mind power | 114 |
|   2. Yogic exercise for improving the eyesight | 115 |
|   3. Cheeks power promoting exercise | 115 |
|   4. Yogic exercises for improving the hearing | 116 |
|   5. Yogic exercises for strengthening the neck | 116 |

| | |
|---|---|
| 6. Yogic exercises for strengthening the shoulders | 117 |
| 7. Chest power promoting exercise | 118 |
| 8. Yogic exercises for improving the mooladhar chakra and swadhisthan chakra power | 118 |
| 9. Yogic exercises for awakening the kundalini power | 118 |
| 10. Engine runnning (gallop/assault) | 119 |

*Various Asanas*

| | |
|---|---|
| 1. Ardhamatsyendrasana | 119 |
| 2. Ashvasthasana | 120 |
| 3. Bhoonmanasana | 121 |
| 4. Chakrasana | 121 |
| 5. Dhanurasana | 122 |
| 6. Garbhasana | 123 |
| 7. Garudasana | 123 |
| 8. Gomukhasana | 124 |
| 9. Gorakshasana | 124 |
| 10. Halasana (Sarvangasana) | 125 |
| 11. Janushirshasana | 126 |
| 12. Kaagasana | 126 |
| 13. Kati-Chakrasana | 127 |
| 14. Konasana | 127 |
| 15. Koormasana | 128 |
| 16. Kukkutasana | 128 |
| 17. Kursi-Asana | 129 |
| 18. Makarasana | 129 |
| 19. Mandookasana | 130 |
| 20. Matsyasana | 130 |
| 21. Mayurasana | 131 |
| 22. Naukasana | 132 |
| 23. Padangushthasana | 132 |
| 24. Pad-Hastasana | 133 |
| 25. Padmasana | 133 |
| 26. Paschimottanasana | 133 |
| 27. Sarpasana (Bhujangasana) | 134 |
| 28. Shalabhasana | 134 |

| | |
|---|---|
| 29. Shavasana | 135 |
| 30. Shirshasana | 136 |
| 31. Siddhasana | 137 |
| 32. Simhasana | 137 |
| 33. Supt-Pavanmuktasana | 137 |
| 34. Supt-Vajrasana | 138 |
| 35. Swastikasana | 139 |
| 36. Tadasana | 139 |
| 37. Tribandhasana | 139 |
| 38. Udrakarshasana | 140 |
| 39. Urdhvahastottanasana | 140 |
| 40. Urdhvasarvangasana | 141 |
| 41. Utkatasana | 142 |
| 42. Uttaan-Koormasana | 142 |
| 43. Uttan-Mandookasana | 143 |
| 44. Uttanpadasana | 143 |
| 45. Vajrasana | 144 |
| 46. Yogmudrasana | 144 |
| Surya namaskar | 145 |
| Pranayama | 148 |
| Nadi | 149 |
| Bandh (Mool bandh, Ashwini kriya, Uddiyan bandh, Agnisaar kriya, Jalandhar bandh) | 149 |
| Shat chakra | 151 |
| Kundalini | 151 |
| Regulations for pranayama | 152 |
| Kapalbhati pranayama | 152 |
| Nadi shodhan or (Anulom-Vilom) pranayama | 153 |
| Surya-bhedi pranayama | 154 |
| Ujjayi pranayama | 154 |
| Sitkari pranayama | 155 |
| Shitali pranayama | 156 |
| Bhastrika pranayama | 156 |
| Bhramari pranayama | 157 |
| Moorchha pranayama | 158 |

| | |
|---|---|
| Kevali pranayama | 158 |
| Mudra | 158 |
| Mahamudra | 159 |
| Mahabandh | 160 |
| Mahavedh | 160 |
| Khechari | 161 |
| Viparitkarni | 162 |
| Pratyahar (control of sense organs) | 162 |
| Dhaarna (concentration) | 163 |
| Dhyan (meditation) | 163 |
| Samadhi (communion) | 167 |
| Yog nidra | 168 |
| Navel centre (solar plexus) | 168 |
| Massage | 172 |
| Hand postures | 174 |
| Acupressure | 178 |

# Part-III
# ANATOMY AND PHYSIOLOGY

| | |
|---|---|
| **Anatomy and physiology** | **190** |
| (1) Digestive system | 191 |
| (2) Blood circulatory system | 197 |
| (3) Lymphatic system | 204 |
| (4) Respiratory system | 206 |
| (5) Skeletal system | 207 |
| (6) Muscular system | 214 |
| (7) Nervous system | 216 |
| (8) Urinary system | 226 |
| (9) Reproductive or genital system | 228 |
| Sense organs | 234 |
| Endocrine glands (ductless glands) | 242 |
| Metabolism | 249 |

## Part - IV
## NATURAL TREATMENT OF VARIOUS DISEASES

| | |
|---|---|
| **Natural treatment of various diseases** | **252** |
| Acidity | 253 |
| Aids | 254 |
| Allergy | 255 |
| Anaemia | 256 |
| Appendicitis | 257 |
| Arthritis/gout | 258 |
| Asthma | 260 |
| Poor eyesight | 261 |
| Backache | 264 |
| Cancer | 264 |
| Cataract | 267 |
| Cervical spondylosis | 269 |
| Chicken pox | 269 |
| Cholera | 270 |
| Cold | 271 |
| Colitis | 272 |
| Conjunctivitis | 272 |
| Constipation | 273 |
| Cough | 274 |
| Dandruff | 275 |
| Dengue | 276 |
| Dental disease | 278 |
| Depression | 280 |
| Diabetes | 281 |
| Diarrhoea | 283 |
| Dysentery | 284 |
| Ear diseases | 285 |
| Eczema | 286 |
| Epilepsy | 287 |
| Epistaxis | 289 |
| Fever | 289 |
| Fissure/fistula | 292 |

*Contents* xix

| | |
|---|---|
| Gas trouble | 292 |
| Glaucoma | 293 |
| Miscarriage | 294 |
| Hair fall | 295 |
| Greying of hair | 296 |
| Magical hair oils | 297 |
| Halitosis (foul breath) | 298 |
| Heart diseases | 299 |
| Hernia | 304 |
| High blood cholesterol | 306 |
| High blood pressure | 308 |
| Hydrocele | 309 |
| Hysteria | 310 |
| Impotency | 311 |
| Indigestion/dyspepsia | 313 |
| Inflammation of nerves (neuritis) | 314 |
| Insomnia | 314 |
| Intestinal worms | 315 |
| Jaundice | 318 |
| Kidney diseases | 318 |
| Leucoderma | 320 |
| Leucorrhoea | 321 |
| Liver diseases | 323 |
| Low blood pressure (hypotension) | 324 |
| Low blood sugar (hypoglycaemia) | 325 |
| Measles | 325 |
| Weak memory | 326 |
| Meningitis | 327 |
| Menopause | 328 |
| Menstrual disorder | 329 |
| Migraine (hemicrania) | 332 |
| Mucus | 333 |
| Multiple sclerosis | 333 |
| Mumps | 334 |
| Muscle cramps | 335 |
| Nervous weakness (neurasthenia) | 335 |
| Obesity | 337 |

| | |
|---|---|
| Oedema (dropsy) | 338 |
| Osteoporosis | 338 |
| Paralysis | 339 |
| Parkinson's disease | 342 |
| Piles | 343 |
| Pimples (acne) | 344 |
| Pleurisy | 346 |
| Prostate disorder | 347 |
| Psoriasis | 348 |
| Pyorrhoea | 350 |
| Rickets | 350 |
| Scurvy | 351 |
| Sciatica | 351 |
| Sinusitis | 352 |
| Skin diseases | 353 |
| Stammering and lisping | 354 |
| Sterility | 355 |
| Stone | 357 |
| Thalassemia | 359 |
| Thinness | 360 |
| Throat diseases | 361 |
| Thyroid diseases | 362 |
| Tonsillitis | 364 |
| Tuberculosis | 365 |
| Ulcer | 366 |
| Urinary tract infection | 367 |
| Uterus diseases | 368 |
| Varicose veins | 369 |
| Venereal diseases | 370 |
| Vomiting | 371 |
| Child diseases | 372 |
| Miscellaneous diseases | 375 |
| Nature cure in sudden accidents | 377 |
| *Ramanama and natural treatment* | 386 |

# Part-I
# NATURAL HEALTH

# Perfect health

Perfect health is to be healthy physically, mentally and spiritually.

## Indicators of perfect health
1. Sound sleep.
2. The body feels energetic and enthusiastic on waking up in the morning.
3. Stool is solid, clean and regular.
4. There is natural appetite.
5. You work actively the whole day.
6. The belly does not protrude as compared to the chest.
7. You do not desire intoxicating products that cause excitement.
8. Your mind feels relaxed and heart is full of heavenly bliss.
9. You have the capacity to work for hours without getting tired.
10. You always remain involved in some creative activity.
11. You talk sweetly.
12. Your face glows.
13. Your eyes are bright and fearless.
14. There is a smile on your face under all circumstances.
15. You feel young and vigorous.
16. You think positively.

## Indicators of unhealthy body
1. Any abnormality in physical activity.
2. Lack of sound sleep.
3. Stool is loose or hard.

# Natural Health

4. Loss of appetite.
5. Desire to eat spicy food.
6. Body odour.
7. Belly protrudes out as compared to the chest.
8. Feeling of discomfort or heaviness after meals.
9. Baldness
10. You have negative thoughts
11. You have interest in destructive things
12. Anger
13. Irritability
14. Lethargic body
15. You are unable to concentrate on anything
16. You get tired fast
17. Addiction to intoxicating products
18. Swelling above the eyebrows, on the eyelids, between eyebrows and eyelids and under the eyes.
19. Spots on the face
20. Headache

## Cause of diseases

All diseases are solely caused by the accumulation of toxins in the body. Although nature keeps extracting toxins out of the body, they get collected when detoxification is less than accumulation.

When toxins increase, various parts of the body become non-functional and germs flourish, but nature takes them out in the form of acute diseases like fever, loose motion, vomiting, cold, cough, etc. When this process is suppressed by medicines, then the disease becomes chronic.

### *Reasons for accumulation of toxins*

1. Lack of balanced diet.
2. Imbalance of alkali and acid in our food.
3. Consumption of unmatchable and contradictory food items.
4. Spicy, heavy and fibreless food.

5. Overeating
6. Consumption of intoxicating food
7. Eating food late in the night.
8. Imbalance of body's five elements (space, air, sunshine, water and mud)
9. Working beyond one's physical or mental capacity and not taking adequate rest.
10. Fear, anxiety, anger and stress.
11. The process of extracting toxins is suppressed by medicines.
12. Suppressing the natural urges of body like defecation, urination, flatus, vomiting, sneezing, belching, yawning, hunger, thirst, tears, sleep, rest, etc.
13. Pollution
14. Remaining seated continuously.

## Cure of all diseases

There is one cure for all diseases and that is detoxification of the body by natural means. There is an unseen force which we call the life force which keeps our body healthy. For all diseases there is one cure, and that is detoxification of body by natural means. To keep our body healthy, there is an unseen force which we call the life force. In spiritualism it is defined as pranic energy and allopathy calls it the resistance power. Elimination of diseases and protection against diseases is due to this inherent force alone. The stronger this healing power within, the sooner the disease will be cured.

Naturopathy enhances this pranic force and hampers accumulation of toxins.

As soon as any sign of illness like headache, loss of appetite, etc. appears, immediately give up eating and clean the body by taking enema, etc.

By doing so the chance of the disease becoming acute will be eliminated. If there is an acute disease (fever, loose motions, vomiting, cold, etc.) treat it as a natural cleansing process and do not suppress it with medicines.

In such a case, one should go for fasting and let the body be detoxified through natural means of cleansing. By doing so, the disease will not become chronic.

If the disease is chronic, it should be treated with various natural means of treatment. Natural means of treatment are:
1. Natural food and related precautions.
2. Five elements (space, air, fire, water and mud) which constitute human beings and other things in this world.
3. Right way of living
4. Removing mental disorder
5. Various yogic exercises

## Naturopathy

Detoxification and enhancing pranic force in the body is called naturopathy. Naturopathy and yoga are two wheels of a cart. Apart from natural health and yoga, there is no medical treatment which can provide complete health. Knowledge of naturopathy makes everyone self-dependent for one's own health.

Naturopathy is not just a treatment but also a way of life. When all treatments fail, there is still a possibility of cure in naturopathy.

Naturopathy is natural, easy and omnipresent. Whoever takes its refuge will find it truly useful as it eradicates the ailment from its root and provides speedy recovery. The mind also feels peaceful and full of vigour.

Naturopathy cures all dormant diseases. There is no need for medication or surgery. Patients, after experiencing relief through its treatment, can get back to their own work. The fear of disease is rooted out of the mind.

Naturopathy works in two ways. First, it makes the patient get rid of his ailment speedily, secondly, it educates him to adopt a natural way of life to remain healthy in future.

## Healing crisis

The speciality of naturopathy is that it does not suppress any disease, on the contrary it, extricates it from its very root.

During the treatment, accumulated toxins are released from the body in the form of loose motions, cold, cough, etc. which is called healing crisis.

Due to ignorance, patients get disappointed when the healing crisis takes place and give up naturopathy to resort to medicine. But it is a mistake.

Healing crisis need not be taken as another discomfort but as a cleansing process which takes the disease out of the system.

Even then if it causes uneasiness then a naturopath must be consulted for advice before giving up naturopathy treatment altogether.

## Mud therapy

Mud digests all the faeces, waste and dirt of the world yet remains pure itself. Faeces buried underground assimilate and become one with mud after a few days.

### *Healing qualities of mud*

1. It has the power to extract poison.
2. It scratches the oldest of faeces stored in the body and dilutes them.
3. It extracts toxins from the body.
4. It is effective for swelling, pain, boils and perforations in the skin.
5. It removes burning sensations, bleeding and tension.
6. It takes out extra heat from the body.
7. It gives required coolness to the body.
8. It acts as a pain killer and deodorant.
9. It provides the body with magnetic force which gives vigour and strength.

### *Selection of mud*

Mud could be of any type but should have been taken from a neat and clean place exposed to sun rays, extracted from 2 to 2½ feet below the ground. It should be dried in sunlight then sieved before use.

The mud from termites hill is extremely effective while for bathing and head bath Multani mud is useful.

## Various uses of mud

1. **Sleeping in mud** – It is extremely effective for insomnia, nervous weakness and blood poisoning.
2. **Mud massage** – By massaging and applying mud on the body, harmful air and poisonous elements can be removed.
3. **Mud bath** – Instead of soap if mud is applied, it helps in removing all diseases.
4. **Walking barefoot on mud** – This helps in curing kidney ailment, improving eyesight and increasing magnetic power.
5. **Mud pack** – It is very important in naturopathy and is used against many diseases. For all the ailments of the abdomen it is very important.

It is used on the lower abdomen, chest, forehead, eyes, head, spine, throat, feet, anus and wherever needed.

**How to make a mud pack** – Mud should be ground, sieved and then soaked in clean water twelve hours before use. At the time of use, spread half an inch layer of this wet paste of mud on a thin cloth and put it on the spot where required, then cover it with a woollen cloth. It should be kept for 20-30 minutes or else the toxin extracted by mud will re-enter the body. Once used, the mud pack cannot be used again.

## Mud therapy for various diseases

1. **Constipation** – Mud pack is helpful in all types of constipation.
2. **Piles** – The portion of anus where moles are swollen up mud pack as thick as a cushion can be stuck. It gives relief in acute pain.
3. **Loose Motions** – Mud has diverse properties. It cures constipation and also loose motions. While suffering

from loose motions, mud pack is to be put on the abdomen.
4. **Cholera** – Mud pack is to be put on the chest and abdomen.
5. **Stomach ache** – Mud pack on the abdomen.
6. **Vomiting blood from the lungs** – Cold mud pack on the chest.
7. **Fever** – Mud pack on abdomen and forehead.
8. **Eczema** – Applying mud clears eczema.
9. **Pimples** – Mud pack on the face cure pimples.
10. **Ailments of the eye** – Tie mud pack on the eyes.

**Hydro therapy**

Two-thirds of human body is water which is present in each part of the body. The excretion of water from the body is a continuous process. When the quantity of water decreases in the body, thirst is experienced. Thus, when thirsty, water must be taken in appropriate quantity.

*Healing properties of water*
1. Stimulant
2. Sedative
3. Tonic
4. Diuretic
5. Diaphoretic
6. Purgative
7. Antipyretic
8. Local anaesthetic
9. Hypnotic
10. Eliminative
11. Anodyne
12. Refrigerant
13. Aseptic
14. Expectorant

15. Antispasmodic
16. Haemostat

## Different uses of water

1. Hip bath
2. Sitz bath
3. Spinal bath
4. Hot foot bath
5. Simple full bath
6. Hot-cold graduated bath
7. Steam bath
8. Wet sheet pack
9. Hot and cold fomentation
10. Pack or bandage
11. Wet bandage on the abdomen
12. Enema
13. Early morning drinking water kept overnight
14. Inhaling steam
15. Compression
16. Kunjal (drinking water on empty stomach and vomiting it out)
17. Jalneti (pouring saline water into one nostril and releasing it from the other and vice versa)
18. Ice therapy

### 1. Hip bath

In a cushioned tub fill water so as to reach up to the navel. Keep feet outside the tub on a small stool. Rest the back on the rear side of the tub. After sitting in the tub stroke the abdomen going from the right side towards the left with a rough towel. This bath can be taken for 5-15 minutes. Gradually increase the duration. After hip bath, dry the wet portion with a dry cloth, wear clothes and go out for a swift walk or do some light exercises. If the patient is too weak, he should lie down in the bed with a blanket on.

**Hip Bath**

*Note* – Hip bath can be taken by women until three months of pregnancy.

*Benefits* – It gives permanent relief in all ailments of the abdomen. It is very useful for reducing excess fat from hips and abdomen. There is not a disease wherein hip bath does not give a positive response.

## 2. Sitz bath

The upper skin on the penis should be stretched over the head of the penis so as to cover it completely. Hold it with two fingers of the left hand – index and the middle one. With the right hand take a piece of soft cloth dip it in cold water and touch it on the area of skin held, repeatedly.

In the tub for hip bath, fill water and sit on a stool or a thick piece of wood. The water should touch only the relevant portion and nowhere else.

In a similar way women can also sit and touch water on the vaginal lips with a soft wet cloth.

*Benefits* – It helps in case of premature ejaculation of semen, leucorrhoea and nervous weakness. Anger is gradually cured. It is specially good for neuralgia and sciatica. In case of women, it helps in curing hysteria and other diseases they suffer from.

*Natural Health*

## 3. Spinal bath

There is a special tub for spinal bath. It is filled with water and the water touches only the spine and the adjoining area.

In the beginning, after 10 minutes of spinal bath, spine should be wiped with a towel to warm up for some light physical exercises.

*Benefits* – It helps in controlling/curing blood pressure, sleeplessness, unconsciousness, fatigue, weakness and nervous tension. It also regulates blood circulation.

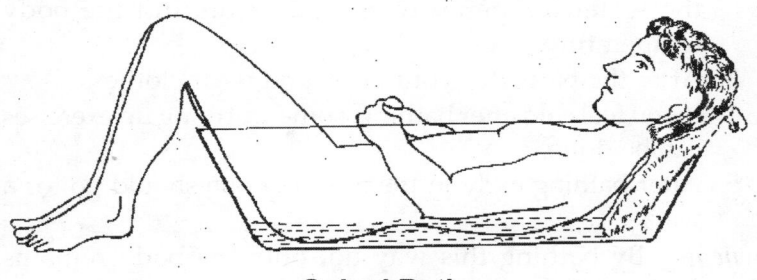

**Spinal Bath**

## 4. Hot foot bath

For hot foot bath a bucket should be filled with hot water, as hot as the skin can bear. Then sit on a stool or a chair, put your feet in the bucket of hot water. Water level should be below the knee.

When the water starts to cool down, take out some of it from the bucket and replenish it with an equal quantity of hot water. Cover yourself with a blanket in such a way so as to cover yourself fully apart from the head. The bucket should also be under. Before beginning this bath drink some hot water and continue to drink in between the bath while covering your head with a towel soaked in cold water. When the bath is over, wipe the perspiring body with a towel, and if necessary take a normal bath in cold water.

*Benefits* – It helps in cold and cough, blood pressure, unconsciousness and attacks of asthma. For women having irregular menstruation, it is useful to have this bath regularly over a period of time.

### 5. Simple full bath

The present way of bathing is only a ritual as the actual benefit is lost. Therefore, while bathing, certain things should be kept in mind:
1. Before bathing, the body should be warmed up by rubbing it with a dry towel.
2. Thereafter, have bath with cold water. In winters the water temperature should be around the body temperature level.
3. After the bath, dry your body and wear clothes.
4. If you feel cold after bathing, some warming up exercises can be done.
5. After bathing early in the morning one should go for a walk.

*Benefits* — By bathing this way not only the body remains clean but experiences vigour and blood circulation improves, skin glows and becomes active, mind is happy and freshness permeates to make one willing to work.

### 6. Hot-Cold graduated bath

Take hot water in a bucket and open the cold water tap into it. Take a handful of water and start bathing by rubbing the nape downwards. Gradually when water gets cold, pour it over the head.

*Benefits* — During winters this bath is extremely useful because only hot water activates the skin. All the benefits of a simple bath are there along with more cleanliness, fast circulation of blood and awakening of appetite.

### 7. Steam bath

There is a special cabin for steam bath which encloses the whole body with only the head protruding out.

Before a steam bath enema is recommended. After drinking water, one should sit barefoot in the cabin with a wet cold towel on the head. In about ten minutes when perspiration is over, dry your body with a towel and have a bath in cold water.

*Benefits* — It opens the pores of the skin, blood circulation increases, red blood corpuscles also increase in number. Steam bath strengthens the lungs and heart, kidney functions properly. Arthritis, stroke, obesity, all types of skin diseases, asthma, inflammation in the bronchial passage, etc. ailments get effected positively.

## 8. Wet sheet pack

On 3 to 4 heavy blankets, put one thin cotton sheet wet with cold water. Then make the patient lie on it with his arms stretched upwards. Then fold the sheet from one side covering the body and press it along the armpit at the other side. Bring down the arms placing them straight along the sides. Then from the other side take the sheet and cover the body over the other arm.

Then cover the whole body including the legs with one or more blankets as per need, leaving only the head open.

As per requirement after 30-60 minutes the pack should be removed and cold water bath.

*Benefits* — In case of fever, extract faeces out of body, to strengthen nerve tissues, and for detoxification, wet sheet pack is used. This pack takes out so much poison that when it is taken off it emits foul smell. In a body which has too much toxins the sheet becomes pale in colour. Four times in a month this can be used. Before using it the body of the patient should be warm enough to produce good results.

## 9. Hot and cold fomentation

A cloth with 3-4 folds wet with hot water should be kept for 2 minutes on the desired spot, then a towel wet with cold water should be kept for a minute. This process should be repeated four times, beginning with hot and finishing with cold.

*Benefits* — To repair a part of the body or to bring relief in pain, alternate hot and cold fomentation is very useful and no other treatment is as effective as this one. On the abdomen, hot and cold fomentation gives relief in chronic constipation, gastric trouble and also removes weakness.

## 10. Pack

Water cushion, pack and binding bandage are ancient practices and even today for relief in various diseases they are used. Sometimes hot pack is used sometimes cold. Usually wounds, caused by burn, injury, sprain, fracture, gastric pains, arthritis, perforated boils, cysts and elephantiasis are treated in various ways with the use of pack.

*Benefits* — This pack can be used in treating all diseases with little variations.

## 11. Wet abdomen pack

Keeping wet pack on the abdomen removes constipation. For immediate relief in any ordinary illness in the body a thick layer of cloth wet in water should be rinsed and kept below the naval for half an hour, or immediately thereafter kept again after wetting. This should be covered with a polythene packet (to avoid clothes getting wet). With this one can continue to work.

*Benefits* — Useful for all ailments of the abdomen.

## 12. Enema

The process of transporting a kind of liquid in the rectum is called enema. This is also called cleaning up of the rectum. While giving enema the nozzle should be greased with Vaseline or oil and put in the anus. The box of enema can be kept at a height of three feet from the person's seat and let the water in it flow into the rectum. If the patient feels pain during this process then the height of the box can be reduced

*Natural Health* 15

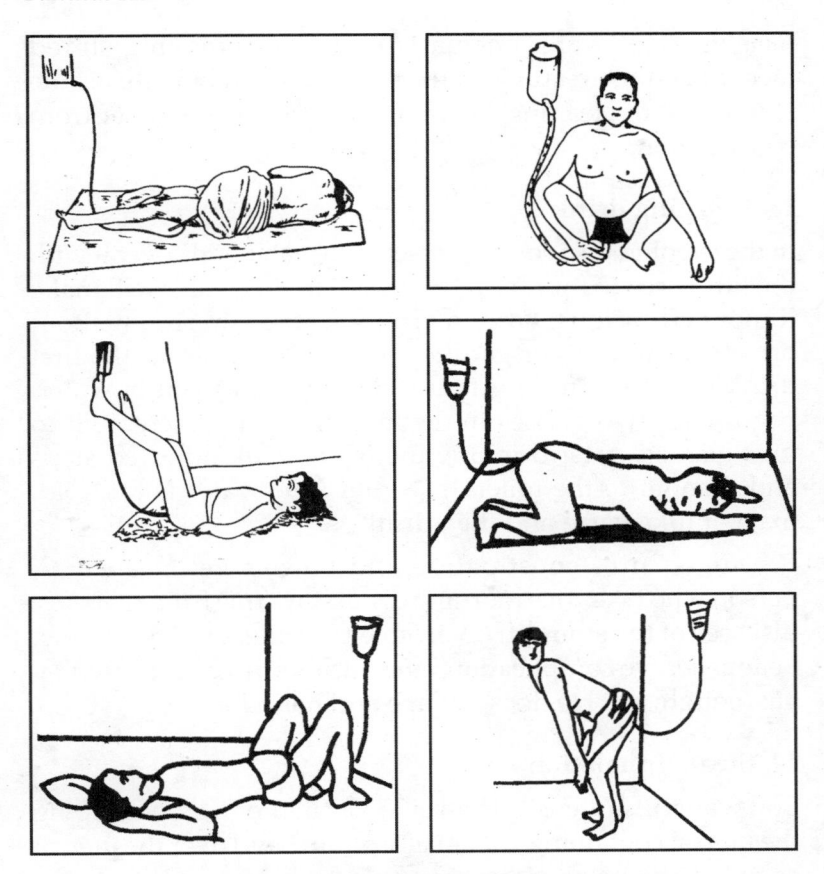

**Various methods of taking enema**

and the flow of water stopped for a while. This will stop the pain. Generally 200 ml water is poured into the rectum. More quantity of water should not be given. For 5 to 10 minutes water can be kept inside, while keeping it inside one should walk to and fro and then gradually let it go in the toilet along with stored stool. The whole water need not be let lose at once in a hurry.

*Types of Enema* – Fresh water enema, hot water enema, honey enema, neem enema, butter milk enema, lemon enema, wheat grass juice enema and many more types of enema can be done.

*Benefits* – Hot water enema is useful in removing stored faeces from the rectum. In the world of medicine this is the safest way of cleaning the intestines. This gives relief from constipation.

### 13. Morning drink

In the evening fill a copper vessel with water and cover it with the lid. Three to four basil leaves put in this water will make it more efficacious. Early morning before sun rise, without brushing the teeth or gargling, drink this water as the first drink in the morning. At once do not drink a lot of water, begin with two glasses in the morning. Then increase it to four glasses. After drinking the water walk hundred steps and then go to the toilet. In winter time water is too cold, make it lukewarm and then drink.

*Benefits* – Cures constipation and bowels get cleaned. A person who takes this morning drink stays free from diabetes, diseases of the stomach, liver, spleen, urine, semen, leprosy, headache, eye complications and various diseases caused by gas, cough, etc. He does not age and has a long life.

### 14. Steam inhalation

Boil water in a utensil. Then sit on a chair or a stool keeping the utensil containing water before you. Bend over the utensil covering the head with a towel and inhale deeply through the nostrils into the throat.

*Benefits* – This is useful in cold, cough, diphtheria, tonsillitis and sinusitis.

### 15. Compress

Take a 7 to 8 feet long and 6 to 7 inch broad wet cotton cloth and rinse and tie it up. Over it take a dry woollen cloth of same dimension and tie that too. Keep this compress for a minimum of one hour. As per requirement the duration can be increased. After removing the compress, wipe with a wet cloth. This is used in various diseases on various parts of the body. For instance throat compress, abdominal compress, chest compress, leg compress, joint compress and girdle compress, etc.

*Benefits* – This is useful in thyroid and parathyroid problems, tonsillitis, asthma, liver problems, diabetes, kidney problems, arthritis, etc.

## 16. Kunjal

Explained later in the book on page no. 108

## 17. Jalneti

Explained later in the book on page no. 110

## 18. Ice therapy

Ice can be used to cure many diseases —
(1) *When Skin gets burnt* – If any part of the skin gets burnt, then immediate application of a piece of ice on that place gives relief from burning sensation and also prevents boil formation.
(2) *When nose starts bleeding* – Due to excessive heat, often the nose of a person starts bleeding. In this state ice is the best treatment.
   If the nose bleeds keep ice, wrapped in a cloth on the nose. Within few minutes the bleeding will stop.
(3) *On bleeding* – If blood flows continuously from any cut portion of the body or it does not stop, then in such conditions use ice on that portion. Bleeding will stop immediately.
(4) *On hidden injury* – If there is any type of hidden injury then applying ice on that area which will prevent clotting and remove pain.
(5) *On swelling* – Often, a swelling occurs after injury. In such state ice fomentation reduces the swelling.
(6) *On sprain* – Applying ice on any area with sprain reduces the swelling and pain.

(7) *In fever* – During high fever keeping ice, wrapped in a cloth on the patient's forehead, palm and soles of the foot helps in bringing down the fever.

(8) *On being stung* – On being stung by honey bee, ice should be applied immediately on that area. This prevents burning sensation and pain.

(9) *On having prickly heat* – During summers, often people suffer from prickly heat. For this ice is an easy treatment. Rubbing ice on prickly heat, gives relief.

(10) *Backache* – Ice can be used to get relief from backache. Take ice pieces in a clean cloth and apply them on the area of pain. Do not keep it for more than 20 minutes. After an hour it can be kept again.

*Note* – While applying ice on head, wrap it in a cloth first.

**Chromotherapy**

Energy received from the sun replenishes micro food, increases life force and makes one free of diseases. It removes nervous weakness and strengthens the muscles. It balances quantity of calcium and phosphorus to keep the bones strong. It keeps the skin healthy, strengthens digestive and excretory activities. Sunshine helps in mental and physical development and gives boost to beauty. Sun rays kill germs. Houses which are not exposed to sunshine have germs carrying diseases breeding in them leading to several diseases.

**Ways of utilising sun rays (sunshine)**

*Looking at rising sun*

(1) By looking at the ruddy glow of the rising sun, eye diseases are cured. By seeing the reflection of the sun in a river or pond, eyesight improves.

(2) While making oblations to the sun early in the morning the sun is seen through the pouring water, it helps in curing physical and mental ailments.

## *Sun bath*

Take sun rays on your bare body with a cloth covering the head and seated on a chair or lying in sunshine not with too many clothes on the body.

If women do not have the convenience of sun bath they could wear very thin clothes and sit or lie in the sun to avail the benefit. While sun bathing the head should be in shade or covered with a wet towel or under green leaves. The timings for this bath should be between 8 to 9 O'clock after sunrise.

Fifteen to thirty minutes of sun bath is sufficient. Thereafter rub the body with a towel and take a bath with fresh water.

## *Benefits*

By sun bathing weak bones, teeth problems, weak digestion, and diseases connected with intelligence and muscles get relief. Massage in sunshine. Once a week at least the body should be massaged scientifically (rubbing and stroking) with mustard oil or sesame oil. While massaging any part it should be kept in mind that the pressure should be directed towards the heart. But for heart patients it should be reverse.

## *Colour therapy*

Apparently sun rays are white, but actually they are a combination of the following seven colours.

1. Red
2. Orange
3. Yellow
4. Green
5. Violet
6. Indigo-Deep blue
7. Sky blue

When our system gets deficiency or excess of any colour, then accordingly there is affliction of a disease. All the above stated colours have medicinal properties which are absorbed in water, oil, honey, ghee, etc. for reaping desired benefits.

## Preparation

To prepare different coloured water, oil, honey, ghee and air, they have to be kept in glass bottles of the desired colour. 3/4 portion filled, bolted with cotton and a cork put thereon. It should be placed in sunshine from morning till evening on a piece of wood. While the process of preparation is on, these bottles have to be shaken every day and the cotton should be replaced regularly. Outer surface of glass bottle should be cleaned every day. If any bottle with a particular colour is not available then on a white ordinary glass bottle a transparent paper of the desired colour can be covered.

Water can be prepared daily. It takes 15 days for honey to get ready for use. Ghee and oil take 1½ months to get ready for use.

Water can be used for three days, honey for six months, ghee and oil can be used for a year.

Oil is only for external use. Ghee is used on the spine and eyes. Honey is specially prepared for using during journeys as water cannot be prepared then.

## The effect and utility of different colours

1. **Red** — This colour is more hot. When the body gets cold, pale, stricken or is in a state of getting blue then this is useful.

   It is useful in cough and cold or to rejuvenate a dead portion. It is only for external use. Application of this oil on genitals removes impotency. Massage on aching joints is a remedy for arthritis. Its application can perforate a steaming boil. It is effective in aches of the lower back and neck.

   During winter it is applied on cracked heels. It is massaged on the chest in case of chronic cough, asthma and pneumonia.

   Paucity of red colour causes laziness, excessive sleep, loss of appetite and constipation. In excess, it causes heat in the body, sleeplessness and loose motions.

2. **Orange** — This is slightly less hot than red. It boosts up the nerves and blood. It is a great remedy for asthma. It is also useful in joint aches also. It increases appetite.
3. **Yellow** — This is less hot than orange. It showers enthusiasm and happiness. It is a slight laxative also and facilitates full excretion of stool and urine. Strengthens the brain, liver and spleen. Develops retarded brain and heals paralysis. It is also useful in curing impotence. Brightens up a dull brain. Yellow ghee is good for eyesight. Also helps in burning sensation in the eyes and redness.

   It should not be used in palpitation, stiffness and nervous disorder.
4. **Green** — This is neither hot nor cold but has a medium effect. It detoxifies the body hence it is useful in every disease.

   It is cooling for the eyes and strengthens them. For women it provides relief in burning sensation in the vagina, and unconsciousness.

   In case of spontaneous ejaculation, green glow and massage of green oil is very effective on the lower part of the spinal cord. It also helps in all kinds of fever, oozing boils, wounds, fissures, fistula and skin diseases.

   It has a magical effect in typhoid, measles, eye ailments, diabetes, high blood pressure, heart diseases, cough, cold, piles, etc. It is beneficial in cancer also.

   In all eye ailments green water can be used for washing eyes. If there are wounds in the stomach or intestines green water should be drunk on an empty stomach.

   Green oil applied on the head of a cataract patient provides relief and also strengthens the mind.
5. **Violet** — It has a cooling effect. It helps in sound sleep. It is very effective when the lungs are damaged acutely. This increases red blood cells and cures anaemia.
6. **Blue** — It is cooler than violet. It is anti-inflammatory, anti pyretic and strengthens the nervous system,

quenches extreme thirst. It is an antiseptic. It is useful in complications of the vagina, rectum, swelling of testes and leucorrhoea. In diseases of the throat gargling with blue water is effective. Paucity of blue colour increases anger.

7. **Sky blue** — This is very cool. Pains caused by burns and heat get relief. This also has antiseptic properties. It is a tonic for nerves. For all kinds of fevers it is extremely efficacious and stops all types of bleeding. It is effective in excessive menstrual bleeding, cholera and heat stroke. Quenches thirst and heals inflammation in the rectum. Ailments of the head and hair are cured.

It should not be used in arthritis, gastric trouble, paralysis and acute constipation.

## Sky blue oil —

1. Strengthens the heart when massaged on the chest.
2. When massaged on the head it cures headaches caused by heat. Removes suspicion, blackens, softens and lengthens hair.
3. If massaged on the lower abdomen it regulates menstrual bleeding and cures hysteria.

## Sky blue ghee —

1. Gives relief by application on ulcer in the mouth.
2. Strengthens nerves constantly if the spinal cord is massaged with it.

Deficiency of sky blue causes anger, irritability, body heat, loose motions, excessive laziness, constipation, weak digestion and excessive sleep.

## Quantity of coloured water prepared in sun – age wise

| Age | Intervals | Quantity |
|---|---|---|
| 1 day to 1 month | after every 2 hours, | Half teaspoon |
| 1 month to 3 months | after 2 hours, | 3/4 of a teaspoon |
| for 3 months to 1 year | after 2 hours, | 1 teaspoon full |
| 1 year to 5 years | after 2 hours, | 2 small teaspoons 5 |
| years to 10 years | after 2 hours, | 4 small teaspoons 10 |
| years to 15 years | after 3 hours | half a small bowl, |
| After 15 years | after 4 hours | one small bowl |

# Natural Health

**Receiving sun rays through clothes** — Clothes should always be white and light so as to absorb sun rays. In a particular disease wearing the relevant coloured clothes is beneficial.

## *Coloured fruits and vegetables*

By using coloured fruits and vegetables benefits of different colours can be taken.

*Note* – Basic colours are only three (1) Red, (2) Yellow, (3) Blue. Remaining colours are formed by combination of these colours.

    Eg.– Orange    (Red + Yellow),
          Green       (Yellow + Blue), Violet (Blue + Red)
          Sky blue   (Blue + White)

**White Colour** — It contains all the colours. It is useful for bone strength.

**Connection of colours and chakras** — On the seven chakras the seven colours affect the body and mind in a special way.

1. Mooladhar Chakra (Root Chakra)     - Red
2. Svadhisthan Chakra (Sacral Chakra)     - Orange
3. Manipurak Chakra (Solar Plexus Chakra) - Yellow
4. Anahata Chakra (Heart Chakra)     - Green
5. Vishuddha Chakra (Throat Chakra)     - Violet
6. Agya Chakra (Third eye Chakra)     - Blue/Indigo
7. Braham Randhra (Crown Chakra)     - Sky Blue

## Air therapy

In the five great elements, air has been placed after space. For protecting life, nature has provided air in abundance. We should make maximum use of pure life giving air and spare ourselves from air pollution. To remain healthy and disease free we should adopt the following means —

1. **Early morning walk** — It is useful to take a walk in the morning. Try to go to open spaces like gardens, water falls, hills. Those who do not breathe fresh air get into the clutches of serious diseases.

1.2. **Pranayama**—Its detailed description is given later on page 148.

1.3. **Air bath**—Exposing the body to air is called air bath. For keeping the skin pores open and activated air bath is necessary. If the body is kept covered with clothes all the time it develops diseases. During summer, wear thin clothes or less clothes in open air in the morning and have air bath at night by sleeping outside exposed to open air. During the rainy season or extreme cold leave a window open while sleeping in the room or verandah, that serves the purpose of an air bath. Never cover the face while sleeping at night, but leave the window open.

1.4. **Swar Yoga**—In yoga breathing is called swar. They are of three types—

   (a) *Chandra swar* (Lunar Breath)—When the breathing is predominant in the left nostril it is known as chandra swar. This provides coolness to the body. Intake of more of liquid and less hard work should be done in this breathing. In day time sleep (if required) in chandra swar.

   (b) *Surya swar* (Solar Breath)—When the right nostril is experiencing predominant breathing it is called surya swar. This provides heat. Eat while breathing this way and do work involving hard labour. At night sleep in surya swar.

   (c) *Sushumna swar*—When breathing both nostrils experience breathing every other second alternatively. It is sushumna swar. While breathing this way practise of yoga and religious activities should be undertaken.

Nature changes the breath in accordance with the requirement of the body. If necessary the swar can be changed.

## Ways of changing swar

1. The nostril which feels predominant breath can be closed by pressing, the other swar will automatically start.

2. Lie on the side which is active, the other side nostril will automatically experience the flow of breath.
3. To make a particular swar active the other nostril could be closed by stuffing cotton.
4. By running, putting in labour and doing pranayam swar is changed. By practising Nari Shodhan Pranayama swar can be controlled in such a way that during winter the body feels less cold and in summer it feels less hot.

*Benefits of knowledge of Swar*

1. A person who is able to change swar willfully lives longer and remains youthful.
2. When experiencing illness if the predominant swar is changed it provides relief in the ailment.
3. While experiencing physical exhaustion chandra swar can be adopted, therefore lying on the right side will help.
4. If there is pain due to nervous disorder changing of swar gives immediate relief.
5. An asthmatic attack loses its intensity if swar is changed.
6. A person who breathes from the left nostril during the day and right nostril at night always remains healthy.
7. At the time of conception if the male breathes through the right nostril and female breathes through the left nostril, a boy is conceived.

## Space therapy

The element of space is the most useful and first among the five elements. Space element is the base element of the five elements. It is the minutest element. Empty space in the body or empty organs exhibit space element. Looking at the sky and sleeping under the open sky generates energy. By fasting we make use of space element naturally.

## *Fasting*

Fasting is a part of the latest way of life. This is an effective means of maintaining good health or rejuvenating best health.

That is why it is necessary for ailing and non-ailing too. As it has exceptional importance from the health point of view, it has got a place in all religious folds. The religious implications of fasting could be various, but the most important aim is eradicating disease from the body. For diseased, it is like a life saving drug. Lately, doctors in the West have also positively supported it, that the effect of medicines worth thousands of rupees is the same as that derived from fasting for a while.

## Benefits of fasting

1. Detoxification from within the body is the main purpose of fasting. Our energy is then utilised in extracting elements causing ailments in the body, relieved from the task of digestion. We know the process of digestion is continuously going on in our body. The nourishing elements of food get assimilated in the form of flesh, marrow, blood, etc. and the remaining stuff is excreted out in the form of stool, urine and cough. Even then some of the contaminated waste remains in the body and gradually accumulates to create toxins and cause diseases. To take out these toxins from the body we resort to fasting. When we eat food the work of extracting is neglected.
2. Fasting provides strength to organs. Churning takes place within the body. Nourishing products get separated and reach to strong tissues of the body. Waste product and accumulated toxins flow into the excretory organs, to take them out of the body easily.
3. By fasting deficiencies in the body get fulfilled.
4. All the organs of the body get rest which increases their efficiency.
5. While fasting cleaning of the body takes place all by itself. Germs breeding in toxins within our body causing diseases take their nourishment from the food we consume. Most of these germs cannot survive without food for a long time. Thus while fasting these germs

start perishing. This way diseases of the abdomen get cured easily. A person who always takes a balanced and uncooked diet need not fast as much as one who eats heavily. For one consuming a diet full of fats and protein, fasting is most essential.

## *Way of fasting*

Do not take any type of food the whole day. Drink 2-2½ litres of water with juice of 2-3 lemons a number of times. If one cannot do it then take fruit or vegetable juice. Those who cannot fast completely may take fruits once in a day.

Fasting can be done for a day or many days. Everyone should fast once a week. A longer period of fasting is recommended depending on the disease, under proper directions.

Never break a fast by eating solid (heavy) food. Orange juice, sweet lemon juice, grape juice or some other fruit or vegetable juice should be taken.

A short duration fast could be broken by eating fruits. These days people break fast by eating heavy foods which proves harmful rather than beneficial.

## *Requirement while fasting*

1. **Air**—While fasting fresh air with maximum oxygen should be inhaled for full benefit to destroy filth in the body.
2. **Bath and cleanliness**—While fasting the filth from within settles down on the skin pores, mouth, nose, ears and reproductive organs. That is why bathing and maintaining cleanliness is necessary. The tongue and teeth should be cleaned a number of times during the day.
3. **Clothes**—While fasting and also otherwise clothes worn should be light, made of cotton and airy.
4. **Exercise**—While fasting exercise only as much as you can bear, like a walk, light exercise, etc.

5. **Enema** — While fasting for internal cleaning enema is essential.
6. **Mental effect** — While fasting do not permit any kind of worry, guilt, anger, fear, disappointment or complication to bother you.
7. **Sunshine** — While fasting the body must be exposed to sunshine in the morning for 15-20 minutes.
8. **Silence** — While fasting maintaining silence is beneficial.
9. **Rest** — While fasting there should be mental and physical rest.
10. **Dry Rubbing** — While fasting rubbing the whole body is very useful.

*Note* — There are some diseases which prohibit fasting, such as diabetes and tuberculosis (TB), etc.

## Food

For the nourishment of body and fulfilling the deficiencies of the body therein, intake of food is essential. By improving the diet alone all diseases can also be treated. That is why it is said that food is medicine. The person is said to be intelligent who takes proper food for a healthy and long life and gives up whatever is harmful to his body. The kind of food we take will determine the state of our body and mind.

By consuming seasonal fruits and vegetables the body remains free from diseases because nature has grown them keeping in view the requirement of that particular season and place.

### Extracting five elements through food

| | | |
|---|---|---|
| Space | — | By liquid diet, |
| Air | — | Leafy vegetables |
| Fire | — | Fruits |
| Water | — | Vegetables |
| Earth | — | Grains |

Classification of food has been done by Lord Krishna in *Gita* into three categories (Satvik, Rajsik and Tamsik), i.e., invoking goodness, passion and mode of ignorance.

## *Satvik food*

The food which facilitates long life, intelligence, strength, freedom from disease, happiness are juicy, greasy and available all the time, naturally dear to everyone.

## *Rajsik food*

The food which is bitter, sour, salty, very hot, spicy, generating heat, promote unhappiness and worries and leads to diseases.

## *Tamsik food*

The food that is half cooked, non-juicy, with a foul odour, stale and impure.

## **Important rules for food**

1. Eat only when you feel hungry.
2. Eat only as much as would satisfy your hunger.
3. Unless the first morsel is fully chewed do not take the second one.
4. In one meal do not take too many food products. Take a few and food should be simple so as not to strain the digestive process.
5. Eat quietly and peacefully.
6. Dinner should be taken three hours before sleeping.
7. There should be a gap of at least 5 hours between two meals.
8. You should not eat immediately after waking up from sleep.
9. Should not eat when stricken with worries, when grieving, tired or in a hurry.
10. While eating need not discuss professional, social or domestic problems.

11. Inflammatory products such as chillies, spices, etc. need not be used.
12. Do not eat when there is a burning sensation in the throat or bad odour.
13. Indigestible and heavy foods should not be taken at all.
14. As far as possible eat only uncooked food (fruits, salad, sprouted cereals, etc.).
15. Stale food causes diseases, hence avoid it.
16. Do not take water while eating. Water should be taken either 30 minutes before or 40-60 minutes after taking food.
17. Drink sufficient quantity of water during the day.
18. White sugar, maida, polished rice, etc. processed products need not be used.
19. Reduce the intake of salt, sweets, spices and ghee.
20. Save yourself from tea, coffee, fried things, smoking, liquor and consumption of tobacco, etc.
21. Once a week live only on juices and sufficient quantity of water.
22. Use flour without straining the chaff.
23. Fruits and vegetables should be washed before eating.
24. Before and after eating food, hands should be washed and also clean the mouth and teeth.
25. Maintain silence while eating.
26. Don't watch television while eating.
27. No physical or mental activity should be done immediately after eating.
28. The habit of urinating after finishing food should be developed.
29. Milk should not be taken at night but can be taken with breakfast in the morning.
30. Eating extreme cold or hot things are harmful for the digestive process.
31. Drinking butter milk at the end of a meal is useful.
32. If after the first meal the body is uncomfortable then forgo the second meal.

33. Curd is more easily digestable than milk.
34. Intercourse should not be done within three hours of having meal.
35. It is harmful to eat within 10 minutes after urinating.
36. After walking in extreme heat while drinking water both the nostrils should be pressed closed with one hand.

## Balanced diet

Our food contains — (1) Proteins, (2) Carbohydrates, (3) Fats, (4) Vitamins, (5) Natural Salts, (6) Roughage, (7) Water.

They are all equally important as they are interdependent on each other for their proper working. Thus food must contain a balanced quantity of these elements in a proper way.

Generally, almost all these necessary constituents are provided in each food product by nature, but some contain less quantity of a particular element and some more. Therefore, it is necessary to find out in which product these elements are available in the right proportion and quantity. Accordingly we should decide upon our mode of food.

### *Protein*

This builds, develops, promotes and fulfills deficiencies in the body.

### *Deficiency of protein*

Its deficiency causes problems like tiredness, weakness, retarded development, nervous disorders, non-healing of wounds. In pregnancy the mother's and foetus's tissues become weak and there is less lactation. Development of tissues is undernourished leading to failure of the body before time.

### *Excess of protein*

As deficiency of protein is problematic so is its excess. Protein deficiency can be cured by giving more proteins, but the ailments caused by excessive protein will require complete cleansing of the body.

Excessive protein damages liver and kidneys. It makes uric acid get collected in joints leading to gout and rheumatoid, the blood gets contaminated. Veins and arteries are blocked with waste deposits leading to pressure on the blood circulatory system. Thus this weakens the heart and sometimes due to high blood pressure there is the danger of blood vessels bursting, consequently leading to paralysis. Apart from these, many minor ailments occur due to excess of protein.

*Means of protein*

Milk, dry fruits, dual seed grains, peas, green leaves, etc. and soya bean contains maximum protein.

*Note*–Generally an old person in accordance with the labour he puts in needs 50-60 grams of protein every day. Approximately the proportion should be one gram of protein per kg of weight.

Children, players, pregnant females and feeding mothers require more proteins.

## Carbohydrates

This gives us strength and heat.

### *Deficiency of carbohydrates*

Deficiency of carbohydrates cause laziness, inactivity and non-enthusiasm.

### *Excess of carbohydrates*

Increases obesity. Carbohydrates get accumulated in the breathing pipe, stomach, intestines, heart and uterus in the form of toxins and gives rise to various diseases. Carbohydrates has two parts:

*Starch*

Starch is a white substance which exists in large amounts in potatoes and particular grains such as rice. All the starch after

getting digested fully converts into sugar. After becoming glycogen, it gets stored in the liver and muscles. It has been divided in to three parts by scientists —
1. Easily digestible (alkaline) — This is derived from banana, potato, sweet potato (Shakar kandi), papaya, chikoo, orange, apple, pineapple and guava, etc.
2. Easily digestible (acidic) — This is derived from rice, barley, maize and other tuber root.
3. Late digestible (acidic) — This is found in all types of single seed grains (wheat, jowar and bajra or millet). If from these grain chaff *(chokar)* is strained it will be hundred per cent acid.

## Sugar

It is of five types —
1. Milk Sugar — It is required right from the time when the baby is in mother's womb. It is found maximum in human milk.
2. Grape sugar — It is found in fine quality of grapes, honey and other fruits. Scientists have called it predigested food as it is easily digestible and the digestive system does not strain much in digesting it. That is why for immediate boost of energy honey and water of raisins *(kishmish)* is given.
3. Fruit sugar or fructose — This is generally in all sweet fruits. This is existent in the juices of plants along with glucose. When the fruit ripens the starch in it converts into sugar. Always eat ripe fruits otherwise instead of getting alkaline one would get acidic food. For a patient of diabetes fruit sugar is harmless as against ordinary sugar. It is digested in the small intestine.
4. Malt Sugar — This is derived from grains eaten daily, for example starchy products like wheat, barley, rice, maize, etc. Apart from sugar they possess many salts, calcium, iron, etc. and vitamins too. The digestive process begins with the saliva in the mouth and ends in the small intestine.

5. Cane Sugar — This is sugar extracted from sugarcane and processed in a mill. It has only the capacity to provide heat. It is very acidic. This is of a low level and harmful. As it is processed more to make it white, thus calcium, iron and other natural salts and vitamins and useful elements get destroyed.

To digest sugar and to replenish its best elements our digestive process takes calcium and iron from within the body, consequently our body becomes deficient of them. It affects the bones, adversely and apparently manifests in decay of teeth. Consumption of too much sugar creates oxalic acid which is not required by the body. When there is insufficient calcium to digest it then creates a havoc in the body.

After having learnt this much, the question arises as to what should be taken instead of sugar. The clear answer is sugarcane in its natural form, jaggery (*gur*), dates (*khajoor*), raisins, banana, figs (*anjeer*) and mango, etc. Sweet fruits available in different seasons should be consumed. Generally an adult person in accordance with the labour put in by him needs 200-500 gms of carbohydrates.

## Fats

Like carbohydrates fats also provide heat. Fats store energy and keep the body warm. Fats are specially beneficial in making the body soft and the bones strong. Without sugar fats do not oxidify properly and continue to burn which causes a feeling of tiredness in the body. To digest fats, liver, pancreas and small intestines must remain healthy for which deep breathing in the open is necessary. Excess of fat creates many diseases and its deficiency is compensated by the body from other foods.

To activate fats in food, the presence of iodine is essential or else thyroid glands get damaged leading to goitre.

## Type of fats

Fat is of many forms but mainly it is divided in two parts.
1. Derived from vanaspati — This is available in all kinds of oils, sesame (til), mustard, olive (jaitoon), sun flower, ground nut, linseed (alsi) and dry fruits (coconut, almonds, cashewnut, and *chilgoza*, etc.).
2. Derived from animals — Milk and milk products. The best quality fats is available in a goat's milk, then cows milk and thirdly it is buffaloes milk.

## Vitamins

Vitamin is any of a group of natural substances which are necessary in small amounts for the growth and good health of the body. It is a invisible micro element and promotes life force, maintains strength and provides resistance power against diseases. It can be bifurcated in many parts.

### *Vitamin-A*

This makes the skin beautiful, important for the ability to see well especially at night and increases resistance power against infectious diseases. Its deficiency causes loss of appetite, weakness, eye, ear and skin ailments and the fear of germs causing infection is there.

### *Sources*

Milk, butter, cheese, yellow fruits and vegetables, carrot, cabbage, pear, green chillies, dates, pineapple, melon, banana, sweet potato, apricot, papaya, mango, turmeric and all type of green vegetables.

### *Vitamin-B*

It is important for our body and our nervous system. There are 18 constituents of this vitamin. They get dissolved in water like sugar or salt. Since water cannot remain constant in the body it should be replenished regularly. Vitamin B are of many types – Vitamin B1 which helps the heart, muscles and nervous system to work well.

Vitamin B2 is found in foods such as liver, milk, cheese and whole grains and is important for the production of energy in the cells and for the production of particular hormones. Vitamin B6 is found in foods such as liver, yeast, fish and bananas and is important in chemical processes in the body and for keeping the skin, digestion and nervous system healthy. Vitamin B12 found in foods such as liver, kidney, eggs, fish and milk is important for a healthy nervous system, normal growth and the production of red blood cells.

This increases the appetite, strengthens digestion and improves health generally. The body develops, nervous system gains strength and resists diseases. Its deficiency causes disturbance in the digestive process, constipation, loss of weight, weakness of the muscles, complications in endocrine glands, pancreas, thyroid gland and liver. The mouth gets blisters. Its deficiency is the cause of beri beri and nervous weakness.

## Sources

Whole grain pieces, milk, roughage of vegetables, cereals, fruits and vegetable chaff, sprout, wheat, green peas, turnip, soya bean, sunflower, honey. By cooking, some of the vitamin B contents get destroyed.

## Vitamin-C

This vitamin is essential for life. This protects against pyorrhoea, scurvy and teeth problems. Keeps the skin intact and boosts up resistance power. Heals the wounds. Regulates the activity of glands. Protects the nervous system and provides protection against poisonous germs. This vitamin cannot be accumulated in the body, therefore, it should be consumed regularly.

Its deficiency causes diseased teeth, pyorrhoea, scurvy, blood pressure and bleeding, etc.

## Sources

Orange, lemon, sweet lemon(*mausambi*), guava, tomato, fresh green vegetables, strawberries, raspberries, pineapple, papaya, aniseed (*saunf*), cabbage, black raisin, green mustard, sprouted grains, amla and mango, etc.

## Vitamin-D

This keeps the quantity of calcium balanced in the body and helps in the assimilation of other natural products and salts. Beautifies the body, balances its shape, whitens the teeth and strengthens them, provides broadness to chest and plays an important role in making hands and feet beautiful. Vitamin D is important for healthy bones and teeth depend on it. It gives rest to the nerves. It is also effective in rickets.

Its deficiency causes infectious diseases, weakness of muscles, weakness of nervous system, weakness of bones and asthma, resistance power degenerates.

### Sources

It is in abundance in milk and sunshine. Children should be massaged with olive oil and exposed to sunshine. Dry fruits grown in sunshine (almond, *chilgoza*, walnut (*akhrot*), sunflower seeds), etc. contain it sufficiently.

## Vitamin-E

For progeny Vitamin E is essential. Vitamin E is required for ordinary growth and development and proper functioning of the pituitary gland. It helps in assimilation of iron. It does not get destroyed at a high temperature but oil destroys it at an ordinary temperature. Its deficiency does not permit formation of sperms in men and ovum among women, consequently leading to impotency and barrenness. Deficiency of Vitamin E causes premature child birth. Vitamin E is important for healthy blood vessels and circulation.

### Sources

Whole grains, milk, vegetables, fruits, dry fruits, soya bean oil. This is available predominantly in sprouted wheat, peas, groundnut and moong daal.

### Vitamin-K

This vitamin resists bleeding. It is important for healthy blood and cells. Its deficiency causes bleeding under the skin as in scurvy and in the muscles and within the stomach also.

In a child this deficiency leads to bleeding causing the child's death. Thus, two weeks before the birth of a child this vitamin should be administered.

*Sources*

Green vegetables, groundnut, top part of a carrot are rich sources of Vitamin K. Soya bean oil and rice grain also contain it. Green grass (*doob*) is its storehouse.

### Vitamin-P

It is necessary to keep blood vessels healthy and blood pressure normal. Deficiency of vitamin reduces resistance power of blood vessels and causes bleeding and tiredness.

*Sources:* Spinach

### Vitamin-U

This protects the membranes of the stomach. It deficiency causes weakness of digestive canal membrane.

*Sources:* Fresh green vegetables and cabbage.

## Natural salts

These contribute in cleansing, creation and development of the body. It is also required for assimilation of the food. There is no cell in this body which can work without these. None of the glands, part of digestive system, digestive juices or any other part can work without natural salts. Without their assistance blood circulation and all the functions connected with the brain cannot be carried on properly. Some essential natural salts are as under—

## Calcium

Calcium is necessary for making the bones strong and balancing blood flow. Its deficiency causes poor development of bones and teeth, bones become brittle, teeth start softening, there is danger of rickets, there can be excessive bleeding, heart beat gets disturbed, nervous weakness is caused, muscles vibrate and get stiffened up. A pregnant woman needs more calcium because it is necessary for the development of the foetus.

### Sources

Milk, carrot, aniseed, cabbage, turnip, beetroot, green vegetables, lemon, sweet lemon, water chest nut (*singhara*), *masoor*, almond, figs, in the chaff of grains. Sesame (White til) is a storehouse of calcium. Green grass has high quality calcium in abundance.

## Magnesium

This helps in utilising fat. Its deficiency causes indigestion, tiredness irritability, nervous weakness, weakness of the brain, stunted physical growth and rapid heart beat.

### Sources

Milk and green leafy vegetables, peas, beans, grains have it in sufficient quantity.

## Phosphorous

This stores strength in the body, along with calcium it makes teeth and bones strong. Its deficiency causes stunted growth of the body, bones and teeth do not develop properly, thinning of the body, loss of weight and generally a feeling of weakness sets in.

### Sources

Milk, beans, whole grains, dry fruits, green vegetables and turmeric have it. With calcium phosphorous is always there.

## Iron

For its assimilation in the body the food must contain copper and chlorophyll. Fortunately iron and copper are always together in food products. This helps in creating haemoglobin, developing the blood bank, carrying oxygen throughout the body and in the formation and reformation of cells, cures jaundice, anaemia and indigestion.

Its deficiency causes acute anaemia, lessening of haemoglobin count, loss of red blood cells, lowering of life force and many other diseases.

### Sources

Green leafy vegetables, cabbage, apple dates, dry fruits, guava, banana, brinjal, pomegranate (*anar*), raisins, grapes, carrot, chaff, coriander, etc.

## Copper

This works along with iron to create haemoglobin. Its deficiency hampers proper utilisation of iron, anaemia, breathing problems, general weakness, stunted growth.

### Sources

This is found in whole grains and food products containing iron.

## Iodine

Iodine keeps thyroid gland healthy. All activities in the body are affected by thyroid gland. It sharpens the intellect, protects against goitre and obesity. It is essential for oxidation of fats and proteins.

Its deficiency leads to inflammation of the thyroid gland leading to goitre which is dangerous. Slightest swelling of the throat should be taken seriously and to remove it, food containing iodine must be consumed.

### Sources

Whole grains, dry fruits, water containing food (kamalgatta, makhana, water chest nuts) pineapple, green vegetables have iodine in them.

## Chlorine

It is found primarily in the form of chlorine in all food products. It cleans up the body. Takes out the waste and purifies blood. Its deficiency causes indigestion, loss of power to retain water, loss of weight and diseases connected with menstrual cycle.

### Sources

Milk, green vegetables, dry fruits and grains have it.

## Sodium

Along with chlorine it is especially important. Sodium is necessary for digestion of calcium and is required for dissolving of many other salts. Its deficiency leads to poor digestive process, loss of weight, nervous disorder, desire to eat salt, general weakness, less water retention, etc.

### Sources

Green vegetables, especially leafy ones, spinach, radish, black gram, turnip, unpeeled fruits, whole grains and unpeeled cereals are its carriers.

## Potassium

It makes glycogen in the liver and muscles. This makes the muscles and tissues flexible, balances acidity in the body, is essential for the brain and for the production of red blood cells. Strengthens the nervous system. Dissolves accumulated toxins and is important for taking them out. Its deficiency leads to slow development, constipation, gastric problems, nervous disorders, sleeplessness and laziness.

### Sources

It is mainly present in almost all complete food products, vegetables, watermelon, white pumpkin (white petha), cabbage, cucumber, etc.

### Silicon

It is together with phosphorous in vegetables. It makes skin and tissues flexible and blackens hair, makes them strong. Its deficiency causes loss of digestive power in the intestines. Development stops and hair start greying.

### Sources

Whole grains, green vegetables and fruits and especially amla.

### Roughage

This works as a broom in the digestive process. Without it, intestines cannot be cleaned. Thus it is necessary to have it with food. Its deficiency causes constipation which is the root cause of diseases.

### Sources

All types of fruits and vegetables, grains, and leaves contain it. It is on the upper layer and seeds of food products. That is why wheat grounded with chaff, unpeeled cereals and among fruits, pear, guava, apple, etc. should be consumed with the peel. Isabgol, figs, *bel*, black raisins, and raisins have it in sufficient quantity.

### Water

70% of our body weight (except fats) is water. Our body needs 1 to 7 litres of water every day. The requirements depend upon our nature of work, humidity, temperature and other conditions. On an average a man needs 8-10 glasses of water every day. We get approximately 20% of water from food. Rest of the 80% is consumed by drinking juice and water.

Water comes out from the body in the form of sweat, urine, stools, and breath.

Water used for drinking and bathing should always be at the same temperature as of the body. Cold water damages the digestive system. During meal we should not take water. Nowadays instead of water, tea, coffee, sugar beverage and synthetic drinks are served. These are harmful to our body. If you want to drink something else instead of water, drink fruits or vegetable juices, coconut water and other organic juices.

## Balance of alkaline and acidic food

All diseases begin from imbalance of alkali and acid in the body and end with it getting balanced. In human body 80% is alkali and 20% is acid. Maintaining this ratio is the primary basis of health. In this aspect only all our physical, mental, practical, natural, capacity of copulation depends, that is why our food must be 80% alkaline and 20% acidic.

### *Alkaline food products*

All types of fruits except plum and berries, lemon, orange, leafy vegetables and remaining vegetables, coconut, fresh milk, sprouted food grains, dates, figs, soaked dry fruits.

### *Acidic food products*

Meat, egg, cheese, butter, cooked food, chapatti and dry fruits, sweets, sugar, grains, coffee, tea, chocolate, sugar syrup, boiled milk, maida, salt, intoxicating drinks, soda water, vegetable ghee, intoxicating drinks, fried and deep fried foods, baked products,etc.

### *Note*

People who eat more of raw food like fruits and salads do not have the problem of alkali or acid. This problem is faced by people consuming cooked food.

## Food combination

It is necessary to know which food products can be combined together. In the sagas of Ayurveda there is a lot of discussion on combinations of food. Sushrut comments that many products when combined together become poison. For instance honey with ghee mixed together in equal quantity becomes poison.

To digest different elements of food different digestive juices are required. Starch is processed in alkaline juice while being digested, while protein is processed in acid. If both types of food products are consumed together then their respective digestive juices will also be created at the same time. Thus alkali and acid on mixing will become ineffective and protein will start rotting, starch will start fermenting. Digestive process will thus get disturbed.

Therefore, at one time eating too many food products like vegetables, fruits, pickle, curd, pudding, sweets, papad, etc leads to chemical reaction and the digestive system gets spoiled.

At a time taking only one food product is ideal. Actually mixed diet is the first wrong step. At a time, the less the number of food products are mixed, the better it will be for the digestive process.

While eating take fruits at a time, then salad (vegetables) the other time and then grain should be taken. This is called mono diet.

## Wrong combinations

1. Banana with milk or curd
2. Radish with milk or curd
3. Milk with curd
4. Honey with hot water or any other hot product
5. Honey and radish
4. Khechadi with sweet pudding
5. Milk with melon, water melon, cucumber.
6. Urad dal and radish
7. Curd and Jamun
8. Curd and Melon
9. Curd and cheese
10. Fruits with vegetables

11. At night radish or curd
12. Heated up curd
13. Ten days stale ghee in a metal pot
14. Pulses with sweet potato, potato
15. Any other food product with melon or water melon
16. Cereals with rice or cereal with chapatti
17. Chapatti with milk or curd
18. Chapatti and tamarind

*Note* — Those who eat chapatti or rice with cereals must eat raw vegetables at the same time in good quantity.

## Ideal combinations

1. Mango and cow's milk
2. Milk with dates
3. Rice with coconut powder
4. Pulse (dal) and curd
5. Guava with *saunf*
6. Radish leaves with watermelon
7. Bathua with curd, i.e. raita
8. Carrot with *methi* leaves
9. Banana with small cardamom
10. Curd with amla powder
11. Leafy vegetables with starch
12. Dry fruits with sour fruits
13. Vegetables with pulses
14. Mixture of vegetables and rice biryani
15. Fruits with a little quantity of dry fruits
16. Green leafy vegetables with chapatti
17. Sprouted pulses and raw coconut

## Precautions in preparing food

To preserve nourishing elements in food the following simple precautions should be observed —

1. Wash vegetables before cutting not vice versa.
2. Put salt, tomato, coriander leaves, etc. after cooking vegetables.

3. Do not leave cut vegetables for too long.
4. Leafy vegetables should be washed before boiling. After boiling them, water need not be thrown away.
5. Cut vegetables should not be fried, in doing so many of the nutrients get destroyed.
6. After cooking vegetables eat within half an hour.
7. Food kept for three hours after cooking becomes tamsik.
8. Chapattis should be cooked of dough containing chaff in it.
9. Instead of making chapatti dough with water it is better to use the juice of methi leaves, *bathua*, white gourd, *chaulai* and green leafy vegetable as it is more healthy.
10. *Ghee* (fats) cooked once, if cooked again becomes poisonous.
11. Do not try to make food very tasty as taste lies not in the food but in appetite. Without appetite nectar also proves to be poison.
12. Make sandwiches with vegetables, do not use butter, cheese, jam, etc.
13. Salad should be cut immediately before serving and do not sprinkle salt over it. Lemon should be used in salads.
14. Oil or ghee heated up a number of times should not be used.

## Sprouted food

Sprouted food is very important for physical, mental and spiritual balances. The starch of the grain sprout gets converted into glucose and protein into amino acid and becomes easily digestible and generates strength in the body. So it is called predigested food.

Sprouted food is a good source of chlorophyll, Vitamin (A, B, C and K), calcium, phosphorous, potassium, magnesium, iron and other minerals.

Sprouted food is an appetising detoxicant and diuretic. Sprouted food is a complete diet to rejuvenate the body, so that human beings look beautiful, healthy and disease free.

It is a good source of instant energy. It is easily absorbed by the body. Sprouted food removes undernourishment. Sprouted food is anti flatulent and a laxative.

It cures diseases. Sprouted food could replace expensive fruits and vegetables. It is simple, prepared easily and is cheap. It is within every body's budget.

Sprouted food generates wholesome new life. It cannot be adulterated. Wheat, *moong, moth,* soya bean, groundnut, maize, sesame, black gram, alfalfa and other grains, cereals and seeds, etc. can be sprouted.

## Ways of sprouting

Dry grains, cereals or seeds, etc. whatever is to be sprouted, should be washed and soaked in water in a utensil. After 12 hours take it out of water and tie it in a piece of cloth in such a way that it is humid and is exposed to air. After 12 to 30 hours (depending on different food products) it will start germinating. Sprouted food is ready. Wash it and use it.

## How to eat sprouted food

1. It is preferable to consume it raw, uncooked without salt.
2. Single seed (wheat, barley, maize, etc.) sprouts can be eaten with sweet products (dates, raisins, honey etc.) and fruits can also be taken.
3. Dual seed (black gram, moong, moth, peas, ground nut, soya bean etc.) sprouted can be eaten with tomato, carrots, cucumber, capsicum, green leaves (spinach, mint, coriander, bathua etc.) other salads and lemon, these mixtures are very tasty and health giving.
4. For infants, children and old people the above stated combinations could be grounded and the paste could be given to lick or drink.
5. Sprouted food should be eaten uncooked because by cooking, its nutritional value and properties get reduced.

## Uncooked food

The basis of naturopathy is food and the main base of food is uncooked food. Uncooked food simply means that whatever food you consume after cooking according to your capacity, should be eaten uncooked.

The main cause of disease is cooking food product on fire. Cooked food takes longer to digest. If the product is fried or deep fried in oil or ghee it becomes more indigestible. While cooking, many elements get destroyed affecting the taste and nutrient value adversely. Taste is restored with the help of artificial means (salt, spices, sugar, etc.) in that case one eats more than the appetite, which causes disease.

In modern lifestyle cooked food is so deep rooted that one cannot think of giving it up. If you do not have the courage and strong resolve to give up cooked food at once, then make an effort to say good bye to cooked food and adopt uncooked food gradually.

For physical and mental health, strength for copulation, efficiency and competence human beings require balanced and healthy food products, and that is possible and can materialise only with consumption of uncooked food.

As per scientific research fresh fruits, sprouted grains, green vegetables and dry fruits contain sufficient quantity of natural salts, vitamins, protein, carbohydrates, fats and other elements essential for development, growth and living a healthy life. By using these, not only physical, mental and spiritual health becomes wholesome, it also protects against diseases, and the mind remains happy, body strengthens, the soul experiences bliss, while sexual strength can be invigorated.

Grains need not be used dry but should be eaten only after they get sprouted. While being sprouted many new nutrients, develop and those already existing get enhanced. These grain may be wheat, barley or dual black gram, moong, masoor or arhar.

Dry fruits (almonds, cashew nuts, groundnut, raisins, figs, black raisins, dry date, etc.) should also be soaked in water for eating. Seasonal fruits and vegetables should be taken fresh.

If you are unable to chew the food products then grind it into a paste and eat it with a spoon or use fingers to lick slowly so that saliva is released for facilitating its digestion.

By cooking, the chemical property of chlorophyll is destroyed in green vegetables and leaves and thus we are deprived of the element, useful for life. Cooking destroys roughage mostly in all food products, consequently constipation occurs and contamination takes place.

A person taking cooked food has some addiction or the other (tea, coffee, betel leaf, tobacco, cigarettes, liquor, etc.)

Apparently persons who do not drink but take chapattis made of maida, tea, coffee, sugar, sweets, salt, roasted fried products over a long period of time fill themselves with as much toxins as a drunkard and over a period of time have to face the consequences.

Uncooked food also has specialities like various salads, vegetables, fruits, various vegetable raitas, chutneys, nutritious milk, milk shakes, juices, sweets (dates) etc. While eating uncooked food weight loss is a sign of strength, therefore we need not be afraid of slimming on an uncooked diet. This gives energy and exalts resistance power. Mind and body feel light like a flower, the face smiles always like a blossomed flower and it invokes purity. A person living on uncooked food does not get tired due to any kind of physical or mental exertion.

## Benefits of uncooked food

1. Consumption of uncooked food gives a feeling of happiness in mind, energy in body and mental bliss, by achieving physical, mental and spiritual health.
2. It removes toxins accumulated in the body, which is the root cause of all diseases and thus prevents acute, chronic and fatal diseases.
3. Removes insomnia, induces peaceful, deep and relaxing sleep and there is a feeling of relaxation and freshness rather than tiredness.

4. Spreads youth, excitement and hope by making arteries, veins and other hard parts soft and flexible.
5. Promotes digestion of food, its absorption and excretion which takes place in our body.
6. Brings freshness, promptness, hope and energy in nervous system and removes its stiffness, tension, burning sensation and stimulation.
7. Increases weight if it is below average and decreases weight if it is above average.
8. Makes the skin beautiful, glowing, soft and flexible.
9. Keeps one away from feeling too hot in summers or too cold in winters.
10. It is very important for endocrine glands in development and proper flow of hormones secreted by them.
11. Pacifies unusually increased sexual urge by inner purification in terms of words, thought and action. Hence there will be no sinful course by religious persons if they adopt uncooked food.
12. Decreases high BP and increases low BP.
13. Removes acidity created in the body and makes the body alkaline.
14. Rejuvenates deteriorating life force.
15. Cures mental pain, disappointment, restlessness and lack of self confidence and it gives healthy, congenial and happy life.
16. Removes impotency and premature ejaculation etc., by keeping the male glands healthy and active.
17. Removes sterility in women and regulates menstrual cycle and makes it painless.
18. Maintains regular creation and growth of foetus during pregnancy.
19. Induces creative and life giving powers into mother's milk. The child becomes very healthy and beautiful, intelligent and promising and gets incomparable resistance power inside him.
20. Provides best quality pure water mainly found in fruits

and vegetables, because of which we do not require water from outside. When uncooked food loses this [...]ing into contact with fire and becomes [...]hen our need for outside water increases [...] the digestion.

[...] rid of bad breath and smelly sweat, dirty [...] smelling stool/faeces.

[...]acity to work manifold.

[...]nced, nutritious and adequate food.

[...]thy element chlorophyll (through green [...]les) and fibre. By cooking food, these [...] destroyed.

[...]al elements of food vitamins, minerals, [...], phytonutrients, enzymes, etc. which [...]essary for health and most of them are [...] heating food.

[...]ple working in call centres as they have such long and erratic working hours that most of them become prey to serious diseases.

27. It is very important for people doing mental work (scientists, students, etc.) as there is no laziness and mind works more.
28. It maintains the genes and avoids cancer.
29. It gives pleasure of various tastes, which gets limited (sweet, sour and salty) in cooked food.
30. Strengthens resistance power of a person by which he remains safe even from contagious diseases.

(For detailed knowledge read the author's book - *Secrets of Natural Diet*)

## Fibrous food

Fibre is that part of vegetables, fruits and grains which does not get digested but keeps the digestive process regulated and plays a main role in cleaning up of the rectum.

This eliminates the possibility of cancer in the intestines, constipation and piles.

Fibre is found in all natural food products (fruits, vegetables, whole grains, etc.). But when they are cleaned and processed then they become bereft of fibre, i.e. rice cleaned in machines, maida, besan, etc. When food is cooked fibre gets destroyed.

## *Chaff, a medicinal fibre*

Food grains are generally ground then strained in a sieve. In straining wheat, maize, the upper layer of the grain remains in the sieve and is called chaff and is thrown away or fed to animals. This way the most nutritious part of grain goes waste. Chaff has such elements which effect the formation of genes. It plays an important role in resisting fatal cancer of the colon, diabetes and reducing the level of cholesterol it is also found that it increases resistance power in the body and quantity of haemoglobin in the blood. Thus its vitality cannot be refuted in fighting against asthma, AIDS, allergy, etc. that is why, it should not be taken out from dough. Chapattis should have chaff in it when cooked.

## Milk

Mother's milk is the best diet for an infant. Till teething is over and the digestive organs become fully active the child requires milk. Thereafter by balanced food all his requirements are fulfilled, then he does not require milk.

Only children have a right over milk which nature has granted them right from the time of birth. Thymus gland is fully developed in a child and by the time he grows young attains his size, it becomes dormant and in a young person completely insignificant. The thymosin excreted from thymus gland helps in proper digestion of milk. That is why milk is food for children only.

Most of the people drink milk at night after dinner before sleeping. This does not permit food to get digested. Never take milk after dinner. In the morning it should be taken with breakfast. These days pure milk is found with great difficulty.

## Pasteurised milk

Vitamins and many enzymes get destroyed due to heating at a high temperature. Its proteins and calcium become so hard that they are indigestable.

## Synthetic milk

Chemically prepared fake milk is adulterated in milk thus making its purity questionable. From the point of view of health it is extremely harmful.

## Effects of oxytocin injection

These days oxytocin injection is administered on the animal by those who are in this trade. The injection affects the animal in such a way, so as to give rise to elements which are harmful to human health and they get assimilated in the milk of the animal, consumption of this milk by human beings leads to mental imbalance among them. This is proved by occurrence of anger and agitation without provocation. Hormonal glands are adversely affected, consequently paralysis, cancer, etc. dangerous diseases occur in the body. It also adversely affects the reproductive power of human beings.

## Alternatives for animal milk

Milk of soya bean, sesame, groundnut, coconut.

## Method of preparing milk

Soyabean, sesame, groundnut or whatever is to be used for making milk should be soaked in water for 12 hours. Then it should be grounded. Add to this paste six times water in quantity and then strain it. Milk is ready. This is how fresh coconut is grounded and milk is prepared from it. There is no need to soak coconut.

## Soya milk

From all angles soya milk is equivalent of cow's milk. It is difficult to find as nutritious product as soya bean in the world.

It is a storehouse of protein and its protein is of excellent quality. This is 80% alkaline. It is a good source of calcium, iron, phosphorous and Vitamin B.

Soya milk is good for children. This reduces cholesterol and is useful for heart patients and those suffering from high blood pressure. This does not permit formation of uric acid and is a better alternative for patients of arthritis.

It is useful in diseases connected with the brain, nervous, weakness, loss of memory, epilepsy, hysteria, lung ailments (mainly tuberculosis) diabetes, anaemia, ailments of the liver, gastric diseases, etc.

It is useful in all the diseases caused by acidity and eliminates the possibility of cancer.

### *Sesame (til) milk*

This is a storehouse of calcium. It also contains proteins, carbohydrates, Vitamin B, C, E, Phosphorous, iron, etc. in sufficient quantity. Knowingly or unknowingly nature has treasured a store house of nutrition in it. It gives all the necessary elements. Its fats do not lead to cholesterol formation.

This is useful in weakness of the brain, weakness of teeth, skin disease and is very beneficial in promoting sexual capacity. This alleviates three defects—vat, pitta and kaph. Because of its properties it has special importance in homes, offerings, worshipping and festivals.

### *Coconut milk*

This contains vitamin A, B, C, calcium, iron, phosphorous, etc. food products in sufficient quantity. It has a high quality alkaline oil and easily digestible proteins and carbohydrates. It improves health. The use of coconut milk cures constipation and all types of internal swelling. Children do not get rickets.

Coconut milk is extremely beneficial for those suffering from ulcer in the stomach, constipation, colitis and weak digestion.

## Groundnut milk

This also contains proteins, carbohydrates, fats, Vitamin A, Vitamin B, calcium, iron and phosphorous in good quantity. This is easily digestible, strength giving and removes weakness of the brain.

*Note* – This way milk can be prepared from almonds, sunflower, melon seeds, etc.

## Juices

The juices taken out of fruits and vegetables contain great nutritious and medicinal elements. They also contain various types of important minerals, vitamins, antioxidants, enzymes and phytonutrients. Therefore juices provide the required elements to the body and purifies the blood. It dissolves and removes the toxins accumulated in the body and provides the necessary elements for new production of cells. Therefore, juices are useful in every disease, independently or in the form of a helper. In fatal diseases such as cancer, juices are specially beneficial. It improves resistance power. It helps in proper functioning of endocrine glands of our body.

For people with weak digestion, juices of various fruits and vegetables are very beneficial.

To obtain necessary elements consumption of fruits and vegetables in large amount cannot be alone but its juice can be had in that quantity. Necessary substances of juices quickly reach to various parts of the body through blood and therefore benefit fast.

To get relief from heat if we consume juices from the market instead of having various types of cold drinks then it will only benefit rather than harm. By changing the types of juice consumed we can enjoy different tastes. For beauty and health, juices should be consumed every day. It is very necessary for children and pregnant ladies.

Juices are a better treatment for removing the addiction of intoxicating drugs.

## Precautions

1. Always drink fresh juice, do not drink juice that has been kept for a long time.
2. Drink the juice slowly.
3. Never heat the juice.
4. Never add salt or sugar to juice.
5. Take the fruit juice and vegetable juice separately.
6. Before taking out juice, wash the leafs, vegetables and fruits properly.
7. Take juices and solid food at different times.
   Note–Due to preservatives, consumption of tinned juices is very harmful.

## Main useful juicy products

Juice of white pumpkin juice of cucumber, green coconut water, pomegranate juice, pineapple juice, juice of banana stem, carrot juice, cabbage juice, sweet orange juice, sweet lemon juice, juice of water melon, juice of grapes, juice of wheat grass, beetroot juice, white gourd juice, amla juice, lemon juice, lemon and honey with water.

Combinations of carrot and cabbage, carrot and spinach, carrot and beetroot are very useful.

## Wheat grass juice

Scientific search and experiments have propounded that the juice of wheat grass promotes life force, and rules out the possibility of any disease in future. Due to its inexhaustible properties, it is incomparable and is called nectar. For its special qualities, a special place is given to it in worshipping also. It is used in all conditions.

Its juice has the capacity to help intestines and blood gets rid of its settled poisonous waste. It has the power to take out toxins so effectively that for all diseases it is recommended as an efficacious medicine.

Wheat grass provides carbohydrates, protein, all vitamins, high quality alkaline nutritious elements and chlorophyll. Its chlorophyll strengthens heart, facilitates the process of blood circulation and benefits specially intestines, lungs and uterus.

If a pregnant woman takes this juice regularly the child born to her will be beautiful, strong and healthy. If a barren woman takes it regularly, her barrenness is cured and she can see the face of her own child. If the child is given daily five drops of it the child will be beautiful and healthy.

If juice of wheat grass is taken along with satvik food all diseases are eliminated from the body.

The treatment of wheat grass juice is effective in incurable gastric trouble, acidity, diabetes, worms, Parkinson's disease, skin disease, stone formation, irregularity in menstrual cycle, heart trouble, cancer, etc.

In ailments connected with teeth and jaws its juice should be taken and jaws massaged with its juice for definite effect.

While suffering from constipation it is helpful to drink this juice and chew the grass. In very chronic constipation it could be given in enema. In ear problems apart from drinking its juice, a few drops should be put in the ear.

## *Preparation*

Fill mud in seven pots and sow some good quality wheat seeds daily in one of them and water it regularly. After ten days the plant will be 6-7 inches high. Then pluck it from first pot, cut the root away and wash the leaves thoroughly and grind into a paste. To this add water and strain it to drink, about half a glass of it. Then again sow wheat in this pot. Thus daily pluck from one pot and sow a new one.

As per need change the mud in these pots.

**Way of consumption** — Juice should be taken immediately after preparation. At a time 20 mgm to 120 mgm of it can be taken four times in a day at regular intervals. Do not eat or drink anything half an hour before or after drinking this juice.

*Note* — Initially it may cause nausea, vomit or loose motions. These are indication of heavy deposits of toxins in the body. One need not get perturbed.

## Less food for better health

Right from the olden days sages have suggested to eat only as much as to satisfy half of the appetite. Food should fill half the stomach, one fourth be kept spared for water to fill and the remaining one fourth for air. But very few people adhere to it.

Most of the people hold that less food will provide less nourishment and consequently the body will become weak. Actually this contention is wrong. Only those food products are good for the body which are easily digestible.

Remember the more you eat, the more you become amenable to diseases. Do an experiment on yourself for two weeks. For three four days you will experience hunger on account of eating less, but within a week the stomach will get accustomed to it. Then observe your body and behaviour. You will find that there is more awareness in your body. Then you will definitely realise the importance of eating less and adopt it for the rest of your life. Long lived people are found to be eating less.

It is not wise to feed without requirement in being host or out of affection.

If people realise the mystery of eating less then the problem of health as well as food problem of this world will be solved.

## *Ways of eating less*

1. Use your self control to decide your diet and take that much only in your plate. First offer it to the lord and eat as His prasad. Prasad is not taken again. Thus the quantity of food will get fixed.
2. Chew your food completely, chewing well gives satisfaction promptly. One person was fond of eating too much. When suggested that each morsel be chewed 32 times, he got satisfied on consumption of two chapattis only.

# Natural Health

3. Talking or entertaining mental tension while eating is always harmful. Unknowingly you tend to eat more.
4. You should eat only juicy, pure, and such food stuff which provides stability, strengthens the brain and heart and is easily digestible. Therefore as far as possible eat only satvik food.
5. Develop a habit of eating only twice a day.
6. Often to consume leftover food we tend to eat more than required, which is harmful to health. This is how gifted sweets are eaten, more than the required, quantity which is too harmful. Thus do not use such stuff.
7. Pickles, jams, vinegar, papad, chillies and spices, sour foods, etc. need not be consumed. They also cause to make one overeat.

## Taste is not in food but in appetite

Appetite is natural to body. If it is natural appetite then all food products will seem tasty. When there is no appetite and we eat, then tasty food is required like pickles, jams, vinegar, chilli-spices, sweet and sour stuff etc., which is harmful for health. This leads to over eating and strains the digestive process.

To make tasty artificial colours, chemicals etc. are also used which are harmful to our health.

It is necessary for human beings to know what, how much and when they should eat and when to stop eating.

Nature has created human beings to eat natural food (fruits, vegetables and dry fruits) but he relishes on unnatural food stuff.

Between two meals there should be an interval of six hours so as to rise natural appetite to find food tasty.

When we get over the habit of eating artificial food and take to fruits, salads, sprouted food, etc., and develop natural taste, then it is indeed a great pleasure in eating and that surpasses all other pleasures.

## White sugar a sweet poison

White sugar is a corrupt form of natural sugar. In its digestion process many important elements, vitamins get drained from the body, hampering other activities of the body.

On scientific analysis it is compared with liquor. It increases acidity in the body.

Excessive consumption of white sugar cause teeth problems. The main cause of arthritis is attributed to it. Its excessive use causes diseases of the liver. The main cause of diabetes is white sugar and food stuffs in which it is used.

Excessive use of sugar can lead to cancer. Sugar causes blood cholesterol.

It causes stomach ailments and also sinus.

Excessive intake of white sugar is the cause of increasing mental diseases in children today.

Its excessive use causes nervous weakness, pain during menstrual bleeding, as leucorrhoea, etc. among women.

To protect health it will be good if white sugar is given up altogether. As the natural sugar available in fruits, vegetables is easily digestible, therefore, good for health. Dates, black raisins, honey and jaggery are good substitutes of sugar.

## Salt is also poison

Excess salt in any substance makes it non eatable. It becomes poisonous. This way salt affects the inner cells, blood vessels and nerves badly. It destroys the natural taste of food.

Failure of kidney and liver is the result of excess salt. It affects soft parts of intestine and stomach. Its excess use results in cancer, obesity, diabetes, cold, insomnia etc. It increase heart beat and blood pressure. It increases acidity.

Salt does not get digested easily. As body excretes the salt dissolved with water so excess use of salt increase the thirst. It works to weaken the bones. It has the nature to dissolve.

The body gets salt from the natural substances (fruits, vegetables, sprouted grains etc.) when eatable substances are cooked their salts gets destroyed. So small quantity of salt may be put in them. With natural substances (fruits, vegetables, sprouts, juices, curd etc.) salt should not be used any way.

Body accepts the salt from the natural eatables in organic form. Other salts are being excreted by the body always and if they store in the body, it results in a severe disease. It is like a burden to our excretory organ. Salt is salt whether it is black or white.

## Food products causing diseases

**Soft drinks**—According to a report presented sometimes ago, soft drinks contain 40 to 72 mgm intoxicating elements, glycerine, alcohol, eastergum, citric acid and glycerol from animals.

If you put any soft drink in the toilet for an hour, it will clean it like phenyl does. If a rusted spot is rubbed with a cloth soaked in a soft drink it will get cleaned. It takes many years for mud to dissolve teeth and bones, but leave them in soft drinks for 10 days and see the devastation.

By drinking such harmful drinks we are only collecting chemicals which damage the liver, intestines, etc.

**Maida**—While preparing maida natural salts, vitamins, roughage, etc. is destroyed and only low quality starch remains. Maida sticks in the intestines and causes constipation and fermentation leading to complications. Many diseases are caused naturally.

**Preserved food**—These contain a chemical preservative which the body has to eject out, straining unnecessarily the body and kidneys.

**Fast foods and Chinese food**—They contain ajinomoto or monosodium glutamate which gradually accumulates and creates toxicity, leading to diseases like cancer.

## Effects of non-vegetarian food

Human beings are not non vegetarian. The formation of their teeth, salivary glands and small intestines and other digestive organs are not similar to non-vegetarian animals.

Human beings can spend all their life without non-vegetarian food, but cannot survive on non-vegetarian food alone.

Non-vegetarians are short lived whereas vegetarian are long lived. Non-vegetarians are not strong and healthy but are weak and diseased. Non-vegetarians get tired early than vegetarian.

The amount of energy, willingness to work, interest, commitment and determination that a vegetarian has is not there in a non-vegetarian.

Non-vegetarian food is acidic. It reduces resistance power causing a number of diseases. Non-vegetarian food has excessive uric acid which gets accumulated in the body and causes arthritis.

Non-vegetarian food can cause heart disease and cancer. Non-vegetarian food causes mental problems, loss of patience, anger and irritability. The propensity of sexual urges and agitation increases. Cruelty and unkindness increases. Criminal propensities are invoked. Surveys have proved that among criminals the number of non-vegetarians is much more than vegetarians.

Non-vegetarian food gives rise to tamsik propensities leading to incidents of mutual differences, domestic scrabbles, fights, snatching, etc.

Egg is also non-vegetarian. It contains a lot of cholesterol which is harmful for the heart.

Flesh or egg of any animals is poison for human body. Although Westerners are non-vegetarians, they are now converting to vegetarianism.

## Food of special quality

The following are special quality products to be used necessarily in daily life.

## 1. Basil

Not only with a religious point of view but from the point of view of medicine, basil has an unparalleled place. The odour of basil spreading in air will purify the atmosphere as far as it reaches and make it health giving. Harmful germs, insects, mosquitoes and flies will not develop.

Basil is of two types:
1. Shyam Tulsi (black stems and darkish leaves).
2. Ram Tulsi (White stems and green leaves).

Both the forms are almost the same in properties and odour. Yet the former is considered a better quality. Whoever eats five leaves of basil daily gets protection against many diseases, mental weakness is taken care of, memory improves and also grasping power gets boosted. An old person does not feel weak on consumption of basil regularly. It also cures infectious diseases. Basil leaves purify blood. From the point of view of curing diseases, basil is not only a medicine but is a great medicine. It is nectar because today humanity is disease stricken, and all those diseases can be singly cured by using basil.

Ayurveda considers it as destroyer of tridosha (gas, acid and cough).

### *Juice of basil*

Every morning if basil juice is taken on an empty stomach with water, then it exhilarates brightness, strength and memory. It increases digestive power and kills worms. Vomiting stops immediately. It is effective in malaria. Increases the functional capacity of kidneys. It helps in acidity, dysentery, white patches, obesity etc. To a patient of fever, cough, running nose and repeated sneezing, asthma—three grams of basil juice is given. It helps perceptibly. Patients having stones should be given basil juice with honey for six months. Cough, cold, fever, loose motions, vomiting can be cured by basil juice. It reduces blood cholesterol.

## 2. Emblimyrobalan (*Amla*)

Emblimyrobalan has the qualities of a fruit and medicine both. It has a lot of importance in Ayurveda. Due to its astringent like quality it destroys vata and kapha and its sweetness and coolness cures pitta thereby removing all the three *doshas*.

It has vitamin C in abundance. Its speciality is that its vitamins do not get destroyed by heating or drying.

Amla gives youthfulness to young and rejuvenates old ones. Experimenting on this, Sage Chyavana regained his youthfulness. The amount of disease resistant, blood purifying and strength giving elements which are available in emblimyrobalan, are not found in any other product or medicine in this world. That is why a person craving for health and happiness must give a primary place to amla in his diet.

Emblimyrobalan strengthens teeth and jaws and makes body and mind energetic. It is very useful in diseases of the nerves, restlessness in the heart, palpitation, obesity, spleen, blood pressure, ring worms, leucorrhoea, weakness of the uterus, impotence, skin diseases, urinary problems and complication of the bones. For weakness of the liver and for curing jaundice it should be given with honey and water as a tonic.

Emblimyrobalan can be used in the form of juice, chutney and powder to be taken with water.

## 3. *Triphala*

One part *Harad*, two parts *baheda* and four parts of *amla* mixed together make *triphala*. This is ordinary food stuff and medicine too.

It has all tastes (bitter, sour, sour and bitter, pungent, sweet and salty) in it.

Triphala cures ailments and boosts up life force, leads to increase in appetite, clears bowels and helps in getting deep sleep.

It is very efficacious if taken with water every day in the morning.

Consumption of triphala cures weakness of the male, and all diseases connected with menstrual cycle among females, leucorrhoea, etc.

Benefits of consuming triphala over a period of twelve years.

| | |
|---|---|
| By using for one year | ..... Overcome laziness |
| By using for two years | ..... Freedom from all diseases. |
| By using for three years | ..... Improvement in eyesight |
| By using for four years | ..... Increases beauty |
| By using for five years | ..... Development of intelligence |
| By using for six years | ..... Strengthens the body |
| By using for seven years | ..... Blackening of hair |
| By using for eight years | ..... Old regain youthfulness |
| By using for nine years | ..... Special power for the eyes |

For Clairvoyance it is necessary to do Ashtanga yoga.

## 4. Neem (Margosa)

Margosa is a very useful tree. Right from its root to stem, flower, leaves and fruits are full of medicinal qualities. Its bitterness is its greatest quality. Neem tree remains throughout the year.

It is generally an antiseptic. Chewing five neem leaves daily provides cure for all diseases, purifies blood and protects against infectious diseases, cures all teeth trouble. Voice becomes sonorous.

Teeth become clean, strong shiny, free from disease if brushed with the stem of its branches.

Neem leaves are ground and the paste is applied on boils and perforations for relief. Leaves of neem are burnt to get smoke which makes insects, flies and mosquitoes run away.

Neem leaves are boiled in water and if that water is used for bathing along with balanced food and habits all skin problems (itching, eczema psoriasis, etc.) can be treated.

Neem oil is used in preparing many medicines. According to Ayurveda neem cures gas, acid and cough.

For allergy, skin diseases, and diabetes the juice of neem leaves is very efficacious. For hair fall and greying two drops of neem oil should be put in the nostril. To get rid of dandruff neem oil should be massaged on the scalp at night.

## 5. Coconut

For its qualities coconut is considered to be an auspicious fruit in the Indian culture and Hindus use it almost on all festivals. Our Vedas and religious books refer to the utility of coconut now and then. Coconut is food stuff and medicine too. It has Vitamin A, B, C, calcium, iron, phosphorous, etc. minerals in sufficient quantity. It has a very high quality alkaline oil, which provides enough fat to the body. The protein derived from it is of very high quality and its carbohydrates help in growth.

Coconut is cooling, easily digestible, diuretic, rejuvenating, strength giving, develops enzymes, red blood cells, removes complication of gas, acid and blood. Its dry kernal is pure, likable and strength giving.

By chewing coconut the possibility of any kind of cancer in the mouth can be alleviated.

If the pregnant woman is fed coconut daily the child would be healthy and strong and during labour it would not be too painful for the mother. The water of fresh coconut is as good as mother's milk from the point of view of its properties. This provides health to children.

Coconut milk is extremely beneficial for those suffering from ulcer in the stomach, constipation, colitis and weak digestion.

## 6. Coconut water

Coconut water is naturally sterilised and is full of minerals. It nullifies the bad effects of medicines. It is a tasty drink which helps in indigestion. It is perfectly safe for children. If taken with honey, it acts as an effective tonic. It is very effective in cholera, it takes out the poisonous germs of cholera from the intestines. During dehydration it should be administered with lemon juice in it.

It contains potassium and chlorine in right proportion. It has special use in kidney ailments, less urination, stone formation, toxaemia in pregnancy, excessive albumin, measles, typhoid, etc.

Among children and pregnant women it could be given for relief with lemon juice in it, in the condition of nausea and vomiting. Mixed with milk it removes constipation and indigestion. In all infectious diseases it is very helpful. It is also efficacious in asthma and ulcer. Washing the face with coconut water removes dark blemishes, black spots and pimples and makes the face glow.

## 7. Honey

Honey is like nectar for human beings. When a human being becomes totally lifeless, weak and loses speech even, administering honey makes new life force flow into the body. It is called predigested food and provides instant energy. Right from birth and till after death it is used. If given with milk to children it not only makes them strong but also free from disease. It makes the human body beautiful, healthy and glowing. Old people experience rejuvenation.

Many chemical elements are found in honey which are extremely useful for human beings. Vitamin A, B, C are in sufficient quantity. Essential minerals like iron, copper, calcium, sodium, phosphorous, iodine are also present in it. It is an antiseptic also.

Regular intake of honey makes the body strong, energetic, fresh and disease resistent. Removes weakness of respiratory system, asthma, weakness of nervous system, digestive system and skin problems. It purifies blood and acts as an expectorant and increases digestive power.

Honey and lemon juice consumption removes tiredness and cholesterol. Honey makes fat people thin and thin people fat.

Water and honey mixed together should be taken on an empty stomach. Mixing it in hot water is harmful. In winters it should be taken in lukewarm water. It should never be heated on fire.

## Indications of pure honey

Pure honey does not get dissolved in water instantly. Pure honey smells nice. It gets frozen in winter and melts in summer. In pure honey if a cotton wick is soaked and burnt it will continue to burn. Pure honey if dropped on a cloth or a paper does not cause a stain. In appearance it is transparent. Pure honey when dropped on a plate false like a snake curling, while impure honey spreads immediately on falling.

## Intoxicating products — enemy of health

A person addicted to drugs can never be healthy or happy. Addiction is like cutting one's own feet.

Pan masala, gutka, tobacco, beedi, cigarette, liquor, opium, charas and smack, etc. fall in the category of intoxicating products.

They are all more harmful than the other. They enter our body like friends and destroy us like enemies.

Tea, coffee and betel leaf are promoted in a civilized society, which are detrimental for life force. All types of intoxicating products are the worst enemies of health. Smoke let out by smoking also harms non-smokers.

Intoxication numbs the nerves of a human being, which makes him feel sleepy, the brain becomes inactive, tongue thickens, loss of taste takes place, mouth does not open, kidneys get damaged, coughing increases. Loss of teeth is prompt. In young age one feels old. Speech gets slowed down.

Different types of diseases befall. It is the root cause of impotency. Nervous tissues and tissues of the brain become inactive. Gradually life force is reduced and addicted person meets his own doom very soon.

## Remedies for giving up addiction

Strong determination, mental strength and the following yogic activity with improved diet can help in giving up addiction.

**Shat karma**—Kunjal, Sutraneti, Jalneti, Kapalbhati, Shankh Prakshalan.

**Yogic exercises**—Breathing kriya, padmasana, swastikasana, gomukhasana, ardhamatsyendrasana, naukasana, ashvasthasana, pad-hastasana, naukasana, katichakrasana, garudasana, tadasana, janu shirshasana, paschimottanasana, bhunmanasana, yogmudrasana, shalabhasana, urdhvasarvangasana, halasana, surya namaskar, shavasana.

**Pranayama**—Nari shodhan, sheetali, seetkari.

**Mahamudra**—Ujjai and vipareet karni.

**Dhyan**—Practice dhyana and yoga nidra daily in the morning and evening..

**Food**—Fruits, salads, sprouted grains should be taken in increased quantity.

Spinach, cabbage, bathua, coriander, mint leaves, clean radish leaves, turnip leaves and other eatables daily 100-200 gms, washed and eaten for helping in getting rid of intoxication.

**Special**—Those who wish to give up smoking, gutka, tobacco, etc. should take a piece of small *harad* in their mouth and suck its juice whenever the desire to take intoxicating drug arises. After a few days they will get over this habit forever.

## How to recognise an addict

1. Less attendance in school, college, office or factory.
2. Keeping awake late in the night without any reason.
3. Leaving old friends for new.
4. Asking for more money to spend.
5. Getting angry all of a sudden without any reason and abnormal behaviour.

6. Tiredness, laziness, restlessness, trembling, sweating and unimpressive face.
7. Swelling below the eyes, sticky red eyes.
8. Non-interest in social festivals and feeling of weakness.
9. Disturbance in sleep repeatedly and change in the time of sleeping and the way of sleeping.
10. Reduction in digestive power, weight and patience.
11. Borrowing money or stealing (domestic items getting disappeared) habitually.
12. Telling lies unnecessarily.
13. Spot of cigarette burns on the body or clothes.
14. Stiffness in the stomach.

## What should you do as parents

1. Assure that the child's health is all right and he eats food properly, sleeps sufficiently and does exercises.
2. Information should pass between parents and teachers, They should help each other for curing intoxication in the child.
3. Medical check up should be done after regular intervals.
4. Prompt the child to work more, exercise and participate in games.
5. Some time should be spent together to promote unity in the family, specially while taking dinner.
6. Be a miser while giving pocket money but give love in abundance.
7. Not only cater to your child's physical needs, but also provide for his mental needs, and promote security in him.
8. Seek children's help in domestic work.
9. Children like discipline which indicates that parents pay attention to them.
10. Discuss their problems of the school sensibly and with patience.
11. Never pressurise the child with hopes which cannot be fulfilled.
12. Be completely strict but behave honourably.

## For a healthy life what to leave and what to adopt

| Leave | Adopt |
|---|---|
| 1. White sugar | 1. Jaggery, honey |
| 2. Maida or fine atta | 2. Rough atta and porridge sprouted wheat. |
| 3. Polished rice | 3. Hand grounded rice |
| 4. Fried vegetables | 4. Raw and boiled vegetable |
| 5. Tea and coffee | 5. Basil, saunf and chaff tea or soup. |
| 6. Pan gutka | 6. Saunf and elaichi (cardamom) |
| 7. Supari | 7. Dry amla |
| 8. Pickle | 8. Fresh chutney |
| 9. Sweets | 9. Dates, raisins, sweet fruits |
| 10. Red chillies | 10. Pepper and green chilli. |
| 11. Soft drinks and canned | 11. Lemon, Honey in water, coconut water, juices. |
| 12. Non-vegetarian food | 12. Vegetarian food |
| 13. Over eating | 13. Eating less |
| 14. Use of salt | 14. Only boiled vegetables |
| 15. Cooked food | 15. Uncooked food |
| 16. Heavy food | 16. Digestive food |
| 17. Bed Tea | 17. Water kept in copper vessel overnight. |
| 18. Fast food | 18. Fruit diet. |
| 19. Atta without chaff | 19. Atta with chaff |
| 20. Rice strained of its water | 20. Rice boiled with water |
| 21. Eating late in the night | 21. Eating three hours before sleeping |
| 22. Eating without appetite | 22. Not eating without appetite |
| 23. Laziness | 23. Hard work |
| 24. Tiredness | 24. Relaxation |
| 25. Negative attitude | 25. Positive attitude |
| 26. Too much sex | 26. Self control |
| 27. Air tight clothes | 27. Cotton and loose clothes |

28. Tooth paste          28. Neem brush
29. Smoking              29. Chewing harad
30. Tobacoo chewing      30. Chewing amla

## Importance of rest

As exercise is necessary for good health, so is relaxation. After eating and a long period of hard work the body needs rest. A person exhausted by hard work recovers his strength immediately after resting. There is no better remedy for tiredness than rest. Both mental and physical rest is required, in that case only the state of complete rest is achieved.

Sleeping is the best means of rest. For resting for a short time shavasana is very effective. Generally people rest physically but mental rest is far from them. For a while stop mental exertion, close the eyes, feel peaceful and without tension. This will give relaxation. In the office close the eyes, cup them with your hands, with your elbows on the table for effective mental rest.

After an interval of three hours, physical and mental rest should be taken, this exalts the capacity to work. If there is no relaxation, physical and mental ailments crop up.

Meditation gives rest to the mind. Complete rest is like medicine.

Note – Unwillingness to do any work is an indication of requirement of rest.

## Sound sleep

Sleep has a very important place as far as health is concerned. After sleeping toxins are emitted from the body and minute cells get replenished which facilitates the flow of fresh vigour in the body.

Not sleeping as per need and remaining awake with the help of artificial means or stimulants like tea or coffee gives rise to various diseases.

Sleeping more than required is also harmful. Leaving children, patients and pregnant women apart, for all the others, sleeping during the day is harmful. By sleeping during the day liver is adversely affected and sexual urges increase.

## Precautions related to sleep

1. Eat three hours before sleeping.
2. Early to bed and early to rise.
3. Before sleeping clean the mouth, teeth, tongue and throat.
4. Before sleeping one should urinate and defecate and wash the excretory organs by washing them with cold water.
5. Do not wear tight clothes.
6. Don't let television interfere with the time of sleeping.
7. The bed should be neat and clean but the mattress need not be soft and pillow should be thin.
8. Bedroom should be airy.
9. While sleeping feet should be towards the north or west and one should sleep turned on the left side or on the belly like a child.
10. Before going to sleep never let the mind wander instead read good books or practise concentration on any of the following
    (1) Breathing (inspiration and expiration)
    (2) Chanting mantras
    (3) Reverse counting from 100 to 1
11. Before sleeping practise self review and decide upon the ways of improvement. Just before sleeping these thoughts can be easily accepted by the subconscious mind and then it will start working accordingly.
12. By eating satvik food and leading a satvik way of life one sleeps peacefully and happily.
13. Sedative pills should not be taken. Although one may sleep well with the help of medicines but over a period of time they prove harmful.

14. Those who indulge in more physical labour need more sleep. For an ordinary person six hours of sleep is sufficient. For old people five hours sleep is enough.
15. For sleeping well, practise yognidra and shavasana.

## Power of silence

In Indian culture and all religions maintenance of silence has been attributed a very important role. Silence increases physical and spiritual strength.

By talking too much, physical energy and strength is dissipated. Maintenance of silence is a process of conserving strength. Silence saves one from useless talks and lies. He overcomes the instinct for fulfilment of worldly wishes, anger, arrogance and greed. Life gets disciplined. The speech is controlled and spiritual development takes place. Silence can help us get rid of mental ailments. To overcome anger there is no better alternative as maintaining silence.

It increases capacity to work. A person should speak as little as possible, in a sweet and controlled manner. Unnecessary arguments, discussions should be avoided. Control of speech is the greatest control. A person who remains silent or speaks sparingly can do something great.

Only participate in creative discourses, as that will help derive new knowledge. If you feel that the talk that is going on is pointless, meaningless and intended to dissipate energy then do not participate, on the contrary listen without any reaction and leave that place as soon as the opportunity arises.

Every day consciously silence should be maintained for sometime. In a week if silence is maintained for a few hours it can generate immense strength and silence for 24 hours will give you such experiences that you will say it is magical.

While maintaining silence stop writing your thoughts on a piece of paper unless absolutely necessary—while maintaining silence do not watch television or listen to the radio.

## Anger — a dangerous disease

The greatest enemy of health is anger. It can also be called temporary madness, as in anger one tends to take wrong decisions one after another. Anger leads to ailment of digestive process, mental disorders, heart problems, etc. Anger causes to reduce the working capacity of our muscles and damages its working process. Anger can make hell the life of an individual, family and society. Anger is the root cause of many crimes.

A person prone to anger can neither be a good fighter nor a good player. He can never succeed in competitive fields. Anger is such a spark, if not extinguished in the initial stages it assumes the shape of such a fire which burns everything leaving the person only to repent.

## *Easy ways of controlling anger*

1. Speak out your mental agony peacefully.
2. Contemplate whether everything can be set right by being angry.
3. Whenever you are angry think of the consequences.
4. By taking Satvik food anger can be controlled.
5. Direct the energy dissipated in anger in creative work after controlling it.
6. By practising yoga, energy generating anger can be channelised.
7. If experiencing extreme anger massage the ears.
8. Do not get agitated after hearing from one side alone, Decide after hearing both the sides.
9. Adopt a positive outlook.
10. Do not force the present generation to think like your own.
11. Do not see who is wrong, see what is wrong.
12. Expecting an outburst of anger, drink a glass of water and change the topic.

13. "One said the other accepted, all say that both are wise" this policy should be adopted by husband, and wife, brothers, brother – sister, sisters, father – son, mother-in-law – daughter-in-law, sister-in-laws, etc. for alleviating the stake of anger.
14. What cannot be cured can be endured smilingly.
15. Write your thoughts in detail.
16. Whatever happens, accept it happily holding the view that whatever the Lord does is for good.
17. A jolly person can control anger easily.
18. Accept change, that is the rule of nature.
19. Silence helps greatly in controlling anger. Nothing else helps as much. Thus maintain silence and contemplate over yourself, do self analysis.
20. Beware of the race of desires because hurdles in the way of fulfilling wishes inflame anger.
21. Remain detached.
22. Learn to forgive.
23. Do not react immediately in a problem.
24. Learn to disagree from others, without getting angry.
25. By not being angry, an enmity can be converted into friendship.
26. As you want from others, do the same to them.
27. Do not have expectations from others. Any good done to them will not go waste, it will come back later in the form of a reward.
28. Remember-the enemy makes you angry to dissipate your strength.
29. Read such literature regularly which will help you to develop physically, mentally and spiritually.

*Note* – Artificial scolding or exhibition of anger is not harmful, you should become normal immediately thereafter.

## Mental tension

For a healthy life it is essential to be without tensions. Tensions have a detrimental effect on the nervous system, digestion, sleep, blood pressure, muscles, etc. leading to toxicity and innumerable diseases.

## Main diseases caused by tension

1. High blood pressure
2. Heart disease
3. Asthma
4. Migraine
5. Spondylosis
6. Acidity and peptic ulcer
7. Menstrual irregularity
8. Insomnia
9. Diabetes
10. Backache and shoulder pain
11. Tiredness
12. Depression
13. Mental weakness
14. Weak eyesight
15. Paucity of semen or early ageing
16. Constipation
17. Cough and cold

It is astonishing that all those who are mentally dull by birth mostly do not have any physical disease because they are free from mental tension.

## Indication of mental tension

1. Sleeplessness or disturbed sleep, nightmares.
2. Irritability and anger
3. Headache and heaviness in the head
4. Addiction
5. Talking about one's own problems
6. Unable to concentrate
7. Wasting time and postponement of work
8. Chewing nails.
9. Negative thinking

10. Erratic thoughts
11. To boast high
12. Get perturbed at any problem
13. Illusion of undesired happenings
14. Memory becomes weak.
15. Driving carelessly.
16. Disinterest in social, family and business matters.
17. Feeling of insecurity
18. Shaking the knees while sitting
19. Repeated intake of stimulating drinks like tea, coffee, etc.
20. Blinking too often
21. Embarrassed nature.

## Causes of mental tension

1. Unhealthy body
2. Comparative point of view and competition, bitterness and feeling of jealousy.
3. Negative attitude
4. Excessive work load
5. Fear of failure
6. Unemployment and other financial problems
7. Unfulfilment of desires
8. Extremely ambitious nature.
9. Any kind of intoxication.
10. Insecure atmosphere and uncooperative colleagues
11. Get influenced with others very easily.
12. Illegal work or occupation
13. Being sentimental (Taking everything to heart).
14. Harsh natured partner
15. Noisy and loud atmosphere at work place.
16. Incapable subordinates
17. Failure in sexual relations or love affairs.
18. Insults, taunts and displeasure.
19. Telling lies.
20. Ill effects of television on subconscious mind.

## Freedom from tension

1. The most easy way to get freedom from tension is positive attitude.
2. Early morning walk, exercise, yogasanas, pranayam, meditation, shavasana and yog nidra are extremely useful in alleviating tension.
3. The remote control of your happiness should be in your own hand not in anyone else. If you get tensed up due to something said or done by others, it indicates that the remote control of your happiness is in other's hands.
4. Try to find out the root cause of problems and find their solutions, as problems come with their solutions also.
5. Don't bother who's wrong or right, instead think about what is wrong or right.
6. Try to understand the other's point of view because you can change yourself not the other.
7. Finish necessary tasks before they become urgent. Learn to divide and choose works.
8. Utilise your time properly.
9. Choose competent workers.
10. Do not do too many things at a time. Take up only as much as is within your capacity.
11. There is always scope for progress in all situations.
12. If someone tells about your faults, welcome him because this is in your favour.
13. Truth never dies, if you are on the path of truth then there is no need to worry in any circumstances.
14. Detachment does not cause tension.
15. Compromise with situations.
16. If you try to bring peace and happiness in others' lives you will feel the same in your own.
17. When a worry bothers, stop thinking on that topic and concentrate on something else, because thinking on one topic for too long causes tension.

18. Be forgivable and tolerable and always keep smiling.
19. Be childish with children and enjoy playing with them.
20. Keep some hobbies which delight you like reading, etc.
21. Soothing and peaceful music also gives relief to stressed and tired mind.
22. To rock on a rocking chair gives the feeling of lightness and mental pleasure.
23. Financial planning should be done by purchasing insurances for higher education of children, their marriage, expenditure on hospitalisation in case of disease and accident, provision of the income in case of accident and disability.

Provision for retired life, emergency fund, untimely death of the earning member, maintenance of income of the family, etc.

## *Impact of thoughts on our health*

Human beings become as they think. Thoughts have a close impact on health. Those who are too indulgent, lustful, vulgar in their thoughts and talk and entertain themselves this way can never possess good health. Worries, anger,

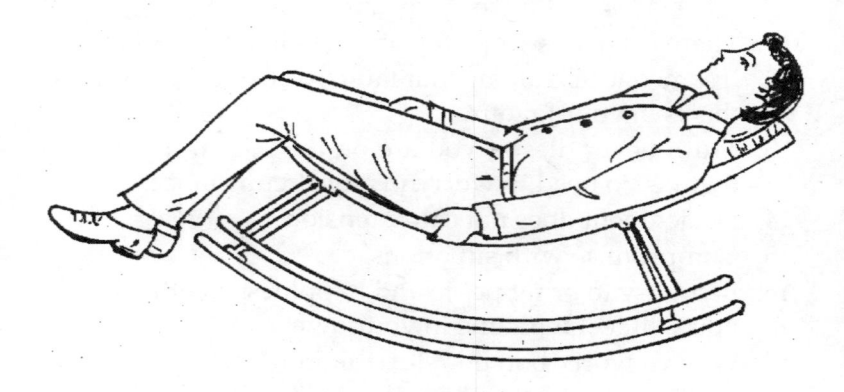

**Rocking Chair**

fear, dissatisfaction, envy, ill feeling, greed, arrogance, etc. ill thoughts are chief causes of diseases.

For instance wrong thoughts cause the following diseases:

*Worries* – cause high blood pressure, heart ailments, diabetes, insomnia, etc.

*Fear* – causes greying of hair at a young age and early ageing.

*Anger* – causes ulcers in stomach and intestines.

*Greed* – causes indigestion and loose motions.

*Disappointment* – causes indigestion and paralysis, etc.

Some people suffer from diseases only because of wrong way of thinking. Such people may be given treatment but they will not improve unless their way of thinking and thoughts improve.

As bad thoughts lead to diseases, good thoughts cure them.

If the subconscious mind is confident that the disease is getting cured then it will definitely. Not only one but many diseases can be cured like this. Thus the patient might be suffering from any ailment but he should practise it to feel healthy.

A disease incurable by medicine can be cured by the feeling of being healthy.

Television has a very bad effect on the subconscious mind, therefore, its programmes and timings should be managed properly.

## Positive thinking

In this world nothing is good or bad only thinking makes it so. Our perception attributes goodness or evil, negative or positive properties to everything. We may have a positive point of view, by taking into account the good qualities or a negative point of view, by looking only at the drawbacks.

In any country, society or family there cannot be unity and love till people are looking for each other's faults.

A clear minded person looks for good qualities in the other person, whereas a corrupt mind always looks for faults. An optimist goes forward keeping in mind the past, a pessimist thinks of the future and reverts back to the past.

If one feels ill one falls ill, although there may not be any sign of illness in him. Negative thoughts drain away 95% of our competence. That is why negative thoughts are our greatest enemies.

As we speak we think. As we think we work. As we work our habits will develop. Our habits will make our character. Our character will decide our fate.

## *Benefits of a positive mental attitude*

1. Tension reduces
2. One experience happiness in all circumstances.
3. Better relationships are maintained, brotherhood is there.
4. Development of complete personality.
5. One reaches the heights of success.
6. No problem causes tension because positive thoughts teach the art of finding solutions for problems.
7. Positive encouragement makes an evil person good.
8. Everyone possesses some unique qualities in him and positive attitude gives the power to recognize those qualities in everyone.
9. Sadness cannot touch a person with a positive attitude.
10. The capacity to work increases.
11. It boosts up patience and self confidence.
12. It increases the decision-making power.
13. Creative way of thought appears.
14. Positive thoughts develop such hormones which help improve the resistance power of the body.

*Remember* – You may be working in any field, the key to success is your outlook.

## How to develop a positive attitude

1. Remember situations with extreme conflicts are a true test for human beings.
2. Remember a critic is our friend and does good for us in life, that criticism makes us alert that we should work properly.
3. Remember every circumstance is an opportunity to learn something new.
4. "Every thing has a dual meaning; adopt whichever is good, and let go whichever is bad." Adhere to this motto.
5. Remember downfalls make a man learn to live life.
6. Accept changes, the change is the rule of life.
7. Do not look at a person or situation's faults but try to look at its positive aspects and his good qualities.
8. Love whatever work you do and make a constant effort to do it better.
9. Whenever a guest comes do not talk about the sorrows of your country, society, family and work.
10. Take interest in other's thoughts and welcome their viewpoints and contentions.
11. Place yourself in the other person's situations and then try to decide.
12. Be optimistic
13. Stop blaming others.
14. Ignore small things.
15. If there is a hurdle then find the way or make the way.
16. Defeat is only the step to success. A child learns to walk only by falling down a number of times.
17. Stay away from people who pinpoint drawbacks in everything, or talk negative.
18. Whatever the Lord does is good, counting on this mental attitude you can find some good in all circumstances.
19. Develop the habit of encouraging others.

20. In your daily life always use positive words, while talking or writing.
21. Read good books and meet good people from whom you may get something to learn.
22. Do not bow your head while walking. Negative thoughts come from walking with bowed head.
23. Whenever a negative thought comes, say "No" to it or convert it into positive.

## Creative thinking

To think creatively is to get fresh thoughts, new concepts and searching for new solutions. Creative thinking sharpens the intellect and removes mental tension.

Thinking power only differentiates human beings from animals. The test of man's intellect is his ability to overcome difficult situations smoothly.

A person without decision making power is one who has not practised good habits. Thus a person with intellect must necessarily think.

Develop your potential, and solve complications yourself, the solution is within you. Your thought process only decides your mentality. Understand the problem from all angles which may take an hour but that will save you many hours while actually doing the job.

We make futile efforts to imitate or equal others. We too must be possessing such powers or qualities which are lacking in others. Everyone in this world has something unique about himself. Do a self analysis. Forget what the others are doing, Do only what you can excel in. Try to discover your inherent qualities. These qualities are your treasure. and may fetch you great rewards.

When we succeed in a job, we should direct our potential towards another direction. If we don't continue in our struggle, it will lead to stagnation which will consequently ruin us.

## *Ways to creative thinking*

1. Either alone or a group of people may keep an object of daily use before them and start thinking what are its other uses. This can be made into a play game.
2. Take up a problem and find various solutions to it.
3. Find the way to reach any destination or make way for it.
4. Think there will be more better ways.
5. Set your aim in life, which is very important, and then with full commitment and determination pursue it. Automatically you will start thinking creatively.
6. Get together with your friends for a study circle for exchange of ideas over different subjects.
7. Change is necessary and the only constant factor in our life that is why we must adapt ourselves to it.
8. Man is master of his fate. He can make it or break it according to his own imagination. Use your imagination in such a way that you may see light in your difficult and unknown sojourns.
9. Keep your mind alert. Do self introspection and always have a positive attitude in life.
   Try to do something which others cannot do.
10. Observe successful people and find out the qualities that make them different and try to adopt them.
11. Suggest the solution along with complaint.
12. Always be curious to discover and learn new things
13. Try to be more in the company of creative people.
14. Everybody walks on the path which has already been made. Try to make some new paths for yourself.

## Memory power

Remember that good health is the basis of good memory..

To keep the brain active, proper exercise and pure air are necessary.

As much efforts are put to exalt memory power it will improve.

We get knowledge of this world through our sense organs. Therefore, it is essential to keep them alert.

Whatever you wish to remember be clear and open about it.

If you wish to remember a name, write it down when alone. Thereafter connect the name with the object.

The mystery of a successful and happy life lies in our interests, and good memory is the basis of our interests. If you learn something with interest and enthusiasm then you will easily remember it.

With the help of Gyan mudra (hand posture) and meditation, the memory power develops manifolds.

## Power of desire and aim

For physical, mental, spiritual and material success in life one should have a desire for it. A person who has no aim in life is like a train without an engine. A person with a weak determination is not competent to take any decision and incapable of executing the decisions already taken.

People with no determination and aim, while doing a job think it would not have been done, and when not doing a particular work think it should have been taken up. Such a person develops lack of confidence. Therefore, they are rather shy in thoughts and deeds, hence do not progress much.

Remember as we mould ourselves the world gives us that shape alone and the way we spend our life, our life takes that course alone.

A person who concentrates on achieving his aim with determination, his mind does not flutter here and there.

To start any work the present moment is the best time for it.

If your drawback in one field hinders your progress, then achieve success in another direction to make up for it. Hindrances can be overcomed.

When we use our discretionary power to fix a time for realisation of our aim and start to fulfil it, then, our sub¬conscious mind works very fast and we automatically find new ways to do it, and success becomes certain.

## Character formation

Only a person who leads a moral life remains free from diseases. Character or morality is such a source of power within a human being which gives him courage in difficult times.

Education of building of character and moral values begins at a tender age only. Just listening to religious messages, moral teachings, etc. are not effective, unless practised. It is better to be a man of strong character than be famous. The way you spend your time and your true thoughts give a review of your character. A person's character is known by his speech. A person's thought process builds his character. Truthfulness is recommended as the best, but character bears a higher place. Character is a tree, and fame is its shadow. A person with character likes to bear his criticism.

**Character of a man is known by the company he keeps or does not keep.**

## Laughing for health

Laughing is such a great quality which is possessed by human beings alone amongst all living beings.

Laughing and smiling overcomes anger. A person who always remains happy is dear to everyone.

If you want to be healthy try to laugh loudly as much as possible. Every day for five minutes practise laughter in different poses before the mirror.

Laughing removes tension, gives peace to the mind, saves you from heart problems, makes the face beautiful. Laughing loudly cures many ailments of the stomach, that is why it is necessary to laugh loudly at least thrice or four times a day.

Always keep a smile on your face even while talking, walking, sitting and standing. This will keep you in a positive frame of mind, relieve tension and keep you cheerful.

**One who learns to swallow poison of sorrow smilingly, has learnt the art of living practically.**

## For an attractive beauty

An attractive beauty is a synthesis of inner and outer physical beauty. With the use of chemically mixed cosmetics temporarily one appears beautiful temporarily, but later on it can have adverse effects on one's skin. According to dermatologists most of the people coming to them for skin problems have been the victims of harsh chemicals used in the variously available cosmetics and beauty products available these days. The hair colours which are used these days have harmful chemicals which can be detrimental to the eyes.

The real secret to a healthy and beautiful skin and body is happiness. There is no substitute to it. Therefore anger and mental tension should be completely avoided and one should be positive in life because that is what brings radiance in your life both internally and externally.

Take to natural Indian means of beautification. Even people in the West are adopting Indian natural means of beautification.

### *Tips for a beautiful skin and a healthy body*

1. Green vegetables, salads, fruits, fruit juices should be taken regularly. Not only will this bring a glow to the skin but will also help you keep wrinkles at bay for a really long time.
2. Avoid taking too much spicy, salty, fried and sweet foods. Preparations of *khoya* are detrimental for your health.
3. Soak 20-25 gms of raisins in water at night and eat these in the morning along with water. This will bring radiance to your face.
4. Constipation, sleeplessness at night, staying up late at night, indigestion are harmful for your health.
5. Light exercises and deep breathing should be practised every day in open air.

6. Try various facial exercises like contouring the face in different directions, making funny faces, raising your eyebrows, etc. All this will help to avoid wrinkles and fine lines that appear on the face.
7. Do not apply powder, creams and cosmetics made of chemicals on your skin. Constant use of these, closes the pores in the skin making it lose its natural beauty.
8. For a healthy glow on the face the soles of the feet should be scrubbed with a stone or scrubber.
9. Have a bath after applying paste of besan, turmeric, mustard oil, lemon juice and milk all over the body. Blemishes on the face will disappear in a few days and your skin will start glowing.
10. Once in a fortnight have a bath after applying fuller's earth (*multani mitti*) all over the body.
11. If powder of dried flowers is mixed with Fuller's earth, it improves the complexion of the face perceptibly.
12. Massaging the face, neck and the whole body with milk before bathing improves the complexion manifolds.
13. If the skin is oily then apply a paste of besan and honey. When slightly dry, rub it off and wash properly.
14. For a dry skin apply a paste of curd, besan and honey and wash it off after 15 minutes.
15. Hair should be washed with curd once in 10-15 days. This prevents hair fall and provides shining to the hair.
16. Boil tea leaves in water, then strain it and mix lemon juice in it. Wash your hair with this concoction for beautiful and shiny hair.
17. Dark circles around the eyes can be treated by keeping fresh potato slices over them.
18. Cucumber juice and lemon juice mixed together if applied on the face makes it glow .
19. For treating dandruff apply a paste of amla, leaves of custard apple (sharifa), shikakai and grounded bhringraj on the scalp and wash it after an hour with lukewarm water and dry the hair in the sun.

20. Cream of fresh milk can be used as cold cream in winters.
21. Wash, dry and, ground orange peel and mix with milk for making a paste which can be applied on the face. This removes dryness of the skin.
22. Boil water and cumin seeds. Let the water cool. You can use this water for washing your face to bring a glow to it.
23. Juice of basil leaves and lemon if mixed together is applied on the face it can help remove spots, patches and blemishes.
24. Blemishes can be removed by applying the cream of milk with turmeric.
25. Once a week give your face steam treatment and then apply lemon juice mixed in water on the face. This opens skin pores and the face starts glowing.
26. For a clear or fair complexion tomato juice should be taken in the morning as well as in the afternoon.

## *Protection of skin in winters*

As soon as winter sets in, many problems concerning protection of skin crop up. The skin starts cracking and gets dried up. If attention is paid before the onset of winter there will be no problem. The main reason for the skin getting dried up is that the harsh weather deprives the skin of its moisture and blood circulation also becomes slow.

In your daily routine observe the following ways to save yourself of these difficulties.
1. In winters massage your skin with oil and then for 15-20 minutes remain in the sun.
2. Do not use soap instead use besan or Fuller's earth for bathing . Also use lukewarm water for bathing and in the end wipe the body with cold wet towel and dry the skin with your palms.
3. Before sleeping at night apply milk cream on the face.

4. Put your feet in lukewarm water for 10 minutes and then massage them with oil.
 5. Mix lemon juice in glycerine and apply on your hands.

## Motherhood and child care

For a beautiful, healthy and an intelligent child, it is necessary that the parents should be physically, mentally and spiritually healthy.

The most important time of a woman's life is pregnancy. Some necessary things should be kept in mind during pregnancy to remain healthy and to give birth to a healthy child.

Husband and wife should lead a proper life and eat good food before conception of a child, and most of all should be mentally prepared for it.

At the time of conception if the male breathes through the right nostril and female through the left then definitely a baby boy is born and vice-versa for a baby girl.

Whether it is a boy or a girl, is not so important. But to have a healthy and talented child is very important. The mother's behaviour and thoughts directly affect the baby in the womb.

### *Tips for pregnant mothers*

 1. Must drink loads of water and increase the intake of fluids.
 2. Try to be happy most of the time and don't take any tension or stress.
 3. Wear loose, thin, cotton clothes.
 4. Should not use any intoxicant.
 5. Give up all kinds of addictions.
 6. Light physical exercises, morning walk, nadi shodhan pranayam are necessary, deep breathing in open air is very important.
 7. Do not suppress natural calls (stool, urine, hunger, thirst and sleep.)

8. For a pregnant woman fear is extremely harmful.
9. Do not criticise anyone and do not hear others do it.
10. Stay away from jealousy, ill-feeling, and feeling of vengeance.
11. Adopt positive, Satvik and creative thoughts
12. Do not sleep too much during the day and do not keep awake at night.
13. Take out collected filth from the body regularly.
14. A pregnant woman should read good books and read about great personalities and think of their ideals.
15. Practice self control during pregnancy.
16. High heeled shoes or chappals need not be worn. This leads to exhaustion and any slip and imbalance can be fatal.
17. To avoid having stretch marks apply grease or anti stretch marks cream on one's belly, this does not permit marks on the skin after delivery.
18. Always sleep on your side with knees folded.

## *Food recommended for a pregnant woman*

1. Wheat atta with chaff, unpolished rice and cereals with the peel should be used.
2. Sugar and salt be used to the minimum. Instead of sugar use jaggery, honey, dates, raisins, figs, dry dates etc.
3. Tinned food products, sweets, fried products, maida etc. heavy and indigestible food need not be taken.
4. Cola, Tea, coffee be replaced with herbal tea, lemon and honey shake. Juice of fresh fruits and vegetables are good for health. If coconut water is taken daily then the child born is good looking.
5. Sprouted moong, gram, groundnut, sunflower seeds, almond, pista, coconut, walnuts, sesame (Til), milk and cottage cheese etc. be eaten.
6. Daily diet should contain regional seasonal fruits (orange, sweet lemon, pineapple, raspberries, phalsa, apple, pear, watermelon, melon, grapes, shahtoot,

# Natural Health

chickoo, guava, lichies, jamun, custard apple etc.)
Fresh vegetables like tomato, radish, carrot, cabbage, turnip, tinda, parwal, cauliflower, spinach, methi, chaulai, soyabean, *bathua,* etc. should be taken.

7. 70% of food should be fruits and vegetables.
8. Using spinach regularly does not permit indigestion, vomiting, abortion etc., the child develops properly in the womb. Similarly sprouted wheat eaten with raisins is better.
9. Mostly pregnant women are fed more than it is required which leads to many diseases.

## *Post natal care*

1. For forty days after delivery, cold water need not be used, not in any form.
2. Chewing aniseeds daily increases appetite, digestion, backache is cured, reduces gas formation and cleans up the uterus.
3. After delivery hot or lukewarm drinks should be taken a number of times like green vegetable soups, etc.
4. After delivery diet should be simple, light and digestible. Milk, dry fruits and honey are very useful.

## *Child care*

1. The place where the child sleeps should be quiet, clean and airy.
2. Do not let the child have anything in his mouth while he sleeps.
3. Do not cover the child's face when he sleeps.
4. Do not wake up an asleep child all of a sudden.

## *Mother's milk*

Doctors have found that no food is better than mother's milk for the child. This not only fulfills all that the child needs, but develops resistance power in him. He cannot take any other food stuff from outside. It has been proved that breast feeding is not only good for the child but also for the mother. It helps the mother lose post pregnancy weight and also saves her from conception during the lactation period and protects her from diseases of the breast, like cancer.

Before feeding breasts should be wiped clean with a wet cloth. Mothers should not feed the child while lying down This can cause various problems in the child's ear. After feeding the child he should be held straight with his mouth on the shoulder of the mother and his back should be stroked to make him belch. By doing so he does not throw off milk. Do not feed milk to child if not hungry.

Whenever the child weeps do not think he is hungry.

Prolonged research has revealed that those children who are fed on mother's milk for a long time are more healthy. They are better in maths than average children and their I/Q level is quite high.

Till the child is one year old the mother ought to breast feed him regularly and take special care of her own diet also.

## *Child's growth chart*

| Age | Height | Weight |
| --- | --- | --- |
| At the time of birth | 50 cm. | 2.75 kg. |
| 1 Year | 73 cm. | 9.50 kg. |
| 2 Years | 84 cm. | 12.75 kg. |
| 3 Years | 94 cm. | 15.00 kg. |
| 4 Years | 101 cm. | 16.75 kg. |
| 5 Years | 104 cm. | 18.60 kg. |
| 6 Years | 111 cm. | 20.40 kg. |
| 7 Years | 117 cm. | 22.30 kg. |
| 8 Years | 122 cm. | 25.00 kg. |
| 9 Years | 127 cm. | 27.70 kg. |
| 10 Years | 132 cm. | 30.40 kg. |
| 11 Years | 137 cm. | 33.10 kg. |
| 12 Years | 142 cm. | 35.80 kg. |

*Note :* There could be slight variation from the above given table.

## Indications of child's development

1. When three months old the child is able to balance his neck.
2. Learns to sit by the time he is six months old.
3. At the age of nine months the child starts crawling on his feet and learns to stand.
4. By the time the child is 10-11 months old he starts walking with support.
5. By the time he is 12-13 months old he starts walking independently, starts uttering syllables like *ma, pa, ta,* etc.
6. When 15 months old can run easily and pronounce small, easy words.
7. By the time he is two years starts talking a bit.
8. Around three years the child can talk properly.

## Teething period

From 8 months to 14 months of age teething begins in children and continues till the child is two and a half year old. These teeth are called milk teeth. Mostly the teeth appear in the lower jaw earlier than in the upper jaw.

In the 1st year   6 teeth
By 1½ Years      12 teeth
By 2 years       18 teeth
By 2½ years      20 teeth

From the 4th to 6th year milk teeth start coming off. In the sixth year, generally, there are 28 teeth. In young age there are 32 teeth but it is not necessary.

## Development of children's qualities

Children have a propensity to imitate and thus make parents their ideal or someone nearby and on the same pattern their qualities are developed.

Building of character and moral values are taught right from the tender age.

If the child remains in an atmosphere of criticism, he learns to criticize.

If the child remains in an atmosphere of appreciation, he learns to appreciate.

If the child lives in an atmosphere of bickerings, then he learns to fight.

If the child lives in an atmosphere of patience he learns to be patient.

If the child remains in an atmosphere of atrocious mocking, then he becomes shy.

If he lives in an atmosphere of encouragement he grows up to be self confident.

If the child lives in an atmosphere of shame then he grows with inferiority complex.

If the child develops in a supportive atmosphere then he learns to appreciate himself.

If the atmosphere is non-partial, than he grows up to be justice loving.

If the child grows up in a secure atmosphere he learns to trust people.

If the child grows up in an atmosphere of consent and friendship he learns to love.

*Note:* If parents do not give their children a congenial atmosphere, good behaviour and conditioning, then they commit a sin.

## As the child grows

1. The child should be encouraged to read good books according to his age.
2. You must share your experiences with your children, without expecting them to agree with you. If they work contrary to your views and that is not against the society, then you should support them.
3. Permit them to respond to telephone calls at home.
4. Permit your child sometimes to purchase small things for his own use.

5. Check by burdening your expectations, you are not obstructing your child's development.
6. Place yourself in your child's place.
7. Encourage your child to talk about one of the important happenings during the daily itinerary and exchange views over it.
8. Take your child to new exhibitions or historical places so that he is able to inculcate new ideas and concepts from there.
9. He should be encouraged to indulge in extracurricular activities, so as to allow complete physical and mental development.
10. Forgive his mistakes and explain lovingly where he has gone wrong so that the mistake does not recur.
11. On small occasions give variety of books to make him creative.
12. Permit some time for T.V. and games, but keep a watch on the daily itinerary.
13. Make him develop respect for his elders.
14. In taking small decisions you must consult your children for suggestions.
15. You should try to read your child's mind. It is not necessary that the child will share his problems always with you. Go near him and offer a solution to his problem. This will bring him close to you.
16. Give time to your child. Make him worldly wise.
17. Get to know your child's friends. See if your child is in good company.
18. Listen to his talk and problems with interest.
19. Do not fulfill all the wishes of your child or else he will become stubborn.
20. Teach him the importance of money and relationships.
21. Find out his interests and encourage him in pursuing them.

## Questionnaire on child problems

Some recurring problems of daily life regarding the health of growing children are stated under with their possible solutions.

Q. It is generally thought that fruits cause cold and cough. Is this contention correct?

Ans. This is just a notion. Fruits are not harmful to children. Fruits give ample quantity of natural salts, vitamins and digestive sugar which is lacking in grains. A small spoonful of orange juice can be given to a child of any age. Children with teeth can chew as much fruits as their fill.

Q. Is there no definite time for stopping breast feeding? What is the ideal time for weaning off?

Ans. The time for weaning off is when the child is 9-10 months of age. That is the time when teething begins. It is considered very important to breastfeed the child till he turns one.

Q. While the child is being breastfed, can the child be given fruits and other useful food products?

Ans. A small spoonful of orange juice can be given through out but orange should be sweet in taste. A six months old child could be given juice of one orange with one fourth water mixed in it. Juice of fresh fruits especially orange, amla, sweet lemon, etc. can be given during the period of breast feeding and thereafter also.

Q. How does a child grow tall?

Ans. Daily massage the child specially the spinal cord. Put a mark on the wall and try to touch it by standing on one's toes daily. After touching it, put a higher mark and strive to touch it. Spend more time in open air. Diet must consist of one litre milk, chapatti made of dough inclusive of the chaff, fruits and vegetables in ample quantity.

Q. What are the causes of stammering in children and remedies for it?

Ans. Due to nervous weakness, and being afraid of admonitions, children start stammering. For this, their way of life and food should be natural, every day exposure to sunlight, massage of the spinal cord and loving treatment is a must.

Q. Should the child be given bottle feed?

Ans. No, it is harmful for the child.

Q. If the newly born child is dark complexioned, then?

Ans. Daily apply *chironji* paste over his body with a few drops of olive oil in it. This will improve his complexion.

Q. A child suffers from loose motions during teething. What should be his diet at such a time?

Ans. Loose motion indicate that there is waste collected within, and is getting extricated. If the child is on breastfeed then he should not be given anything apart from that. Otherwise, food stuff containing calcium predominantly, green vegetables, honey and fruit juices should be given, four times a day. Bowels should be cleaned.

Q. What should be the diet of a breast feeding mother?

Ans. Fruits and vegetables should be there in ample quantity. Intoxicating and agitating products like tea, coffee, sweets, pickles, vinegar, etc. need not be taken, otherwise the mother will be unhealthy which will affect the child adversely.

For keeping the stomach and blood clean fruits, vegetables and sprouted cereals should be taken in ample quantity so as to provide necessary roughage and alkali.

Orange is also important due to its superior quality of sugar, properties and effects. It also provides roughage. The food must have a big spoonful of chaff or a fruit like apple, guava, must be taken.

If there is less lactation, then two and a half litre of water should be consumed daily, juices, vegetables and fruits and almonds could be taken. Roasted cumin seed must be taken. Chapatti made of flour containing chaff is also good.

Q. Is it harmful for children to suck their thumb?

Ans. This habit is very harmful. For this the child's thumb should be covered with paste of neem leaf or with some covering which will prohibit him from sucking the thumb. The child does so because of deficiency of calcium in mother's milk. The mother should increase fruits, vegetables, milk, curd in her diet.

Q. How to save children from getting exposed to hot waves in summers?

Ans. The child should be given a wash twice a day or should be bathed in water as warm as the body temperature and should be left in the open in the morning to play.

Q. Children pass stool after eating and drinking milk. Is it a disease?

Ans. It is not a disease. While eating and drinking the digestive process becomes active and that leads to muscle movement, consequently bowels get cleaned.

Q. A weeping child becomes quiet on getting a soother in his mouth. Is it proper to put soother?

Ans. No, it is absolutely wrong. It causes infection. Through the soother the child gets germs and diseases.

Q. Should the child be given any tonic or not, if yes, when should it be started?

Ans. If the child is being breastfed and is healthy then there is no need of tonic. If the child's stomach is not all right, is prone to aches, then a good gripe water should be given.

Q. What should be given to a child aged two years in his diet?

Ans. A child's diet should have green vegetables, milk, curd, butter milk and some grains. Instead of sugar and sweets, honey or jaggery can be given. This alleviates the possibility of any kind of complication. Water should be given a number of times, 100-150 ml at a time. A child should be taught to chew the food properly instead of swallowing up immediately. Do not feed the child whenever he cries. This can cause ailments.

Q. Often it is observed that once a child is three months old he throws up milk, how to avert it?

Ans. Children are tossed immediately after feeding, or put on the shoulder or elbow. This causes throwing up of milk. A child should not be shaken too much.

He should be made to lie down. If the child vomits regularly then he should be made to lie down restfully. The cause of this is feeding more and at short intervals. Before feeding the child, it is better to give 2 to 4 teaspoonfuls of water.

## *Daily routine*

(1) Get up early in the morning after turning to the left side before sunrise.

(2) Immediately after waking up fill the mouth with clean water and sprinkle water on both the eyes at least forty times. This prevents weakening of the eyesight and those wearing spectacles get rid of them.

(3) Drink up to four glasses of water kept overnight in a silver or copper vessel before going to the lavatory in the morning. This prevents constipation, piles, plethora, eye ailments, cough and other diseases.

(4) Early morning tea on an empty stomach is very harmful.

(5) Go to the lavatory at a regular time. While urinating or evacuation of bowels press the jaws tight, this strengthens teeth and tooth ailment do not occur. Remember relieving yourself before bathing, and one must urinate, before sleeping, after meals and exercise.. After cleaning the bowels the anus should be contracted 8 to10 times. This prevents any kind of ailment of the anus and also premature ejaculation.

(6) Never urinate before the sun as it causes skin diseases.

(7) If possible, daily or once in a week the body must be massaged with oil.

(8) Margosa stick is beneficial for brushing the teeth. While brushing the teeth and cleaning the tongue the palate must be cleaned with the thumb and gargle with saline luke warm water. This prevents eye, throat, ear and nose ailments.

(9) Whenever you get a chance, try to be expose yourself to the sun rays.

(10) Go for brisk walk in the morning and practice deep breathing and yogasanas.

(11) Before bathing rub the body with a dry towel for 10 minutes and after the bath rub the body dry with one's own palms and then use a towel to wipe.

(12) Do not eat if not hungry and eat slightly less than your appetite.

(13) One must practise meditation regularly.

(14) Eat only twice during the day and your diet should contain mostly uncooked food (fruits, vegetables, fresh green leaves, sprouted cereals, honey, etc.). If taking three meals in a day then take fruits and fruit juices in the breakfast.

# Natural Health

(15) Sit in vajrasana after meals or breathe eight times lying on the back, then sixteen times after turning to the right side and thirty two times on the left side. This will digest the food speedily and gastric problems will not occur. The accumulated gas will eject out. After having dinner one must walk at least hundred paces.

(16) After meals head should be scratched with a wooden comb. This prevents early hair fall, greying, headache and itchy scalp.

(17) Whenever tired must rest. After working continuously relax, by doing shavasana, etc. Weekly holiday must be observed.

(18) Sometimes sip the water.

(19) Must laugh loudly once or twice daily.

(20) Clothes should be simple and clean and preferably of cotton. Tight woollens should not directly touch the skin.

(21) Every month put a few drops of pure mustard oil in the ears.

(22) Eating a few basil leaves and margosa leaves daily prevents one from many diseases.

(23) Do not inculcate the habit of sleeping during the day.

(24) Good thoughts should be nurtured in life and positive thinking developed. This will keep mental tension at bay.

(25) Do not entertain disappointments in the mind. Be optimistic.

(26) Only one who loses courage, fails.

(27) Before sleeping drink water and wash your feet.

(28) Before sleeping clean the throat and the palate too.

(29) While sleeping the feet should be either towards the north or west.

(30) Sleep on a slightly hard bed and do not use a pillow, or if necessary use a thin one.

(31) Develop the habit of sleeping on your left side or on the belly, like a child.
(32) The bedding should be exposed to sun light sometimes.
(33) Sleep only when you feel sleepy.
(34) Lying on the bed waiting for sleep is like inviting diseases.
(35) Do not cover the face while sleeping.
(36) Do not take medicine for getting sleep.
(37) One must sleep on time at night, maximum by 10'o clock.
(38) The house should be well lit, airy and clean.

# Part-II

# YOGA

## THE SCIENCE OF HAND POSTURES AND ACUPRESSURE

# Yoga

Lord Shiva is the eternal inspirer of Yoga

"योगश्चितवृत्तिनिरोध:" Opposition of propensities of the mind is yoga.

"योग: कर्मसु कौशलम्" Efficiency in working is Yoga.

"समंत्वयोग उच्चते" To remain stoic is yoga.

Yagyavalka Samhita calls the communion of soul with the Supersoul as Yoga.

Yoga protects religion and education. One can attain knowledge by yoga only. There is no strength as there is in yoga and without yoga, moksha (salvation) is impossible.

The body feels light, becomes disease free and starts glowing, voice becomes sweet, the body emanates a nice odour, discharge of waste from the body in the form of faeces and urine reduces in quantity. These are some indications of first step to mastery of yoga.

There are eight parts of Yoga therefore it is called "Ashtang Yoga" by sage Patanjali which includes (1) Yama (behaviour), (2) Niyama (regulations), (3) Asana (postures), (4) Pranayama (controlling breath), (5) Pratyahara (control of sense organs), (6) Dhaarna (concentration), (7) Dhyan (meditation), (8) Samadhi (communion).

## (1) Yama (behaviour)

Yama leads to pure and good behaviour with others. It has five parts.

  (i) **Ahimsa** (non-violence) — Not to afflict pain on anyone in thought, speech or action is non-violence or ahimsa.
  (ii) **Satya** (Truthfulness) — One should be clear and not treacherous in one's behaviour.
  (iii) **Asteya** (Non stealing) — Non stealing is Asteya. Not paying appropriate wages is also stealing.

(iv) **Brahmacharya** (Celibacy) — All sensual pleasures should be given up mentally, in speech and physically under all circumstances, to protect semen in every way. This is Brahmacharya.
(v) **Aparigrah** (Non hoarding) — Non collection of unrequired things.

## (2) Niyama (regulations)

Niyamas are connected with the individual's body, senses and conscience. By adhering to them regularly the mind becomes truthful and pure. This also has five parts —
  (i) **Shauch** (Cleanliness) — Internal and external cleanliness of the body.
  (ii) **Santosh** (Contentment) — Contentment in the fruit you reap.
  (iii) **Tapa** (Dutifulness) — Perform your duties with diligence.
  (iv) **Svadhyaya** (Regular Practice) — Regular study of own life which will enable to realise one's own duty.
  (v) **Ishwar Pranidhan** (Surrendering to God) — Seek refuge in the Lord.

## (3) Asana (postures)

Asanas are connected with physical activity. They remove restlessnes, instability, laziness and obesity from the body and provide satvik glow and grandeur. In the world, no other activity than the asana have been found which would so minutely affect the endocrine glands especially.

**Shat Karma** (Six Actions) — For doing any asana cleansing of the body is essential, practise of shat karma removes the waste from the body.
  1. **Basti** — After doing Ganesh Kriya — (Apply oil with your fingers into the anus) put a hollow bamboo into the anus. Sit in water in Utkatasana and

**Basti**

hold the position in uddiyan bandh to pull water upto the large intestine, then take out the bamboo and twist the anus and pass stool repeatedly. Repeat this activity four to five times and then go into Mayurasana to get rid of the remaining water and air.

*Benefits* – Gas problem and constipation get over. The face glows, spleen, liver, anus and stomach get free from diseases. These days instead of basti water enema is given.

*Note* – These days instead of *basti* water enema is given.

2. **Kunjal** – Sit in Khagasana (on heels) and fill your stomach with hot water, then stand and bend down. Then keep the left hand on the stomach and with three fingers (index, middle and ring finger) of the right hand, touch and move the inner tongue. When water starts coming out then take out the fingers. As long as the water is being vomited out keep the fingers outside, thereafter immediately again move the three fingers on the back of the tongue, till all the water is vomited out. Do it repeatedly. In the end if sour or bitter water comes out, then immediately drink two glasses of hot water and take it out again. Water should neither be too hot nor too cold. Bathe either two hours before kunjal or two hours after. Do not mix salt or *saunf* in the water for kunjal. Do it after having passed stool otherwise it can cause constipation.

**Kunjal**

*Benefits* – This act helps to get free from skin problems, dental problems, constipation, acidity, gastric trouble, cough, night blindness, asthma, drying of the mouth and throat, etc.

*Caution* – Heart and High blood pressure patients should not do it.

Yoga – The Science of Hand Postures and Acupressure 109

3. **Vastra Dhauti**—Take a soft thin muslin cloth almost 7.5 cm broad and 5 meter long. Wash it nicely, boil it in water and then dry it. Then roll it up like a bandage. Put it in a clean utensil having boiling water. Sit in Khagasana catch one end of the dhauti in your right hand with the index and middle finger and take it up to the small tongue in the mouth

**Dhauti**

and leave it. Then try to swallow the bandage as if using food. For swallowing if need, one or two sips of water can be taken. While swallowing it if one feels nausea then close the mouth and sit still for a while. First day you should not swallow more than one feet. In a week's time gradually increase it to 5 meter. Then immediately thereafter pull the dhauti out from the other end slowly, as long as it comes out easily pull it, when obstructed drink a bit of water and pull again.

*Benefits* – This brings out both acid and cough from the body. Ailments caused by cough and acid get cured, lisping and leprosy can also be overcomed. Asthma patients must practise it.

## 4. Neti

*Sutraneti*—Sit in Khagasana, put the thread in hot saline water and wet it completely. Make the twisted portion into a semicircular shape and put it gradually in that nostril from which you are breathing predominantly. When the thread reaches the throat then hold it with index and middle finger and pull it out gradually. Similarly do it in the other

**Sutraneti**

nostril. After sutraneti it is essential to do jalneti. First time when sutraneti is done it is advisable to put a few drops of pure ghee in each nostril on previous night.

*Jalneti* — For doing jalneti take lukewarm saline water in a barrelled tumbler and put it in that nostril which is breathing predominantly and bend the head on the other side. This will fill water in the first nostril and then water will flow out from the other nostril. Similarly put water in the other nostril and let it flow out of the first one. While performing this act keep the mouth open and breathe through the mouth only. After performing jalneti it is essential to take out the remaining water out of the nostrils. Therefore after doing it Kapal Bhati must be performed.

**Jalneti**

*Kapal Bhati* — Stand with both feet together, make the left hand into a fist and take it behind the back and catch the wrist of it by the right hand. Bend forward at an angle of 90°. Move the neck right and left, up and down and breathe out with great force while doing it. The body or back should not move, only the neck should move. Repeat this act a number of times.

*Benefits* — All ailments of the neck and head (headache, sleeplessness, excessive sleep, hair fall, boils within the nose or protruded flesh growth, cold, running nose, eye complications, impaired hearing, epilepsy, etc.) are cured.

## 5. Nauli

Stand straight with both the legs apart maintaining a distance of one foot with both hands on the knees. Exhale and then in the state of retention pull the belly in completely. Then put pressure on the hands and loosen the belly slightly, now while pulling on the chest try to pull out the nauli or midriff. While doing this act watch the belly whether nauli or the midriff comes

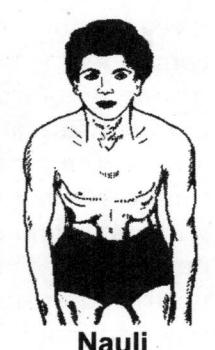

**Nauli**

out or not. By practising repeatedly the nauli will definitely come out. Thereafter nauli can be moved to the right and left and shaken with speed.

*Note* – This should be done only on an empty stomach. Before doing nauli exhale and inhale repeatedly. Repeat this act again and again.

*Benefits* – This does not leave faeces in the belly, gas is under control. Many diseases like fever, enlargement of spleen, gastric balls causing pain do not occur, internal parts of the stomach get massaged. All ailments caused by gas, acid and cough are eliminated.

## 6. Trataka

Concentrating the eyes on a particular unseen object is called trataka. There are many ways of doing it.

Padmasana, Siddhasana or Vajrasana can be adopted for sitting. Make a round spot of the size of a small coin on a thirty square centimeter white paper, placed at a distance of one meter and stare at it without blinking.

**Trataka**

Stare at it till tears are about to come out. Close the eyes then. By practising it for a few days, a kind of light will be seen, which will cover the spot.

*Benefit* – This cures eye ailments. Spiritually it is very efficacious. For mental concentration there is no other better method.

## Shankh prakshalana

Apart from the said shat karma, shankh prakshalana is a process of cleaning the whole digestive system.

Sit in Khagasana. Then drink two glasses of hot saline water and immediately do sarpasana four times. In the posture of sarpasana look towards your feet from left side and then from the right side. Then do urdhva-hastottanasana,

**(1) Sarpasana**  **(2) Urdhva-Hastottanasana**

**(3) Katichakrasana**  **(4) Udrakarshasana**

katichakrasana and Udrakarshasana four times. Then again drink two glasses full of hot saline water again and repeat all the asanas in the same sequence. By doing so first faeces, then loose stools, then yellow water and finally white water will come out. Till white water does not start coming out continue to repeat the above stated process doing all the asanas four times. After white water has come out, drink two to three glasses of water and perform Kunjal.

*Note* – Don't take bath with cold water after shankh prakshalana. Take bath with hot water in a closed bathroom and come out after wearing the clothes.

Thereafter do not remain hungry for more than an hour and eat porridge or khichadi with 25-50 grams of pure ghee in it. After shankh prakshalana rest is necessary and within 24 hours milk or curd should not be consumed.

*Benefits* – It gives relief to the body. Its practice cures ailments of the head, eye, ear, nose, pyorrhoea, tonsils, ailments related to stomach and anus, etc. Its practice also helps in appendicitis, damage in the intestines, swelling, etc. Among females all ailments of the uterus are cured like leucorrhoea, dysmenorrhoea, irregular menstrual cycle, non appearance of natural complexion, etc. Barrenness among women can be cured effectively by doing shankh prakshalana. Intestinal worms also come out.

## *Rules for asanas*

1. After passing stool do asanas on an empty stomach.
2. For doing any asana the time should be appropriate.
3. Asanas are performed in the open. If doing it in a room it should be clean, open and airy.
4. As far as possible do asanas bare bodied. The body should have minimum clothes.
5. Asanas should be done on a mat or a carpet on the floor.
6. Before doing asanas have a bath. One who sweats too much should bathe after half an hour of doing asanas.
7. Choose some useful asanas for yourself and practise them.
8. Do not eat immediately after doing asanas or vice versa. Have meals after half an hour of doing asanas or perform asanas after three to four hours of having meals.
9. Those who do heavy exercises and hard labour need not perform asanas.
10. During menstruation women should not do asanas. In the first 3 to 4 months of pregnancy they can do few light asanas, thereafter it should be stopped. After four months of delivery they can start it again.

11. At the end of the asanas doing shavasana is necessary.
12. Practise asanas under the guidance of a competent yoga practitioner.
13. Before beginning asanas get a medical check up done, if there is a disease first get it treated or practise asanas on the advise of the yoga teacher.
14. Maintain silence during asanas.
15. Both sided asanas should be performed for equal times and out of those asanas which are performed by lying down, one lying on back and another lying on belly must be done to maintain the balance on the spinal cord. Uttanpadasana-Naukasana,, Halasana-Dhanurasana, Paschimotanasana-Bhujangasana are few examples.

## *Yogic exercises*

Before starting to do asanas some of the following yogic exercises should be performed. Their practice will take care of physical and mental disorder, refresh the body and make it feel light.

### 1. Yogic exercise for improving mind power

These are of two types—

1st— Stand and look straight, inhale deeply and exhale with the same force. It is important to exhale as forcefully as the inhalation, then only this act will have favourable effects.

2nd— Bend the neck backward and look upward towards the sky with your eyes open. Then similarly inhale and exhale forcefully with equal force.

*Benefits*— This extracts accumulated of mucus from the head. Breathing through the nose becomes easy. Lungs get pure oxygen in them. Those who have cough accumulated in their lungs or suffer from breathing problem must practise it regularly. This will clean the lungs and will be able to receive oxygen in great quantity. It is very efficacious for asthma patients. This activity could be indulged in by people of any age and could also be practised by healthy persons and ailing as well. Its practise increases memory power and eyesight.

For those suffering from mental diseases it is extremely efficacious. It also helps heart patients and those suffering from high blood pressure.

## 2. Yogic exercise for improving the eyesight

Keep both the feet together. Keeping straight the portion from feet to shoulders, tilt the neck backwards completely and remain standing. Keep looking at the sky with both eyes. When the eyes feel tired, close them before tears come out. Open the eyes and resume the practise. Do this for five minutes.

*Benefits* – Practise of this exercise removes all the defects of eyes and eyesight improves and one gets vulture sight. By practising this exercise regularly for minimum 40 days, spectacles get removed and natural eyesight is obtained.

## 3. Cheeks power promoting exercise

Put your feet together shaping the body straight, join the front portion of the eight fingers of both the hands, close both nostrils with the thumbs, of both the hands. Make your face into the shape of a crows beak, keep the eyes open, inhale from the mouth creating the sound of sur-sur forcefully. Then inflate the cheeks and keep the chin on front thymus. As long as breath can be held it should be retained with the tongue placed normally. Looking forward open the nostrils and exhale through your nose.

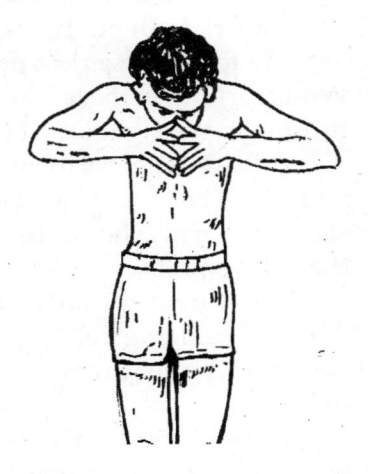

*Benefits* – This makes the cheeks pink, the need of artificial cosmetics is eliminated. It gives glow to the face and makes it attractive. Problem of bad breath is also overcomed. Pimples, boils do not occur. Hollow and wrinkled cheeks fill up, pyorrhoea and other diseases of the mouth are cured.

## 4. Yogic exercises for improving the hearing

Join both the feet, keeping the body straight, keep the mouth closed and then close both the ears with both thumbs. Close both eyes with both index fingers. Close both nostrils with both middle fingers. Close mouth with both ring and little fingers. Now make the mouth like a crow's beak, suck the outside air, inflate the cheeks and perform jalandhar bandh. Maintain kumbhak as per capacity, after that bring the neck in normal position, remove both hands, open both eyes and slowly take out the inside air through nose. Do it five times.

*Note* – During kumbhak, keep the cheeks completely inflated.

*Benefit* – Practise of this exercise removes ear related diseases. Hearing power improves and undeveloped hearing starts developing.

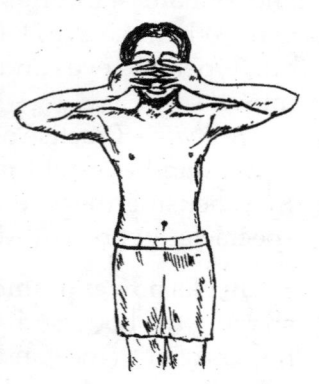

## 5. Yogic exercises for strengthening the neck

This can be done in three ways —

1st — Stand and look straight, then move the neck with a slight jerk to the right and then bring it to the centre, then again with a slight jerk to the left and come back to the center. While turning to the left look behind the left shoulder, while turning to the right look behind the right shoulder.

*Note* – While performing this act keep the shoulders straight. There will not be any kind of movement in the shoulders. This should be done at least 15-20 times on both the sides equally.

2nd — Stand and look straight, then move the neck with the head hanging behind, and then bend it forward resting the chin on front thymus. This act should be practised 15-20 times.

*Note* – Those who suffer from neck or back pain should not bend the neck forward while practising it.

3rd — Stand straight, rest the chin on the front thymus, move the neck from right to left and left to right in a circular motion.

*Note* — While doing this act the shoulders need not be pushed upwards. This should not be practised by those suffering from neck pain. This should be performed 15 to 20 times equally on both sides.

*Benefits* — This makes the neck shapely and thin. Those who have excessive fat on their neck should practise it. Its practice eliminates diseases connected with the neck. Those who suffer from pain in the neck should learn it properly and then do it.

## 6. Yogic exercises for strengthening the shoulders — This can be done in two ways.

Ist — Stand straight and take the right hand above straight in such a way that the arm is sticking to the ear. Then bring it down. Repeat this motion of right hand 10-15 times. Similarly do this exercise with the left hand. Thereafter practise with both the hands moving simultaneously. Remember while being lifted palms of both hands must be outwards.

*Note* — Begin this exercise with 15-20 times and then increase its duration gradually.

*Benefits* — Excessive fat on the shoulders is reduced, the muscle there get massaged; shoulders become strong. Those people whose shoulders become erect must practise it gradually. The practice of this exercise makes the hands shapely and beautiful.

2nd — Stand straight and then put the left hand thumb on the palm and make it in to a fist. Thereafter move the hand in a circular motion from the shoulder first beginning in the front then the same way backwards. Then repeat this with the right hand and thereafter both the hands simultaneously. Remember while doing it only the arms should move and the rest of the body should remain erect.

*Note* — This exercise should be done 10 to 15 times in the beginning. Then its practise should be increased in accordance with the body's capacity.

*Benefits* – The practice of this exercise removes stiffness of shoulders. Muscles are massaged. Shoulders become shapely and beautiful.

**7. Chest power promoting exercise** – Keep both the feet together, body straight from feet to head, open the fist and keep the fingers together. Bring both hands from front side towards back by inhaling and bring the chest back. Remain in this position for some time and by exhaling come back in the original position. Repeat it for five times.

*Benefits* – This exercise removes all lung problems, chest becomes broad. Breast become sturdy and firm. Heart becomes strong. Tuberculosis, asthma, cough and other Kapha defects are removed. Those who have a weak heart or a heart ailment should practise this for five minutes daily after passing faeces and taking bath.

**8. Yogic exercises for improving the mooladhar chakra and swadhisthan chakra power**

Stand straight by keeping both feet and thighs together. Keeping hips strongly together, pull the anus upwards by internal force and keep it for five minutes.

Now repeat the same by keeping about 8 cm distance between both the feet.

Now repeat the same by keeping about 50 cm distance between both the feet.

*Benefit* – It is useful in all diseases of anus and genitals. Piles, fistula, bleeding piles are cured very quickly. Problems related to sperm count, leucorrhoea, other sexual problems, uterus problems are removed. Erection power is increased. This exercise also helps in maintaining celibacy.

**9. Yogic exercises for awakening the kundalini power** – Keep a distance of 8-10 cm between both the feet, body straight from feet to head. Hit or stroke the hips by both the heels one by one. On returning, feet should come on the ground in original state. Repeat this 25 times.

*Benefit* – Kundalini power gets awakened.

**10. Engine runnning (gallop/assault)** — By keeping both the feet together stand straight from feet to head. Fold the hands from elbow and make your hands into a first with the thumb beneath the four finger. Now move the hands alternatively towards front and back like a engine shaft and after that hit the hips by feet alternatively. Keep in mind that same leg and knee will be bend and the feet will be on the ground of same side whose hand is towards the front. Do this by jumping on the ground. Inhale and exhale by making sound like engine.

Elbow should not go behind the body and the heel must touch the hips. By increasing gradually do it fifty times.

*Benefits* — Body becomes beautiful, healthy, strong and fit. Lungs become more strong. No tiredness is felt even after having done a lot of work. Surprisingly power flows in the body. Chest becomes broad. Thigh and calves become strong and firm. Obesity can also be overcomed with the help of this exercise. Face starts to glow. This exercise if done for 5 minutes has the same benefit as can be derived from jogging for approximately 5 kms. This exercise is very useful for military, police persons and sprinters.

## Various asanas

There are as many asanas as the number of living beings on earth. But here we have described some asanas which are useful and important for normal life.

**(1) Ardhamatsyendrasana** — Sit with legs spread ahead. Then fold the left leg and place the foot next to the right hip and then put the right leg next to the left knee. Remember the toes should be beside the knee not ahead of it. Then take the left arm turning over the shoulder and bring it over the right leg under the knee

**Ardhamatsyendrasana**

in such a way that it holds the toe of the right foot. Right hand should be taken behind the right shoulder in an effort to bring it around from behind to touch the navel. Similarly repeat it on the other side also.

*Benefits* – This asana is specially efficacious for diabetes. Its continuous practise gives a massage to the pancreatic glands which start producing insulin which is necessary for people suffering from diabetes. The internal organs of the abdomen get massaged well and start working efficiently. Indigestion gets cured. Appetite increases. Constipation and gastric problems do not occur. Worms like round worm, tape worm, thread worms, etc. die during the course of continuous practice of this asana. The waist becomes flexible and excessive fat on the stomach gets reduced. Muscles get massaged. Shoulder become strong. Excessive fat on the neck is removed. Those who have pain in the knee should practise this asana slowly.

**(2) Ashvasthasana**—Stand on both the feet. Lift the left hand upward with the palm facing forward. Then lift the right foot backward and the right arm should be lifted up to the shoulder. In this state the palm of the right hand will be facing downward. The body should remain straight. Remain in this position as long as possible. Then change to the other foot and practice the asana similarly for some time.

*Benefits* – The practice of this asana increases the capacity of lungs to inhale more oxygen and more oxygen enters the lungs leading to cure of breathing

**Ashvasthasana**

problems. Asthma patients should practise this asana continuously. Shoulders become strong and broad. This asana is good for pregnant women. They should practise this asana for first three months of their pregnancy.

**(3) Bhoonmanasana** — First sit down on the floor and spread both feet like a hawk's feathers. Bending forward hold both the toes with both the hands. Then while exhaling gradually bend forward to touch the forehead on the ground. Then even shoulders and chest should touch the ground and lie in this position.

**Bhoonmanasana**

*Benefits* — This asana makes the waist flexible. The body becomes like rubber and can be moulded and folded easily. This asana is good for dance artists. The lower portion of the body below waist becomes shapely. Fat people become thin. Those who are unable to perform should practise it gradually and not strain the waist too much. It cures piles. It is efficacious in urinary problems also.

*Note* — This asana should not be performed by patients of high blood pressure, heart trouble and people who have backache and neck ache.

**(4) Chakrasana** — Lie on the ground on your back with both thighs together then keep both palms behind the shoulders and lift the middle portion of the body. The weight of the whole body should be on both the hands and feet equally. Remain in this state for a while and then lie down.

*Note* — While lifting the body leave the neck loose or else there is fear of a sprain in the neck. The neck should remain loose so that it hangs below.

*Benefits* — This asana can make one remain young and active for a long period of time. It directly affects the spinal column and makes the body so flexible that it becomes like rubber. Navel centre naturally gets into its place. This gives steadiness to 72864 nerves in the body. Waist becomes beautiful and attractive. This asana should be practised gradually.

**Chakrasana**

**(5) Dhanurasana** — Lie on your stomach and fold both feet upward from the knees towards the head and hold both calves with both hands, then while inhaling deeply pull both the legs with both the hands towards the head. In this position the weight of the whole body will be on the abdomen.

*Benefits* — This is one of the most important asanas connected with the navel. By practising regularly displaced navel centre comes into its place. Spine becomes flexible. This asana is specially beneficial in pain in the waist and neck. Breathing problems also find relief. This should be practised after learning how to do it properly. It increases the capacity to breathe. Shoulders become broad and strong. Excess fat is removed from the abdomen. Constipation

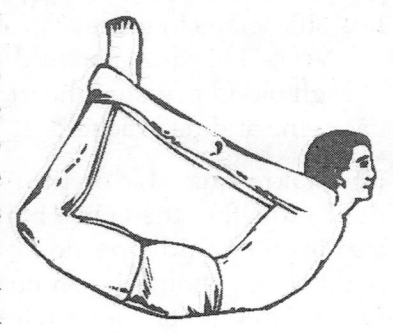

**Dhanurasana**

is cured and appetite increases. For it is a good asana for diabetics.

*Caution* – This asana should not be performed by one suffering from high blood pressure, heart problem, ulcer and hernia.

**(6) Garbhasana** – In lotus posture take out both hand up to the elbow from between the thighs and calves and then fold the elbows and lift both knees upwards. Balance of the body should be maintained. Keep both palms on both the cheeks. In this state the balance of the body will be on the hips.

**Garbhasana**

*Benefits* – This asana provides exercise of each part of the body. The body feels light and blood circulation improves. This asana is specially beneficial for women. All ailments of the uterus are cured. If practised from the age of fourteen the possibility of any ailment of the uterus would be eliminated. After 40 days of the delivery it should be practised and within three months the body recoups its strength. Facial beauty is restored. Its regular practice keeps men and women away from ageing.

**(7) Garudasana** – Stand straight and then lift the left leg and put it around the right thigh encircling it so that the left foot goes around the right calf. Then lift both hands in the front and keep the left arm on the right. In this state both the arms will look like a Garuda's beak. Then bending down closely try to keep the toes of the lifted feet on the ground.

**Garudasana**

*Benefits* — Practice of this asana cures jointaches. Patients suffering from arthritis must practise it regularly. Those who tremble and are thin benefit from this asana. By practising it enlarged scrotum gets into size.

**(8) Gomukhasana** — Bend the left leg from the knee and sit on the sole of the same foot and bending the right leg place in on the left leg. Lift the right arm over and behind the back and fold it in such a way that its inner portion touches the ear.

Elbow should remain close to the hair tuft. Take the left hand back and make a grip of fingers with the right hand. Similarly repeat the action on the opposite side.

**Gomukhasana**

*Benefits* — It is useful in the ailments of lungs. Patients of asthma and tuberculosis must do it. Apart from this shoulders become strong. Elbow, upper leg joints, knees, ankles gain strength. Those who suffer from knee pain must practise it regularly. Those who suffer from ailments of the anus should practise it. This should be practised equally on both sides.

**(9) Gorakshasana** — Sit on the floor, unite both feet and sit over them with both knees touching the ground. Keep both hands on the knees and straighten the spine and neck and remain steady.

*Benefits* — This asana is useful for anal and urinary ailments. Practice of this asana effects the lower portion of the waist. It is very useful to remove stiffness of knee, ankle and hip joints. Its regular practice makes the knees

**Gorakshasana**

flexible and ankles do not ache. Excessive fat from the legs is shed down.

**(10) Halasana (Sarvangasana)** — Lie on the ground on the back. Bring both the toes and ankles together. Keep hands beside the thighs then gradually lift the feet together and without bending the knees bring them beyond the head and place them on the ground. In this state the chin will touch the throat. Soles of feet will point towards the sky. Remain in this position for as long as possible.

*Benefits* — This asana is very good for the spinal cord. It massages each vertebrae in the spinal cord. The spinal cord becomes flexible like a rubber. It invigorates blood circulation and purifies blood leading to elimination of skin trouble. Thyroid and parathyroid glands get massaged well. All throat ailments find relief. Heart and brain get full flow of blood in this asana, which strengthens the heart and memory power also increases. Greying and falling of hair stops. The face glows and becomes beautiful. Ailments of the eyes are cured. Shoulders become strong and powerful. All the organs of the abdomen get massaged. For patients of indigestion, constipation and gastric trouble it works wonders. Appetite increases. It is an extremely useful asana for diabetes. It removes obesity. Excessive fat from the abdomen and hips gets removed.

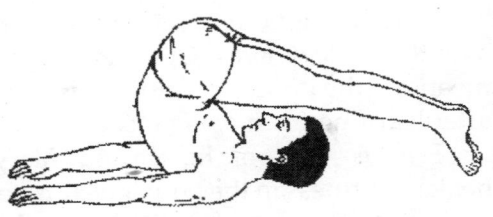

**Halasana (Sarvangasana)**

This asana is very beneficial for women. Those women whose uterus is not stable must practise it with uddiyan bandh.

*Note* — Patients of high blood pressure, heart trouble, ache in the neck and backache should not practise it.

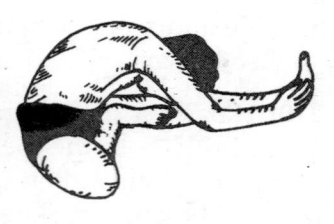

**(11) Janushirshasana** — Sit with both feet in the front. Then pull the left foot above with the right ankle touching the loin at the inner thigh of the right leg. Then gradually exhale and bend down to hold the right toes with both the hands and rest the head on the knee of the right leg. In this state both the elbows will touch the ground. Then repeat it on the other side.

It can be done in another way. The ankle could be put over the naval where the portion is uplifted and swollen. That means on the uplifted hernia. This asana should be practised after learning from a yoga teacher.

*Benefits* — Chronic hernia and enlarged scrotum are easily healed. Stiffness in the body goes and body becomes flexible. Excessive fat is removed. Gastric problem is cured. Pimples, acne and ailments of the tongue find relief. Infectious fevers get cured. It is beneficial in skin diseases also.

*Note* — High blood pressure, People suffering from back pain and those suffering from cervical spondylosis should not do this asana.

**(12) Khagasana** — First sit with legs folded with 30 cm distance between both the feet. Place both hands on the knees and look straight ahead.

*Benefits* — This asana is very useful for all the kriyas of Shatkarma as they are performed in this asana only. Knees become flexible. It is useful for the lower part of the body. Although it is easy to perform yet it is regretful that in large number people cannot perform it because they mostly use western toilets. Use of Indian toilets would automatically make one practise this asana.

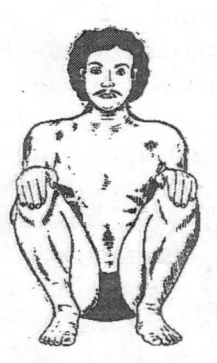

*Yoga – The Science of Hand Postures and Acupressure* 127

**(13) Kati-Chakrasana** – Stand with both feet one foot wide open on the ground. Lift both arms up to the shoulder's height. In this position both the palms will be facing each other. Then twist the waist to the left side. In this state the right hand will be straight and left hand half folded. Repeat it on the other side.

*Note* – While twisting the waist, knees should not be bent and body below navel region should not be twisted.

**Kati-Chakrasana**

*Benefits* – It is important for the process of Shankhprakshalan. It massages the intestines which removes constipation. Continuous practice of this asana makes the waist flexible like rubber. Shoulders broaden and the waist becomes shapely. It is best for ladies and diabetics.

**(14) Konasana** – Stand straight and spread both the feet 25-35 cm wide. Then keep the right hand on the side of right knee and raise the left hand upward. Keep the elbow of the left hand on the left ear and bend the body to the right side. In this position palm of the left hand will remain towards the ground and right hand will touch the right feet. Repeat the same on the right side.

**Konasana**

*Note* – While doing this asana bend from the waist only and elbows and knees should remain straight.

*Benefits* – This asana should be performed by those suffering from sciatica. It massages the entire nerves and muscles of the body leading to increased blood circulation and purification of blood. Body and face glows. It is good for backache. Those who have heavy thighs and waist, should practise it for getting rid of excessive fat. This is specially useful for women. Even pregnant women can do it till six months of pregnancy but slowly.

**(15) Koormasana** — The way a tortoise pulls all his organs together within the body. Similarly this asana is practised, that is why it is called koormasana. Fold your feet and keep them apart at the back with toes together. Sit on the ankles spread apart. In this state the knees will be together and the waist and neck straight. Thereafter make fists of both the hands with thumbs within. Fists should face the sky. Unite both the elbows together and place them on the navel. Then while exhaling bend as much so that the chest touches the arms. Sit in this state between the heels. The back portion should not be raised from the heels.

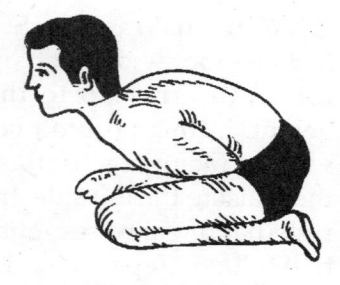

**Koormasana**

*Benefits* — Its continuous practice is efficacious in many diseases of the stomach like constipation, gastric trouble, indigestion, etc. It is very beneficial for diabetics..Those who do not have an appetite must practise it continuously. Its practice for 15-20 minutes generates fire in the body, which leads to perspiration. For awakening the kundalini koormasana is very useful.

*Note* — Its practice should not be done by those who have neck ache and backache.

**(16) Kukkutasana** — First sit in padmasana then keep both the hands on the loins and slip them out from the space between calves and loins in such a way that they are out up to the elbow. Then put both hands on the ground and on their strength lift the whole body up. Practise it for as long as possible..

*Benefits* — The practise of this asana strengthens the whole upper body like — hand fingers, wrists, arms, elbows and shoulders. It makes the body strong and

**Kukkutasana**

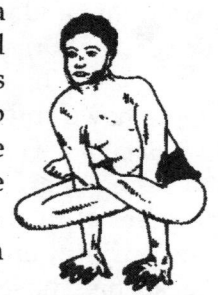

steady. Its continuous practice increases appetite and like a cock one wakes up early in the morning. For those whose hands shake while writing and get tired very easily should practise this asana.

**(17) Kursi-Asana** — Stand with both heels and toes together and lift both hands in the front at shoulder height facing the ground. And then gradually bend at the knee in the front so much as if seated on a chair. Keep the neck and back straight in this position.

**Kursi-Asana(1)**      **Kursi-Asana(2)**

This asana can be practised in another way. Stand with both toes together and arms stretched at 180° with the palms facing downward. Standing on your toes begin to bend down slowly. As you bend both the knees should come forward.

*Benefits* — This asana is efficacious in knee pain, pain in the calves. The waist becomes strong. Those who have to stand and walk too much while working must do this asana as it is very useful for them.

**(18) Makarasana** — Lie down on the stomach and keep both hands one upon the other on the earth in front of the body or bring them in front of the head and put the forehead on

**Makarasana**

it. Then open the feet with a distance of 60-90 cm between them. Remember that both the heels should face inward.

*Benefits* — This asana removes fatigue. It is a very good asana for the stomach. It increases the strength of the body and the whole body becomes solid like a crocodile. Practitioners of this asana have softness invoked in their behaviour. The process of Sastang Dandavat followed by yogis and great souls is similar to this asana. This asana is also useful like shavasana. This asana removes mental and physical fatigue.

**(19) Mandookasana** — Put together both your feet behind and keep the heels apart, and sit on the open heels. Keep the waist and neck straight and the knees together. With both thumbs folded make fists and keep them together on the navel centre as shown in the picture, the side of the thumb should be on the navel. Then while exhaling slowly bend down gradually to touch the chest on the knees. In this state the rear portion should not leave the heels. Then lift the neck and see ahead, as shown in the picture.

Benefits — The practise of this asana helps in most of the stomach ailments. It is very effective in indigestion and gastric problems. It is especially beneficial for patients of diabetes. All the parts of abdomen get massaged. Knee pain, aching of calves, aching muscles are cured through its continuous practice. Its practice makes the body fit for jumping.

*Note* – Those suffering from backache and neckache, high blood pressure and heart troubles should not do it.

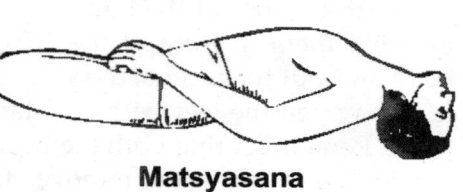

**(20) Matsyasana** — First of all lie down in padmasana on your back with both your palms beside the head. Thereafter lift the neck set the head back on the ground and then bring back both hands in the front towards the feet and hold the left toe with the right hand and right toe with the left hand. In this state both the elbows will stick to the ground. After practising this both hands should be taken back to the rear of the head. Straighten the neck, hold the waist with both the hands, putting pressure on the elbows gradually get up.

*Benefits* — This is an extremely useful asana for patients suffering from breathing problems. The neck becomes shapely. Those who have too much fat on their neck must practise this asana. It is very effective in curing pain in the neck and waist. Indigestion, constipation, gastric complications are also cured. Defects of the eye are cured. Knee pain, gout and other aches also get relief. Dryness of skin is removed. Skin becomes beautiful and attractive. The face glows. If in this asana a person lies down in water, he will float, that is the speciality of this asana. This asana removes women's ailment connected with uterus speedily and regulates menstruation.

**(21) Mayurasana** — Put both the heels and toes together and sit on the heels with knees spread apart touching the ground. Then place both hands on the floor near the knees with a distance of four fingers between them. Bring both the elbows together and place them on the navel. Then bend a bit and raise your feet from the ground. In this state the weight of the body will be on the stomach. Gradually balance and straighten both the legs and look ahead.

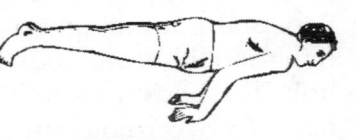

**Mayurasana**

*Benefits* — Continuous practise of this asana cures indigestion, constipation and gastric troubles. Internal organs of the abdomen get massaged. There is increase in appetite. The capacity to digest more and heavy food is invoked. The energy to digest is so much that even venomous food could get digested. Apart from this hands, arms and shoulders become very strong. Defects of the eyesight are cured by its continuous practice.

**(22) Naukasana** — Lie on the belly and stretch both arms in the front and keep the hands together and the toes and ankle together. Then gradually while inhaling raise the top portion of the body and legs as well. In this position the weight of the entire body will be on the belly. In this state the body will appear like a boat as shown in the picture.

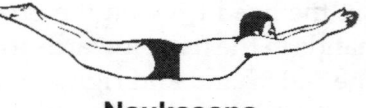

*Benefits* – Continuous practice of this asana leads to speedy blood circulation in the vessels. Muscles become flexible. Lungs receive more oxygen. It cures diseases concerned with breathing. It is good for backache and neckache also. Continuous practice leads to removal of excess fat from the abdomen. Body feels light and energetic.

*Note* – Those suffering from ulcer and colitis should not do it.

**(23) Padangushthasana** — Sit on the floor and put the right feet on the left thigh and the heel of the left feet should hold the body pressing the seevani nerve (between anus and genital). Then keep both hands on the waist and look straight ahead. Upper part of heel must press the seevani nerve otherwise it will not be so beneficial. Then do it again with the other feet for the same time.

*Note* – While performing the asana the entire weight of the body should be on the toe of the feet. This asana should be performed carefully after learning from a yoga teacher for best results.

*Benefits* – Practise of this asana makes a person achieve complete celibacy. Swapnadosh gets cured. Celibacy is possible because the seevani nerve (which carries semen) get under the practitioner's control by practising this asana. This cures all types of seminal complications. Man can control his urges. That is why young men and women are advised to practise this asana more. Those who tremble must practise it for speedy relief. Proper practice of this asana will make one mentally strong and cure venereal diseases.

**(24) Pad-Hastasana** — Stand with the toes and ankles together. Lift both hands upward. Then slowly exhaling bend the body forward gradually putting the forehead on the knees and both hands next to both feet on the ground.

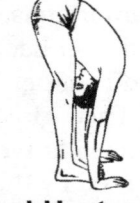

*Benefits* — Those who have heavy hips benefit from this asana. Nerves get massaged. Waist thins down and shoulders broaden up. Excessive fat from the abdomen gets removed. It is good for diabetics. Spinal column becomes soft and flexible.

*Note* — While practising this asana knees should be kept straight. Those suffering from backache and ache in the neck should not do it.

**(25) Padmasana** — Keep the right foot on the base of left thigh and the left foot on base of right thigh. Keep hands in gyan mudra (index finger and thumb together with palms facing upward) on the knees. Keep the spine straight.

*Benefits* — This asana also is good for meditation, bhajan and worship. Pranayama is not effective without padmasana. This increases digestive power, and loins and calves get strengthened.

**(26) Paschimottanasana** — Sit with both the legs in the front. Both ankles and toes will be side by side. Then while exhaling bend down and hold both toes of the feet with both the hands and place the forehead on the knees. Both the elbows will touch the ground.

*Benefits* – Continuous practice of this asana makes the spinal cord flexible. Blood circulation improves, muscles of the waist and calves get toned up which makes them flexible. Paschimottanasana is effective in obesity. Those who have a heavy lower back, must practise it regularly. Waist becomes thin and shapely. It cures skin disease and foul smell in the body. Face glows and there is stimulation of energy. Its practice kills worms and purifies blood. It should not be performed by those suffering from backache and ache in the neck.

**(27) Sarpasana (Bhujangasana)** – Lie down straight on the stomach and keep both hands under the shoulders. Ankles and toes should be kept together and then while inhaling raise the body upto the waist in such a manner that the body takes the shape of a snake. Waist should be raised up to the navel.

**Sarpasana (Bhujangasana)**

*Benefits* – The practice of this asana makes the spinal cord flexible. Diseases like asthma and breathing problems get cured. This asana is important for the kriya of Shankh prakshalana. Excess fat on the belly gets removed. Waist gets thin and chest broadens. It is very beneficial for patients of cervical spondylosis.

*Notes* – This asana should not be done by those suffering from ulcer, colitis and hernia.

**(28) Shalbhasana** – Lie down on the stomach on the ground. Keep both toes and ankles together, and both the palms under the shoulders. Then gradually inhaling raise the neck and feet so much that the weight of the whole body is on the belly. In this state raise both hands or put them under the thighs.

In Shalbhasana the neck should be kept upturned and feet stretched together in the air as shown in the picture.

**Shalbhasana**

*Benefits* – This asana is also better for breathing problems. The practice of this asana makes the chest broader. Oxygen is received in great quantity. It is efficacious for diseases like asthma, neckache, backache. Those who experience trembling of the body can cure it by practising this asana. This asana should be done regularly for stability and strength of the body. Excess fat on the belly is reduced. By practising it even the navel remains in its place. Constipation is also cured.

**(29) Shavasana** – Lie on the floor on your back. Shift the hands slightly away from the thigh with palms facing the sky. There should be a distance of almost 45 to 60 cm between both feet. Thereafter gradually relax the body leaving it absolutely loose. Practise it in such a way that there is no movement or activity in any other part of the body. This asana is called shavasana because as there is no movement in a shava (corpse) similarly with practise the body has to remain completely still. Lie down comfortably and put the left hand palm on the stomach. Then take 8-10 deep breaths, as inhalation is on, the belly will inflate and when exhalation is done it will sink in.

Similarly feel the movement in the belly. After 8 to 10 times breathing will be normal and the movement of the belly will also be normal. Feel it continuously. If your mind wavers after some time then again speed up your breathing which would affect the movement of the belly and again bring

**Shavasana**

it back to normal speed. This way practise it continuously. After a few days meditation time will increase. It appears to be very simple but it should be practised after learning it properly, then only it is beneficial.

*Benefits* – As you feel fresh after sleeping for 7-8 hours, similarly if this asana is performed properly for half an hour you will feel equally fresh. Practise of this asana leads to removal of mental and physical fatigue. Those who suffer from excessive mental tension must practise for 40 minutes. Heart patients must practise it. It is very good for students also. Constant practice of this asana increases concentration. Mind becomes strong. Those who have an inferiority complex get strength of mind by doing this asana properly. This asana is done after having done all other asanas which leads to speeding up of blood circulation and relieves physical fatigue. Those who do not sleep well or have scanty sleep, must practise it continuously.

**(30) Shirshasana** — Sit on the ground and intertwine fingers of both the hands to make a pillow for the head. Then keep the head on this with elbows straight on both the sides of the head. Now gradually lift the body up and straighten it. The entire weight of the body will be on the arms and elbows. Eyes should be half open. To practise shirshasana fully, it takes months and years. Before doing it should be learnt from an experienced yoga practitioner. If done wrongly it can cause a number of diseases. Those whose nasal passage is blocked should not do this asana.

**Shirshasana**

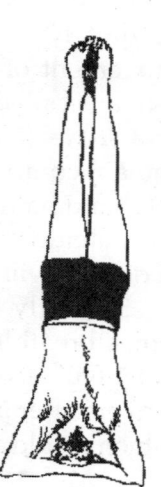

*Benefits* – Shirshasana is the king of asanas. It has a beneficial effect on all ailments. It rectifies blood circulation, eye problems, greying of hair, hair fall, women's menstrual problems, etc. Cough and cold and mental diseases are cured. Lunacy is also cured. The face glows and eyes brighten up. Shavasana must be performed after this asana.

*Note* – This asana must not be done by heart patients and those suffering from constipation.

**(31) Siddhasana** – The heel of left feet should be placed amidst the anus and genital so that the sole should touch the right thigh. Similarly the right heel should be placed above the base of the genital so that the right sole should touch the left thigh. Then put the toe of the left foot placed between the right thigh and calf. Similarly keep the toe of the right foot between the left thigh and calf. Those who have pain in their knees and ankles.

*Benefits* – This is the most important asana of all asanas. This asana cleans 72864 nerves. For meditation it is very easy and appropriate.

All ailments connected with semen are cured.

**(32) Simhasana** – Join both heels the brows and place both hands in gyan mudra over the knees. The spine should be erect while the body is in this asana.

*Benefits* – This asana is specially beneficial in ailments of the throat, tonsils, thyroid gland, etc. One should practise it to boost confidence. Its practice cures ailments of the anus.

**(33) Supt-Pavanmuktasana** – This asana should be done on right foot first then on the left foot and thereafter on both the feet. Lie down on the back with both ankles and toes together. Keep your chin up and look straight ahead.

*Benefits* – This asana is very good for gastric trouble. Those who belch too much, suffer from gastric ailments and

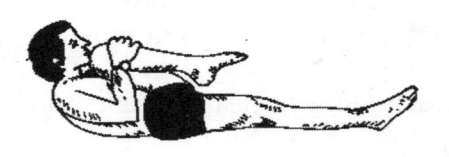

**(with one feet)**      **(with both feet)**

**Supt-Pavanmuktasana**

should do it as it removes gas immediately. Indigestion and constipation are also removed. Digestive power increases. This asana cures knee pain and arthritis. It has a good effect on the vertebral column.

*Note* – Those who have backache or neckache should not do it.

**(34) Supt-Vajrasana** – Sit in vajrasana. Place both the palms behind close to the waist on the floor. Then fold the elbows and slowly lie down. Shoulders and neck will touch

**Supt-Vajrasana**

the ground. Then keep both the palms under the shoulder and raise the head in such a way that it touches the ground. Thereafter put both the palms down on the thighs. In this position both the knees will be together.

*Benefits* – Continuous practice of this asana broadens the chest and makes the waist shapely. It is good for breathing trouble like asthma and bronchitis. While practising it lungs expand fully. This increases the breathing capacity, which helps in curing breathing trouble. Throat and its organs get massaged. Those who have excessive fat on their belly and have a broad waist can benefit from the continuous practice of this asana. They should practice it gradually. Blood circulation gets toned up and blood gets purified, the body feels light. For those whose navel gets displaced, the practice of this asanas will bring it back into its place.

**(35) Swastikasana** — In this asana both the toes have to be hidden between the thigh and the calves behind the knee. Both hands are to be placed on the knees and look straight. In this asana both ankles should cross each other.

*Benefits* — This asana is also good for meditation. This gives relief in pain in the feet, sweating in the feet and smelly feet. Those who feel very cold in the feet in winters and sweat too much in summer must practise this asana for 20 minutes daily.

**Swastikasana**

**(36) Tadasana** — Stand and lift both hands upward with the palms facing the reverse on the sides and then stand on the toes keeping the feet together and pull the body towards the sky as much as possible.

*Benefits* — As the tree of Tad is tall similarly this asana increase height that is why it is called tadasana. Practice of this asana circulates blood fast in all the nerves and this is the only asana which can be practised by a pregnant women for her entire pregnancy. This reduces the labour pain considerably and the child born is healthy.

**Tadasana**

Those who walk too much and have to keep standing in their routine, must practise this asana. This asana can be done by lying posture also.

**(37) Tribandhasana** — In this asana three bandhs have to be performed, i.e., moolbandh (closing up of anus), uddiyan bandh (pulling in the stomach), jalandhar bandh (resting the chin on the chest) simultaneously and that is why it is called tribandhasana (three bandh in the asana).

**Tribandhasana**

First sit in padmasana and keep both hands on the knees. Then applying pressure on the hands pull the anus up (mool bandh), then while breathing out pull the stomach in towards the spine (uddiyan bandh) and then rest the chin on the throat (jalandhar bandh) and close the eyes.

*Benefits* – Practise of this asana leads to cure of all ailments of the throat. The face glows. Asthma, acidity, weakness, constipation, indigestion are removed. All ailments connected with the chest find relief. The contaminated air in the lungs comes out. Constant practise of this asana increases the working capacity of the heart. Faeces and urination decrease in quantity. All ailments connected with the anus like piles, fissure, etc. are cured. Best for reproductive organs. Practitioner of this asana has a long life.

*Note* – Spondylosis patient should not do it.

**(38) Udrakarshasana** – Sit on the ground as in case of Khagasana. Keep both hands on both knees and press the left hand on the left knee towards the right foot so that the knee just touches the ground. After that press right knee on the abdomen and see at the back of the right shoulder similarly. Repeat reverse from the other side.

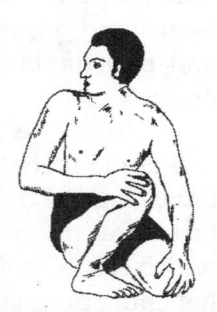

**Udrakarshasana**

*Benefits* – Indigestion, constipation gets cured. Pain in the feet is cured and limbs become strong. By practising this the possibility of any kind of trouble in the joints below the waist cannot arise.

**(39) Urdhvahastottanasana** – First stand and keep both toes and ankles together. Then intertwine all the ten fingers of both hands and raise it upwards above the head. In this position the palms should be facing the sky. Thereafter bend to the right side and then left alternatively.

*Note* – This asana must be practised on both sides equally. While in the position both elbows and knees should remain straight.

*Benefits* — The practise of this asana massages all the intestines and cures chronic constipation. Those suffering from constipation should drink two glasses of lukewarm water in the morning and then perform tadasana. After tadasana they should practise this asana four times on each side. Then they should perform katichakrasana which would clean the intestines. This asana is very good for those suffering from sciatica pain. Those whose back and thighs are heavy must practise this asana. This is one of the main four asanas of shankhprakshalan. Without it shankhprakshalan is not possible. This asana is good for pregnant women. They can perform it till three months of pregnancy.

**Urdhvahastottanasana**

**(40) Urdhvasarvangasana** — Lie down on your back and keep the toes and ankles together. Keep both palms on the waist and lift both feet gradually. Hold the waist with fingers at the back and thumb in the front. Lift the body up taking the support of the arms and straighten it towards the sky. Remember the feet should not be taken behind the head but remain straight. Hold it for as long as possible in this position. To come back bring the feet down to the back of the head and place both the hands on the floor. Gradually putting down each disk of the spinal column one by one, bring back the legs straight on the floor without moving the neck and shoulder.

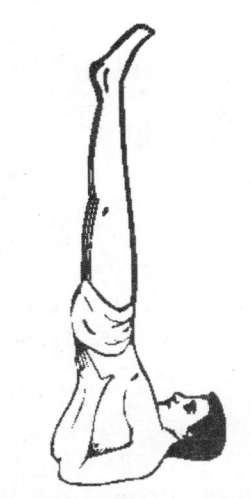

**Urdhvasarvangasana**

*Benefits* – This asana supplies ample blood to the heart and brain, which strengthens the heart and improves memory power. Greying and falling of hair is cured, eye sight improves. Throat ailments like tonsilitis are averted. It massages thyroid and parathyroid glands. The face glows and looks beautiful. Neck and shoulders become strong and powerful. The odour of sweat is removed from the body. It keeps the body agile. Blood circulation is invigorated and is purified. It is good for skin diseases. This is good for woman. By doing it with uddiyanbandh displaced uterus comes into its place.

*Note* – Shavasana must be performed after doing this asana. It should not be done by patients of high blood pressure and neck pain.

**(41) Utkatasana** — First sit down with both the toes and ankles together. Then lift the ankle sitting on the toes. Then keep both hands on the knees and join the fingers of both the hands together and place the chin on the hands and look straight.

*Benefits* – This asana cures ache in the joints below the waist. Toes of the feet become strong. Venereal diseases are cured. State of celibacy is achieved. This asana helps in some yogic exercises. It also brings freshness to the brain.

**Utkatasana**

**(42) Uttan-Koormasana** — Sit in Vajrasana and keep both the palms on the ground behind the back and fold the arms from the elbow and gradually lie down. In this state shoulder and head will touch the ground. Then keep both the hands on both thighs.

**Uttan-Koormasana**

*Benefits* — This asana is good for diseases connected with breathing like asthma, bronchitis, T.B. etc. It is good for the waist muscles. Waist becomes slim and flexible. Its practice removes excessive fat. Knee pain and pain in the calves finds relief. Spinal cord becomes flexible. Blood circulation in the vessels becomes easy and blood is purified.

*Note* — The practice of this asana should not be done by those suffering from ulcer, colitis and blood pressure.

**(43) Uttan-Mandookasana** — Sit in Vajrasana and keep both hands on the ground. Then fold arms from elbow and gradually lie down. In this state the neck and shoulder will touch the ground and then bring both hands behind the head and hold each elbow with each hand.

**Uttan-Mandookasana**

*Benefits* — This asana like uttan koormasana is good for breathing problems. Its continuous practice purifies the lungs, waist becomes flexible and thin. Those who have drooping shoulders must do it regularly. It broadens the shoulders and strengthens them. Excessive fat on the body gets removed. Thighs thin down and become shapely.

*Note* — Those suffering from ulcer, colitis, high blood pressure should not do it.

**(44) Uttanpadasana** — Lie on your back on the ground then put both the hands on the sides of both the thighs and raise the head and feet one foot above the ground. In this state the entire weight of the body will be on the back and waist. Thereafter keep the hands on the thighs. Remember that the portion above the waist should not touch the ground. Only the waist should be on the ground.

**Uttanpadasana**

Both the parts of the body upper and lower part should be equally raised from the ground.

*Benefits* – This is one of the four asanas to keep navel centre in place. The practice of this asana massages 72864 nerves of the entire body. Blood circulates properly. Nervousness gets cured. In the beginning while practising this asana there will be trembling in the body but continuous practice strengthens the body.

*Note* – Those suffering from high blood pressure, cervical spondylosis should not do this.

**(45) Vajrasana** — Keep soles of the both feet against the posterior (hip projection) with toes of both feet together and ankles apart and sit on them. Lower portion of knees to fingers of the feet should touch the ground. Keep the neck and spine straight and keep the knees joined together in the front.

Benefits — This asana is also very good for meditation and worship. This makes the body strong, as Indra's weapon vajra. That is why it is called vajrasana. It is efficacious in too much sleep and sleeplessness also. If done after meals food is immediately digested and, gastric ailments do not occur. For high blood pressure, tension, heart disease, spondylosis it is very good. Pain in the knees, ankle, legs and calves is cured. Apart from this it is very good for students. This removes laziness from the body, provides strength and solidity. A student should practise it for 15-20 minutes with closed eyes, and mind still. Those who are disinterested in studies will be able to study with concentration by practising it regularly.

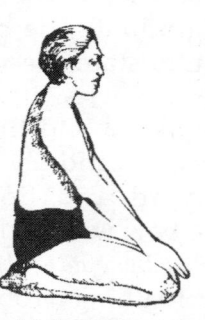

**(46) Yogmudrasana** — This asana is called Yogmudrasana because out of the 84 lakh asanas this is the only asana which includes pranayama also. In this asana retention of breath is also done and leads to awakening of kundalini. By awakening of the kundalini the practitioner reaches the zenith of yoga.

First of all sit in padmasana and bring both hands from behind to hold to the toe of each foot; this means left hand will hold the toe of left feet and right hand will hold the toe of right feet. Keep the waist and neck straight and then exhaling gradually bend down and touch the forehead on the ground. Practise this as much as possible.

**Yogmudrasana**

*Benefits* – This asana increases digestive power, constipation is cured, there is no gas formation after a few days of practice. The face glows and the person becomes soft in his behaviour and anger is reduced. For breathing trouble this asana is very useful. Even tuberculosis gets cured by doing this. For mental development this asana is very good. It benefits in case of fever in the bones.

**Surya namaskar** – This is the best exercise which alone gives the benefit of asana, mudra and pranayama. It affects all the parts of the body and they perform their functions smoothly. Its practice makes the lungs receive pure pranic air in ample quantity and the body of the practitioner glows like the sun.

*Procedure* – Surya Namaskar has twelve steps.

1. Fold both hands together in front of the chest while standing erect with feet together.

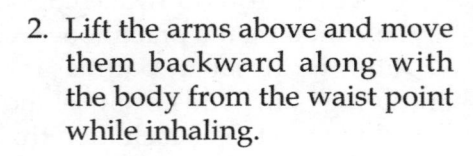

2. Lift the arms above and move them backward along with the body from the waist point while inhaling.

3. Then exhale keeping the portion from foot to waist straight and touch the ground with both the hands and put the forehead on the knees.

4. With both the hands on the ground push the left foot behind stretching it fully and fold the right. Bend backward from the waist and look straight ahead.

5. Inhaling bring both the arms towards the back and bend backward from the waist as much as possible.

6. While inhaling bring back both the hands on the ground with right leg fully stretched behind and left folded in the front, look straight ahead.

Yoga – The Science of Hand Postures and Acupressure

7. Inhale and take back both the arms backwards and bend the body above the waist towards the back as much as possible.

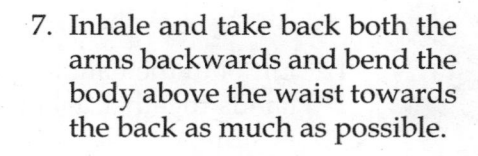

8. While exhaling pull the middle portion upward with the body resting on palms on the ground in the front and feet behind. The body should be mountain shaped.

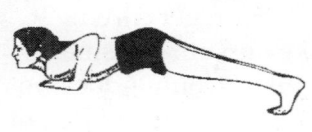

9. While inhaling bend down the body stressing on the palms and feet with the middle portion not touching the ground.

10. Pressing on the palms under the shoulder downward lift the upper portion of the body above the waist and look above concentrating on the centre of the eyebrows.

11. From foot to waist keep the body straight while standing and bend down the portion above the waist to touch the forehead on the knees and both hands on the ground beside the feet.

12. Lift both the hands, stand straight and fold the hands together against the chest as in the first posture.

*Benefits* – Surya namaskar increases mental, physical and spiritual strength. Body's rigidity decreases and one feels light and energetic. It improves eyesight and memory power and leads to mental development. Lungs become strong. Tuberculosis, cold and cough, asthma palpitation, etc., find relief. Complication in the vertebral column get cured.

The face of a practitioner glows like the sun. The smallest part of the body gets affected by it. Skin trouble does not occur. Surya namaskar is helpful in increasing the height also.

*Note* – It should be done in the morning. Hernia patients should not do it.

## 4. Pranayama

Pran (breath) control is pranayama. If the pran is in one's control then longevity of life, strong resolve, peace and happiness can be achieved. In the exalted state of pranayama the inherent power of Kundalini gets awakened.

Padmasana is the only best asana in which Pranayama can be done. It has three parts –
(1) Rechak – Exhaling
(2) Poorak – Inhaling
(3) Kumbhak – Retaining the breath Kumbhak is divided into three parts –
   (i) Antah Kumbhak – Breathing in and then retaining.
   (ii) Bahya Kumbhak – Breathing out and then retaining.

# Yoga – The Science of Hand Postures and Acupressure

　　　(iii)　Kaivalya Kumbhak – Retaining the breath as it is.

Before Pranayama it is necessary to know about nadi, bandh, shat chakra, kundalini, maatra and des.

**Nadi** – The body has 72864 nerves out of which three are very important.

(1) Ida Nadi (Chandra Nadi) – This begins at the left nostril and goes up to the base of the spine.

The breath coming from the left nostril is called chandra swar (moon rhythm). This provides coolness to the body.

(2) Pingla Nadi (Surya Nadi) – Pingla nadi begins from the right nostril and goes up to the base of the spine. The breath from the right nostril is called surya swar (sun rhythm). It provides heat to the body.

(3) Sushumna Nadi (Spinal cord) – Between ida and pingala nadi is placed sushumna nadi. This begins from the medulla oblongata in the brain and goes upto the base of the spine.

**Bandh** – Amongst yogic exercises it is very small but it is the great releaser of energy like the atom. It is a process of controlling and hardening different organs of body but in a phased manner with all precautions. Bandhs are of three types –

**1.　Mool bandh** – The muscles of the anus should be pulled upward using strength internally. Remaining in this position is called mool bandh.

*Benefits* – Diseases of the anus (piles, fissures, etc.) are cured. People suffering from high blood pressure, heart troubles and hernia patients find special relief through it. Night fall, premature ejaculation and other complications of this sort have an effective remedy in mool bandh. Even old become like young.

If men and women practise it regularly then their marital life will be full of inexplicable happiness. It is helpful in awakening the kundalini.

*Note* – Before doing mool bandh practise of ashwani kriya is much better.

**Ashwini kriya** – Doing contraction and expansion of anal muscles in any asana while sitting, lying or standing is called Ashwini Kriya. It should be practised on an empty stomach. It is more beneficial if practised in bahya kumbhak (Breathing out and than retaining). It should be practised for 25-100 rounds.

*Benefits* – This kriya is helpful in celibacy (brahmacharya). It cures piles, urinary problems and makes the anal region healthy. Its practise keeps reproductive organs of male and female strong and healthy. Uterus remains healthy and strong. If a pregnant lady makes regular practise, the delivery will be normal and comfortable..

*Note* – It should not be practised by the patients of constipation.

2. **Uddiyan bandh** – Exhale and pull the stomach within so that the belly becomes a pit against the back. Remain in this position as far as possible.

*Benefits* – It strengthens the organs of the abdomen, removes acidity, constipation, and indigestion. Its practice is good for gastric complications. Asthma can be cured and lungs become powerful. The working capacity of the heart increases. It removes worms from the digestive tract and is good for diabetes.

*Note* – Heart patients and those with mental problems should not practise it. Before doing uddiyan bandh practice of agnisaar kriya is much better.

*Agnisaar Kriya* – Sit in Padmasana and exhale the breath than inflate and deflate the abdomen. Repeat this act again and again. Initially start with 15-20 times and increase gradually.

*Note* – Those unable to sit in padmasana can do it while sitting in swastikasana or vajrasana.

This act can also be done while standing by spreading both legs with a gap of about 30-40 cm between them and with bending forward keep both hands on the knees. Thereafter looking in forward direction similarly inflate the stomach while inhaling and deflate while exhaling. People with backache should not perform in this way.

*Benefits* – Digestion takes place smoothly. All ailments related to stomach are removed and the appetite increases. Obesity, diabetes, urinary problems are cured. Burning sensation in urine is lessened. Excess urination is also lessened by this act.

*Note* – Patients having constipation or ulcer should not do this.

3. **Jalandhar bandh** – In this the chin is rested on the throat.

*Benefits* – Ailments of the throat do not occur. Removes diseases of the tonsils. Voice becomes sonorous. Beneficial for thyroid and parathyroid glands. The face starts glowing and kundalini also gets awakened.

*Note* – Those ailing from backache and neckache should not do it.

## Shat chakra

(1) Mooladhar chakra – It is at the anus, the base of the body.
(2) Swadhishthan chakra – It is at the root of the genital.
(3) Manipurak chakra – It is placed at the navel.
(4) Anahat chakra – It is placed at the heart.
(5) Vishuddh chakra – It is placed at the throat.
(6) Agya chakra – It is placed between the eyebrows.

**Kundalini** – Kundalini is the inherent spiritual strength which lies dormant at four and a half fingers (approximately 8 -10 cm) above the Mooladhar with 3½ turns holding its tail in the mouth at the beginning of the spinal cord. As long as it is dormant a human being is ignorant and those who are able to awaken it get enlightened. By practising shatkarma, asanas, pranayama and mudra this power of the kundalini gets awakened.

**Maatra** – The ratio of time duration for poorak, kumbhak and rechak, i.e. inhalation, retention and exhalation is called maatra. Maatra should be in the ratio of 1:4:2.

**Des** — While inhaling the breath goes up to the very root so its place is up to the mooladhar. While retaining it is up to the navel and while exhaling it is at the beginning of the nostrils. So this is what is called *des* or place where breath is stationed.

## Regulations for pranayama

(1) The place for pranayama should be clean, airy, peaceful and pure.
(2) Pranayama should be performed in padmasana, siddhasana or vajrasana, etc.
(3) Spinal cord, neck, waist and chest should remain straight.
(4) Morning and evening are the right times for pranayama.
(5) Pranayama should be done on an empty stomach or at least four hours after meals.
(6) If one is too hungry pranayama should not be performed.
(7) While suffering from high fever or disease or in case of pregnant women speedy pranayama is prohibited.
(8) While practising pranayama the food consumed should be nutritious and digestive.
(9) Stomach should be kept light and without faeces, i.e. clean.
(10) After practising pranayama one should take rest.
(11) Celibacy is to be practised with special attention.
(12) 4.30 in the morning, 12.30 in the afternoon, 4 to 6 O'clock in the evening and 12 p.m. to 2 a.m. at night are recommended as the ideal time for pranayama.

*Note* — Before main pranayama it is necessary to perform additional pranayama kapalbhati and nadi shodhan or anulom vilom.

**Kapalbhati Pranayama** — In kapalbhati pranayama the emphasis is totally on rechak (exhaling forcefully). Effort is not put on inhaling, but the amount of air one can normally breathe in is allowed and the entire concentration is on exhaling. While doing so there is natural deflation and inflation in the abdomen and it has a special effect on muladhaar, swadhisthan and manipurak chakras.

Initially starting with 3 minutes it should be practised till 5 minutes. In the beginning if one experiences fatigue while doing kapalbhati then shavasana can be done in between. After practising for one or two months this pranayama can be done for 5 minutes continuously.

While doing this one must think that as he is exhaling all the diseases of the body and negative thoughts are also being excreted.

*Note* — Initially one may experience stomach or backache. This will gradually go away. Those having acidic tendency should practise this for approximately 2 minutes during summers.

## Benefits

(1) Face glows and looks beautiful.
(2) Removes allergy, cough, asthma, sinusitis, etc.
(3) Removes diseases related to heart, lungs and brain.
(4) Obesity, diabetes, constipation, gastric trouble, acidity, prostate and kidney related diseases are removed.
(5) Keeps stomach, pancreas, liver, spleen and intestines disease free.
(6) Mind remains stable, calm and happy. Negative thoughts are destroyed which help in getting rid of diseases like depression, etc.
(7) Chakras are purified and there is flow of divine power in all the chakras from root chakra (mooladhar chakra) to crown chakra (brahma randhra).

**Nadi Shodhan or (Anulom-Vilom) pranayama**—Sit in padmasana and keep the waist and neck straight. Eyes will remain steady. Hands will be in anjali mudra (place left hand near the navel, and on its palm the right palm, both palms should face skyward).Then lift right hand in mudra (with index and middle finger on the left side of the nose and the thumb on the right side of the nose) and place it on the nose. From the left nostril exhale and without making any noise inhale. While inhaling the belly should expand like a pitcher and apply jalandhar bandh and mool bandh. Then close the eyes and keep the right hand again in anjali mudra and retain that position. In case breath cannot be retained then bring the right hand again on the nostril. Open jalandhar bandh and mool bandh. Open the eyes and exhale from the right nostril and apply uddiyan bandh and then inhale from the same nostril. Again similarly retain and exhale by the left nostril then one cycle is complete. Repeat it as many times as one can. Inhalation, retention and exhalation should be in the ratio of 1:4:2.

*Benefits* – All the nerves of the body get toned up. Blood is purified. The face glows and eyesight improves. Skin trouble is cured. Energy to digest is invoked.

Main pranayama are of eight types—
**(1) Surya-bhedi pranayama**—It is called surya bhedi because in this inhalation is done by the right nostril alone, i.e. surya swar is used.

Use surya swar for inhalation and chandra swar for exhalation without sound and remaining method is like nadi shodhan.

*Benefits* – Diseases caused by cold (cold, asthma, cough etc.) are cured. Good for diabetics in diseases of the brain, gastric trouble, gout, constipation and worms. Removes imperfections in the blood, it is good for the skin diseases. It is good for low blood pressure. In the body spiritual energy flows and the kundalini is awakened.

*Note* – It is prohibited for heart patients. Asthma patients need not do retention in it. This should be practised in winters only.

**(2) Ujjayi pranayama**—By practising this pranayama control over pran is achieved that is why it is called ujjayi pranayama. Sit in padmasana and keep your hands in the anjali mudra.

Without making noise inhalation and exhalation is to be done by both the nostrils. After inhaling apply jalandhar and mool bandh and retain that position. In case retention cannot be done then make mudra with the right hand and open mool and jalandhar bandh. Then applying uddiyan bandh exhale from the left nostril. Inhalation, retention and exhalation should be in 1:4:2 ratio.

*Benefits* – All throat ailments (glands in the neck, mumps, tonsillitis, goitre, irritation in the neck) are removed. Thyroid, parathyroid glands are affected. Blood is purified. It is considered best for venereal diseases. Women ailments (Leucorrhoea, dysmenorrhoea, uterus and menstruation problems) get cured. Ailments of men (night fall, impotency, etc.) also get cured. Constipation, indigestion and gastric complications find relief. Cough, fever and disease of the spleen get well. It is good for low blood pressure. Kundalini power also gets stimulated and awakened.

*Precautions* – High blood pressure patients and heart patients should not practise it.

**(3) Sitkari pranayama** – In sitkari pranayama the inhalation is through the mouth producing a 'ssssss' type of sound, that is why it is called sitkari pranayama.

Sit in padmasana and keep both hands in anjali mudra. Take the tongue inward and close the jaw and then inhale from the mouth creating loud noise like 'ssssss'. After inhalation apply mool and jalandhar bandh. Retain this position. If breath cannot be retained then open mool and jalandhar bandh and exhale from both the nostrils. The time ratio of inhalation, retention, and exhalation should be 1:4:2.

*Benefits* – This makes the body beautiful like Kaamdeva's. Cures diseases caused by heat in the body. It keeps the system of the body cool. It is good for high blood pressure patients and heart patients. Its continuous practice removes mental tension and appetite, thirst, lethargy and sleep do not torment the practioner. It cures complications of the blood and dysentery. Strengthens eyes and ears. Activates liver and spleen. It is best for acidity. It also helps in awakening of Kundalini.

**(4) Shitali pranayama**—In this pranayama excessive cold is experienced. Sit in padmasana. Keep your hand in anjali mudra. Keep the waist and neck straight. Keep eyes straight. Take out the tongue from the mouth folded round and inhale through it making a noise. As inhalation is done the belly should expand like a pitcher. Thereafter apply jalandhar bandh and mool bandh. Shut the eyes. Retain your breath in this position. While exhaling thereafter open jalandhar bandh and mool bandh. Open the eyes exhale from both the nostrils and in this state apply uddiyan bandh. Practise it this way in accordance with one's capacity.

*Benefits* – The practice of this pranayama gives strength and beauty. Many diseases are cured. Blood gets purified. Control over hunger and thirst is achieved. Fever and tuberculosis get cured. Effect of venom is lost. Once expertise in its practice is achieved even snake bite does not have any effect on the person. The power to live without water or food is also achieved. Acidity does not occur if it is practised regularly. This pranayama is good for liver and spleen. It is efficacious in diseases occurring due to complications in them. It helps in awakening of kundalini.

*Precautions* – This pranayama should not be practised in winter or extreme cold. It is not good for those suffering from cough.

**(5) Bhastrika pranayama**—While practising this pranayama inhalation and exhalation creates the noise of a blacksmith's apparatus, and that is why it is called Bhastrika pranayama.

Sit in padmasana and place the right hand on the nostril in apan mudra. Exhale noisily from any one nostril and inhale from the same nostril. Then exhale from other nostril and also inhale from the same nostril and now exhale from other nostril. Thus a cycle is completed. Take long, deep breaths and make sure that the belly expands at every inhalation and contracts at exhalation. At a time it should be practised 20 to 25 times. Then inhale from the right nostril, while inhaling the belly should expand, apply jalandhar bandh and mool bandh. Close the eyes and retain breath in this position. In case of inability to retain the breath right hand should be in apan mudra over the nostrils. Relax mool bandh and jalandhar bandh and open the eyes. From the left nostril without creating any noise, exhale and apply uddiyan bandh. This way one cycle of pranayama is completed and should be practised as per ones' capacity.

*Benefits* – This is the best pranayama. All ailments caused by cold find relief. Venereal diseases among men and women are cured. Weakness, constipation, gastric complications, etc. are cured. It is best for awakening the kundalini. It is also the best for worms and diabetes.

*Note* – High blood pressure and heart patients should not do it. This can be practised in any season.

**(6) Bhramari pranayama** – In practising this pranayama inhalation should be done like a male black bee (bhanwra) and similarly exhalation also in the sound of female black bee done. That is why it is called Bhramari Pranayama.

Sit in padmasana and keep your waist and neck straight. Eyes must be still, keep both the hands in anjali mudra. Inhale from both nostrils creating the sound of a bumble bee. During inhalation the belly should expand like a pitcher. Then apply jalandhar bandh and mool bandh. Close the eyes. As far as possible retain this position. Relax mool and jalandhar bandh and breathe out from both the nostrils creating the sound of bumble bee. While exhaling apply uddiyan bandh. Practise it as per one's capacity.

*Benefits* – Continuous practice of this pranayama gives peace of mind and increases concentration. Imperfections of the blood are cured. It is best for removing mental tensions. Mind shifts away from material. Practitioner of this pranayama becomes capable of samadhi.

*Precaution* — High blood pressure and heart patients should not practise it.

**(7) Moorchha pranayama** — After any pranayama if on removing jalandhar bandh while exhaling gradually one feels as if unconsciousness is descending upon him it is called Moorchha pranayama. According to yogis during any pranayama if breath is retained from 5 to 10 minutes and while exhaling thereafter the feeling of unconsciousness is experienced then it is moorchha pranayama.

*Benefits* — By continuous practise of this pranayama one gets freedom from mental tensions and fears. This is the first stepping stone for achieving samadhi. It gives happiness and joy to the mind. The practitioner roams about in spiritual arena. This should be practised under the guidance of a competent teacher.

**(8) Kevali pranayama** — In any pranayama when the practitioner is able to retain in the position of outer breath outside and inner breath within, with the pran stationed at the crown, then this particular state is called kevali pranayama.

Practitioner is able to give up inhalation and exhalation and accepts the air happily. There is no need for inhaling or exhaling in this state.

*Benefits* — After excelling in the practice of Kevali retention the practitioner can get anything from the three lokas. Sweat does not smell. The body becomes beautiful like Kamadeva. Astasiddhis can be achieved. Control over all terrestrial beings is achieved. Yogi can become invisible, and the body disappears. It enables to foresee the future. The practitioner becomes a clairvoyant. His curses and boons are influential. The urine and faeces of such a person if applied on iron can convert it into gold. All the qualities of raaj yog are inculcated.

# Mudra

To achieve the ultimate goal of yoga, along with asanas the process of pranayama is carried out, it is called mudra.

Sage Gherand described 25 mudras out of which 3 mudras have been described i.e., mool bandh, uddiyan bandh and jalandhar bandh and 5 special mudras are described here.

**(1) Mahamudra**—This has been called Mahamudra by yogic sages because it destroys the five points of suffering (attachment, envy, ignorance, pride, fear of death) and the practitioner is able to get control over death.

First sit in the asana with your feet stretched forward, then fold the left leg and keep the heel on the seevani nerve. In this position the left sole would be touching the right thigh. Then hold the right toe, with the left hand and with the right hand make apan mudra over the nostrils and start inhaling from the nostril of the same side as the outstretched leg without making any noise. The belly should expand forward. After inhaling apply jalandhar bandh and mool bandh. Bending forward touch knee with head and hold the right feet with the hand employed in mudra till now. In this position both knees and elbows will touch the ground. As far as possible hold the breath and remove the hand of mudra from the out stretched foot and keep it on the nose in mudra. Straighten the back and neck and relax mool bandh and come out of jalandhar bandh. Then exhale from the side of the folded foot and apply uddiyan bandh. Repeat the same process on the other side, keep the ratio of inhalation, retention and exhalation 1:4:2.

*Benefits*—Mahamudra's practice removes tuberculosis, diseases of the anus, piles, piles with bleeding, fissure, weakness, etc. All the five causes of suffering are destroyed. By practising this mudra regularly one can achieve super soul. Semen is procured. Venereal diseases get cured. Night fall does not occur. Leucorrhoea, dysmenorrhoes, discolouration in menstrual bleeding, etc. find relief. The face glows, helps in awakening of the kundalini. Ulcer, colitis, gastric complications, etc. are cured. Physical, mental and spiritual discipline is achieved. Diseases of the lungs, stomach, kidneys get relief. It is beneficial for mental diseased, cures pimples and aches, diseases related to the throat are removed. Infectious fever gets over. It is beneficial in skin diseases.

*Precautions* – People with high blood pressure, heart patients and those with a backache should not do it. This should be practised on both the sides equally.

**(2) Mahabandh** – Sit in Gomukhasana. Cross both the hands and hold the shoulders. Keep the waist, neck, straight and look in front and inhale with both nostrils without making any noise. While inhaling, the belly should expand. Apply jalandhar bandh and close the eyes. Retain breath as far as possible in this position. Mool bandh will be applied automatically. Then open the eyes. Remove jalandhar bandh. Exhale from both the nostrils and apply uddiyan bandh. In this also the maatra ratio should be 1:4:2. Repeat the same process changing the foot position. It is generally practised by discerning persons.

*Benefits* – Mahabandh gives freedom from the fear of death. Ida, pingla and sushumna nerves unite to give concentration of the mind. Power is derived from Shiva. This mudra is extremely helpful in concentration of the mind and kundalini getting awakened. Pran enters the mooladhar chakra to reach the crown chakra after one by one. Diseases of the lungs like asthma, etc. get cured. Diseases of the throat get cured. Removes mental tension. This is the greatest bandh and that is why it is called maha bandh. It helps in all ailments of the anus.

*Precautions* – High blood pressure and heart patients need not practise it. Waist is to be kept straight always. Practise must be from both sides.

**(3) Mahavedh** – Mahavedh is a combination of two words Maha + vedh meaning thereby greatest piercing. The arrow of Pran pierces through the Brahma gland, Vishnu gland and Rudra gland, i.e. the gate of sushumna while practising this madavedh.

Sit in Padmasana. Keep both the palms beside the thighs. Keep your waist and neck straight and without making any noise inhale from both the nostrils. Apply jalandhar bandh and mool bandh. Close the eyes, put the entire weight of the body on both the arms and lift the whole body. In this state of retention hit the hips repeatedly. When unable to retain the breath any more stop hitting the hips. Remove jalandhar bandh, relax mool bandh, open the eyes, without creating a noise exhale from both the nostrils. The above stated process can be done repeatedly.

*Benefits* – Practise of Mahavedh makes one achieve many siddhis. The practitioner does not get wrinkles on his face. Hair do not get grey. Old age and death is conquered. Mahabandh and mahamudra are not fruitful without mahavedh. It is good for curing tonsils and stammering. Falling of hair gets over. Pran resides in sushumna and awakens the kundalini.

*Precautions* – This mudra should not be practised by high blood pressure patients, heart patients, asthma patients and those suffering from back ache.

**(4) Khechari** – 'Khe' means sky and 'Chari' means roaming, i.e. roaming in the sky. Turn the tongue inward in the throat and concentrate between the brows with your eyes. According to the Yoga granth first churning is to be done.

Rock salt, big harad, black pepper and saffron are ground together in equal quantities. Then strain the powder in a thin cloth. This powder should be applied under the tongue and to make the tongue long it is pulled with both hands. Tongues are of three types.

(1) Snake Tongues, (2) Tortoise Tongues ,(3) Cow Tongues Those who have snake tongue, their tongues takes three days to achieve success in khechari. Tortoise tongued take three months to perform khechari successfully and cow tongued take six months to do it. Once excellence is achieved in khechari the tongue is able to reach the kapal kuhar then the

practitioner can experience six tastes. They are salt, bitter, sour, milky, like ghee and honey.

*Importance* – The body becomes beautiful like an angel and divine qualities are inculcated. The point on the forehead stabilises. While in this world one gets freedom from worldly matters. As the root holder of this universe is God, similarly khechari is the most important among all the mudras. By practising khechari the practitioner can achieve the state of samadhi. Khechari is the best source to close all the seven openings. Churning of tongue is good for stammering.

## (5) Viparitkarni

Lie in urdhva sarvangasana and chin should be on the chest (juguler knotch) so that the position of surya (navel) and chandra (crown) is reversed, that is why it is called viparitkarni. Practise deep rhythm breathing.

*Benefits* – The secretion in the throat through kapal kuher is saved. Digestive energy is invoked. All ailments of the neck get cured. Pronunciation becomes sweet. The face glows. Permanent celibacy is achieved. Venereal diseases are cured. It is good for hernia and hydrocele. Greying of hair, falling of hair, etc., is cured. It gives relief in skin diseases and practitioner is able to conquer death. It is very good for mental ailments.

*Note* – Heart patients, high blood pressure patients and those having backache should not do it.

## (6) Pratyahar (control of sense organs)

When senses for their own satisfaction go after the material object, controlling them by not letting them to go to the material object is called pratyahar.

Eyes are for sight and nose is for odour. The tongue perceive six tastes, and sonorous words are perceived by the ears and touch is felt by the skin. To separate senses from their respective material objects is pratyahar.

As the pran gets under control, so does the mind. When senses get under control then the material objects lose their importance. That is why first pranayama is to be done.

## (7) Dhaarna (concentration)

Concentrating wholly on a single point or on a task in which one is completely engrossed is concentration. The practise of dhaarna should move from tangible to intangible and from visible to invisible.

## (8) Dhyan (meditation)

Keeping the mind continuously in concentration is called dhyan.

*Method* — Dhyan can be performed in any dhyan asana. If one is unable to sit in an asana then one can even sit in a chair with legs hanging below. The spine and neck should remain straight.

Dhyan can be performed in many ways. A person should adopt the way which he has faith in. Remember according to the Gita the way of living and food habits should be extremely regular.

First concentrate on the front of nostril and feel the touch of breathing air. After this practise and feel the difference in the temperature of the air inhaled and exhaled. After this, concentrate between both the eyebrows and feel something like palpitation, etc. After this practise, concentration can be done any where.

According to *Gherand Samhita* dhyan is of three types.

(1) **Sthool Dhyan** — concentration on a place, garden, etc.
(2) **Jyotirmaya Dhyan** — concentrating on the centre between the brows.
(3) **Suksham Dhyan** — it is for those who have reached the zenith of dhyan. According to Bhakti sagar there are four types of dhyan.
   (i) **Padastha Dhyan** — concentrating on the nails of the feet of one's own deity, placed in one's own heart and then see his shape up to the top.
   (ii) **Pindastha Dhyan** — Practise Yama, Niyama, Asana, Pranayama, Pratyahar, Dharna to clean the mind, then

**Braham Randhra (Crown Chakra)**

**Agya Chakra (Third eye Chakra)**

**Vishudh Chakra (Throat Chakra)**

**Anahat Chakra (Heart Chakra)**

**Manipurak Chakra (Solar Plexus Chakra)**

**Swadhishthan Chakra (Sacral Chakra)**

**Mooladhar Chakra (Root Chakra)**

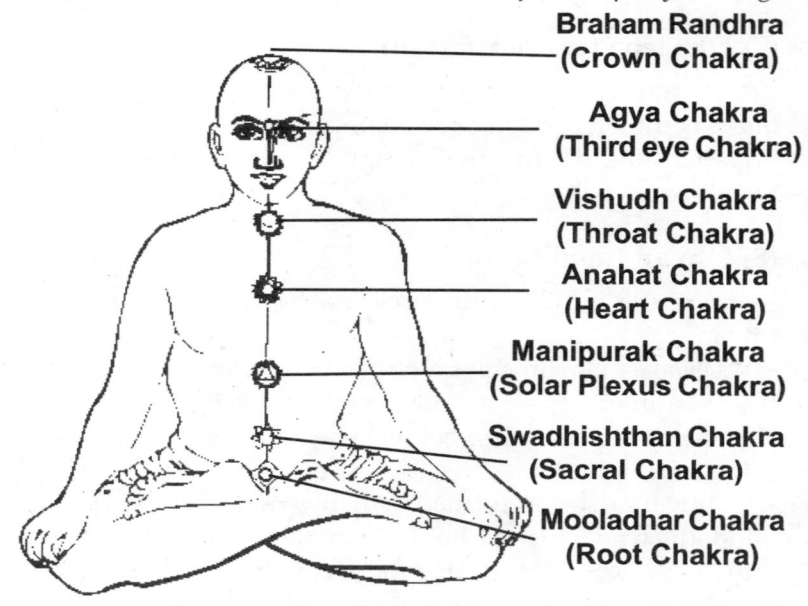

go through the six chakras to the crown and concentrate there.

The points of union of ida, pingla and sushumna nerves are called chakras.

*Mooladhar chakra* – This is placed in the middle of anus and the genitals. This is the place of earth element. Concentration on this chakra leads to its activation and increases physical vigour.

*Swadhishthan Chakra* – This is at the root of the genitals. This is the place of water element. By concentrating here this chakra gets activated and arrogance, greed, jealousy and anger, etc., are destroyed. The person becomes active.

*Manipurak Chakra* – It is situated in the line of navel. This is the place of fire element. Concentration on this chakra leads to its activation, by which qualities of courage and growth are imbibed.

*Anahat Chakra* – This is placed in the line of heart. This is the place of air element. By practising this, desirous practitioner get materialistic achievements and non desirous practitioner gets perfection in yoga.

*Vishudh Chakra* – This is placed in the line of throat. This is the place of sky element. By concentrating on this chakra one gets a lot of peace, happiness, knowledge and the voice quality also improves..

*Agya Chakra* – The place of this chakra is in the middle of the eyebrows. This had the fruits of all the chakras. *Gita* also suggests concentration on this chakra. Its activation leads to foresightedness and heavenly knowledge. Therefore it is also called the third eye.

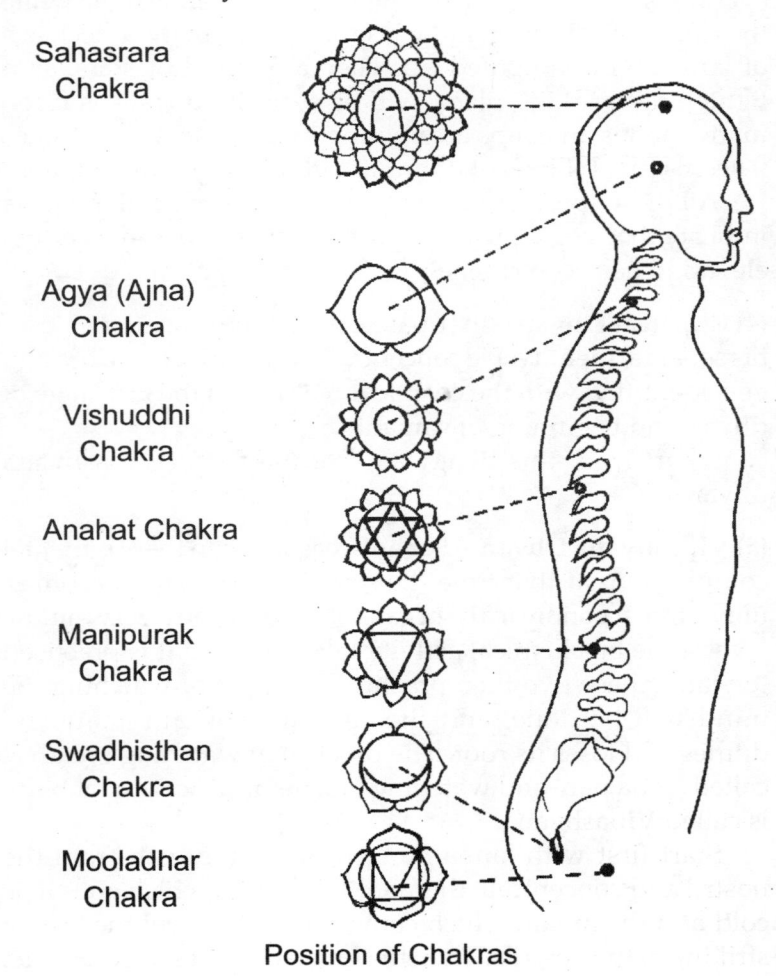

Sahasrara Chakra

Agya (Ajna) Chakra

Vishuddhi Chakra

Anahat Chakra

Manipurak Chakra

Swadhisthan Chakra

Mooladhar Chakra

**Position of Chakras**

Through all chakras dhyan reaches the crown. This cuts the practitioner from the outer world and becomes one with the creator.

As per need one could do dhyana on a particular chakra but the effective way for doing it is to begin from the mooladhar chakra to crown gradually one by one and from crown to mooladhar chakra.

**(3) Roopastha Dhyan—** Try to concentrate in between the eyebrows. First small fire particles will be seen. After a while the flame of a lamp will be seen and gradually a necklace of lamps will be lighted up. Then a garland of stars, as if lightening is taking place, will be seen. It appears as if too many moons and suns are shining in the space and at times it seems that billions of atoms are glowing on both hands.

All these spectacles and other glimpses of similar nature indicate that yogic pursuit is well-maintained and a certain elevation has been reached.

**(4) Rupateet Dhyan—** In rupateet dhyan the practitioner loses his separate identity. He concentrates on brahma randhra and gets identified with the cosmic force. This is the last stage of dhyan and beginning of samadhi.

Apart from this Bhagwan Buddha found Vipashyana dhyan.

**(5) Vipashyana Dhyan—** For any reason when there is mental complication at that time the speed of breathing becomes, unnatural, secondly in the organs of the body on a very minute level some biochemical activity takes place. If it is practised to watch these two then practically the job of watching the mind will be done, and the complication automatically dilutes and loses its root. The practice of watching breath is called 'aana pan' and watching biochemical activity of body is called Vipashyana.

Start first with 'anna pan', watch the breath from the nostril and concentrate thereon. The breath which goes in is cold and the breath which comes out is hot, feel the breath striking at the nostrils. Then the touch becomes very minute.

Then concentrate on that minute place and that minute activity.

After 3-4 days start Vipashyana. Take the mind concentrating on breath to the head area, move there slowly then come to face, neck, hands and feet. Having completed the observation from head to foot the process is repeated in reverse order and in this way the cycle continues.

During this there will be many sensations, pain, touch or trembling, etc.

These feelings should not be taken to be pleasant or unpleasant.

They should be felt like an observer. The feelings come like the wavelets of a river flow or the ebb and tide of the ocean.

Vipshyana is a spiritual practice of sublime order to cleanse the mind of avarice, attachments and envy.

## *Benefits of Dhyan (Meditation)*

Dhyan controls the mind and its wavering gets absolutely over. The spiritual happiness experienced during dhyan breaks all mental blockages and the person feels light. Its regular practice removes nervous weakness and increases memory power. Foresightedness, creative thinking and problem solving skill are developed.

A person practising dhyan regularly has an attractive personality. Those who come into his contact are inspired by his effective speech, brightness in the eyes, healthy body and good behaviour.

## Samadhi (communion)

Samadhi is the last stage of Hath Yoga. In this the individual soul becomes one with the universal soul. This is termed as moksha.

As long as the practitioner's five senses are awake or conscious one is in the dhyan state and when these sensations are completely lost then the state of dhyan converts into samadhi.

When in the state of samadhi one does not experience hunger, thirst, smell, taste, beauty, touch, sound, hot, cold, honour, dishonour, happiness and unhappiness, etc. A person who has achieved this state cannot be cut or pierced by a weapon, no human or violent animal, venomous being can harm such a person. He is not affected by mantra or tantra, maaran or uchchatan. No propensity can grip him. Even astha-siddhis can also be achieved through yoga.

Before learning to attain samadhi mastery of yama, niyama asana, pranayama, pratyahar dharna, dhyan and right way of eating and living is essential.

## Yog nidra

Yog nidra is a simple way of putting a restless mind at peace. Yog nidra is that state of dhyan whose practice removes mental and physical tension and gives a lot of mental peace.

Lie down in Shavasana and do not move and try to relax. Loosen up all the body parts and try to concentrate on your breathing. Keep your eyes closed and then concentrate on the toe of one feet and from there come towards the heart. Similarly concentrate on the toe of other feet and slowly come to the heart. Similarly concentrate on the fingers of both the hands one by one and come to the heart. Try to concentrate on the other body parts one by one at the same time. Continue taking deep breaths. This gives physical rest to the body. While lying down in shavasana one can also try imagining various things like mountains, trees, sunrise, chirping of birds, any deity one worships, etc. This will bring a lot of peace and tranquility.

Yog nidra removes sleeplessness, mental tension, etc.

## Navel centre (solar plexus)

Each part of the body has its own importance and navel is a very important part of our body. It is considered to be the centre of all the organs of the body. If the body can be divided in two the navel will fall at the centre. Approximately 7 cm beneath the navel an egg shaped lump of flesh is there. From there 72,864 nerves (nadi) are spread all over the body. It is normally pulled by some tissues, which keep it in place. If for any reason these tissues get pulled then the navel gets displaced. Consequently various ailments crop up.

**Reason for Displacement of Navel**—Displacement of navel usually happens in childhood and can happen due to various reasons. Running, climbing the stairs, lifting weight with a jerk also leads to the displacement of navel. People who while standing lean on one foot more than the other or those who while lifting weights put pressure on one side of the body are likely to have their navel displaced. Accumulation of toxins in the navel region is also one of the main cause. Generally it is seen that men have their navel displaced on the left side and women on the right side.

**Symptoms of Displacement of Navel**—If the navel is displaced upward then the following diseases occur—constipation, heart trouble, palpitation, etc. If the navel is displaced downwards then it causes loose motions, night fall, indigestion, etc. If it is displaced to either left or right side then it can lead to stomachaches.

Similarly women get various diseases due to displacement of navel, e.g. Leucorrhoea, dysmenorrhoea, complications of the uterus and irregular menstruation.

Generally displacement of navel is considered normal. But when it acquires serious dimensions then it cannot be cured by modern medicines also. But yogic exercises can easily rectify it.

## Ways of examining navel displacement

(1) If the navel is displaced in case of a man or woman make him or her do Uttanpadasana and then lie down in shavasana. Sit next to the patient in khagasana. Then bring all the five fingers together and place the tip of the fingers on navel of that person, if throbbing is felt right under the navel then the navel is in its place., If it is felt above or below to the right or left it may have been displaced.

(2) Take a thread, tie it on the index finger of the right hand and place it on the navel and then the other side of the thread can be held with the left hand and taken up to the left nipple of the patient. Thereafter carefully measure the right nipple with the thread. If the thread falls short then it may be known that the navel is displaced upwards and if it is bigger then it may be confirmed that the navel is displaced downwards.

*Note* – In case of women the test should be done by taking the thread from the navel to the toes of the feet (The heels of both the feet will remain together and the toes will be separate.)

(3) Tell the patient to lie down on his back and join the big toes of both legs. Both legs should remain straight. If navel is displaced then both the big toes will not be of same size, one may be bigger and other smaller.

(4) Open the palms of both hands facing upward and join them in such a way so that the little fingers touch each other. If their are not together the navel is displaced. If the little fingers of both the hands are not of the same size then the navel is displaced.

*Note:* Keep the portion of both palms from little finger to wrist together.

## Methods to bring the navel center in order –

(1) For this do uttanpadasana then dhanurasana and chakrasana followed by matsyasana.

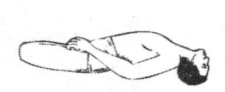

Uttanpadasana   Dhanurasana   Chakrasana   Matsyasana
      1.                    2.                   3.                   4.

*Note* – One who practices uttanpadasana has his navel always in place.

2) Lie down on your back.

Keep your legs apart so much so that there is a distance of almost one foot. Now fold your knees. Put

(1)

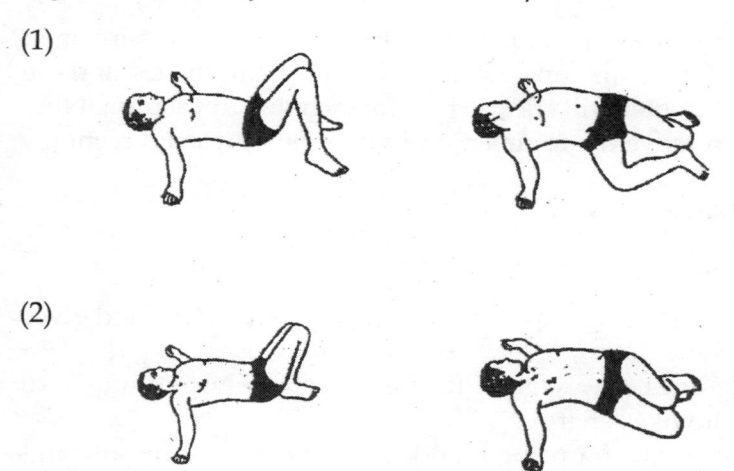

(2)

both the hands on either side parallel to the ground. Now turn both the knees to the left side on the ground. In this position the right knee will touch the heel of the left foot. Turn the head to the right side on the ground.

Now repeat the same procedure towards the right side with both the knees turned towards the right side and turn the head on the left side. Do this ten times on both sides. Now do the above exercise with both knees and feet together, i.e. touch both the knees on the ground to the left side then right knee will be on the left and the head will remain turned to the right side. Now do this on the other side.

(3) Put a rug or a blanket on the floor. Lie down on your chest. Take a plastic ball under your navel and lie over it for four to five minutes. Get up and sit for sometime and have a fruit.

(4) Lie down on your back and cycle by moving your legs forward and backward. Do this every day.

(5) Lie down the patient on his back with an empty stomach. Pull the big toes of both the feet and simultaneously pull the small fingers of both the hands.

Similarly pull that little finger of the hands.

(6) Lie down the patient with empty stomach on his back. Light a small oil lamp or candle and keep it on his navel.

Keep a tumbler made of glass with little pressure on it. After sometime the flame will be extinguished and the tumbler will stick to the stomach due to vacuum. Now remove the tumbler straight in the upward direction.

## Massage

### *Benefits*

1. Massaging makes the nervous system strong and gives relief to it.
2. Gives new vigour to the digestive system and also invokes energy.
3. Speedens up the blood circulation in all organs and takes out toxins along with sweat and urine.
4. It strengthens lungs, kidneys, liver, skin, etc.
5. Reduces fat in the body.
6. Exercises the muscles which make them shapely and active.
7. Removes fatigue and body becomes strong, eyesight improves and one gets good sleep.
8. Boosts body's resistance power.
9. Regular massage keeps ageing at bay.

### *Things to remember before going for a massage*

1. After attending to the natural calls, one should get the massage done in a lonely, peaceful, airy room or open place.
2. Massage should be done in the morning sunshine for better results, or else try to sit in the sun for 15-20 minutes before the massage.
3. One should get the massage done from a person with a happy frame of mind.
3. Massage should be done on an empty stomach.
4. For massage mustard oil, coconut oil, sesame (til) oil, castor oil, almond or olive oil, etc, can be used but pure mustard oil is more beneficial.

5. The person doing massage should be in a happy frame of mind and healthy because it has an effect on the recipient.
6. While massaging no talking should be done.
7. Massage should not be given to those suffering from fever, constipation, any kind of skin trouble, jaundice, swelling, and during menses.
9. Massage should be done in such a way so that the blood flows towards the heart. But in case of people with high blood pressure it should be reverse.
10. While giving massage the movement of hand should be from bottom to top.

## How to massage?

Make the person lie down on his back. Apply oil on the sole of one foot and start massaging. Press the sole of the foot with thumb. Massage the toes of foot, press them, turn them clockwise and anti-clockwise and pull them.

Massage thoroughly on the heels in all directions. For massaging the calf keep the knee upwards. For massaging the thighs, keep the legs straight.

In the same way massage the other leg starting from sole of the foot to toes, heel, calf and thigh.

Similarly do hand massage starting from palm to the shoulders.

For massaging the abdomen, fold the legs. Press the abdomen around navel in a circular movement.

Apply oil on the chest and massage each bone of the chest. Use fingers or thumb to rub and massage between bones.

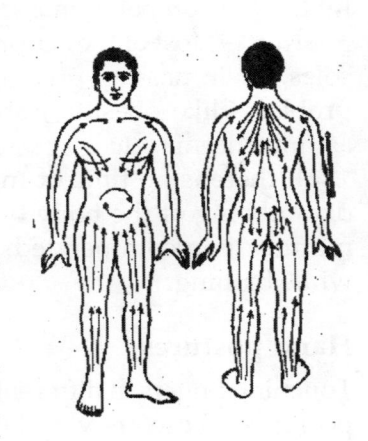

Special care should be taken to massage the breast of a woman. From the base of the breast, move the hands in circular motion and bring up to the tip of the breast. By doing so the shape of the breasts becomes proper.

For massaging the back, lie down the person on his stomach. Apply oil on the back. Press the backbone with friction and use the thumb to press from lower back towards the neck. Then press by giving friction on both sides of backbone using the thumb, from downward to upward direction. Join all the fingers and with their tips move them in a circular movement on the spine and bring them towards the neck.

For massaging the neck and head, make the person sit. Massage the neck and throat, move the thumb around the eyes. Massage the eyebrows. Press the bones of the eyebrows lightly with fingers. Press near the ears and massage. Massage the forehead. Massage the top of the head.

Only applying oil and rubbing is not sufficient. During massage apply pressure on the organs and pat them slowly. The tips of fingers (without nails) should be poked and pressed at the desired spots. Make palms into half fist and hit the portion being massaged.

*Note* – Most of the acupressure points are on the palms or soles. Their massage gives relief and is helpful in combating problems like obesity, imbalance of hormones, joint pain, asthma, hernia, etc.

If there is no time or means for getting massaged, then dry rubbing of the body before a bath with a towel for ten minutes is recommended. Soles should be rubbed nicely while bathing.

## Hand postures

Touching fingers in different ways together is known as hand postures. These are very helpful in keeping one healthy or to cure many diseases.

Our five fingers in the hand stand for five elements in the following way:

Yoga – The Science of Hand Postures and Acupressure  175

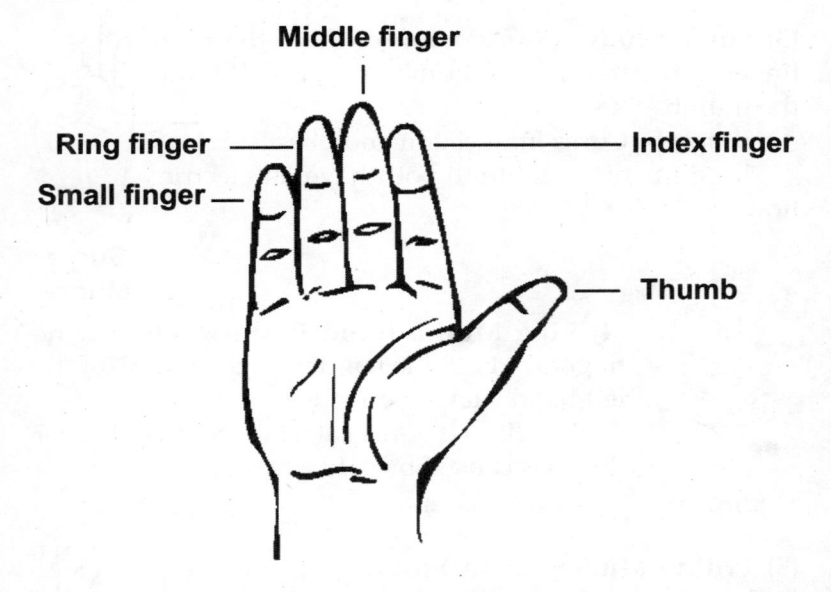

**Middle finger**
**Ring finger**
**Small finger**
**Index finger**
**Thumb**

By hand positions, balance can be maintained in the five physical elements and health can be monitored and lost health can also be restored.

**(1) Gyan Mudra (Knowledge Posture)** – Top of the thumb and index fingers should be united to make this posture.

*Benefits* – Memory power improves, mental diseases, irritability and sleeplessness can also be overcome. Memory power gets invoked by this hand posture. It is a boon for students and intellectuals and is extremely efficacious in mental diseases.

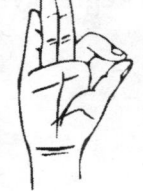

**Gyan Mudra**

**(2) Vayu Mudra (Air Posture)** – Keep the index finger on the root of the thumb and press it with the thumb to make this mudra.

*Benefits* – This mudra cures all types of ailments caused by air imbalance, gout, tremble, paralysis, gastric pain, creeping pain, etc.

**Vayu Mudra**

**(3) Surya Mudra (Sun Posture)** — Place the ring finger at the root of the thumb and press it with the thumb.

*Benefits* — Cures indigestion and obesity.

Ring finger and thumb both have an electric flow.

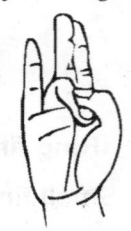

**Surya Mudra**

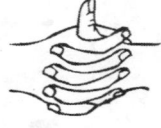

**(4) Ling Mudra (Stud Posture)** — Interwine fingers of both the hand with the thumb of the left hand sticking outside.

*Benefits* — It cures catarrah, cold, and other diseases caused by cold.

**Ling Mudra**

**(5) Prithvi Mudra (Earth Posture)** — Unite the upper portion of ring fingers and thumb.

*Benefits* — For a lean and thin person it is beneficial and brings a glow on the face. Regressive thoughts also get changed.

**Prithvi Mudra**

**(6) Pran Mudra (Soul Posture)** — The top portion of small finger and ring finger should touch the top of the thumb.

*Benefits* — One becomes so powerful physically and mentally that no disease can attack such a person. Blood circulation improves and any blockage in the blood vessels is removed. Any eye defect can also be rectified by this mudra. The mudra also brings in a lot of vigour and enthusiasm.

**Pran Mudra**

**(7) Apan Mudra (Ether Posture)** — Touch the middle and ring finger together to the thumb.
*Benefits* — Reduces gas formation in the abdomen and cures pain or any complications occurring due to it.

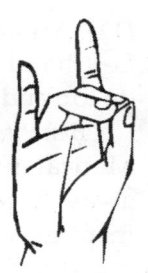

**Apan Mudra**

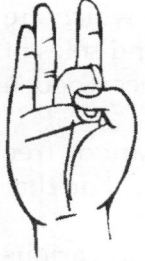

**(8) Shunya Mudra (Vacuity Posture)** — Fold the middle finger and press it with the thumb.
*Benefits* — Gives relief in case of any ailment of the ear. By practising it regularly diseases of the ear can be cured. (If the person is deaf and dumb since birth then it is of no use).

**Shunya Mudra**

**(9) Hridaya Mudra (Heart Posture)** — Put the index finger at the bottom of the thumb and the middle finger along with ring finger should touch the top of the thumb.
*Benefits* — This mudra works as an injection in averting a heart attack. Regular practice of this mudra can remove heart diseases.

**Hridaya Mudra**

**(10) Varun Mudra (Sea Posture)** — Touch the top of the small finger on the top of the thumb to make Varun mudra.
*Benefits* — This cures diseases caused by paucity of water element in the body. It cures ailments of the skin and blood.

**Varun Mudra**

**(11) Anjali Mudra (Meditation Posture):** Left hand is kept below the right which is on top and placed on the lap facing skyward.

*Benefits* – This gives peace to the brain. Mental tension and complications flee away. Its practice generates new energy and inspiration in the body.

**Anjali Mudra**

## Acupressure

Acupressure is a treatment for pain and illness in which pressure is applied on various pressure points which are present mainly in the palms, tips of the hands and soles of the body. Sometimes soles are not soft so sometimes wooden hooks are used to apply pressure.

Acupressure brings instant relief but it cannot free the patient of toxicity that causes the disease. For that improvement in food and life style is necessary.

**Diagnosis** – For diagnosis of any disease the various pressure points which are present in the palms and soles of the body are pressed by the therapist. By pressing a particular point a lot of pain is caused which makes the therapist understand the organ affected.

**Treatment** – For treatment the disease stricken points are pressed for 4-5 seconds then a break of 2 seconds is given. This process is repeated for two to three minutes, and three or four times a day. Pressure is put on the thumb and fingers clockwise for better effect.

## *Precautions*

1. Apply as much pressure which the patient can bear.
2. Heart patients should be gently pressurised.
3. Acupressure should not be given half an hour before bathing and half an hour after it.
4. Treatment through acupressure should not be given during menstruation and during pregnancy.
5. Do not give acupressure on broken organs.

# Yoga – The Science of Hand Postures and Acupressure

6. After taking any medicine wait for two hours before starting the treatment.

**Recognition of pressure points –** For this body has been divided differently.

(1) The body if divided from right to left in two parts, the organs that will fall on the right side will have pressure points in the right palm and sole of the right foot. Those organs that will come on the left will have pressure points in the left palm and left sole. Those organs which are present on both the sides, their pressure points will be in both the palms and soles.

(2) Keeping the fingers of hands and feet as the base the body is divided length wise into the ten equal parts. (Five parts will fall on the right side and five on the left) then whenever a part falls in a particular zone, it's connected pressure points will be in the same zone in the hands and feet.

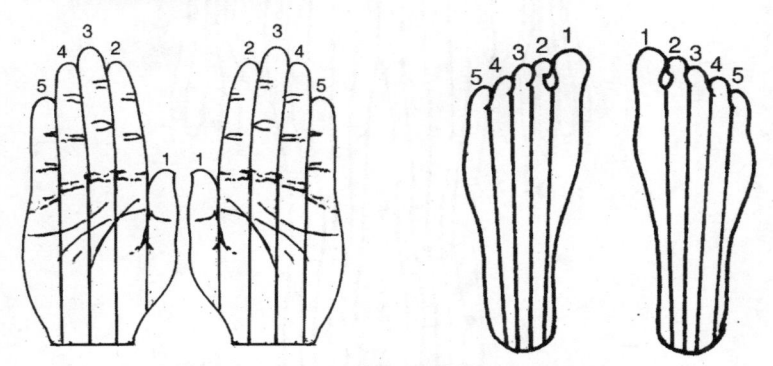

**Five parts of each hand and foot**

(3) If the body is divided width wise, then the first part is head and neck, the second below the neck upto the diaphragm, the third is abdomen and below it. Similarly hands and legs can be divided and the organ in a particular portion will be accordingly placed in the palms and feet soles with its pressure points.

180    Secrets of Naturopathy and Yoga

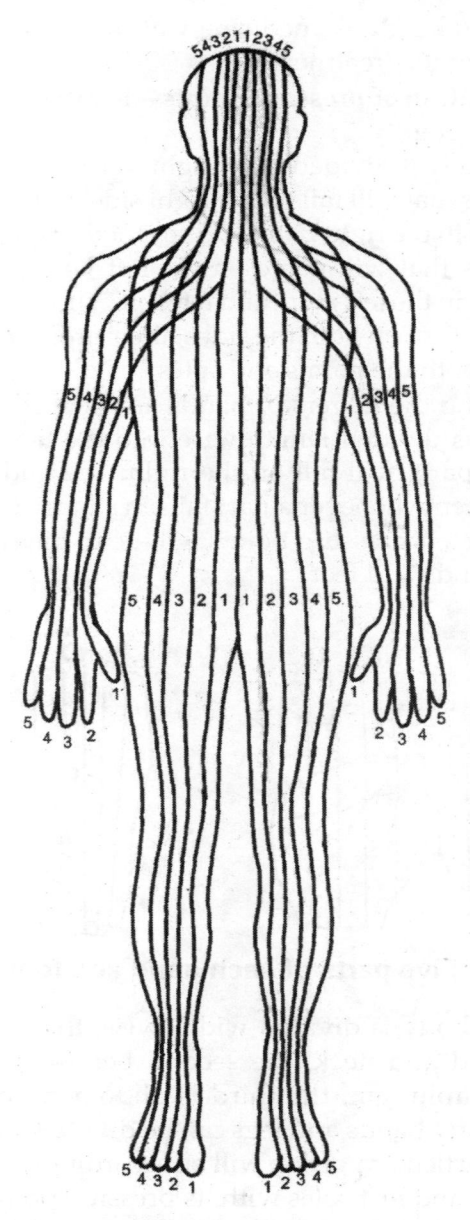

**Length wise ten equal parts of the body**

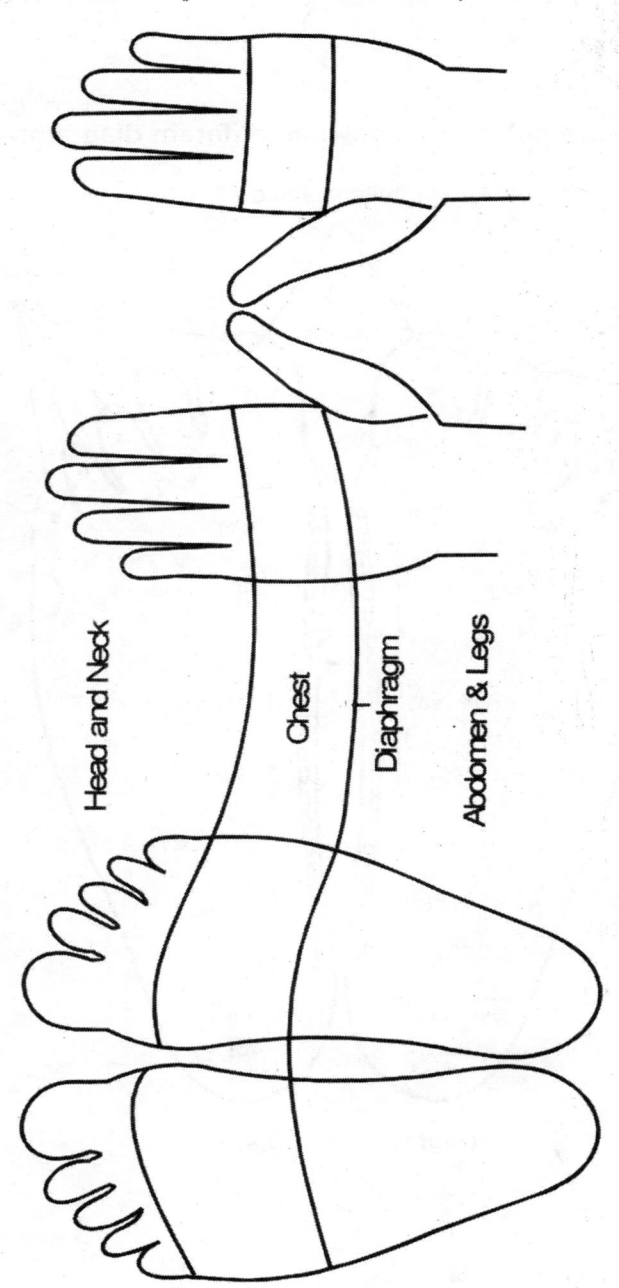

*Yoga – The Science of Hand Postures and Acupressure* 181

**Width wise three Parts of the Body**

- Head and Neck
- Chest
- Diaphragm
- Abdomen & Legs

## Pressure points are shown in different diagrams—

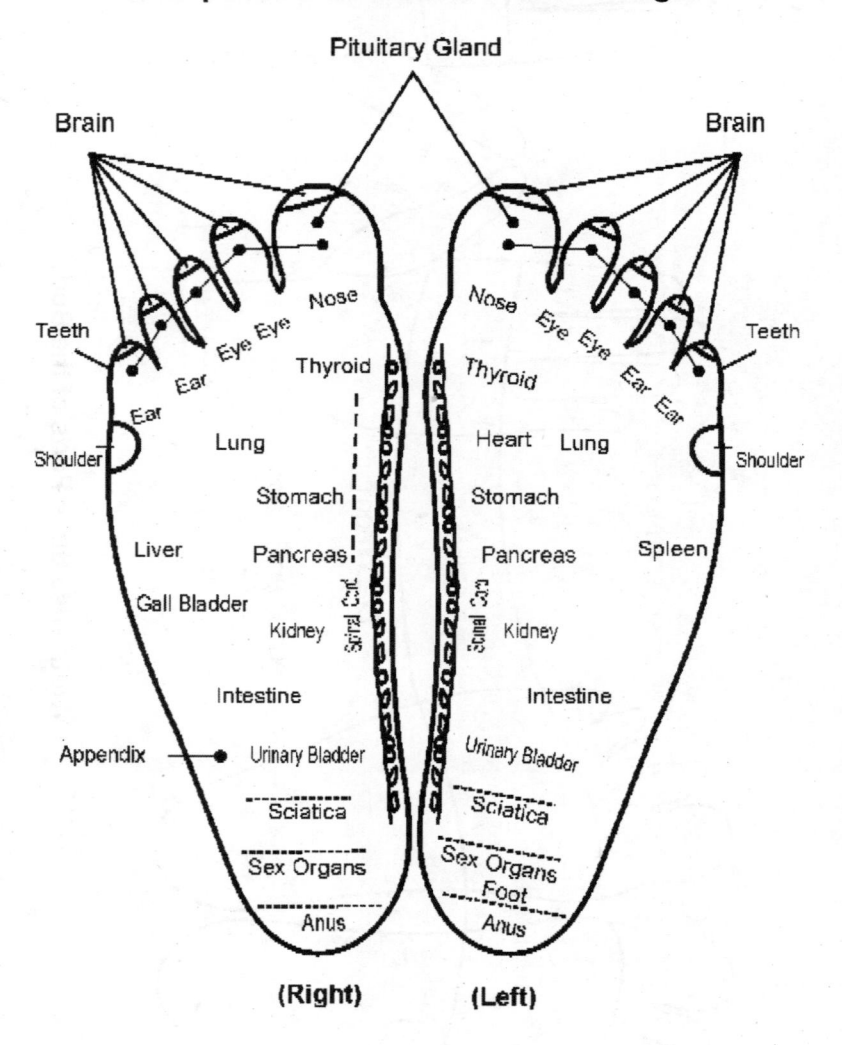

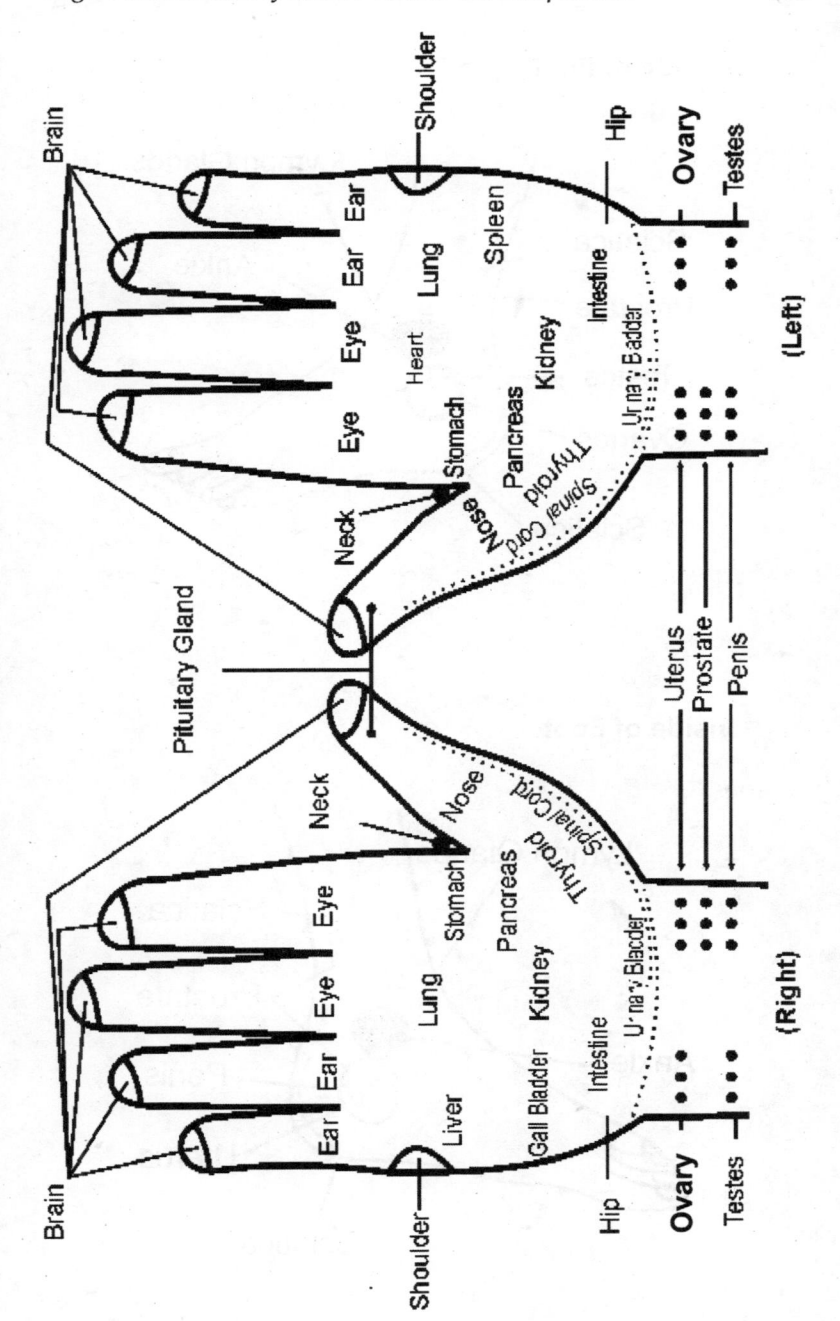

Yoga – The Science of Hand Postures and Acupressure 183

## Outside of Foot

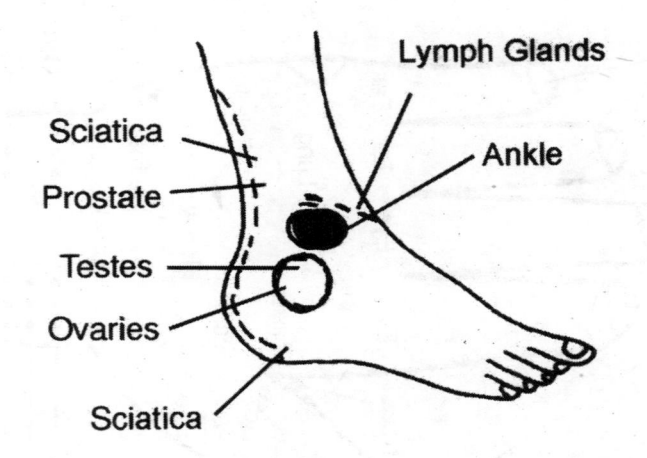

- Lymph Glands
- Sciatica
- Ankle
- Prostate
- Testes
- Ovaries
- Sciatica

## Inside of Foot

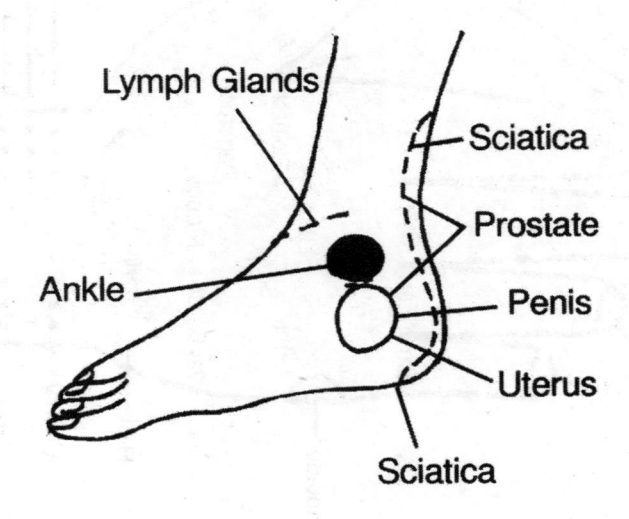

- Lymph Glands
- Sciatica
- Prostate
- Ankle
- Penis
- Uterus
- Sciatica

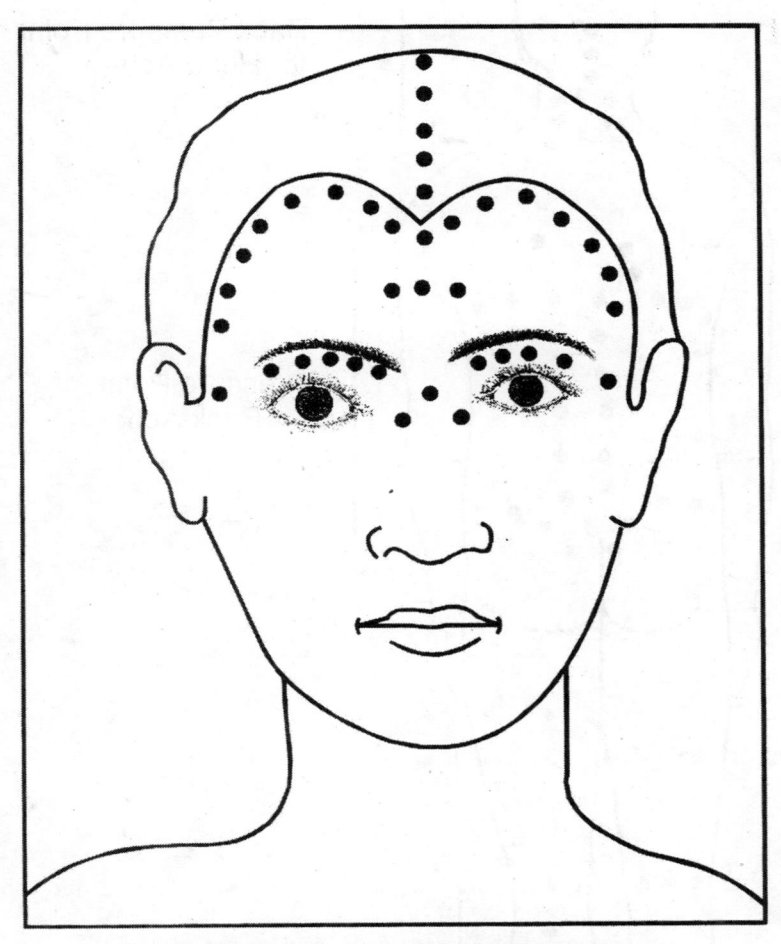

Yoga – The Science of Hand Postures and Acupressure 185

**Front pressure point for Head Ache**

Back Pressure Point for Head Ache

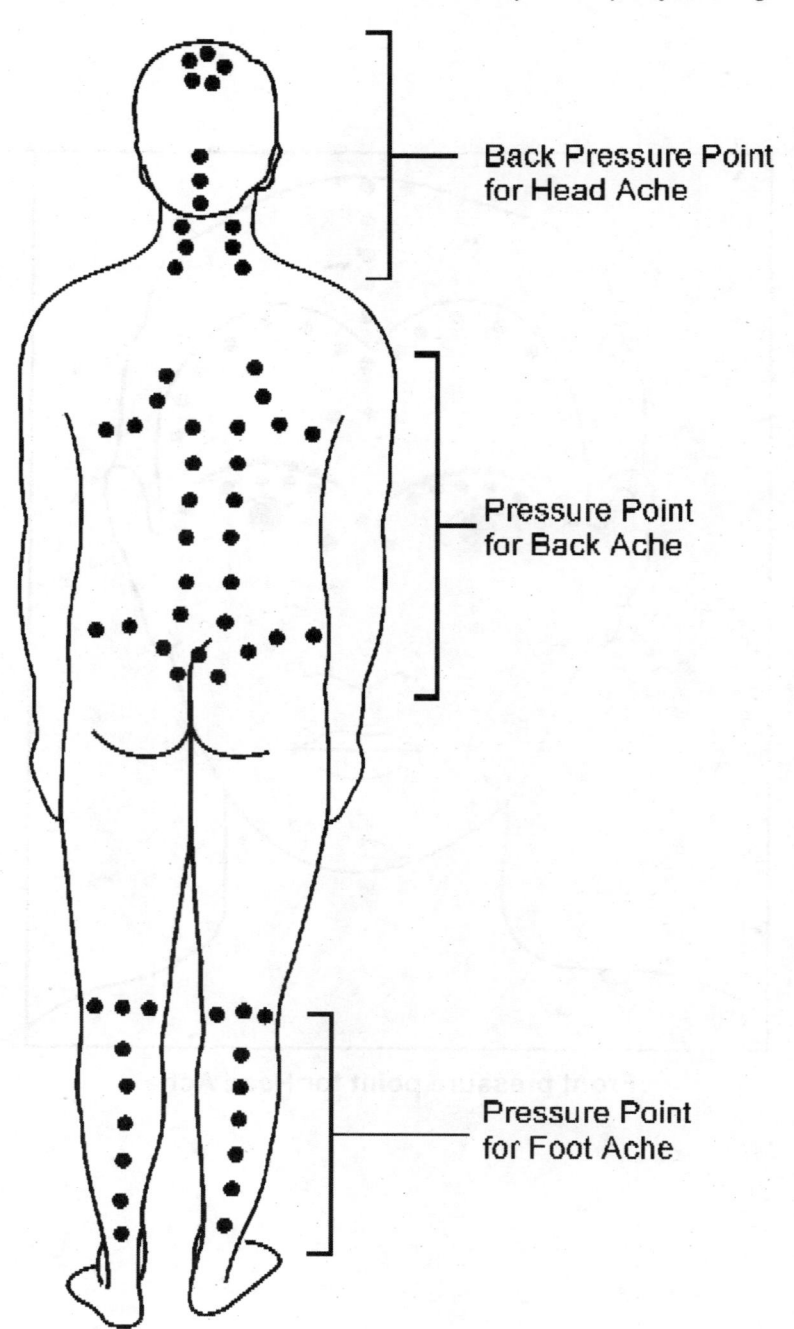

Pressure Point for Back Ache

Pressure Point for Foot Ache

To maintain youthfulness for a longer period and delay the old age: there are pressure points on front of the right hand between the wrist and elbow.

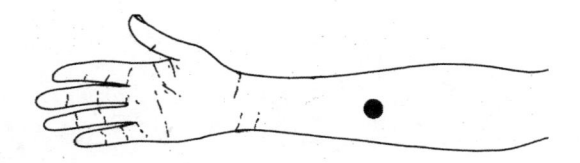

## Acupressure through clapping

Clapping itself is a type of acupressure therapy. By clapping all the reflecting points present on the hands get pressed. This practice is helpful in treating many diseases.

Clapping is an excellent exercise through which dullness is removed, one becomes more active and the blood circulation in the body also improves tremendously.

*Method of clapping* – Keep a distance of 30-45 cm between both hands. Now clap in such a way that fingers and palms of both hands hit each other continuously. Try to clap at a speed of 60-100 claps per minute.

*Precautions to take while clapping*

(1) Apply mustard oil on both the hands.
(2) Wear socks and shoes, so that energy produced during clapping does not escape.
(3) Do not wash your hands for up to 10 minutes after clapping.
(4) Nails of both hands should be trimmed.
(5) Do not clap under the fan or in a closed or an air-conditioned room.
(6) After clapping immediately go for urination.

*Note* – The benefits of acupressure can be received if a person claps for two minutes every day and rubs the soles with a brush. This will make the body agile. Traditional use of ornaments in Indian culture is also a type of acupressure.

# Part-III

# ANATOMY AND PHYSIOLOGY

# Anatomy and physiology

**Anatomy** is the study of structure and interrelationship of structure within the body.
**Physiology** is the study of the functions of various parts of the body.

Our body is made of innumerable minute cells which can be seen by a microscope. Each cell is a unit of life and it keeps on dividing. Due to division of the cell many cells are created. A group of cells forms a tissue of which the organs of the body are made.

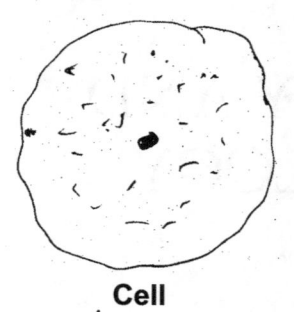

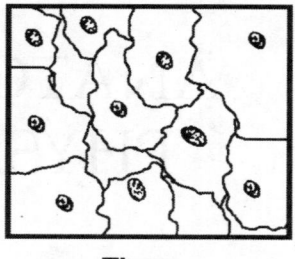

**Cell**            **Tissue**

Many organs have similar function so they group together to form a system. In our body there are 9 systems, 5 sense organs and 9 endocrine glands.

## *Systems*

1. Digestive system
2. Blood circulatory system
3. Lymphatic system
4. Respiratory System
5. Skeletal system
6. Muscular system
7. Nervous system
8. Urinary system
9. Reproductive system

Anatomy and Physiology

## Sense organs
1. Eyes
2. Ears
3. Nose
4. Tongue
5. Skin

## Endocrine glands or ductless glands
1. Pituitary Gland
2. Thyroid Gland
3. Parathyroid Glands
4. Thymus Gland
5. Adrenal Glands
6. Islets of Langerhans in the Pancreas
7. Spleen
8. Pineal Gland
9. Gonads or Sex Glands — Testes and Ovaries

## (1) Digestive system

Digestive system is attributed to the work of ingestion of food and its digestion and absorption. Thereafter assimilation in the food, excretion of indigested and unprocessed food product in the form of waste from the anus.

The main constituent of digestive system is the alimentary canal which is almost ten metres long. It has the following parts —

(1) Mouth
(2) Pharynx
(3) Oesophagus
(4) Stomach
(5) Small Intestine
(6) Large Intestine
(7) Rectum
(8) Anal Canal

Apart from the alimentary canal there are some organs which help in digestion—
- (i) Salivary Glands
- (ii) Pancreas
- (iii) Liver
- (iv) Gall-Bladder

*Peristaltic movements* — These are movements like a slow moving symphony, which make the food move forward in the system.

(1) **Mouth** — It has three main parts connected with digestion.
   - (a) *Tongue* — This is the main organ which accepts taste. This helps in chewing, swallowing and talking.
   - (b) *Teeth* — These are for eating, chewing and grinding our food.
   - (c) *Salivary glands* — These are three pairs. The secretion of these glands is called spit or saliva which converts starch in the food to soluble maltase, saliva works in an alkaline medium only. Saliva makes food more soft and easy to swallow. It keeps the mouth and tongue clean and the tissues in the mouth soft.

(2) **Pharynx** — It is a 12 cm tube which transfers food from the mouth to the food pipe. From this alone air also goes through the nose to the larynx.

(3) **Oesophagus** — This is a tube connected also with pharynx and opens up down in the stomach. Through this food reaches the stomach.

(4) **Stomach** — This is like a temporary store for food. In the mucus membrane of walls of the stomach are gastric glands which secrete gastric juices containing hydrochloric acid. This makes the food acidic. The minute organisms in the food also die. Gastric glands secrete three types of enzymes.

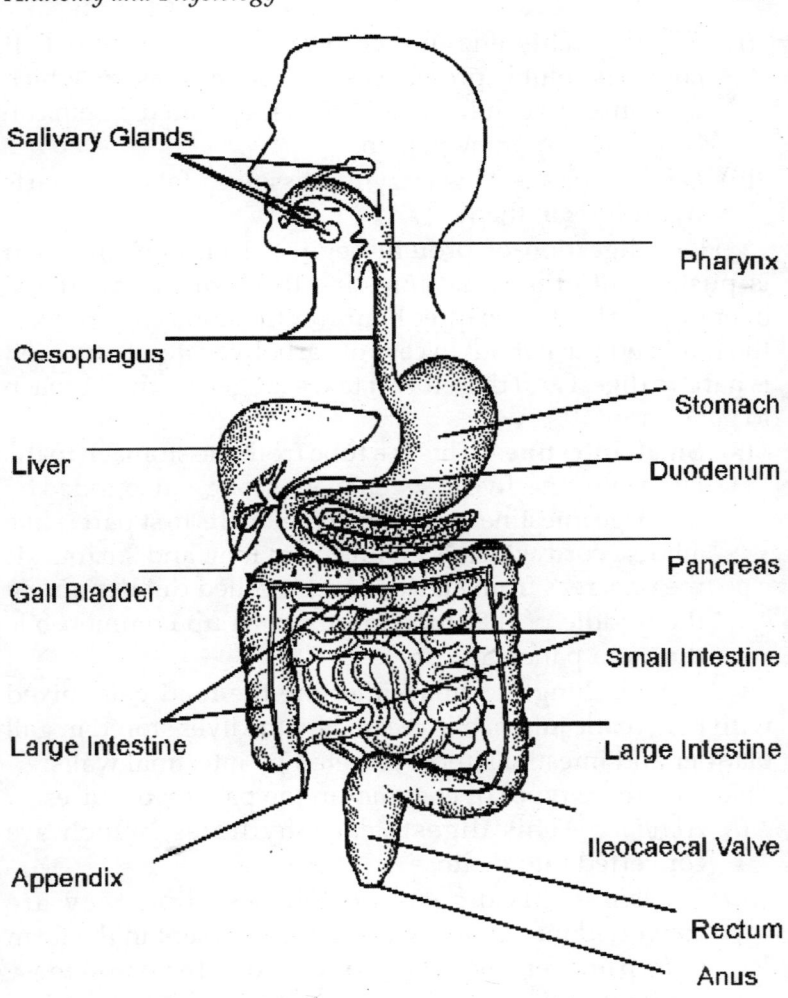

## Digestive System

(i) *Pepsinogen* – In the presence of hydrochloric acid this converts into pepsin. Pepsin converts protein into peptone. Peptone is made of amino acid and is easily soluble.

(ii) *Rennin* – This enzyme converts milk into curd. It converts soluble protein caseinogen into casein, which is an insoluble milk protein. Thus separated casein can be reacted upon by pepsin.

(iii) *Gastric Lipase* – This enzyme dissolves fats and starts hydrolysis in them.

Here digestion of protein begins, from here the food is pushed into the small intestine through the duodenal opening. It takes two to three hours for the stomach to process the food and push it out in case of carbohydrates. Fatty food is hard to digest and therefore it takes longer for the stomach to get clear of it.

**(5) Small intestine** – This is a tube from the stomach to the large intestine, five to seven metres long, surrounded by the large intestine in the navel region. Its first part is like a horse cord which is about 25 cm long and surrounds the pancreas from all sides and is called duodenum. In the middle of the duodenum opens up common bile duct and pancreatic duct.

After reaching the small intestine the food gets mixed with pancreatic juices, bile created by the liver stored in gall bladder and intestinal juices secreted by intestinal walls. There are three types of enzymes in the pancreatic juices.

(i) *Amylase* – This digests carbohydrates, which are converted into maltose.

(ii) *Trypsin* – This digests proteins, so that they are converted into amino acids. This is present in the form of trypsinogen and when combined with enterokinase (present in intestinal juices) is converted into trypsin.

(iii) *Lipase* – This digests fats, which are converted into fatty acids and glycerols.

The acidic food received from stomach to duodenum gets mixed with pancreatic juices and bile and becomes alkaline.

Bile does not have digestive enzymes. But through this the fats are emulsified in the small intestines so that the pancreatic enzymes lipase can act over it properly.

Intestinal juices have the following enzymes which complete the digestion—

*Enterokinase* — This activates inactive trypsinogen present in pancreatic juices and converts it into trypsin. This digests proteins.

*Erepsin* — This converts protein into amino acids.

*Sucrase, lactase and maltase* — digest carbohydrates and convert it into glucose, fructose, galactose and dextrose.

(6) **Large intestine** — The last part of small intestine ileum disappears in the large intestine. Here Ileocaecal valve is placed which takes the food from small intestine to the large intestine but does not come back to the small intestine from the large intestine. Large intestine which reaches the rectum and anal canal is almost 1.5 metre long and much broader than the small intestine.

The large intestine does not have the digestion and assimilation process in it. The large intestine gets remaining part of the food, which is waste and is in the form of fluid. While moving through the large intestine the water out of this fluid gets absorbed which leads to solidification of faeces. The mucus membrane in the large intestinal wall secretes mucous to make faeces greasy and to cause their mobility.

(7) **Rectum** — When rectum gets filled with faeces then the urge to defecate arises.

(8) **Anal Canal** — From this faeces is defecated.

(9) **Pancreas** — This is a 12-15 cm long gland which is situated behind the stomach and extended from duodenum to the spleen.

*Functions of the pancreas*

(1) It is an exocrine gland, which secretes pancreatic juices to digest the food.

(2) In the pancreas there is a group of cells scattered around called Islets of Langerhans. They are endocrine glands which secrete insulin hormone.

**(10) Liver** — Liver is one of the largest organ in the body. It is present in the uppermost part of the abdominal cavity on the right side below the diaphragm. It is largely protected by the ribs and diaphragm.

It is a metabolically active organ and largest biochemical factory in the body. It carries out most of the intermediate metabolic activities.

*Functions of liver*
- (1) It secretes the bile about 800-1000 ml per day.
- (2) It synthesizes glycogen from the glucose derived from the carbohydrate present in the food. Glycogen is stored temporarily in the liver and converted back into glucose when needed by the body.
- (3) It separates the amino group ($NH_2$) from amino acid derived from protein in the food and converts them into ammonia which is then converted into urea. Urea is removed and excreted in the urine through kidneys.
- (4) It stores the fat and utilises when needed.
- (5) It stores the iron and vitamin $B_{12}$ (which are necessary for the formation of RBCs).
- (6) It also stores Vitamin A, D and K.
- (7) It synthesises plasma proteins (albumin and globulin).
- (8) It also synthesises prothrombin and fibrinogen which are necessary for clotting of blood..
- (9) It synthesises heparin which is the natural anticoagulant.
- (10) It is the main organ to produce heat in the body.
- (11) It inactivates toxic metabolies.
- (12) It synthesises blood also in intra-uterine development of the foetus.
- (13) It disintegrates the products of breakdown of haemoglobin (bilirubin and biliverdin) into the bile which are eliminated in faeces.

(14) It synthesizes cholesterol as well as lipoproteins for the transport of fat to other body tissues.

**(11) Gall Bladder** — Gall Bladder is a pear shaped bag like organ which is situated under the liver. It measures 8-10 cm in length and its holding capacity is about 60-100 ml.

*Functions of Gall Bladder*

Gall bladder stores bile and also concentrates it. Bile is a liquid secreted by the liver cells. The main function of the bile is to emulsify the fats and to help in their digestion.

## (2) Blood circulatory system

This consists of the heart, blood vessels and blood. Heart works like a pump, whose pumping motion makes blood flow into the arteries which carry it throughout the body to each cell and comes back to the heart, flowing through veins. Thus the blood circulates in the whole body.

**Heart** — Heart is empty, muscular, spongy, shaped like a fist, placed behind the sternum bone, between the two lungs, slightly to the left side in a triangular tilt.

The wall of the heart has three layers, the outer layer is called pericardium, the middle layer is called myocardium and the inner layer is called endocardium.

There are four chambers in the heart. On the right the right atrium and right ventricle are there, the left atrium and the left ventricle are on the left side. Between the right atrium and right ventricle is the tricuspid valve and between the left atrium and ventricle is the mitral valve. Between the heart and the pulmonary artery and between the heart and aorta also there are valves. These valves prevent the reverse flow of blood.

**Functioning of Heart** — The heart systoles and diastoles almost 72 times in a minute. This process of contraction and relaxation sends impure blood received from various parts of the body through two big veins called superior vena cava and inferior vena cava in the right atrium. From here the blood goes through tricuspid valve to the right ventricle, then from here through pulmonary arteries it goes to the lungs. From the lungs pure blood goes through pulmonary veins to the left atrium. From here through the mitral valve it is taken to the left ventricle. From here the aorta with its branches, and sub-branches, circulates the blood to various parts of the body.

**Blood Vessels** — These are of two types - arteries and veins.

**Arteries** — They take blood from the heart to the other parts of the body. Their walls are much thicker than the walls of the veins. They have pure blood in them, which reaches all the parts of the body and its cells through aorta, arterioles and capillaries.

Only pulmonary arteries have impure blood taken to the lungs for purification.

**Veins** — They bring impure blood from cells of different parts through capillaries, venules and venae cavae to the heart. Only pulmonary vein takes pure blood from the lungs to the heart.

In an adult there is almost 5-6 litres of blood. 55 to 60% of the blood is a fluid called plasma. 40% to 45% is the solid part of blood cells. Plasma is constituted with 91% water and rest of it is protein, mineral salts, nutrients, waste material, hormones, antibodies, enzymes, pigments, gas, etc.

**Blood Cells** —

*Red Blood Cells (Corpuscle) (RBC)* — These are the major constituents in blood. In a healthy person they are 40-50 lakh per cubic mm. Their cytoplasm has haemoglobin which makes the blood red coloured. Iron is its main component. Red blood cells carry oxygen all over the body.

Haemoglobin count is generally 11-16 gm per 100 ml. blood among men and 11-14 gm per 100 ml blood among women.

*White Blood Cells (Corpuscle) (WBC)* — These are the biggest cells in the three types of cells, but are less in number. In

*Anatomy and Physiology* 199

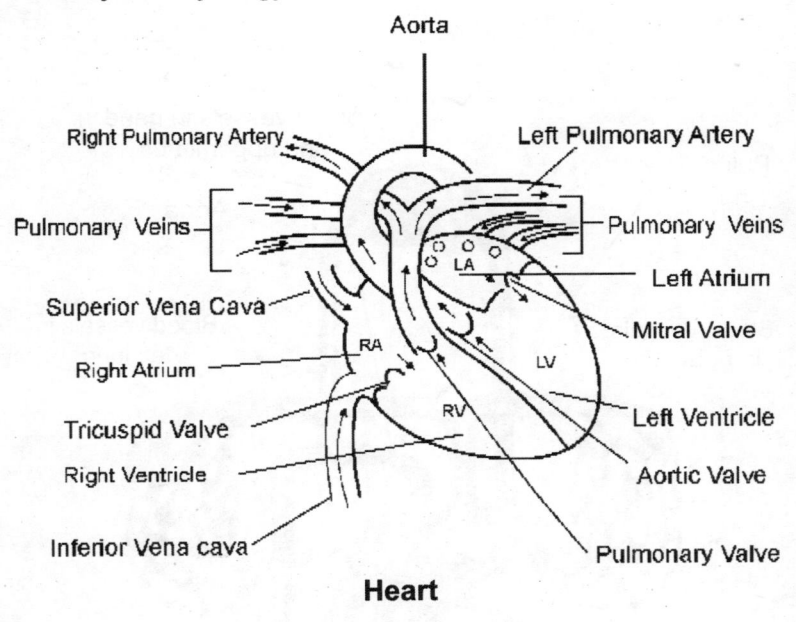

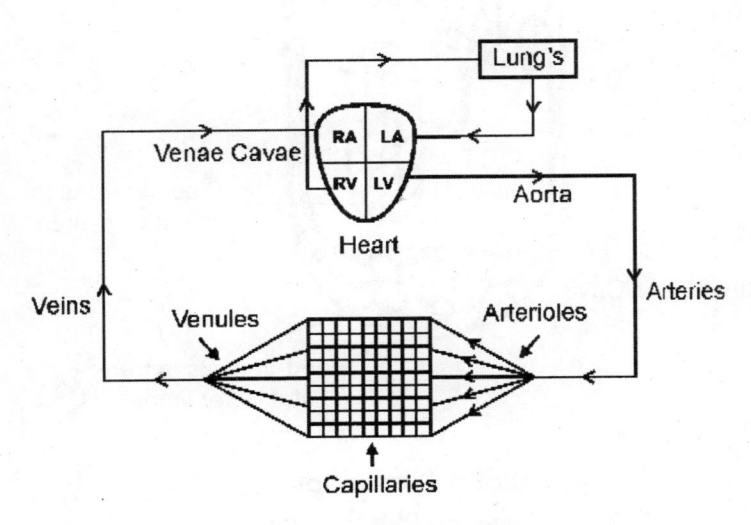

**Heart**

Labels: Aorta, Right Pulmonary Artery, Left Pulmonary Artery, Pulmonary Veins, Pulmonary Veins, Superior Vena Cava, Left Atrium, Mitral Valve, Right Atrium, Tricuspid Valve, Left Ventricle, Right Ventricle, Aortic Valve, Inferior Vena cava, Pulmonary Valve

**Blood Circulation**

Labels: Lung's, Venae Cavae, Heart (RA, LA, RV, LV), Aorta, Veins, Venules, Capillaries, Arterioles, Arteries

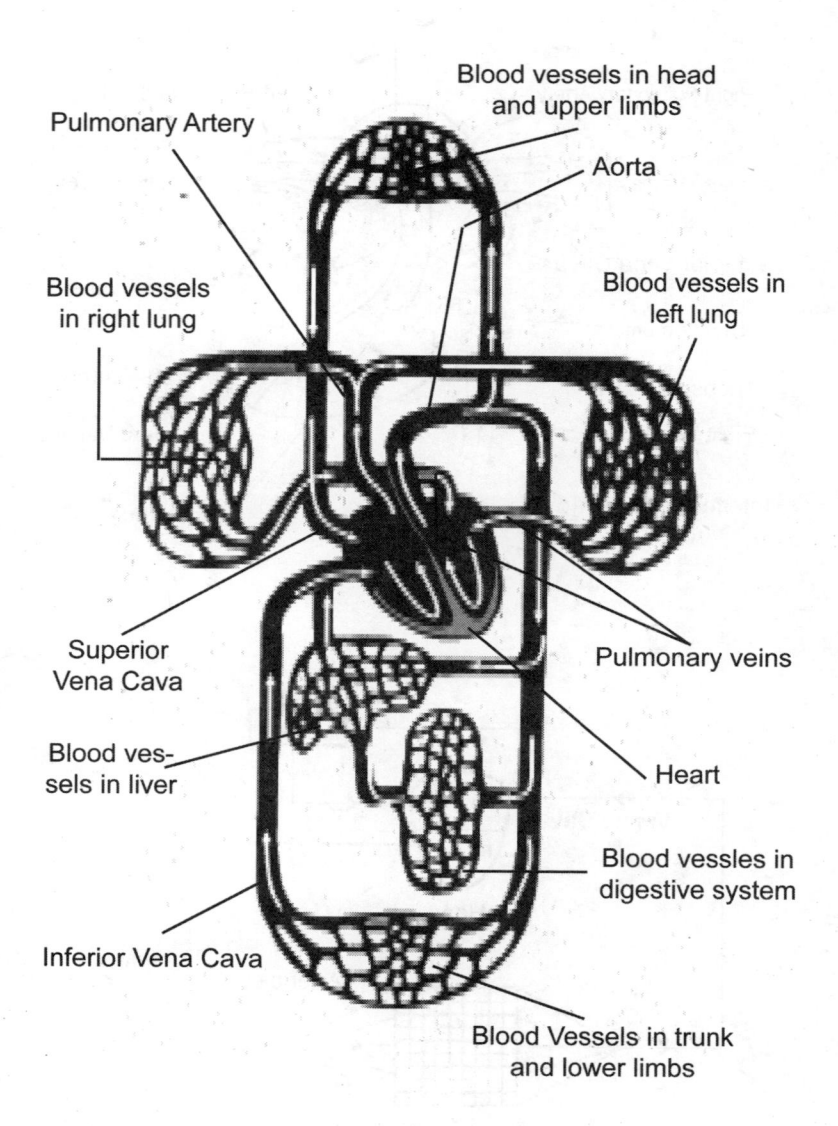

**Blood Circulation**

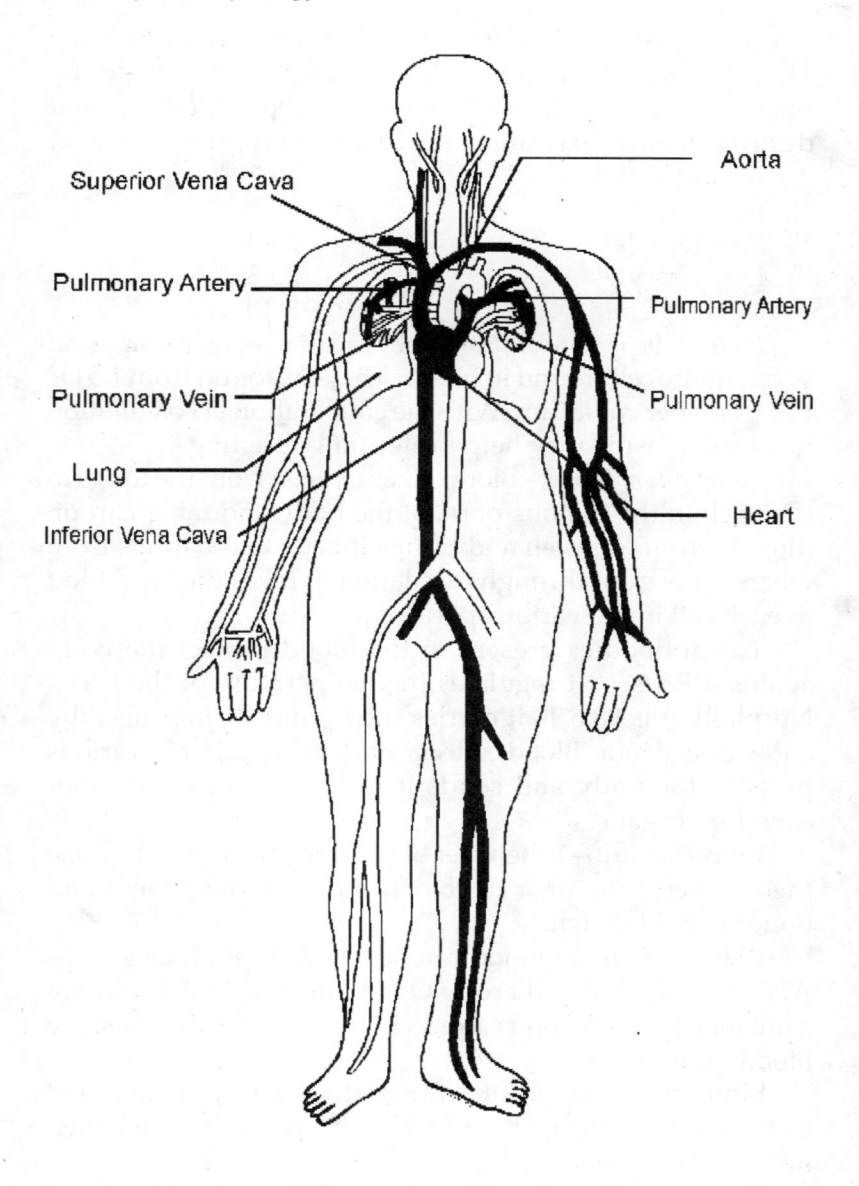

*Anatomy and Physiology*

**Blood Circulatory System**

a healthy person 5000-10000 cells are there per cubic mm. They are actively mobile which changes their shape. By phagocytosis it swallows germs and carbonic particles and destroys them. These are of the following types —

| | |
|---|---|
| Neurotrophils | 60-70% |
| Bosophils | 0-1% |
| Eosinophils | 3-4% |
| Lymphocytes | 25-30% |
| Monocytes | 5-10% |

*Platelets or Thrombocytes* — They are of irregular shape and very minute cells found in blood. They are found from 1.5 lac to 5.5 lacs per cubic mm. With the cooperation of coagulation factors in plasma they help in stopping bleeding.

*Functions of Blood* — Blood takes oxygen from the lungs to each cell in the various parts of the body and takes carbon dioxide from each cell and brings it back to the lungs from where it goes out through exhalation. It takes digested food to each cell in the various parts of the body.

The antibodies present in the blood protect the body against diseases. It regulates the temperature of the body. Normally it is 98.6°F. It carries the hormones produced by endocrine glands. Blood collects waste material from various parts of the body and sends it to the kidneys and other excretory organs.

**Blood Group** — Whenever blood transfusion is to be done then it is essential that the blood group of the patient and donor should match.

(ABO) — Human blood can be divided into four groups A, B, AB and O. Blood group O is a universal donor but not a universal accepter and can accept blood only from the same blood group.

Similarly a patient of AB blood group can take blood from anyone with any blood group. That is why he is called universal recipient.

Rh Group — There are two groups, RH positive (Rh+) and RH negative (RH-).

**Pulse** — The pulse indicates the cardiac output of the heart. The pulse rate is equal to heart beat. To feel the pulse

# Anatomy and Physiology

the wrist is the right place as here the redial artery is present. In fever the temperature increases by 1° F over 98.6° F, then the pulse rate gets pushed up by 10. In an adult generally pulse rate should be 72 per minute.

**Blood Pressure** — The pressure that blood exerts on blood vessels is called blood pressure.

*Systolic Blood Pressure* — When the heart contracts while pumping blood, at that point the maximum pressure created is called systolic blood pressure. This is normally 120.

*Diastolic Blood Pressure* — When the heart diastoles then the lowest pressure is called diastolic blood pressure. This is normally 80.

## Blood analysis

| Test | Normal | Result | Disease |
|---|---|---|---|
| Sugar (F) | 80-120 mg/100ml | More | Diabetes |
| Sugar PP | 140 mg/100ml | More | Diabetes |
| Uric Acid | 2-6 mg/100ml | More | Arthritis |
| Urea | 15-45 mg/100ml | More | Kidney disorder |
| Creatinine | 0.5-1.4mg% | More | Kidney disorder |
| Calcium | 9-11 mg/100ml | More | Parathyroid disorder |
| RBC | 4-5 Million/mm3 | Less | Anaemia |
| Haemoglobin | 11-16 gm/100ml (Male) | Less | Anaemia |
|  | 11-14 gm/100ml (Female) | Less | Anaemia |
| Platelets | 1.5-5.5 lac/mm3 | Less | Clotting System Decreases |
| TLC (WBC) | 5000-10000 /mm3 | Less | Malaria, Measles |
|  |  | More | Infection |
| DLC |  |  |  |
| (A) Neurotrophil | 60-70% | More | Infection |
| (B) Bosophils | 0.1% | More | Allergy |
| (C) Eosinophil | 3-4% | More | Allergy |
| (d) Lymphocytes | 25-30% | More | T.B. (Tuberculosis) |

| | | | |
|---|---|---|---|
| (e) Monocytes | 5-10 % | More | Infection |
| ESR | | | |
| Male | 1-10 mm/1st hr. | More | Infection |
| Female | 3-15 mm/1st hr | More | Infection |
| Clotting Time | upto 10 minutes | More | Bleeding Disorder |
| Prothombin Time | 1 : 3 | More | Jaundice |
| Bilirubin | 1.0 mg/100 m. | More | Jaundice |
| Clotting Time | upto 10 minutes | More | Bleeding Disorder |
| Prothombin Time | 1 : 3 | More | Jaundice |
| Bilirubin | 1.0 mg/100 m. | More | Jaundice |
| Total Cholestrol | 130 to 200 mg/dl | More | Heart Attack possibility increases |
| HDL Cholesterol | 30-65 mg/dl | Less | |
| LDL Cholesterol | 50-120 mg/dl | More | |
| VLDL Cholesterol | 12-35 mg/dl | More | |
| Triglycerides | 60-160 mg/dl | More | |

## (3) Lymphatic system

Lymphatic system is like blood circulatory system and is greatly interconnected with it. This includes lymphs, lymph vessels, lymph nodes, lymph tissues, spleen and thymus gland.

**Lymph** — This is a colourless fluid which has blood plasma and lymphocytes in it. Protein it less in quantity in them. Tissues full of waste matter, give away some of its liquid to blood and the leftover is taken by lymphatic tissues which creates lymph.

**Lymphatic Capillaries** — Small lymphatic capillaries join together to make big lymphatic vessel which opens up in the regional lymph node and in the end it opens up in two big tube — Thoracic duct and right lymphatic duct which puts lymphs in the subclavian vein.

**Lymph Nodes** — These are 1-25 mm in size. Generally they remain regulated in groups. They are found mainly in the neck, armpit, elbow, chest, between stomach and in the joints of legs and behind knees.

**Lymphatic Tissues** — Apart from lymphatic nodes following lymphatic tissues are found.

*Anatomy and Physiology*                                    205

   (1) Tonsils
   (2) Thymus
   (3) Spleen
   (4) Vermiform Appendix
   (5) Peyer's patches in intestine.

**Functions of lymphatic system** — It maintains normalcy of fluids in the body. It takes out waste from tissues and takes it to blood. Lymphocytes are created in lymph nodes.

Lymph nodes work as a filter, to remove outer harmful agents and germs. Lymphocytes destroy germs causing diseases. Once the infection sets in the body lymphocytes are created which protect the body from that infection in future.

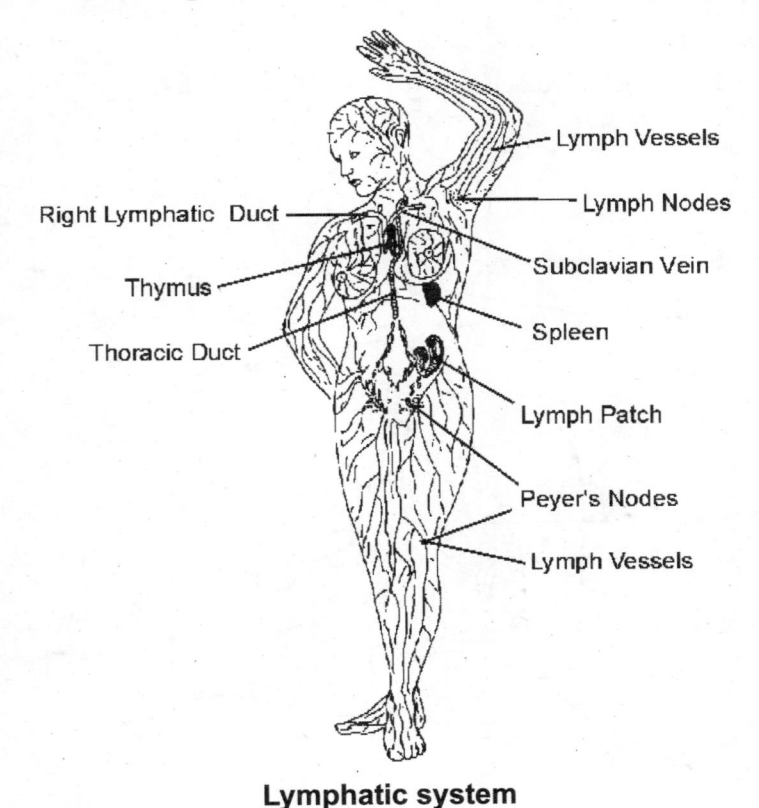

**Lymphatic system**

## (4) Respiratory system

The process of inhaling oxygen from air and exhaling carbon dioxide as a waste matter is called respiration. The organs which make it possible for us to breathe form the respiratory system.

In the respiratory system the following parts are included —

Nose
Larynx
Trachea
Both side bronchus
Bronchioles
Lungs
Pleurae
Inter costal Muscles (Muscles between Ribs)
Diaphragm

**Respiratory System**

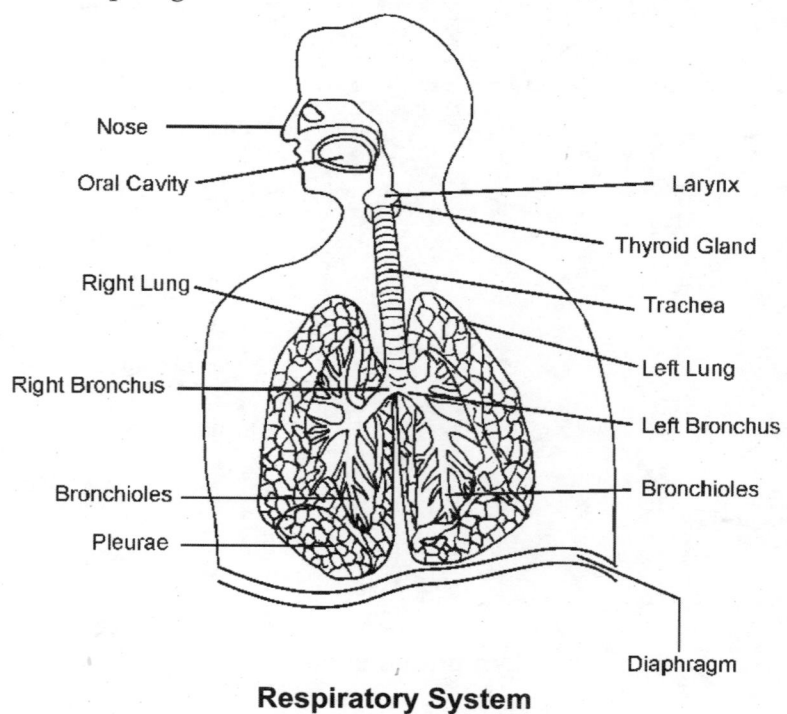

In the respiratory path there is a mucus membrane which has mucous flowing in it on which dust particles and germs that are inhaled get stuck. Breathing in is called inspiration and breathing out is called expiration. In inspiration oxygen received in the air inhaled reaches the blood cells and crosses its walls and gets into the blood capillaries and carbon dioxide crosses the walls of blood cells and reaches the lungs, from here it is exhaled through expiration.

Respiratory system throws out other violent disposable fluids and evaporated water from the body. In the process of respiration contraction of intercostal muscle and diaphragm works as a pump.

## (5) Skeletal system

Bones and joints make the human skeleton. Skeleton gives a definite shape and support to the body.

It provides surface for joining muscle tendons, ligaments, etc. It protects the soft parts in the body. Bone marrow creates red blood cells. In the bones almost 97% of body's calcium and phosphorous is stored.

In the skeleton there are some flexible bones which are called cartilage. They become stiff due to calcification, Various bones together make the following parts of the skeleton—

(1) Skull
(2) Vertebral column
(3) Thoracic cage
(4) Shoulder girdle and upper limbs
(5) Pelvic girdle and lower limbs.

**(1) Skull—** Bones of skulls are in two parts, cranium and face.

*Cranium—*consists of 8 bones which are connected together with fixed joints called sutures.

1 Frontal Bone
2 Parietal Bones
1 Occipital Bone

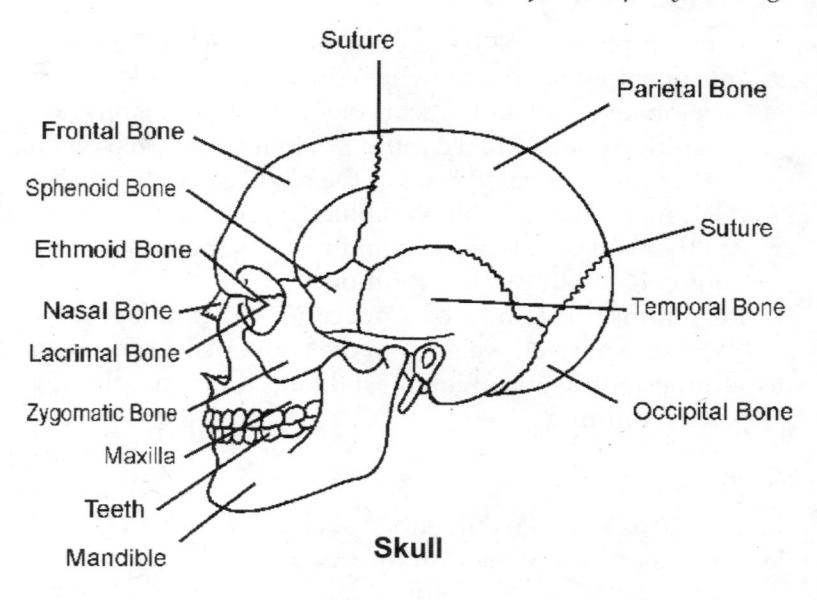

```
                    Suture
                              Parietal Bone
    Frontal Bone
    Sphenoid Bone
                                    Suture
    Ethmoid Bone
                                    Temporal Bone
    Nasal Bone
    Lacrimal Bone
    Zygomatic Bone                  Occipital Bone
    Maxilla
    Teeth
    Mandible         Skull
```

- 2 Temporal Bones
- 1 Sphenoid Bone
- 1 Ethmoid Bone

*Face* – consists of 14 bones.
- 2 Zygomatic bones (cheek bones)
- 2 Maxilla Bones (Upper Jaw bones)
- 1 Mandible bone (Lower Jaw bone)
- 2 Lacrimal Bones
- 2 Nasal Bones
- 1 Bone in the nose called Vomer Bone
- 2 Palatine Bones
- 2 Turbinae Bones

Apart from these there is one bone at the base of the tongue like a horses cord called hyoid bone and six other bones for hearing called auditory ossicles which contribute in making the skull. If these are also included in the skeleton then there are a total of 213 bones.

**(2) Vertebral column**—This is a flexible structure of 33 bones called the spinal cord or vertebral column. The bone of vertebral column are called vertebrae. These are as follows.

*Cervical Vertebrae* – These are vertebrae of the neck. They are 7 in number.

*Thoracic Vertebrae* – These are below the neck at the back of the chest, they are 12 in number.

*Lumbar Vertebrae* – These are lumbar vertebrae which make the lumbar region under thoracic vertebrae. They are 5 in number.

*Sacral Vertebrae* – These 5 vertebraes are below the lumber vertebrae which join with the youthful person and make a sacrum.

*Coccygeal Vertebrae* – They are the lowest 4 vertebrae of the vertebral column which join the youthful person to make a coccyx.

*Functions of a vertebral column* –

(1) All the vertebraes together make the vertebral canal which has the spinal cord present therein and this vertebral canal protects it.
(2) It keeps the skull erect.
(3) The vertebral column makes the axis for the body and bears the body's weight. With this the ribs, shoulder girdle, upper limbs, pelvic girdle and lower limbs are connected.
(4) Presence of cartilage in the vertebrae makes the vertebral column flexible which does not permit too much damage while running or jumping.
(5) Various spinal nerves come out between the vertebrae which go to different parts of the body.

In the vertebrae the presence of cartilages bring about flexibility which enables the body to bend in the front and back, move to the right and left, and perform other movements.

Women, men and children must keep their spine straight while sitting, getting up, walking and sleeping to be healthy as this saves us from many diseases. Those who keep their spine bent, age fast. As long as the spinal cord remains erect and flexible the person remains young and healthy. While meditating, if the spinal cord is erect then concentration is better.

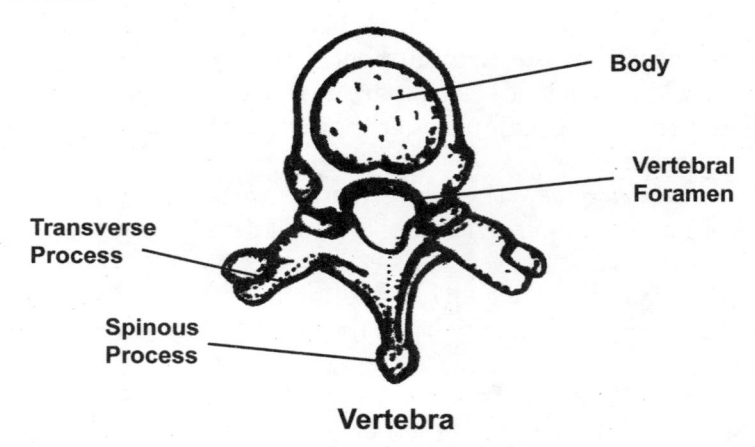

**Vertebra**

- Body
- Vertebral Foramen
- Transverse Process
- Spinous Process

If students would keep their vertebral column erect while studying, then they will be able to memorise faster. To keep the vertebral column flexible simple exercises and yogasanas should be done.

**(3) Thoracic Cage** — This consists of a chest bone called sternum and 24 ribs.

The upper seven pairs of ribs are visibly connected with the chest bone, i.e., sternum and the eighth, ninth and tenth pair of ribs is connected invisibly. Eleventh and twelfth pair are not connected.

## (4) Shoulder girdle and upper limbs

Shoulder girdle is constituted of the following bones— 2 Clavicle, 2 Scapula Upper Limbs—Both upper limbs have 30 bones each -
1 Humerus - bone in the upper arm.

*Anatomy and Physiology*

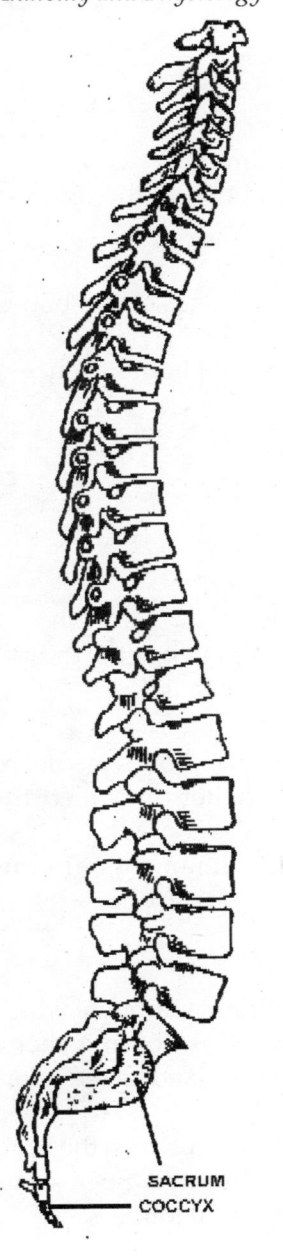

Cervical Vertebrae
(7)

Thoracic Vertebrae
(12)

Lumbar Vertebrae
(5)

Sacral Vertebrae
(5)

Coccygeal Vertebrae
(4)

SACRUM
COCCYX

**Vertebral Column**

1 Radius  } Bones of the forearm
1 Ulna

8 Carpal Bones – Bones in the wrist
5 Meta Carpal Bones – Bones of the palm.
14 Phalanges – Three in each finger and two in the thumb.

## (5) Pelvic Girdle and Lower Limbs

*Pelvic girdle* – There are two innominate bones or hip bones, which are connected in the front.
*Lower Limbs* – Both the lower limbs have 30 bones each.
1 Femur Bone – Thigh bone

1 Tibia Bone } Leg bones
1 Fibula Bone

1 Patella Bone or knee cap
7 Tarsal Bones, (ankle bones)
5 Meta Tarsal Bones, (bones in the sole)
14 Phalanges – three in each foot finger and two in the thumb.

## Articulatory system

The meeting point of two or more than two bones is known as the joint. All the joints grouped together are called the articulatory system.

Joints are made of bones, cartilage, ligaments, fibrous tissues and synovial membrane.

## Joints are of three types

(1) *Fibrous Joints* – These joints have a thin membrane which is a fibrous tissue between the bones, joining them. These joints are called immovable or fixed as the joints of cranium.

(2) *Cartilaginous joints* – There is a cushion between the head of two bones which keeps them connected. Such joints are slightly movable like intervertebral joints.

*Anatomy and Physiology*

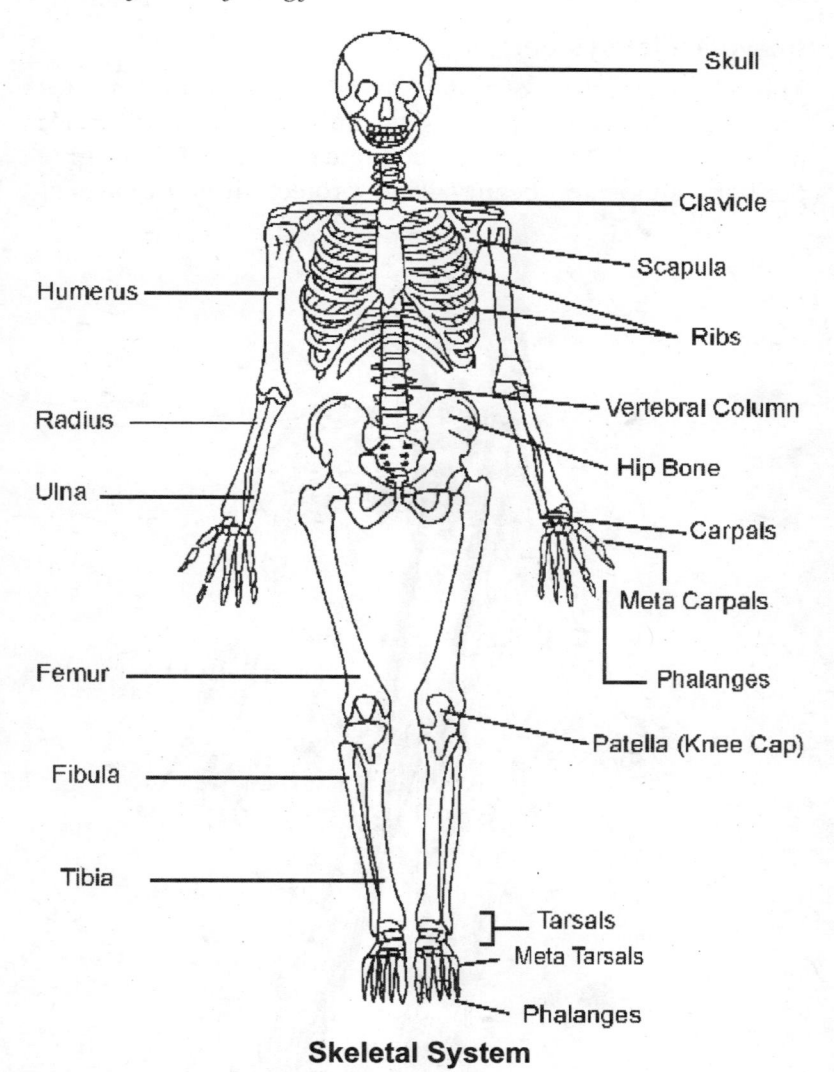

**Skeletal System**

Labels: Skull, Clavicle, Scapula, Humerus, Ribs, Vertebral Column, Radius, Hip Bone, Ulna, Carpals, Meta Carpals, Phalanges, Femur, Patella (Knee Cap), Fibula, Tibia, Tarsals, Meta Tarsals, Phalanges

(3) *Synovial joints* – Bones are connected by a thin membrane called synovial membrane. This is a thin greasy membrane and secretes a sticky oily fluid, which keeps the joints oily and there is free movement of the joints, i.e. shoulder joints, elbows, hips, knees, hands, feet and finger joints.

## (6) Muscular system

The whole structure of this body is covered with muscles which is collectively known as the muscular system. Muscles are tissues which contract to facilitate movement. They give the body shape and beauty. They protect different parts of

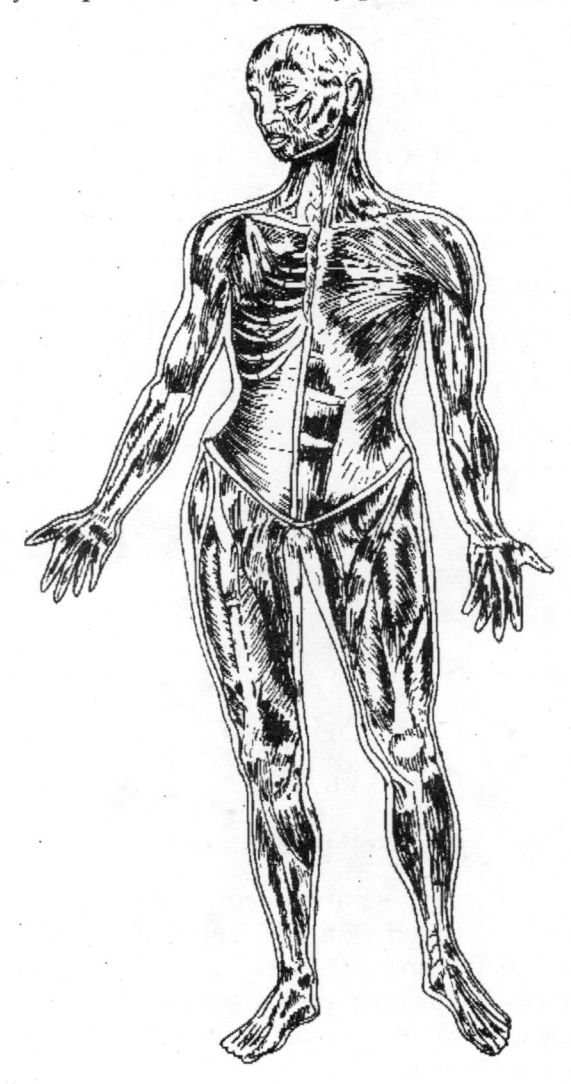

**Muscular System (Front)**

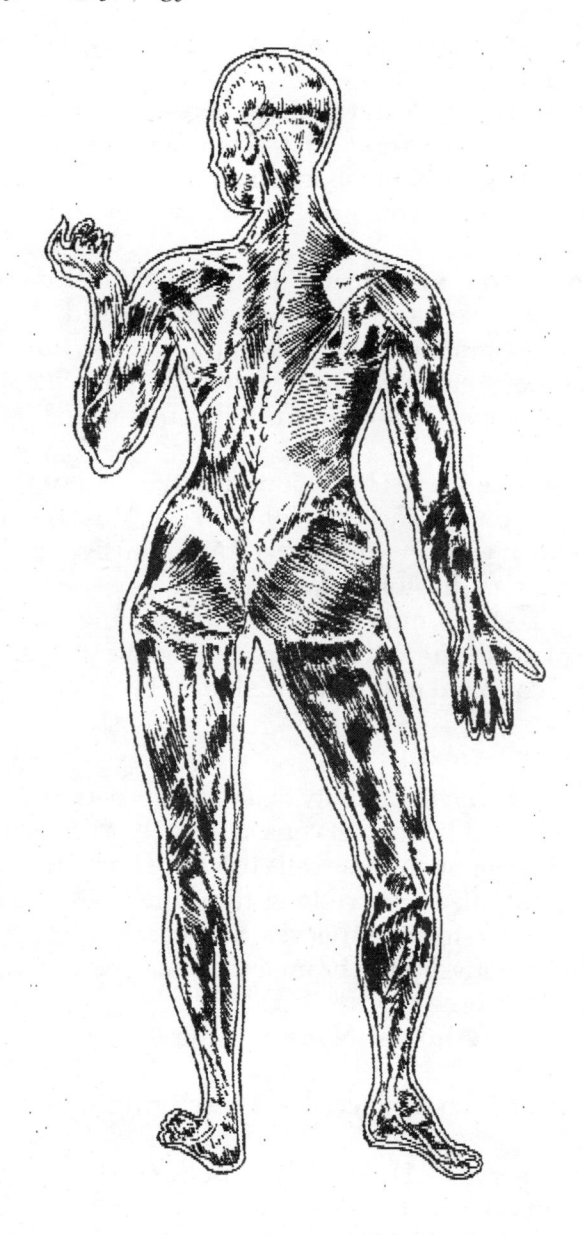

*Anatomy and Physiology* 215

**Muscular System (Back)**

the body. They keep the joints at the right place. They provide movement in the body.

**Voluntary or skeletal muscles**—Such muscles are connected with bones and can be contracted or expanded as desired, leading to movement in their connected parts. These muscles are found in the neck, shoulder, hands, chest, back, hips and feet, etc.

**Involuntary or visceral muscle**—These cannot be contracted or expanded whenever desired. They are connected within solid internal parts like the lungs, liver, spleen, kidneys, etc. or walls of the empty organs like stomach and the intestines. They are in the skin and wall of blood vessels.

**Cardiac Muscle**—This is found in the wall of the heart. Our discretion has no control over it. This is a unique muscle which works without rest continuously for 24 hours, contracting and diastoling for the whole life span.

*Note*—To keep muscles strong and young the muscles must be made to work. If muscles are inactive then gradually toxins get collected and take the shape of a disease.

## (7) Nervous system

In the whole body, the activity of its various parts is regulated and coordinated by the nervous system. Nerve cells are the base of this system. In these cells there are fibres which bring and carry impulses. These long thin thread like structures group together to form nerves that carry information or instructions between the brain and other parts of the body. Nerves are of three types.

Sensory or Afferent Nerves—These carry impulses to the brain.

Motor or Efferent Nerves—These bring impulses from the brain.

Mixed Nerves—These carry impulses on both directions.

Nervous system has three parts—

**(1) Central nervous system**—This includes the brain and spinal cord.

They remain protected by meninges and are surrounded by cerebro spinal fluid or CSF, which pressurises all around the brain and the spinal cord equally and also works as a shock absorber between the brain and the cranium bones. It gives nourishment to the brain and spine and takes out the waste product from them.

**Brain—** Brain controls the whole body. Following are its main parts

(i) *Cerebrum*—This is the frontal and the biggest part of the brain. It receives all sensory impulses (sense of sight, hearing, smell, taste, touch) for their appreciation and interpretation.

This is the centre of intelligence and knowledge and makes the capacity of thinking and understanding, memory, responsibility and morality in the body.

Here emotions like anger, love, hatred, fear, sorrow and happiness are borne. Its right side controls the left side of the body and left side controls the right side of the body.

(ii) *Cerebellum*—This is the back portion of the brain. This establishes coordination in the movement of muscles. It maintains the body's posture and equilibrium.

(iii) *Mid Brain*—This is under the cerebellum. It takes care of balance of the body and has very important reflex centres for seeing and hearing.

(iv) *Pons Varolli*—This is placed under the mid brain. This is mainly made of nervous cells which connects the two parts of the cerebellum.

(v) *Medulla Oblongata*—It starts at ponsvarolli and is merged in the spinal cord.

It has the cardiac centre controlling the movement and strength of the heart contractions. It has a respiratory centre which controls the speed and depth of breathing.

It has a vasomotor centre which controls the diameter of blood vessels.

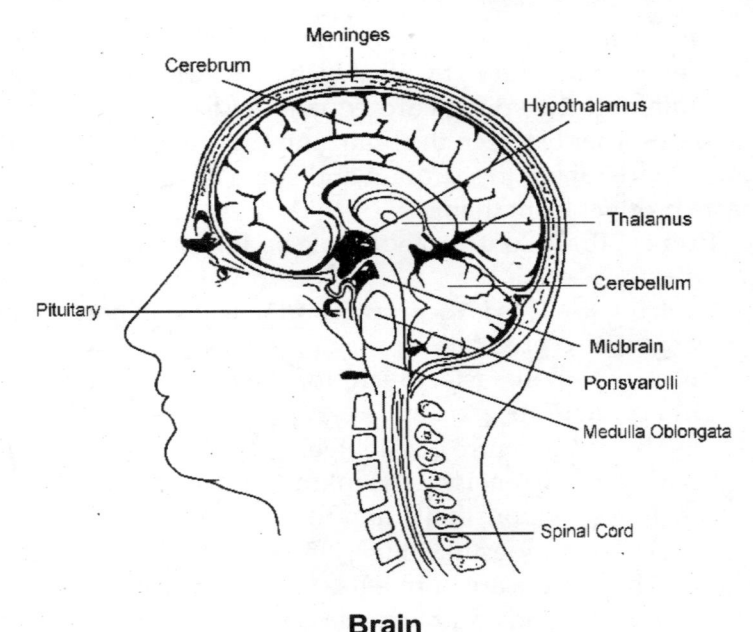

*Diagram labels: Cerebrum, Meninges, Hypothalamus, Thalamus, Cerebellum, Midbrain, Ponsvarolli, Medulla Oblongata, Spinal Cord, Pituitary*

## Brain

It has reflex centres which control reflex actions like, in bright sunshine or falling of a dust particle in the eye the pupil contracts. The action of eye immediately getting shut, on a loud noise or when one gets startled, or immediately removing hands on touching a hot vessel, etc.

Mid brain, ponsvarolli and medula oblongata together make the brain stem.

**Spinal Cord**—This starts from medulla oblongata and goes through the vertebral canal to the lower end of the first lumber vertebra which is almost 45 cm long in an adult and as thick as the small finger of the human hand.

From each vertebra the small and big nerves come out which spread all over the organs and muscles. Spinal cord impulses from different parts of the body comes to spinal cord and then to brain. Similarly message comes from brain to spinal cord and then to the different parts of the body.

**(2) Peripheral Nervous System**—This includes 12 pairs of cranial nerves which come from the brain and 31 pairs of

*Anatomy and Physiology* 219

spinal nerves which are connected with the spinal cord. From these branches come out to reach various organs and tissues.

**Cranial Nerves** — In these nerves are some sensory nerves and some motor nerves and some mixed nerves.

(1) Olfactory Nerves — These are sensory nerves for smell.
(2) Optic nerves — These are sensory nerves for sight.
(3) Oculomotor nerves — These are motor nerves. These supply to most of the external muscles of eye and control to the upper eyelids for getting lifted up, converting into the shape of lenses, contraction of the eye balls, etc.
(4) Trochlear nerves — These are motor nerves for the external oblique muscle of the eye.
(5) Trigeminal nerves — These are mixed nerves and the biggest of cranial nerves. It has three main branches —
   (a) Opthalmic nerves — These are sensory nerves supply to the eyes, upper eyelids, forehead, front of the head and in the mucous membrane of the nose.
   (b) Maxillery nerves — These are sensory and supply to the cheeks, upper jaw, upper teeth and lower eyelids.
   (c) Mandibular nerves — These are mixed and supply to lower jaw, lower teeth, pinna of the ears, lower lip and the tongue.
(6) Abducent nerves — These are motor nerves which supply to lateral rectus muscles of eye balls.
(7) Facial nerves — These are mixed nerves. Their sensory cells perceive taste and motor cells supply the facial muscles of expression.
(8) Auditory nerves (Vestibulo cochlear nerve) — They are sensory and are in two parts.
   (i) Vestibular nerves — These are concerned with equilibrium.
   (ii) Cochlear nerves — These are concerned with hearing.

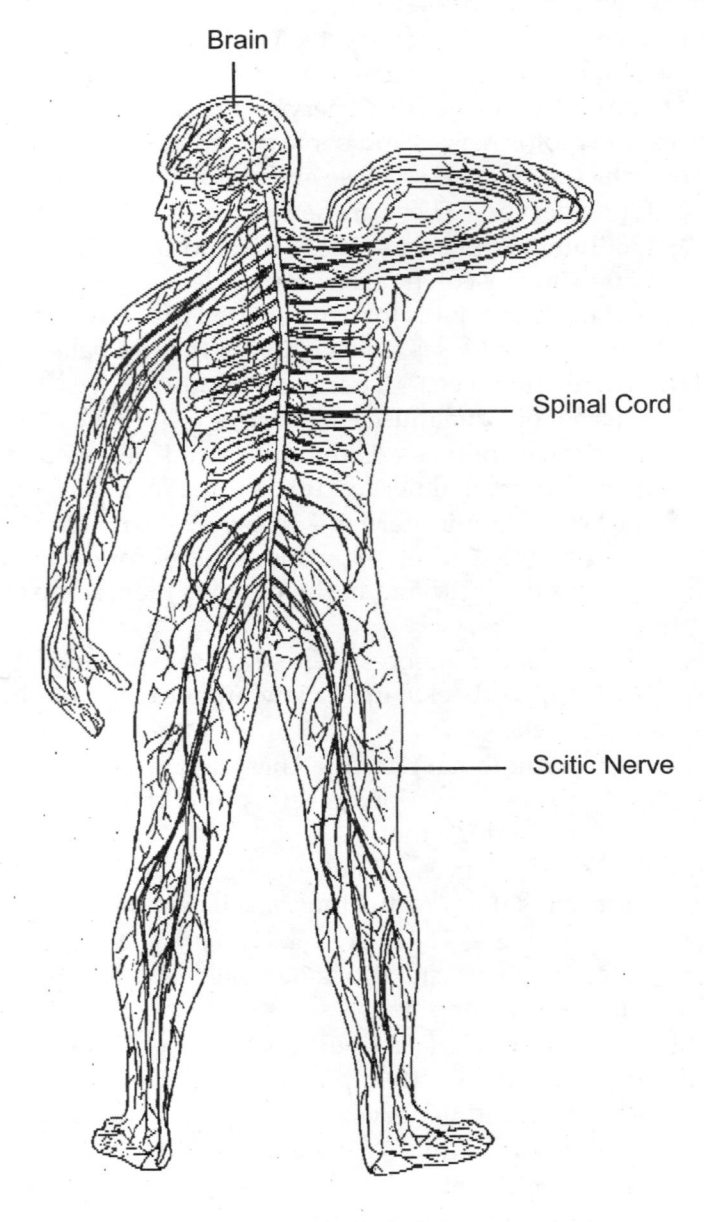

**Nervous System**

(9) Glosso pharyngeal nerves—These are mixed. Their sensory cells are concerned with taste buds of the back portion of the tongue, tonsils and pharynx. The motor cells are concerned with the pharynx muscles and the secretary tissues of parotid gland.

(10) Vagas nerves—They are mixed. They begin at the medulla oblongata, then through the neck, go to the chest and abdomen. As compared to other cranial nerves they are more spread out. Their sensory cells receive the perceptions of pharynx, larynx, trachea, heart, oesophagus, stomach, intestines, gall bladder, bile duct, pancreas, spleen, kidneys, urinary tracts and the inner layer of blood vessels and take them to the brain and the motor cells give directions to the oily and secretary muscles of these organs.

(11) Accessory nerves—These are motor nerves and start from medulla oblongata and the upper portion of the spinal cord. One part of it serves to larynx and pharynx and other part to the muscles of the neck.

(12) Hypoglossal nerves—They are motor nerves which supply to the muscles of the tongue.

**Spinal nerves**—From the spinal cord 31 pairs of nerves come out, they are named after the vertebrae they are connected with—

Cervical – 8 pairs
Thoracic – 12 pairs
Lumbar – 5 pairs
Sacral Nerves – (5 pairs)
Coccygeal nerve – (1 pair)
Sacral – 5 pairs, coccygeal – 1 pair, spinal cord is upto the end of first lumbar vertebrae.

Thus lumbar nerves, sacral and coccygeal nerves come out in a group at the end of the spinal nerves from their vertebrae.

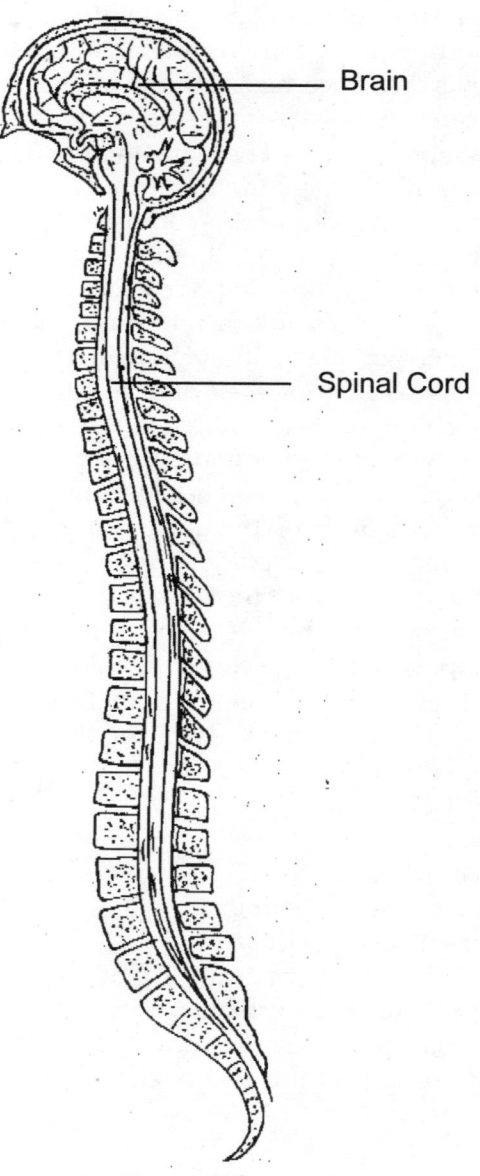

Brain and Spinal Cord

Cervical Nerves
(8 pairs)

Thoracic nerves
(12 pairs)

Lumbar nerves
(5 pairs)

Sacral Nerves
(5 pairs)

Coccygeal nerve
(1 pair)

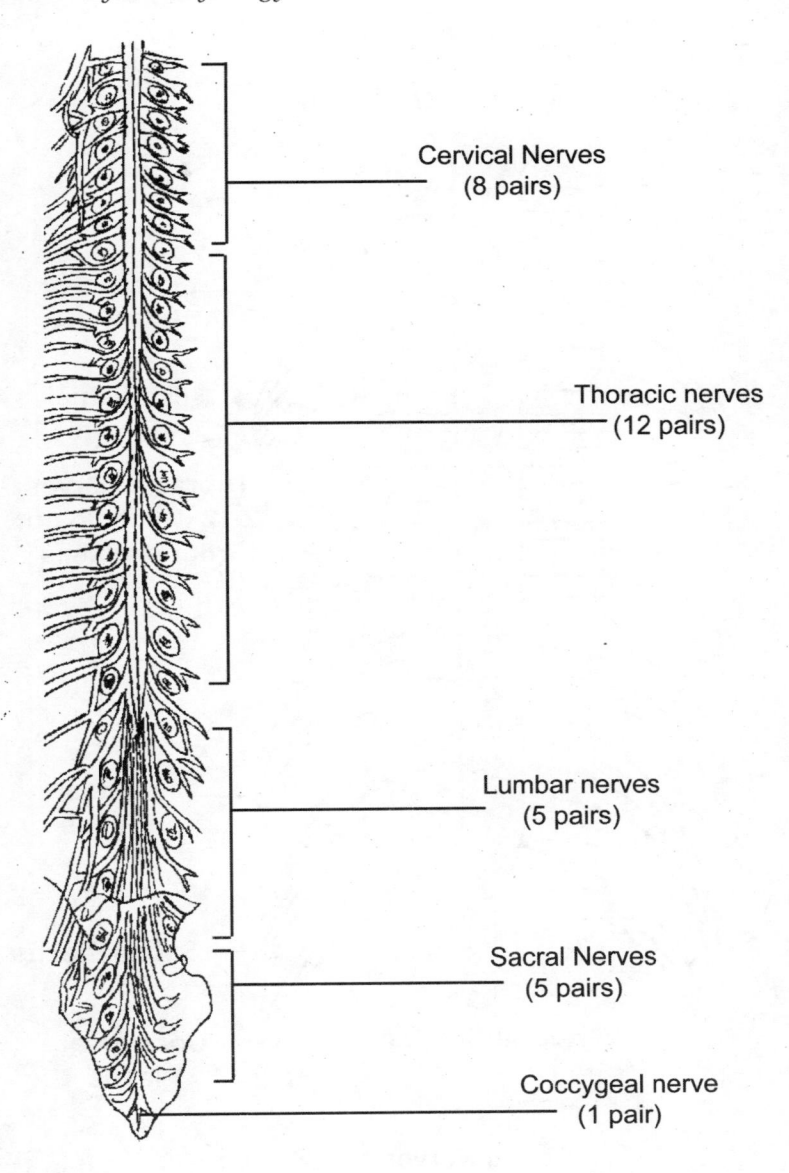

**Spinal Nerves**

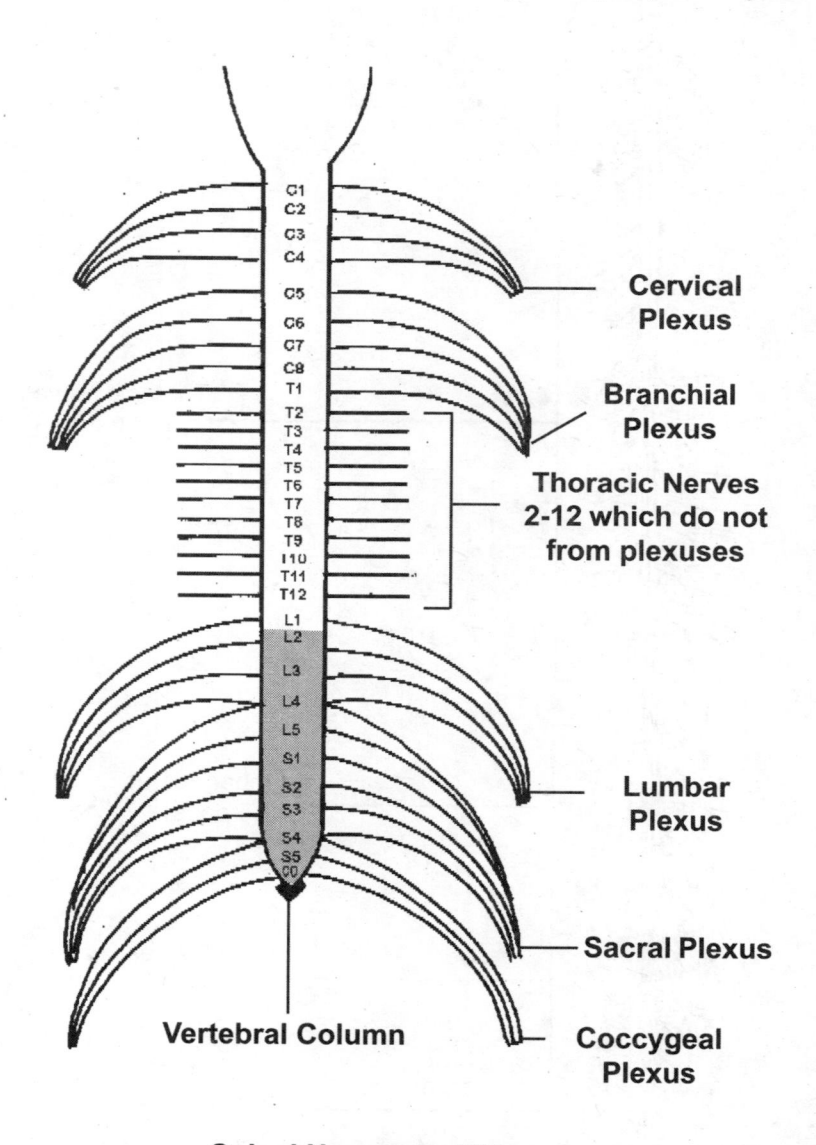

224　　　　　　　　　　　　　　　　*Secrets of Naturopathy and Yoga*

- C1, C2, C3, C4
- C5, C6, C7, C8
- T1
- T2, T3, T4, T5, T6, T7, T8, T9, T10, T11, T12
- L1, L2, L3, L4, L5
- S1, S2, S3, S4, S5, CO

**Cervical Plexus**

**Branchial Plexus**

**Thoracic Nerves 2-12 which do not from plexuses**

**Lumbar Plexus**

**Sacral Plexus**

**Vertebral Column**

**Coccygeal Plexus**

**Spinal Nerves and Plexus**

# Anatomy and Physiology

Spinal nerves are mixed. They get divided into two parts after coming out from the intervertebral foramina—
(1) Posterior primary ramus—They supply to the muscles of the back and skin.
(2) Anterior primary ramus—They unite in groups, out of which five nervous plexuses are formed. The frontal branches of thoracic nerves do not form a plexus. Thoracic nerves supply to the chest, muscles of both sides of chest and skin.

**Five plexuses are as follows:**
   (a) *Cervical plexus*—This is formed by the frontal branches of the first four cervical nerves. The branches coming out from here supply to the neck muscles and skin, one of its branches called the phrenic nerve supplies to the diaphragm.
   (b) *Branchial plexus*—This is formed by frontal branches of the last four cervical nerves and the first thoracic nerve. The branches coming out from here supply to a few neck muscles, chest muscles, skin and arms.
   (c) *Lumbar plexus*—It is formed by the frontal branches of the first three lumbar nerves and a part of the branches of the fourth lumbar. Coming out from here supply to the frontal part of thighs and skin.
   (d) *Sacral plexus*—This is formed of fourth (one part) and fifth lumbar nerve and first three nerves of the sacral nerves with the frontal part of a branch of the fourth one. Many of the branches coming out here have main branch called sciatic nerve which goes to the feet via back of the thigh. Branches coming out of the sacral plexus supply to the rear muscles of the thigh, skin and legs.
   (e) *Coccygeal plexus*—This is formed by a part of the fourth sacral nerve the fifth sacral nerve

and coccygeal nerve. This is a small plexus and supply to the skin of the coccyx region, muscles of the rectum, urinary bladder, genitals and their muscles.

(3) **Autonomic nervous system** — This system deals mainly with involuntary or automatic nervous control of viscera. It is also called involuntary nervous system. Autonomic nervous system has many ganglion also.

The autonomic nervous system is divided functionally into two following parts:

(i) Sympathetic nervous system or thoracco-lumbar outflow — The working process of this is vast and spreads out and faces emergencies instantly, sympathetic nerves come out from the 1st thoracic vertebra or T1 to 2nd Lumbar vertebra or L2.

(ii) Parasympathetic nervous system or craniosacral outflow — Their working process is divided and faces prolonged emergencies. In this system there are four pairs (third, seventh, ninth and tenth) of cranial nerves, which have been described already and sacral spinal nerves are there supplying to the large intestines, rectum, urinary bladder and genitals.

*Note* — Most of the body organs have sympathetic and parasympathetic nerves. They work contrary to each other. Sympathetic nerves accelerate the activity and parasynthetic nerves slow it down. Thus, two mutually opposing effects cause the balance in either becoming very active, or in a state of becoming extremely relaxing.

## (8) Urinary system

The waste products at the end of the food metabolism enter the blood and from blood reach the excretory organs which eject them out from the body. Kidney, skin, lungs, are excretory organs and kidney is the main excretory organ

# Anatomy and Physiology

among them that is why urinary system is the main excretory system.

Urinary system includes the following main four organs—

**Kidneys**—They are two in number. Its main job is to strain blood and after straining it, reabsorb useful products like glucose, amino acids and the remaining waste products, harmful products and water, etc. are converted into urine.

**Ureter**—They are also two in number. Through them urine reaches the urinary bladder from the kidneys.

**Urinary bladder**—This is one in number. Here urine gets collected temporarily.

**Urethra**—The urethra is a narrow canal which leads from the bladder to the exterior.

Female urethra is short and transmits urine only. Male urethra is long and transmits semen and urine. Composition of urine—In urine 95% is water, remaining 5% is solid stuff

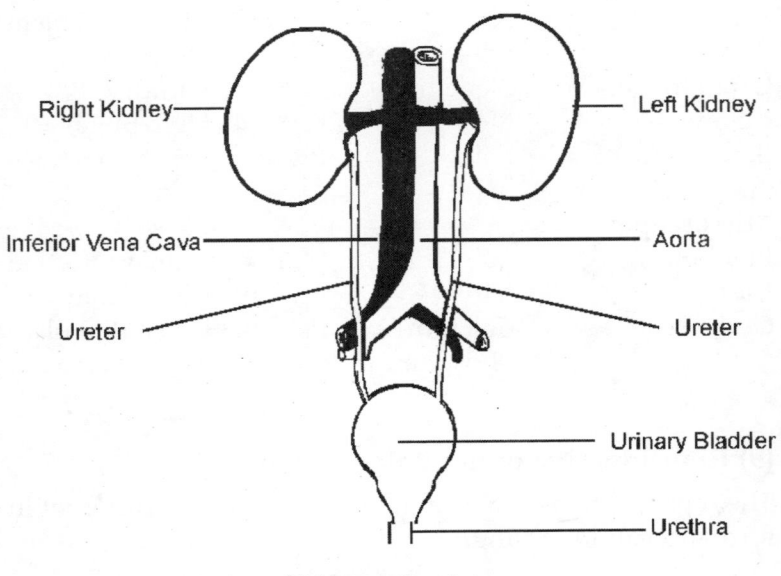

**Urinary System**

which is mixed in water. Out of the 5% solid product 2% is urea and 3% is carbonic (uric acid, ammonia, criatinone, protein or albumin, etc.) and acarbonic (sodium chloride or salt, potassium chloride, calcium phosphate, sulphate and oxejeeate, etc.)

## Urine Analysis

|  | Normal | Result | Disease |
|---|---|---|---|
| **Physical** |  |  |  |
| Colour | Light Yellow | Red | Kidney Disease |
|  |  | Black | Destruction of RBC |
| Transparency | Clear | Opaque | Infection |
| Specific Gravity | 1020 | Less | Kidney Problem |
| PH | 7.4 | Less | Infection |
| **Chemical** |  |  |  |
| Albumin | Nil | Present | Kidney Problem |
| Sugar | Nil | Present | Diabetes |
| Urobilinogen | Negligible | Present | Jaundice |
| Ketone | Nil | Present | High Sugar |
| Blood | Nil | Present | Stone infection in kidney |
| **Microscopic** |  |  |  |
| Pus Cells | 0-2/HPF | More | Kidney Infection |
| Casts | Nil | Present | Kidney Infection |
| Crystals | Calcium/ Phosphate | Present | Possibility of stone Increases |

## (9) Reproductive or genital system

The reproductive organs of male and female are different in formation and working.

## Male reproductive organs or genitalia
This is divided into following parts:

## Male external reproductive organs
(1) *Penis* – It also has involuntary muscles which are formed like a sponge. There are many chambers within, which keep the penis empty when it is flaccid but at the time of sexual excitement fill up with blood and inflate which leads to extension, gaining size and erection.
(2) *Scrotum* – The hanging balls below the penis is called scrotum. Left part is hanging more than the right part. Each part has a testis and epididymis.

## Male internal reproductive organs
(1) *Testes* – These are in scrotum and two in number, and have thousands of small tubes in them. Sperm and male sex hormones are formed here.
(2) *Epididymis* – Behind each testes sticking to it is a small formation called Epididymis. Sperm comes out of the testes and gets collected here and assimilated in its fluid which is called spermatic fluid.
(3) *Spermatic cords* – In both the scrotum testes hang by a spermatic cord.
(4) *Vas deferenses* – The vas deferenses are the ducts passing from the lower aspect of the epididymus, to the ejaculatory duct of seminal vesicles and carry the spermatic fluid from epididymus to seminal vesicles. These join with ejaculatory duct which is situated near seminal vesicle.
(5) *Seminal vesicles* – On both sides of the prostrate glands there is a 4-5 cm long bag which stores spermatic fluid in it, coming from the testes through vas deferences. In this a seminal fluid is also formed which is sticky and provides nourishment to sperm in the spermatic fluid and helps them keep alive and mobile. It gets mixed up with the spermatic fluid. Till ejaculation sperms remain

in seminal vesicle only. Each seminal vesicle opens up in a small ejaculatory duct.

(6) *Ejaculatory ducts* – When the ducts coming out of seminal vesicles join the vas deference of their side, they look like tubes measuring almost 5 cm long. They go through the prostate glands and open up in its prostatic urethra. Through these seminal vesicle fluid and spermatic fluid reaches the urethra.

(7) *Prostate gland* – This surrounds the tip of the urinary bladder and the first part of the urethra. Prostate gland secretes a thin, oily and acidic fluid which reaches the urethra through many ducts and gets assimilated with spermatic fluid to form semen. It makes semen look milky.

(8) *Cowper's glands* – These are glands below the prostate gland, on both sides of the urethra. There are tubes coming out of them which open up in the urethra. Before intercourse when sexually excited the penis ejects an odourless, colourless, thick fluid, that is the secretion of cowper's glands which is alkaline. Urethra is acidic which can destroy sperms so before intercourse these gland's secrete makes the urinary track alkaline so that sperm is not destroyed.

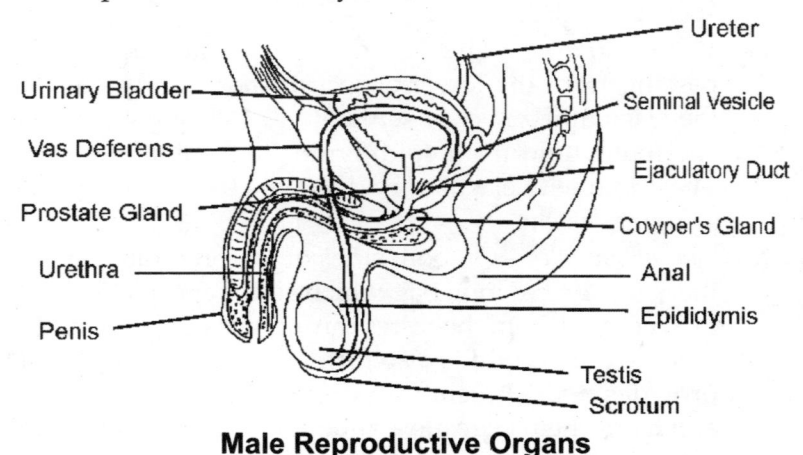

**Male Reproductive Organs**

# Female reproductive organs

These are divided in two parts:

## Female external reproductive organs

(1) *Mons pubis* – Above the pubic bones joint covered with skin is the ascended portion called mons pubis. When puberty begins then hair start growing there.

(2) *Labia majora* – These are two thick long layers of skin under mons pubis. When the girl is small the divided part is adjacent to each other. These have many types of glands and also have hair on them.

(3) *Labia minora* – These are two thin folds of skin, pink coloured which lie in the space enclosed by labia majora. They are very sensitive covered on top by clitoris. Both the Labia minora are hidden under labia majora among small girls and cannot be seen without pulling labia majora apart.

(4) *Clitoris* – It is a small erectile body which is situated at the apex of vestibule. This is the main centre of sexual excitement and at that time gets erect like the penis.

(5) *Vestibule of the vagina* – This is surrounded by labia minora, about 4.5 cm long and 2 cm broad triangular region. On top of it is the clitoris and at the end below is fourchette under the vaginal hole where the labia minora join together. In this area opens the outer urethra vaginal orifice and several ducts of Bartholin's gland and various mucous glands.

(6) *Bartholin's glands* – This is on the base of the labia majora near the vaginal hole a red coloured gland. It opens up into the front of the vagina. At the time of sexual excitement it secretes a pale fluid which keeps the vagina and the surrounding area lubricated.

(7) *Hymen* – It is a thin layer mucous membrane which is slightly within the vaginal orifice, covering the vagina. There is a hole in it from where the monthly bleeding

comes out. This gets ruptured at the time of first intercourse.

(8) *Vaginal orifice* – The part from the hymen to the outer end is known as vaginal orifice.

(9) *External urethral opening* – Above the vaginal orifice there is a small hole from where urine comes out.

## Female internal reproductive organs

(1) *Vagina* – This is about 8-10 cm long circular tube covered with stratified epithelium. It is fibrous and begins at the vaginal orifice and reaches right up to the uterus. It has the quality to expand.

(2) *Uterus* – The uterus is a thick, hollow muscular pear-shaped organ situated in the pelvis between the rectum behind and the bladder in front and almost 7.5 cm long and the upper part is almost 5 cm broad. The upper part is called body of the uterus and the lower part is narrow and is called cervix of the uterus. Some of its portion protrudes out in the vagina. It contains the child after conception.

(3) *Fallopian tubes or uterine tubes* – From the upper part of the uterus, two tubes about 10-12 cm long and 1 cm

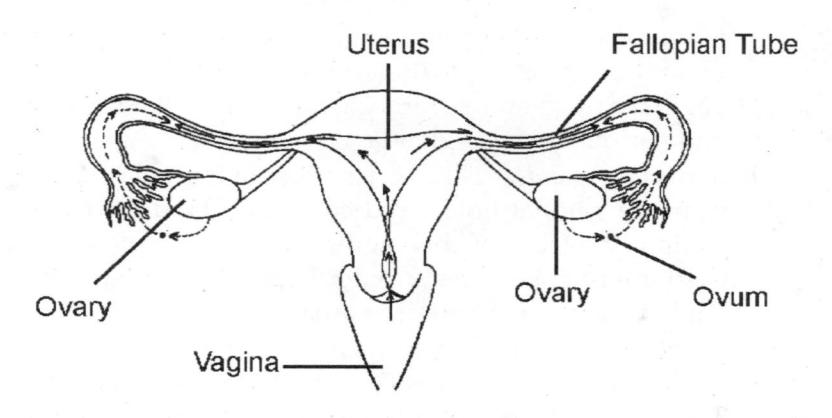

**Female Reproductive Organs**

broad arise and open near the ovaries. The opening point is funnel shaped and is surrounded by finger like processes. Their job is to bring the ovum from the ovaries to the uterus. The ovum is formed every month in one of the ovaries and if sperm enters ovum then it is fertilised. The fertilised ovum settles in the uterus by piercing its wall only or during the menstrual bleeding flows out.

(4) *Ovaries* – On both the sides of the uterus there are almond shaped, light brown coloured reproductive glands called ovaries. These produce ovum and female sex hormones.

**The Mammary Glands** – The mammary glands or breasts are accessory to the female reproductive organs. In the male these glands are rudimentary. These are found on the chest. In females they enlarge at puberty and increase in size during pregnancy and after delivery. They atrophy in old age.

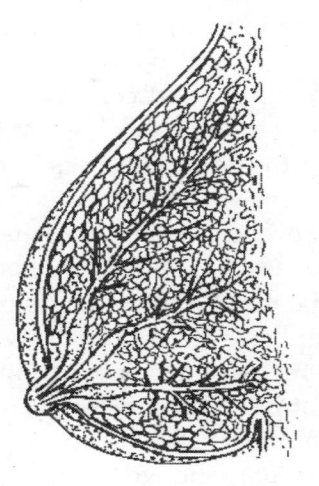

**Mammary Gland**

*Functions of Mammary Glands* – After delivery, lactation or the secretion of milk and its discharge from the breasts during suckling is the function of the breast.

## Sense organs
Human body has the following five sense organs:
1. Eyes
2. Ears
3. Nose
4. Tongue
5. Skin

## *Eyes*

Eyes make us see things of this world. These are about 2.5 cm in diameter. They are on the right and left in the skull placed in the orbital cavity. This bone structure protects the eyes from outside injuries. Eye is like a camera, whose main parts are as under—

(1) **Sclera**—This is the white portion visible from outside in the eyes. This is a white layer. This layer protects the tender parts of the eyes and gives shape to them.

(2) **Cornea**—This is in the frontal region of the eye, a transparent layer and has a convex anterior surface. It has blood supply, but cornea is richly supplied by sensory nerves.

(3) **Iris**—Behind the cornea there is a round hanging veil called the iris. Iris is a pigmented membrane and the colour of the eyes is dependent on its pigments because of which the eyes look black, blue or brown.

(4) **Pupil**—In the middle of the Iris is placed a small hole called the pupil. Depending on the brightness of light its diameter increases or decreases, controlled by two types of muscles of iris. Circular muscle contracts, then the pupil gets contracted, when the radial muscle contracts then it gets dilated. Between the iris and cornea is the anterior chamber and between the iris and lens is the posterior chamber.

(5) **Lens**—It is right behind the pupil an extremely flexible, round, biconvex, transparent formation which does not have blood vessels. This hangs from a ciliary body

*Anatomy and Physiology* 235

through a suspensory ligament. At the requirement of seeing from different distances, the ciliary muscles and suspensory ligament make the thickness of the lens increase and decrease. When an object is closer the thickness of the lens will increase. Lens is closed in a transparent capsule. The lens focuses light entering through pupil on the retina.

(6) **Aqueous Humour** — Between the cornea and the lens in both the chambers there is a fluid secreted by ciliary body called aqueous humour. This is constantly created and excreted. This provides nourishment to the frontal formations of the eye (cornea, lens and lense capsule etc.) which do not have blood vessels and also take out their waste matter. Aqueous humour keeps on forming and getting excreted out. If for some reason this excretion stops then this fluid increases, causing glaucoma.

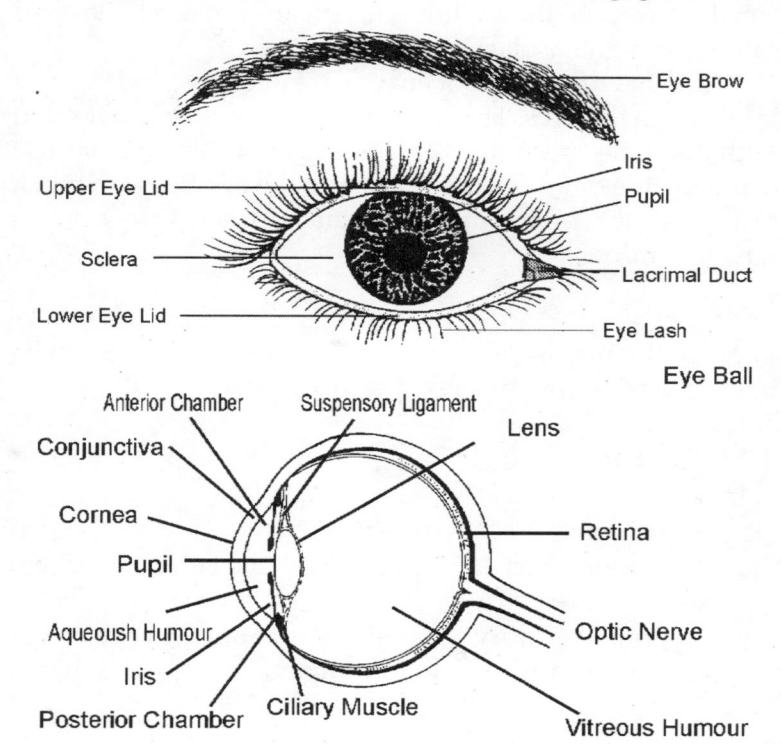

**Retina** — This is the inner layer of the eye ball made of nervous tissues and extends up to the ciliary body. This is extremely sensitive towards light. The objects seen appear small and inverted on the retina when received by the brain appear normal. All the nervous tissues of retina appear on the optic disc and reach the optic nerve which reaches the brain.

**Vitreous Humour** — Behind the lens in the remaining portion of the eye ball there is a colourless, transparent, jelly like substance called vitreous humour. It prevents the walls of the eye balls from getting stuck together by maintaining intraocular pressure.

**Conjunctiva** — To protect each eye there are eyelids. The inner part is a pink membrane which is called conjuctiva.

**Lacrimal Glands** — Each eye has a lacrimal gland in the upper corner, in which tears are formed which through very small ducts reach the eye lids. These tears also reach the nasal cavity through nasolacrimal duct.

Tears have disinfectant enzymes, kill germs, and prevent infection in the eyes. The speed with which tears are formed with the same speed they flow out also. But when a particle from outside or any irritant falls into the eye then too much tear burst out. In an emotional state also tears flow out in large quantity.

### Ears

Ears are the organs of hearing and maintain balance of the body. There are three parts of an ear:
1. External Ear
2. Middle Ear
3. Inner Ear

(1) **External Ear** — It has two parts.
  (a) Auricle or Pinna. It protects the ear and helps in catching sound waves.
  (b) External Auditory Meatus — It is about 2.5 cm circular canal from the auricle to tympanic membrane. It has

*Anatomy and Physiology* 237

some glands, the secretion of which prevents dust particles and minute germs from going inside the ear.

(2) **Middle ear** or tympanic cavity This has the following parts:
   (i) Tympanic Membrane or the Ear Drum
   (ii) Auditory Ossicles — These are three types of bones — (1) Malleus; (2) Incus (3) Stapes, which are connected with each other from tympanic membrane to oval windows and make a chain of movable joints.
   (iii) Pharyngotympanic Tube — Through this tube, tympanic cavity is connected with nasopharynx. This is 3 to 4 cm. long. By this the pressure of air on the ear drum from both the sides is maintained equally.

(3) **Inner Ear** — It has hearing and balancing organs. There are two parts of the internal ear.
   (i) Bony Labyrinth — It is a chain of tubes which has a fluid in them called perilymph.

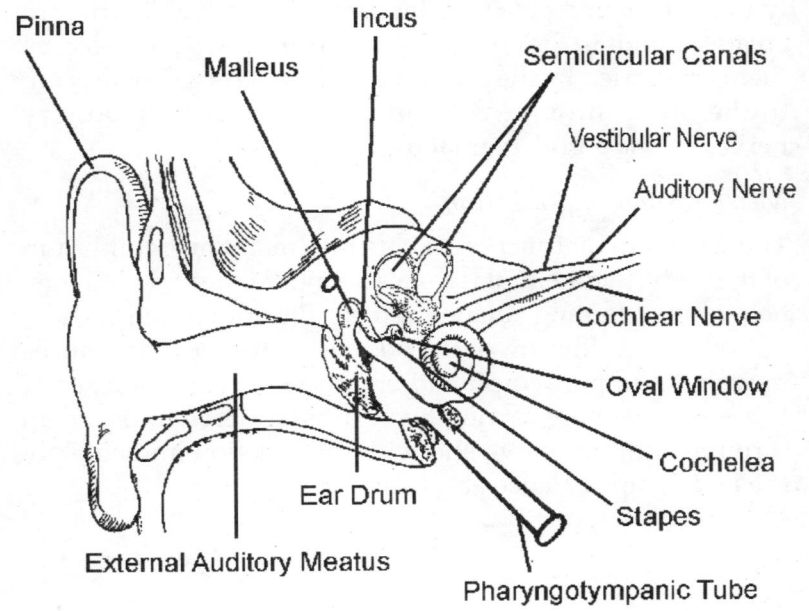

**Ear**

(ii) Membranous Labyrinth—These are similar in shape of bony-labyrinth but is smaller and get fitted into it like one tube gets fit into another. There is a fluid in membranous labyrinth called endolymph.

It has three parts:
(1) Vestibula—Towards the middle ear it is a spread out part with which other parts are connected. It has an oval window and a round window.
(2) Cochlea— Cochlea is the main organ of hearing. This appears like the shell of a snail. Its base is broad, which disappears in the vestibula.
(3) Semicircular Canals—There are three semicircular canals above the vestibula which open in the vestibula.

**The process of hearing**—Whenever there is a sound, it creates sound vibrations which cause a tremor on the tympanic membrane. Tremor reaches the oval window through the auditory ossicles. This creates tremor in the peri lymph which press the membranous labyrinth which in turn creates tremor in the endolymph. The impulses produced by them are carried by the cochlea which is the organ of hearing to the brain through vestibulo cochlear nerve (auditory nerve), or the eighth cranial nerve.

## *Mechanism of Equilibrium*

The second main function of ears is to maintain equilibrium of the body. Semi-circular canals are not for hearing but they help in maintaining balance and equilibrium in the body.

When equilibrium of the body is disturbed, it produces movement in perilymph and endolymph. The impulses of this movement are carried by vestibular nerve to the brain through auditory nerve and with reflex action immediately the body gains balance and equilibrium.

## Nose

The nose along with breathing gives us perception of smell. The receptors of smell are the filaments of olfactory nerve which are spread out in the mucous membrane of upper part of nasal cavity. The sense of smell is stimulated by gases inhaled or by small particles.

It is a very delicate sense and becomes easily deadened when exposed to any odour for some time. The sense of smell is also lessened if the nasal mucous membrane is very dry, very wet or swollen. Smell are described as pleasant or unpleasant.

## Tongue

The perception of taste is received by the tongue. The tongue has four sets of papillae. Each papillae in its inner portion has the end of the nervous tissues which perceives taste. Papillae of three types.

**Vallate Papillae** — They are 10-12 in number. They are at the base of the tongue and are the biggest and easily visible.

**Fungiform Papillae** — They are smaller than the former but are more in number. They are mainly found on the edges and corner of the tongue.

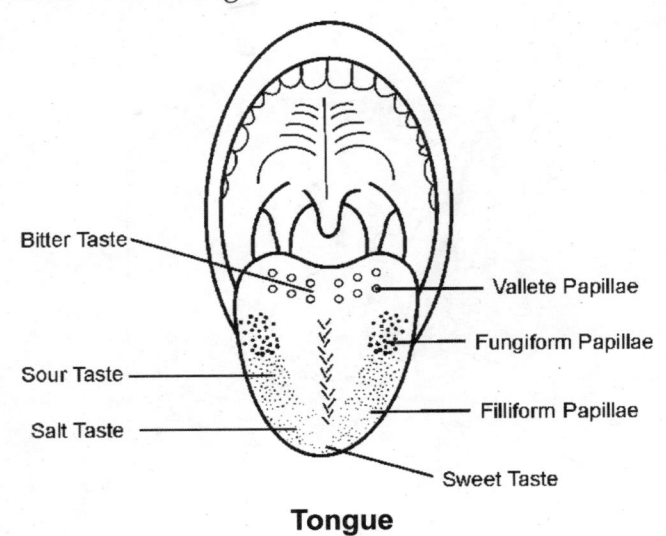

**Tongue**

**Filli form or thread like Papillae** — They are the smallest and maximum in number, which are found on the 2/3rd part of the frontal surface of the tongue.

**Taste** — Sweet taste is felt at the tip. Bitter taste is felt at the back. Sour taste is felt at both the edges. Salt taste is felt at the mid of the tongue.

The tongue also makes out whether the food is hot or cold. Apart from perceiving taste the tongue also takes part in chewing and swallowing the food and also in speaking.

## *Skin*

Skin is the outer covering of human body. The skin is formed of the undernoted two layers:

(1) Epidermis
(2) Dermis

**1. Epidermis** — It is of variety of thickness on various part of the body. It is thickest on the palms and soles. There are no blood vessels or nerves in it.

Mostly there are hair on its surface. Ducts of sweat glands open on its surface. On the surface of the epidermis there are many lines and projections, which correspond the papillae of the dermis lying beneath. These are different in each person. That is why finger prints have importance.

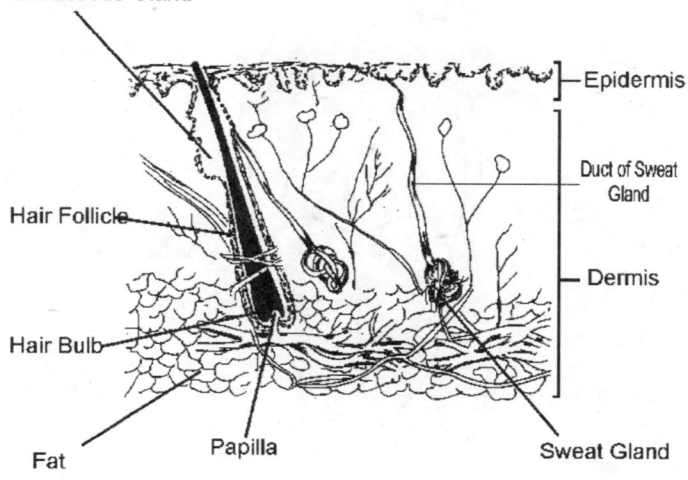

**Skin**

## Anatomy and Physiology

In the Epidermis there are four layers of cells.
  (i) Stratum corneum — This is the outer surface of epidermis. Its tissues are constantly being cast off. They come up from the lowest layer of epidermis, i.e., germinative layer gradually, and new ones constantly keep growing.
  (ii) Stratum lucidum — This is the glistening layer. This is a layer of well defined cells containing nuclei and granules.
  (iii) Stratum granulosum — This is a layer of well defined cells containing nuclei and granules.
  (iv) Germinative layer — In this skin cells are multiplied which gradually climb to the surface and go on changing. Melanocytes are also present here, which create melanin pigment, responsible for a particular colour of the skin.

**(2) Dermis** — This has collagen and elastic fibres which make dermis rigid and flexible. Under this are the subcutaneous tissues which have fats collected in them leading to obesity of the body. It has a network of arterial and venous capillaries.

The following formations are found in it:
  (i) Sweat Glands — Sweat glands are found deep in the dermis and subcutaneous tissues. The ducts of these glands open up on the surface of the skin. These are maximum in the palms and soles. In these glands sweat is formed which consists of water, salts, little urea and other waste products.
  (ii) Sebaceous Glands — These are flask shaped small glands opening up in the hair follicles. These are found in the skin of all parts of the body except palms and soles. The secretion of these glands 'sebum' reaches the hair follicles and makes the hair and skin soft and oily. Sebum also works as a disinfectant and prevents the skin from any infection. Sebum also protects the skin. from drying and cracking.

(iii) Hair Follicles — Hair follicles are like a narrow pit from subcutaneous tissues to the epidermis. On the base of the hair follicles there is a group of cells called hair bulb. When the cells of this bulb grow then a hair is formed.

At the bottom of the hair follicle there is a papilla which has a group of blood cells and they give nourishment to the cells of the bulb. As cells are pushed upwards in the form of hair, they move away from nourishment and thus die. The ducts of sebaceous glands open up in the hair follicles. Small involuntary muscles called Arrector Pilorum, are attached with hair follicles. On the contraction of these the hair stands straight. The colour of the hair depends on the presence of quantity of a special pigment called melanin. When this disappears, hair becomes grey.

There are two appendages of skin — (1) Hair, (2) Nails.

## Functions of skin

(1) Skin perceives sense of touch.
(2) Protects the various parts of body against injury.
(3) It resists germs from entering the body.
(4) It also works as an excretory organ.
(5) The skin has a fat product called dehydro-cholesterol which is converted into vitamin D by the sun's ultraviolet rays.
(6) The skin regulates the temperature of the body. Without sweating, the body remains warm, on sweating the body becomes cool.

## Endocrine glands (ductless glands)

Gland is an organ of the body which secretes or produces liquid chemicals that have various purposes.

**Exocrine Glands** — In these type of glands there are ducts, through which the secretion reaches the appropriate part, like salivary glands, sweat glands, liver and pancreas, etc.

**Endocrine Glands** — These type of glands are ductless, the secretion of these is called hormones and pass directly into the blood stream and is distributed to relatively remote sites throughout the body. These hormones are secreted in a very small quantity and each hormone has a definite purpose. Both less or excess of these hormones is harmful for health.

There are 9 types of endocrine glands in the body:

**(1) Pituitary Gland**—This is the main endocrine gland. It is like a pea in shape, brown in colour at the base of the brain. Its has in front the anterior lobe and at the back posterior lobe.

**Anterior Lobe**—This produces the following main hormones.

(i) Growth Hormone (GH)—This is essential for the growth of body. Its deficiency hinders growth and the person remains dwarf. Its excess makes the person too much taller..

(ii) Adrenocorticotropic Hormone (ACTH)—This controls the activity of the adrenal glands in the production of cortisol from the cortex of the gland. Deficiency of this hormone is rare, and if it ever happens then the efficiency of adrenal gland is reduced.

If it is excessive then abnormal hair growth is caused. Among women hair grows on abnormal spots, raises blood pressure, skin gets thinned and internal bleeding causes blue spots on the skin.

(iii) Thyroid Stimulating Hormone (TSH)—This hormone regulates the growth and working of thyroid gland. A deficiency of this hormone causes hypothyroidism. In this the body becomes weak, it is difficult to bear cold, the skin gets dried and hair start falling, mental retardation sets in, muscles and joints start paining, one becomes hard of hearing, anaemia is caused and menstrual bleeding increases among women. Its excess causes hyperthyroidism, the thyroid gland increases in size and eye balls protrude..

(iv) **Gonadotrophic Hormones or Sex Hormones (GHSH)** — Among males and females following two sex hormones are found:
  (a) Follicle Stimulating Hormones (FSH) — This hormone controls the growth and maturity of ovarian follicles among women and in men controls the seminiferous tubules which generate sperms.
  (b) Luteinizing Hormone (LH) — This regulates progesterone hormones in ovaries and testosterone hormones in testes.

(v) Prolactin or Lactogenic Hormones — This develops breasts along with oestrogen and progesterone hormones during pregnancy and promotes lactation.

**Posterior Lobe** — This produces the following main hormones.
  (a) Antidiuretic Hormone ADH or Vasopressin — This controls reabsorption of water in the kidneys, so that a regulated quantity of urine is excreted. If there is deficiency of this hormone then urination is excessive and blood pressure gets low. Its excess causes less urination and high blood pressure.
  (b) Oxytocin Hormone — Among women oxytocin's activity is restricted to breasts and uterus. Among men its activity is unknown. This compresses the Myoepithelial cells of a woman's breasts leading to immediate excretion of milk outside. It also compresses Myometrium muscle of the uterus to make the delivery easy.

**(2) Thyroid Gland** — This is situated in the lower part of neck and front of trachea. Its both lobes are spread out on both the side of trachea. The thyroid gland regulates

Anatomy and Physiology

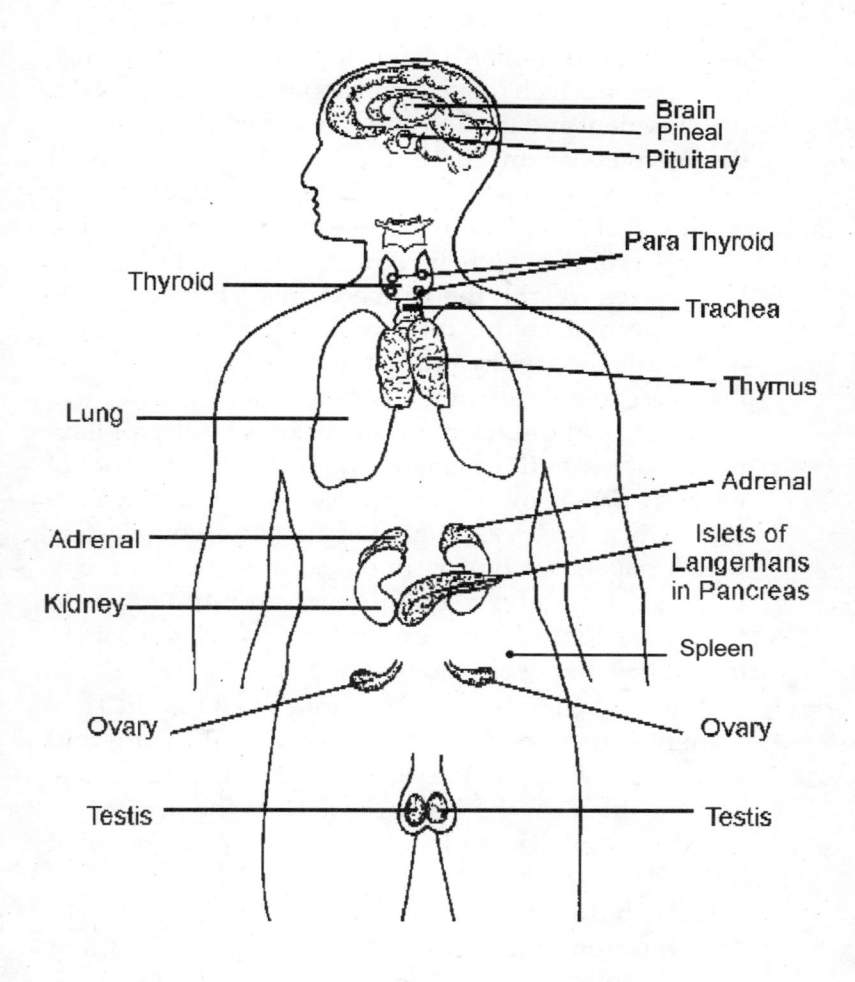

**Endocrine Glands**

many metabolic processes including growth and energy use. Triiodothyronine T3 and thyroxine T4 hormones are excreted which regulate metabolism, and control the development and growth of tissues, specially tissues of the nervous system. For the creation of these hormones iodine is required which is available in food and water.

The deficiency of these hormones cause Hypothyroidism which reduces the metabolic rate. It increases weight, the temperature of the body falls below normal, cold is intolerable, the skin gets dried, hair start falling, pulse rate gets low and among women it causes irregularity of menstrual cycle.

Excess of these hormones cause Hyperthyroidism which increases the metabolic rate. The temperature of the body rises above normal, pulse rate gets fast, weight loss is caused, increases agitation in the nervous system which makes the figure tremble, palpitation is there. If this continues for a long time it can cause goitre in which the thyroid gland expands. The neck appears to be swollen and eyes tend to pop out.

(3) **Parathyroid Glands** — These are four small glands. They are embedded on the posterior surface of the thyroid gland, two lying on each side. One is on the upper side and the other on the lower side. Thus the upper two glands are called superior and the lower two are called inferior.

Here paratharmone hormone-PTH is created. This hormone increases absorption of calcium and phosphorous in the small intestines. This also increases reabsorption of calcium and phosphorous from the bones. It maintains the levels of calcium normal in blood and increases excretion of phosphorous in urine. This increases lactation in both the lactative glands of women.

Its deficiency causes lack of calcium in blood. This results in painful muscular spasms.

Its excess increases calcium in blood because of which calcium get deposited in the kidneys and hence leads to stone formation. Bones become soft and brittle due to decalcificaton.

(4) **Thymus Gland** — This is placed at the dividing point of trachea. There are two lobes in it. There are innumerable lymphocytes in the thymus gland. It is mainly active in childhood. By the time of puberty it is fully developed. Thereafter this gland shrinks instantly. Its main role is to create antibodies and maintain immunity in the body. Before the time of puberty, thymus glands do not permit the sex glands to mature in childhood.

(5) **Adrenal or Suprarenal Glands** — These are in the lumbar region adjoining the upper corner of the kidneys. It has two parts —

    1. **Adrenal Cortex** — Many hormones are created here which are collectively called corticosteroids.

       Their deficiency causes anaemia, low blood pressure, diarrhoea, loss of appetite, loss of weight, weakness and pigmentation of skin.

       Their excess causes brittle bones specially the spinal cord, irregular menstrual cycle, men become impotent, there is abnormal growth of hair, diabetes, high blood pressure, deficiency of potassium in the blood leading to numbness in the body, sensation as if worms are crawling or a pricking sensation and too much urination at night, abnormal growth of hair on the face in a woman.

       These hormones can be divided into three main categories —

       (a) *Glucocorticoids* — They control the metabolism of carbohydrates, protein and fat. They put an end to allergic reactions. They are anti inflammatory.

       (b) *Mineralocorticoids* — They regulate the metabolism of minerals. They also increase reabsorption of sodium in the renal tubules.

    *(c) Sex Steroid* — They influence sexual development of the body and reproduction.

  2. **Adrenal Medulla** — It is important to protect the body from getting infections from outside. Its deficiency lowers the blood pressure, causes hypoglycaemia. Its excess causes high blood pressure, headache, too much sweating, increased palpitation and creates hyperglycaemia in the body.

(6) **Islets of Langerhans in the Pancreas** — The exocrine secretion of pancreas i.e. pancreatic juice (enzymes) reach the duodenum promote digestion of carbohydrates, proteins and fats. In the pancreas there are many groups of cells scattered around called islets of langerhans. These islets secrete insulin and glucagon hormones. Deficiency of these hormones causes diabetes and their excess causes hypoglycaemia.

(7) **Spleen** — This gland is close to the stomach. It is purple in colour and mostly made of lymph tissues. This creates white blood cells, excretes dead blood cells and protects the body against germs.

(8) **Pineal Gland or Pineal Body** — This is a small round brown coloured gland, situated in the brain whose utility is not known exactly. This gland gets atrophied after puberty.

(9) **Sex Glands or Gonads** — Ovaries are almond shaped glands light brown in colour on both the sides of the uterus. In them oestrogen and progesterone hormones are created. They regulate monthly menstrual cycle, growth of breasts and, bring out changes in the uterus to facilitate reproduction.

Testes are in both the scrotums of men. In these androgen hormone is produced. This regulates production of semen, development of sexual organs, bring about hoarseness in voice on puberty, growth of beard, moustache and hair on the chest and hardness of the chest and they make the body capable of sexual activity.

## Metabolism

It is defined as all the chemical processes in our body, especially those that cause food to be used for energy and growth. Metabolism is classified into two parts:
1. anabolism
2. catabolism

(1) **Anabolism** — This is a constructive process which leads to building up of fresh tissues from the nutritive materials of food. This helps in the repair and growth of body.

(2) **Catabolism** — It is the breaking down of substances taken into cells to produce energy and waste products. Catabolism is a destructive process.

*Note*— Normally a balance remains in anabolism and catabolism. Our health is affected when this balance is upset.

During growth or recovery from illness anabolism is predominant. During starvation or illness catabolism predominates.

*Energy* — Energy is the power and ability to be physically and mentally active. For normal activity of the body energy is received by oxidation of the nourishing elements present in the body. Carbohydrates and fats are sources of energy. Protein leads to growth and repair of the body.

*Calorie* — Calorie is a unit of energy which is used as a measurement for the amount of energy which food provides. One calorie is that much quantity of heat which is necessary in 1 litre water to raise the temperature by 10°C. It is estimated that every day a hard working labour needs almost 3500 calories, a person who remains sitting while working needs 2500 calories, while resting 1500 calories are needed. Infants and growing children need more calories than adults.

These above stated calories are estimated. Actually a person needs calories in accordance with his weight, age, gender, profession, climate, health, etc.

Metabolism of 1 gram of carbohydrates gives 4 calories.
Metabolism of 1 gram of protein gives 4 calories.
Metabolism of 1 gram of fat gives 9 calories.

*Basal Metabolism* – It is defined as the minimum amount of energy required by the body during the period of complete rest. After 12 hours of taking food, in a state of complete physical and mental rest, only some amount of energy is required to maintain the vital functions of the body like breathing, beating of the heart and digestive functions, etc. An average individual weighing 60 kg will require 100 calories for basal metabolism.

# Part-IV

# NATURAL TREATMENT OF VARIOUS DISEASES

# Natural treatment of various diseases

Diseases can be categorised into two parts:
(a) acute diseases
(b) chronic diseases

**Acute Diseases**—When the nature takes out toxins accumulated within the body then it is called an acute disease like fever, loose motion, vomits, cough, cold, etc. While suffering from any acute disease the symptoms usually are of loss of appetite, bitter taste of mouth, dirty tongue sore throat, blisters in the mouth, slight fever and headache, etc.

Acute disease are our friends not foes, because they clean up the body of the accumulated toxins and protect us against chronic diseases. We should observe fast, apply mud pack on stomach, get enema and take proper rest.

If acute diseases are suppressed with medicines then the body gets afflicted by chronic diseases later on.

**Chronic Diseases**—When toxins are not taken out of the body then their quantity increases then they can manifest themselves in the form of a chronic disease. The name of the diseases could be different but the cause is the same and the treatment is also same, i.e. detoxification of the body.

For this fasting and intake of juices, fruits and uncooked food is recommended. Other natural means, through which the body can be cleansed should be adopted.

As long as the cause of disease is not extricated, no medical treatment can cure the patient completely.

If the patient does not have full faith in the treatment then it is not fully efficacious. Through naturopathy every disease can be cured but the response of each patient depends on his or her internal state.

(1) Before applying cold therapy, warm the body by rubbing with your palms, and after the treatment, warm the body by walking or by some exercise.
(2) Before taking any hot water therapy one should drink a lot of water.and put a wet towel on the head.
(3) Hoping for a greater benefit, prolonging the treatment for a longer duration is actually harmful.
(4) By treating the body with cold water therapy, bath should be taken only after 30-35 minutes of the treatment.
(5) The treatment should begin two and a half hours from taking the meals..
(6) Eat something only after half an hour, once the treatment is over.

## Acidity

*Symptoms* – Burning sensation in the abdomen, nausea, vomits and sour belches.

*Causes* – Constipation, mental tension, worry, fried and roasted food, spicy food, eating more than your appetite, intake of coffee and tea, liquor, smoking and consuming tobacco, excessive use of salt and sugar, etc.

*Treatment* – Go on a weekly fast on the juices of carrot, cucumber, cabbage, bottle gourd (ghiya), petha, etc. and fruits, vegetables and sprouted foods for one to three weeks. Do not use sugar or salt. Chew the food properly.

Have coconut water, lemon and honey water, fruit juice and vegetable juice, etc everyday. Carrot, cabbage and wheat grass juice is very useful. Eat cardamom also.

Fresh amla juice or dry amla powder with a bit of turmeric in honey should be taken. Drink water from sky blue bottle which has been charged in the sun whole day frequently.

Pass the urine after meals and sit in vajrasana.

After every meal eat one cardamom and one clove.

Regularly take enema, kunjal, dry friction (rubbing of the body with a dry towel) before bath, take deep breaths in open air, and mud pack on the abdomen, hip bath, hot and cold fomentation on the belly, hot foot bath. Wet sheet pack once a week also removes the above noted causes.

Raise the pillow, if more burning sensation is felt in the chest.

*Note* – Do not take milk because milk will give relief but the stomach will have to secrete more acids to digest it. If suppressed by medicines acidity later on can take the form of ulcers and is the main cause of eye ailments and heart trouble.

## AIDS

AIDS is a short form of Acquired Immuno Deficiency Syndrome.

*Cause* – This is due to a virus named HIV which breaks the immune system making the human body lose its power to fight disease. The person succumbs to common diseases.

*Symptoms* –
(1) Prolonged fever
(2) Frequent diarrhoea
(3) Mouth lesions
(4) Weight loss
(5) Ineffectiveness of medicines even to common diseases.

HIV – (Human Immuno deficiency Virus) is the virus which causes AIDS. It is so small that it can't be seen through naked eyes.

This virus enters the human body and gradually damages the immune system that fights infections and diseases.

AIDS can take 5-10 years to manifest itself after the person has been infected with the virus. A HIV positive person can live a symptom free life for years.

It is still not certain that everyone with an HIV infection will get AIDS. In a dry state the virus becomes inactive in a

few seconds. In a wet state it can survive for several hours. The only way to clear this is by getting a blood test called HIV test done. How does HIV spread—
(1) Unprotected sexual contact
(2) Infected needles/syringes
(3) Transfusion of infected blood
(4) From infected mother to child

Ways by which HIV cannot be transmitted—
(1) Casual contacts
(2) Shaking hands
(3) Sharing utensils while eating together
(4) Coughing or sneezing
(5) Embracing
(6) Any insect or mosquito bite.

*Treatment* – There is no treatment for AIDS in modern science. Only awareness and precaution is the best way. But by the help of yoga and nature cure patients may live a better life.

In the food, juices and uncooked food (fruits, vegetables, sprouts, etc.) are necessary. Use of basil, neem (margosa), turmeric, ashvagandha, giloe and wheat grass juice, etc. increases resistance.

Base of the infection is accumulation of toxins in the body. Hence detoxification of body is necessary. For which take mud pack on abdomen, enema, hip bath, steam bath, wet sheet pack, etc. Do exercises and yogasana, do kapalbhati, anulom-vilom and bhastrika pranayama.

Leave all addictions and do meditation.

## Allergy

*Symptoms* – Pricking sensation in the skin, itching, rashes or patches on the skin, reddening of eyes, running nose, restlessness, too much sneezing, itchy nose, cough, breathing problem, migraine, headache, etc. Allergy is the mother of many other diseases like diabetes, depression, heart ailment, ulcer, asthma, eczema, etc.

*Causes* – Allergy is indicative of low resistance power, worms in the stomach, use of intoxicating products, use of cosmetics and synthetic clothes. It could be caused by a particular food product or medicine. Excessive consumption of sugar or mental tension.

*Treatment* – For three to four days fast on lemon juice, coconut water, fruits and vegetable juices, etc. Thereafter take uncooked food for a week. Tinned food, salt and sugar should not be consumed.

Drink soya milk. For a few days drink water of margosa (Neem) leaves on an empty stomach in the morning, and do not eat anything for half an hour.

Similarly take 5 drops of castor oil mixed with fruit juice or with water on an empty stomach, which is very effective. During the day take amla powder with a bit of turmeric.

Drink water from a blue bottle processed in sun rays.

Nadi-shodhan pranayama and ardha-matsyendrasana, sarvangasana, shavasana, etc. should be practised.

The peel of arjun tree should be soaked in water overnight, and crushed the next morning and consumed after decoction.

## Anaemia

Paucity of haemoglobin in the blood is called anaemia.

*Symptoms* – Paucity of blood in the body, weak memory, lethargy, fatigue, breathlessness, vertigo, depression, white patches on nails and paleness.

*Causes* – Deficiency of iron element, protein and vitamin and also due to any other complication, red blood cells are not formed. Excessive flow of blood due to severe injury, piles, excessive menstrual bleeding, etc.

Excess of worms in the stomach leads to anaemia. Mental tension and worries affect the digestive juices which leads to non-absorption of necessary elements and vitamins.

*Treatment* – Spinach juice with honey, pomegranate juice, carrot juice, grapes, orange, sweet lemon, guava, banana, tomato, apple, beetroot, cabbage juice, should be consumed. Spinach, mint, green leafy vegetables should be eaten. Figs are extremely useful.

Drink water from violet colour bottle processed in sunlight.

Dates, black raisins, turmeric and methi seeds are very good. Wheat grass juice should be taken. Two to three margosa leaves should be eaten daily.

Kunjal, enema, hot and cold fomentation on the belly, dry rubbing of the body, deep breathing, pranayama, sun bathing. Surya namaskar, gyan mudra and pranmudra should be adopted.

Yogasana (sarvangasana, paschimottanasana, uttanpadasana, shavasana), dhyan and yog nidra should be practised.

## Appendicitis

*Symptoms* – Appendix situated at the junction of small intestine and large intestine gets inflamed. It pains severely on the right side of the abdomen and gets inflamed like a gland and stiffens up. By pressing it slightly also it pains terribly. Then there is vomiting, nausea, bad breath, constipation, fever, etc. If not treated within time the swelling increases leading to its bursting which is dangerous.

*Causes* – Its root cause is chronic constipation. Eating food which is difficult to digest. Intake of excessively fried food products and non-vegetarians have this ailment more frequently.

*Treatment* – Treating constipation and to detoxify the body is the treatment for this ailment. The patient must take complete rest and only take water slowly. Twice or thrice enema should take be administered. Hot and cold fomentation on the belly should be done a number of times. Due to excessive pain if the weight of wet mud cannot be borne then keep wet sheet pack on the abdomen. From the third day give fruits, vegetables juices and lemon with water. Beetroot and cucumber juice is efficacious, uncooked food (fruits, vegetables and sprouts) should be taken for a week. After the ailment is cured, take normal food. Avoid constipation in future.

## Arthritis/gout

Depending on the part of body affected more than 100 different kinds of arthritis are there. Some of the following are the most common.

(1) **Osteoarthritis** — This occurs with ageing and is normally caused due to cartilages getting obsolete and chipped off. Usually knees, hips and vertebral column get affected, sometimes it happens in the fingers also.

(2) **Rheumatoid Arthritis** — This affects small joints. Fingers, wrists, elbows, knees, knuckles, etc., have pain and become stiff. There is inflammation in the joints which harm the cartilages. Muscles, tendons and tissues are incapacitated which invalidates the patient. This is more common among women as compared to men.

(3) **Gouty Arthritis** — From time to time it causes excessive pain in toes and fingers and it is so much that even slight touch makes the patient withdraw his hand or foot with a jerk. When it gets chronic, the bone connected with cartilage gets damaged. Ten per cent patients of gout also suffer from stone formation, this is more common among men.

(4) **Cervical spondylosis** — In this the bones of the neck and lower back are affected.

*Symptoms of arthritis* — Joints start aching, swelling and stiffness occur, there is hair fall. The problem becomes more acute around the change of season.

*Causes* — Accumulation of uric acid in the joints is the main reason for it. This disease is more common among those consuming heavy protein diet. Excessive intake of acidic food (like meat, fish, egg, pulses, milk and milk products, salt, spice and chillies), gas and constipation, less physical activity and rest and excessive use of medicines cause this disease.

## Natural Treatment of Various Diseases

*Treatment* — Extracting the accumulated uric acid in the body by dissolving it with potassium dominated diet like cucumber, white gourd, water melon, cabbage, spinach, white pumpkin juices for three days. Pineapple, amla, orange and lemon juice should also be given.

For a few weeks thereafter uncooked food (seasonal fruits and salads), etc. should be taken. Vegetable soup should be taken, juices can be consumed regularly, coconut water is also good. Among fruits grapes and custard apple (*sharifa*) is recommended. Wheat grass juice or raw potato juice is also good. Two to three figs, ten to fifteen black raisins should be soaked at night and eaten in the morning. *Khubani* is also good for consumption daily.

Pulses, milk, curd, fried food, sugar, etc. should not be taken.

Drink a lot of water. Put water in a copper vessel throughout the night and consume that the next morning.. Garlic is also useful, sprouted methi seeds and honey should be taken, dates and sesame (*til*) can be made into *laddoos* and eaten. Ginger and basil juice with lukewarm water should be taken. Keep a weekly fast on juices.

Daily drink 250 ml water from a green bottle processed in sunlight a number of times during the day. On the affected portion fomentation by red sun rays should be given. Mud pack, enema, hip bath, sitz bath, steam bath, sun bathing, dry rubbing of the body, hot foot bath, hot pack, hot mud pack, hot and cold fomentation and yog nidra are extremely good.

Joints should be rubbed slightly, lemon juice massage and in case of excessive swelling ice cold water pack is recommended.

Affected area should be massaged with mustard mixed with camphor to reduce stiffness. A pinch of turmeric should be taken with water. Four or five leaves of haar singar ground in a glass of water taken twice in the morning and then in the evening for two to three weeks can cure the disease.

Put salt in a tub filled with water and lie down in it for 30 minutes. Breathing exercise, pranayama (bhastrika, nadi shodhan, suryabhedi, ujjayee), padmasana, vajrasana, siddhasana, gomukhasana, gorakshasana, simhasana are useful. Do cycling exercise with hands and legs.

## Asthma

Air passages of the small bronchi become clogged and constricted with mucus, thus making it difficult to breathe. Asthma can only be cured by naturopathy.

*Symptoms* – The symptoms of asthma are coughing with a wheezing sound and erratic breathing attacks. Normally the attacks are intense after 2 0'clock in the night. But sometimes it occurs at other times also. Cough is hard with a foul smell and is string like.

Asthma is of two types.
  (1) *Bronchial Asthma* – the bronchial tubes shrink causing difficulty in breathing.
  (2) *Cardiac Asthma* – In this the heart becomes weak hence the heart does not circulate sufficient quantity of blood. So oxygen received is also less. Because of this the person has to struggle a lot to breath and sometimes his face becomes red due to the strain. Cardiac asthma is more common among men.

*Causes* – Dried up cough due to medication and erratic eating habits, impure air, mental tension, fear, anger, defect in the blood, use of intoxicated products, cough and cold, copulating during cough and cold, heavy food, chilly and spices, fried food products and dust can cause asthma.

*Treatment* – One day fast on lemon juice and honey water. For a week, be on fast on juices and soups of green vegetables, coconut water, pumpkin juice, cabbage juice, carrot and beetroot juice, grapes juice, doob (a kind of grass) juice wheat grass juice are very effective. Then for two weeks take uncooked diet (only fruits, salads and sprouts). Thereafter take normal food and stay away from heavy food. Take soaked methi seeds and drink the water with a little honey mixed in it.

Do not take milk or milk products. If necessary take soya or sesame milk.

Juice of basil leaves and ginger should be taken with honey. A spoonful triphala with lemon juice and water is also helpful. One cup of hot water with honey is recommended.

Asthma patients should have their dinner early, and should have a glass of hot water before going to sleep. Steam of water boiled with carom seed (ajwain) in it is very effective.

Abdomen mud pack and enema, chest pack, steam bath is very useful. Spinal cord, back and chest should be massaged with mustard oil mixed with camphor in a warm but airy room.

When the asthmatic attack is at its peak then one should change the breathing (swar) and take hot foot bath.

Nadi shodhan, kapal bhati, without retention pranayama, uddiyan bandh, mahamudra, breathing exercises, gomukhasan, matsyasana, uttanamandookasana, uttankoormasana, ashvathasana, chakrasana, shalabhasana, makarasana, yogmudrasana, bhujang asana, dhanurasana, etc. should be practised.

## Poor eyesight

*Causes of defect in eyesight* – Unnatural way of life and food habits, imbalanced diet, acidic and agitative, fried and spicy foods, maida, sour, roasted, excessively hot and cold things being eaten, peel less pulses and dough without chaff in it, eating in a hurry, sleeping immediately after meals, keeping awake till late in the night, getting up late in the morning, having bed tea, wearing high heels, watching television excessively, lack of exercises, deficiency of vitamin A and natural diet, any injury or diseases (constipation, diabetes, high blood pressure tension, etc.)

*Treatment* – Mainly uncooked food is its treatment. The food should contain sprouted wheat and moong gram, green vegetables, milk, curd and fruits. Soaked figs, raisins, black raisins, dry dates should be taken along with their water.

Carrot and amla juice are especially efficacious for eyes. Spinach and carrot juice is good for night blindness and improvement of eyesight. Wash 10-15 black raisins and two figs and soak them in water overnight and eat them in the morning. Orange, grapes, cabbage, green vegetable juice is specially beneficial. In breakfast eat pepper and almonds and drink cow's milk or carrot juice thereafter. Chew four almonds for ten minutes. Take cardamom mixed with honey.

Do jalneti daily in the morning. Get up in the morning and fill the mouth with water and splash water at least fifty times on the eyes. In the morning take deep breaths in the open air and walk barefoot on the grass.

Put 1 spoon trifla in water in a mud or glass vessel at night and strain it in the morning and drink some water and wash the eyes with the remaining water.

Daily sit out in the sun with your eyes closed from 1 to 5 minutes. Drink water from a green bottle processed in sun rays and also wash eyes with this water.

Enema, jalneti, sutraneti, stomach pack, kunjal, hip bath, Sitz bath, spinal bath.

Simhasana, Trataka, bhastrika pranayama should be practised.

Daily massage the soles and apply oil on the toes of feet, while brushing teeth clean up the palate and tongue also.

*Netra Jyoti* — Daily put netra jyoti in the eyes.

Method of preparing netra jyoti — Nine parts of honey, one part of lemon juice, one part of onion juice and one part of ginger juice mixed together and kept in a bottle forms Netra Jyoti. Shake the bottle before use. Every day in the morning and at night put one drop in each of the eyes. Regular use of this does not allow cataract in the eyes and if it is there then with consumption of uncooked food and application of netra jyoti it will be cured. It should not be used if it is more than 20 days old. Keep it in the fridge in summer.

## Relaxation for the eyes:

*Palming* – Sit straight on a easy chair, sofa or any other chair with table in front with such a height so as to keep the elbow easily on it with the spine absolutely straight. Cover the right eye with the right palm and left eye with the left palm. Eyes will remain closed and the fingers of both the hands will cover the eyes over the forehead. Eyes should neither receive any light nor should get pressed too much.

While palming the eyes try to relax all the eye muscles and tissues. Try to concentrate on any black thing with your eyes closed.

If the body and mind and specially the eyes are healthy then while palming one would experience pitch darkness. But if eyes are weak and the body and mind is under pressure, different colours or light will be seen. Once the sight and strength of eye improves then more darkness will be seen.

Whenever convenient during the day palming can be done twice or more. When afflicted by hunger, fatigue, mental instability, worries and anger, palming should not be done.

## Exercises of the eyes:

(1) Close one eye tightly with as much force as possible. Then repeat it on the other eye. Then after some time do it on both eyes simultaneously. Tightly close your eyes and then open them slowly and not suddenly or quickly.

(2) Keep your head and neck straight, then look to the right, then to the left, then towards the sky, then on the ground. Then move the eyes around clockwise and thereafter anticlockwise.

(3) Rub the corners of the eye near the nose then pressing them around gently and then pressing them downward.

(4) Focus on a distant object for sometime and slowly refocus your eyes on a nearby object in the same direction. Repeat this for five times.

(5) Yogic exercises for improving the eyesight are given on page no. 115

## Backache

*Symptoms* – Backaches mostly attack the middle or the lower portion of the back. Ache in the lower back is called lower spondylitis.

*Causes* – Sitting, getting up, lying or walking in wrong posture, wearing high heels, lazy and sedentary lifestyle, menstrual irregularity, lack of nutrients, muscular weakness, obesity, defect in the spinal cord, paucity of rest and exercise, arthritis, osteoporosis or other diseases, sleeping on too soft bed, lifting heavy weight or any injury, use of medicines such as steroid, etc.

*Treatment* – Eat fruits, salads, sprouts, etc. Take juices. Do not eat fried, roasted and oily products, curd, sugar, chillies, spices, tea and coffee. Calcium, vitamin C and Vitamin D rich food products should be eaten. The best for this is milk of sesame. Daily drink at least 2-5 litres water. Take sunbath and consume white bottled water processed in sunlight. In case of severe pain massage with ice. Mud pack on abdomen, enema and steam bath should be given. On the back give hot and cold fomentation, spinal bath and massage on the affected portion. Relax on a hard bed. Spinal cord should be kept straight and flexible. Asanas like bhujangasana, dhanurasana, shalbhasana, etc., in which bending backwards is required should be preferred. Asanas involving bending forward should not be done.

## Cancer

Cancer is a dangerous disease, which crops up in any part of the body in the form of a growing tumour. By the time this disease is detected it has already spread largely in the body. By adopting a nice way of life one can save himself from this disease. As soon as it is diagnosed, patient should resort to naturopathy immediately.

## Symptoms
1. Urinary habits undergo change.
2. Wounds do not heal easily.
3. Unnatural bleeding or discharge.
4. A lump in the breast or any other part of the body.
5. Indigestion or difficulty in swallowing.
6. Change in a wart or mole in size or colour
7. Cough or repeated hoarseness in the throat.
8. Loss of weight for no reason.
9. Change in the colour of skin.
10. Change in menstrual cycle and intermittent bleeding.
11. Loss of appetite
12. Blood or pus coming out with the stool.
13. Constant itching or infection on a particular part.
14. Constant fever
15. Bad taste of mouth
16. Constant pain in the breast.
17. Clear visibility of blood vessels on a breast.
18. Nipple may shrink inside and secretion of any liquid other than milk.

It is not necessary that one has cancer if one or more symptoms are there.

*Causes* – There can be any cause for this disease like –
1. Contaminated food
2. Active smoking or passive smoking.
3. Consumption of pan masala, gutka, tobacco, liquor, etc.
4. More consumption of tea, coffee, sugar, salt, tinned food, meat, etc.
5. Fear, worries, tension
6. Use of excessive medicines and too many x-rays.
7. Unnatural and food lacking roughage.
8. Adulterated food
9. Oily and spicy food
10. Wrong way of cooking and eating

11. Use of chemicals and colours
12. Synthetic and tight clothes
13. Overeating
14. Constipation
15. Deficiency of vitamin A and C
16. Paucity of work and relaxation.
17. Consuming stale food or food stored in fridge for a long time.
18. Oil and ghee being used after heating it repeatedly.
19. Lack of cleanliness of the skin, teeth, ears, eyes, anus and urinary organs.
20. Finely ground wheat, refined rice, maida, etc.
21. Polluted water
22. Use of plastic and aluminium utensils.

*Treatment* – Even though cancer appears in a particular organ in the body it affects the whole body. That is why along with local treatment the whole body should be treated.

As long as possible for a few days fast on lemon juice water. Then for a few days only on grape juice. If a cancer patient lives only on grape juice for six weeks, he can be cured. In case of non-availability of grapes other juices can be given, like coconut water, pineapple juice, orange juice, carrot juice, wheat grass juice, spinach juice, tomato juice, cabbage juice, mint (*pudina*) juice, cucumber juice and green vegetable juice.

After juice therapy, uncooked (without putting on the fire for cooking) food should be taken, like all type of fresh seasonal fruits, vegetables, raw coconut, sprouted cereals (green gram, moth, alfalfa, etc.), soaked raisins, black raisins and figs, etc.

Fruits and vegetables of various colours are very useful as they contain anti-cancer phytonutrients.

In this treatment if one has to remain on uncooked food for a long time, it should be done happily. Uncooked food should not be overeaten also.

Everyday consumption of one gram of turmeric cures cancer.

One spoonful of basil juice and one spoonful of honey should be taken every morning and evening.

Five basil leaves and five margosa leaves must be eaten daily.

In throat cancer a piece of small harad should be sucked twice after meals during the day.

On the belly hot and cold fomentation should be given and then mud pack and enema should be administered. Hip bath for 5-10 minutes is also beneficial. Twice a week wet sheet pack on the body, and steam bath once a week can be given. Sun bathe every day for some time.

Keeping the level of disease in mind, some walking and slight asanas should be performed. Keep ice cold water pack on the affected portion to reduce swelling and pain.

Open air, mental and physical rest is also necessary.

With mental strength and keeping the mind cool, this disease can certainly be overcomed.

Cow's urine is also useful for curing this disease. Consume soya bean milk in place of animal milk.

## Cataract

This is caused by cloudiness on the eye lens. This can be at any age. Gradually it develops into blindness.

*Symptoms* – Hazy (blurred) vision, difficulty in looking with focus, difficulty in seeing in excessive light, rapid and frequent change in the number of lens power of spectacles, double or multiple vision. In the final stage, there is a greyish-white coloration in the pupil.

*Causes* – Increase of toxins in the body, constipation, malnutrition, deficiency of vitamins A, B and C, excessive use of salt, sugar, liquor, smoking, anaemia, reading small prints for a long time by lying or in less light, other diseases like diabetes, thyroid, parathyroid, etc., using medicines such as steroids.

*Treatment* – Once cataract is fully developed then there is no cure in naturopathy. But in the initial stage or to keep the eyes safe from it naturopathy can be resorted to.

Remove the causes of cataract first. For first two to three days live on juices (amla, carrot juice, orange juice, pineapple, juice, white pumpkin juice, lemon water, lemon and honey water, coconut water, etc.). Then for three weeks uncooked food (fruits, vegetables, sprouts) should be taken. Thereafter for three weeks take a balanced diet and fast weekly.

As long as the disease is not cured, repeat this way of eating. Take mostly foods containing vitamins A, B, C and take green vegetables daily. Eat seven soaked and grounded almonds with pepper and honey.

Do not eat maida, sugar, refined rice or consume tea, coffee, alcohol, chillies, spices, meat, etc.

Take amla juice with honey every morning and evening. Take basil leaves or its juice daily.

Jalneti, hot and cold fomentation on the eye, a number of times during the day fill the mouth with water and splash water on the eyes. Weekly sun bath, hot and cold fomentation and mud pack on eyes, mud pack on abdomen, enema, hip bath also mud pack on the spine or wet pack. Every morning or evening netrajyoti (nine parts honey, one part lemon juice, one part ginger juice, one part onion juice should be mixed and kept) should be dropped in the eyes. Keep it in the fridge in summers and more than 20 days old should not be used, it should be thrown away and fresh one prepared. In the morning and evening one drop should be put after shaking the bottle well.

Walk barefoot on green grass in the morning. Avoid flashing light. Eye exercises (palming, tratak, moving of eye ball right and left, up, down, clockwise and anti clockwise, neck exercises and shoulder exercises should be done.

Avoid any kind of mental tension. Practise shavasana and yognidra. Drink water from green bottle processed in the sunlight.

## Cervical spondylosis

In the upper region of the spinal column, i.e., the cervical region consisting of seven vertebrae which get shrunk, rubbed off or the gap between two vertebrae gets narrowed down or toxins get accumulated there, creates this disease.

*Symptoms* – Pain in the neck, stiffness, vertigo, headache and restlessness, grip of the hand gets weakened. In turning the neck there is resistance or pain. It can be detected through X-ray also.

*Causes* – Sleeping on foam cushions and pillows, using more or thick pillows, remaining bent for a long time or keeping the neck raised for a long time, wrong posture of sitting, tension, worries, wrong way of life and eating habits, lack of exercise, using too many medicines, injury and all those causes that are responsible for arthritis.

*Treatment* – Remove the above noted causes. By practising yoga and special exercises this disease can be got rid of completely. Padmasana, vajrasana, siddhasana, gomukhasana, strengthening the neck by various exercises, and other exercises like –
(1) Moving the shoulders up and down, forward and backward, in clockwise and anti clockwise direction.
(2) Intertwine fingers behind the neck and press the neck on intertwined fingers and move the elbows forward and backward.

*Note* – Don't do any exercise which involves bending forward. Other treatments are those recommended in arthritis.

## Chicken pox

*Symptoms* – This is an acute infectious disease spread by a virus. It starts with slight fever, vomiting, backache, cold, headache, etc. Within 24 hours the skin starts getting boils and they get filled up with pus in another two days, which get dried into dark brown peels or scabs and fall off leaving marks on the body.

*Causes* – Accumulation of toxins, wrong food habits, feeding mother's improper diet, eating more than appetite, consumption of white sugar, refined food stuff, maida, ice cream, etc. lack of hygiene and low resistance power.

*Treatment* – Complete rest in an airy room. Nails should be cut to avoid unintentional scratching, because scratching leaves darker marks. First two days only juices should be consumed specially coconut water and lemon water. Drink honey mixed in water. Soaked black raisins and raisin's water be given. Drink as much water as possible. Coriander and carrot soup is very beneficial. Thereafter have fruits salads, sprouted food etc. and vitamin-E dominant food. Coffee, chocolate, fried stuff, sugar, sweets and maida products be avoided. Drink water from green bottle processed in sunrays. Hot water enema, mud pack on abdomen, daily twice chest pack be administered. Basil must be consumed in any form.

## Cholera

Cholera is a highly infectious, often fatal disease occurring in hot countries.

*Symptoms* – In this vomiting and loose motions occur. Cramps in the abdomen and legs are experienced, fever is there, but the body remains cold apparently. The pulse slows down. Cholera leads to dehydration and loss of salts in the body and can be dangerous.

*Causes* – This is an infectious disease, spread by flies or through water. But its real cause is erroneous way of life and food habits leading to accumulation of toxins in the body.

*Treatment* – Drink water lots of in small quantities. Lemon water and coconut water must be given even if it is thrown off by vomiting. Drink mint water. Water boiled with cloves (laung), basil leaves and black pepper ground together should be taken. Drink lemon juice and juice of onions with hot water. Apply wet pack on the abdomen, do enema, kunjal, hip bath, etc. Till the disease is fully cured fast on lemon water, followed by juices, fruitarian diet and then normal food.

## Cold

*Symptoms* – Running nose, sneezing, heaviness in the head, problem in breathing. Sometimes there slight fever and one gets angry over minor things, etc.

*Causes* – Wrong way of living and food habits, indigestion, constipation, more work involving mental attention, smoke, overeating. Eating too much of ghee, oil, white sugar, fried food stuff, maida products, tinned foods, overcooked food and unbalanced diet. Lack of exercise, keeping awake at night, pollution, exposure to cold, etc.

Actually cold is a simple way or process of cleansing the body of the toxins accumulated in it over a period of time.

*Treatment* – One day fast only on hot water, lukewarm water with lemon and honey can be taken. Ginger juice in water, basil leaves juice and honey mixed together should be taken. Lemon juice in water is also recommended. Ten to twenty soaked black raisins and two figs should be eaten. Vitamin C dominant food is useful.

Apply mud pack on the abdomen and do enema. Practise jalneti, kunjal, hot foot bath, steam bath, sun bath, dry rubbing is beneficial. Gargle with saline water.

Water from green bottle processed in sunrays should be taken. If the cold is chronic then take water from a yellow bottle.

Breathing exercises, gomukhasana, sarvangasana, paschimottanasana, surya bhedi pranayama, etc. can be done in open air.

## Colitis

Colitis is of two types:
  (1) **Mucous colitis**
      *Symptoms* – Constipation, abdominal discomfort and irregular bowel habits with mucous.
  (2) **Ulcerative colitis**
      *Symptoms* – Passing of bloody stools with pus and mucous.

*Causes* – Chronic constipation, use of acidic food, pepper, spices, alcohol, other intoxicating products and stress, etc.

*Treatment* – Keep fasting on hot water and juices for 2-7 days. Juices of carrot, cabbage and papaya are very useful. Citrus juices should be avoided.

After that remain on uncooked food for a few days.

Take wheat grass juice.

Daily abdominal mud pack and enema is necessary.

Enema of butter milk is very useful. Hip bath, deep breathing, blue bottled water processed in sunrays are very helpful.

## Conjunctivitis

*Symptoms* – Swelling in the eyes, eyes becoming red, burning sensation in the eyes, watery and sticky eyes, on waking up in the morning.

*Causes* – Exposure to cold, smoke, irritant falling in the eyes, infection in this part due to accumulated toxins.

*Treatment* – Depending on the state of the patient, fasting from one to three days on juices (carrot and spinach juice, orange juice, pineapple juice, coconut water, etc.). After that consume only uncooked food for a week.

Irritants like tea, sugar, chilly and spices should not be used. Food products dominant in Vitamin A, B and C can be taken.

Keep mud pack or wet pack on the eyes.

Open sticky eyes by stroking them with a wet cloth.

Lemon water or margosa water enema can be given. Hot foot bath and jalneti must be performed. Put rose water in the eyes. Water processed in sunrays in a green bottle can be used for washing the eyes.

## Constipation

*Symptoms* – Timely defecation is not there, difficulty in passing stool, it is less in quantity or with hardened pieces in it. After passing stool the feeling of lightness is not experienced. The tongue becomes white or dirty.

This consequently leads to many other diseases and their symptoms occur (foul gas, bad breath, loss of appetite, headache, laziness, under eye circles, nausea, pimples, ulcer in the mouth, acidity, irritation, gout, cataract in the eyes, high blood pressure, etc.)

*Causes* – Wrong way of life and eating habits, not eating on time, stale and heavy food is taken, use of more oily stuff and maida, food without roughage, lack of physical exercise, insufficient intake of liquids, too much medication, worries, fear, mental tension, insomnia, laziness in passing stool, etc. Constipation is the mother of all other diseases.

*Treatment* – Never take any laxative.

Chapatti should be made of wheat containing chaff in it and green leafy vegetables should be chewed well. Uncooked food (fruits, vegetables and sprouted cereals) can be taken. Guava, grapes, papaya, orange, dates, coconut, spinach, methi seeds, cabbage, apple, cucumber, carrot, beet root, tomato, wood apple (bel), walnut and figs, etc. should be consumed.

Lemon water, coconut water, fruits and vegetables [cucumber, bottle gourd (*ghiya*), white pumpkin, carrot and spinach (palak)] juices should be taken during a weekly fast.

Raw spinach juice can be taken in the morning, it cures chronic constipation in a few days.

20-25 soaked raisins can be eaten daily in the morning along with its water.

Wheat grass juice cures chronic constipation. Lemon juice in warm water should be taken at night for clear motions. Triphala powder also cleans up the stomach. Immediately after getting up in the morning drink two to four glasses of water from a copper or silver utensil.

On an empty stomach for 20-25 minutes apply wet mud pack or wet pack. For a few days take enema regularly and have a hip bath. Drink water of soaked amaltas.

In the morning walk for three to four kilometers.

In the evening and morning drink water from a green bottle processed in the sunlight, it works wonders in constipation. For immediate relief take Isabgol chaff. But it does not have any food potential.

Maida, besan, fried food and chillies and spices must be kept at bay.

After meals sit in vajrasana for five minutes. If vajrasana is practised after waking up in the morning then clearing bowels becomes easy.

After drinking water practise sarpasana, urdhva-hastottanasana, katichakrasana, udrakarshasana, padhastasana.

Drink water and perform the exercises for setting the navel at its proper place.

## Cough

Coughing is to make harsh sound when bringing air or harmful matter from the lungs or throat.

Coughing is a vital body defense mechanism. It ejects everything from germs to foreign bodies from the lungs and wind pipe.

Whooping cough is common among children and a sound of hup hup is heard. There is secretion from the nose and the mouth. This type of cough bothers for a long time.

*Causes* – Wrong way of life and food habits, heavy foods, lack of fruits and vegetables in food, excessive medication, indigestion, excessive use of sweets, lack of pure air, smoke and dust, etc.

*Treatment* – Keep one day fast completely on hot water. Then for two to three days take uncooked food. Juices like white pumpkin, white gourd, etc. are useful. Basil juice and ginger juice mixed with honey and licked twice or thrice a day is useful. Pomegranate's peel can be kept in mouth for sucking. With a spoonful of lemon juice take four spoons of honey. Turmeric piece can be kept in the mouth for sucking. Fresh amla juice should be taken, one spoonful thrice or four times a day. Four spoonful of honey can be mixed with cardamom and dry ginger powder should be taken thrice a day.

For dry cough big harad's peel can be kept in the mouth for sucking. Do not use fats. Take green vegetable soup. Ground pepper can be taken with honey.

For whooping cough garlic juice should be mixed with honey and consumed. Take water from a violet coloured bottle processed in the sunlight. Orange juice can be taken mixed in lukewarm water. Keep two to three cloves in the mouth and chew them. Basil leaves can be boiled in water to drink.

Saline water gargles, wet pack on the neck and upper chest is very useful.

Practise suryabhedi pranayama, sarvangasana, paschimottanasana, enema, jalneti, kunjal and breath from the right nostril (surya swar).

## Dandruff

*Symptoms* – On the scalp there is dryness and dead skin. The dandruff comes out if rubbed more with a brush or comb. It also comes out in the form of perforations and thin layers. If not cleaned out it can close the skin pores there.

*Causes* – Wrong way of living and food habit, accumulation of toxins, low blood circulation, the head not being cleaned properly, lack of resistance power, emotional tension.

*Treatment* – Squeeze lemon in water and apply in the roots of hair on the scalp and then wash the hair after a while. Put 4% camphor in coconut oil, and after bath when the hair is dry massage the scalp nicely with it. Reetha, Amla and Shikakai should be soaked in water and the same can be used for washing hair. Daily give dry massage to the scalp. Wash the head with a bit of mustard oil mixed in curd. For half an hour massage the scalp with curd, and then wash it. Soak methi seeds at night, grind it into a paste in the morning, apply on the scalp and wash it after an hour.

Mix lemon juice in coconut oil and apply on the hair.

The scalp be given slight sunlight. If possible shave the head with a razor and apply mud pack and wash the head after an hour, or wash the head with multani mud.

Massage can be done with oil from blue bottle processed in sunrays. Keep weekly fast for removing toxins having only cabbage juice, spinach juice, pineapple juice. For a week consume uncooked food and then take normal food which should include fruits, salads and sprouts in an ample quantity.

Tea, coffee, chillies, spices, refined food products, maida, etc. should not be taken. Try not to get constipated. Take enema when required.

## Dengue

Dengue is a viral disease. It is of two types:
(1) Dengu Fever – It is a severe, flue like illness.
(2) Dengue Haemorrhagic Fever – It is more severe and may cause death.

### *Signs and symptoms of dengue fever*

(1) Abrupt onset of high fever.
(2) Severe frontal headache.
(3) Pain behind the eyes which worsens with eye movements.
(4) Muscle and joint pains.

(5) Loss of sense of taste and appetite.
(6) Measles like rash over chest and upper limbs.
(7) Nausea and vomiting.

## Symptoms of dengue haemorrhagic fever

(1) Symptoms similar to dengue fever.
(2) Severe continuous stomach pains.
(3) Skin becomes pale, cold or clammy.
(4) Bleeding from nose, mouth and gums and skin rashes.
(5) Frequent vomiting with or without blood.
(6) Sleepiness and restlessness.
(7) Patient feels thirsty and mouth becomes dry.
(8) Rapid weak pulse.
(9) Difficulty in breathing.

*Causes* — This is transmitted by the infective bite of Aedes aegypti mosquito. This mosquito is comparatively large than other mosquitoes. Symptoms develop after 5-6 days of being bitten by the infective mosquito. Dengu virus are of four types. Hence a person may get dengue four times in life.

*Treatment* — Drugs like aspirin, brufen should not be used. If bleeding starts or platelets get reduced to below 20,000 then infusion of platelets is required. Dengue patient should drink more water.

One or two days only juice (lemon water, juices of apple, pomegranate, pineapple, etc.) should be prescribed.

Wheat grass and giloe juice is much better to increase the platelets also. Take juice of papaya tree's leaves. Take ginger juice mixed in water.

Consume five leaves of basil twice a day. Eating neem (Margosa) leaves is also very useful.

After juice therapy take uncooked food (fruits and vegetables) for few days.

To clean the large intestines, have mud pack on the abdomen and get enema done.

A dengue patient requires complete rest.

## Dental disease

Teeth are mainly afflicted by the undernoted diseases:

### Dental caries

*Symptoms* – The touch of hot and cold food causes stinging pain. This goes on increasing and remains constant. If not treated in time the tooth may have to be extracted.

### Pyorrohoea

*Symptoms* – In the first stage mouth bears a foul smell. There is bleeding when the gums are pressed or brushed. In the second stage the gums get swollen up and bleed along with pus. Along with food this secretion reaches the stomach and causes other complications. In the third stage pus, bleeding and foul smell reaches its extreme and teeth start shaking. Now this secretion after reaching the stomach causes ulcer, indigestion, inflammation of the throat, fever, eye complications, etc., and when it gets mixed up with blood then the heart, brain, liver, kidneys and lungs get infected.

*Causes of diseases of the teeth* – Lack of dental hygiene which includes not brushing your teeth regularly after meals makes the teeth hollow and the gums become weak.

Betel leaf, supari, tobacco, smoking, gutka, etc. are also cause of teeth problems.

Constipation and other diseases in the body also affect the teeth.

Vitamin C, D and calcium deficiency, excessively hot or cold food, not chewing the food properly and eating only soft things which do not permit the required exercise for the teeth, use of sweets, chocolates, toffees, etc.

When we eat sugar or sugar containing products, then calcium is needed for its digestion which is extracted out of teeth and bones of our body. This weakens the bones and teeth. This is the reason why many children have weak bones and teeth because of the consumption of a lot of chocolates.

## Natural Treatment of Various Diseases

*Treatment* – Remove the above noted causes. As per need fast for a few days on juices which includes carrot, amla, lemon, orange, sweet lemon, spinach, coconut water, white pumpkin, etc. Spinach and carrot juice is especially efficacious in pyorrhoea. For a few days take uncooked food which includes fruits, salads, sprouts, etc. Than get back to normal diet which should contain vitamin C, D and calcium rich diet like carrots, green vegetables, spinach, methi, chaulai, salads, onions, green peas, raddish, lemon, cucumber, long cucumber, tomato, papaya, apple, guava, pomegranate, grapes, orange, banana, amla, raisins, figs, coconut, sesame, etc. Sugar, sweets or tinned food products should not be taken.

Gargle with lukewarm saline water. Inculcate a habit of rubbing gums with one's own fingers. Boil Margosa leaves in water and wash the mouth with it. After getting up in the morning and before sleeping at night margosa should be used for brushing the teeth. With the fingers rub the gums not teeth with lemon juice or amla juice.

Mustard oil with salt and turmeric powder mixed in it should be used daily for rubbing the gums with fingers and also clean the teeth by rubbing them.

While urinating or passing stool keep the jaws pressed to strengthen the roots of weak teeth and by practising this regularly the roots become strong. Patients of Pyorrhoea should eat ten margosa leaves every day.

The ashes of almond peel and the same quantity of alum should be mixed and ground together. This tooth powder rubbed on the teeth cures toothache, shaking of teeth and bleeding gums.

Open the mouth and inhale steam. Clean the mouth after every meal or drink.

Chewing doob (a kind of grass) makes the jaws strong and gums do not bleed.

Around the mouth on the chin if mud pack is applied it gives relief in pyorrhoea.

Along with local treatment of the teeth the whole body should be detoxified by natural means (fast, enema, mud pack, hip bath, throat pack, sun bathing, Jalneti etc.)

Shitkari and shitali pranayama be practised. Viparitkarni mudra, and sarvangasana, matsyasana, paschimottanasana are useful.

If teeth have too many cavities then they can be filled. If the cavity has reached upto the pulp then the tooth will have to be extracted.

## *For instant relief in toothache*

(i) Gargle with guava leaves boiled in water.
(ii) Keep clove in the mouth and suck.
(iii) Turmeric powder can be rubbed on teeth.
(iv) Cotton soaked in clove oil be kept pressed over the teeth.
(v) Basil juice and camphor be applied with cotton.
(vi) The aching tooth should be covered with camphor and pressed.
(vii) Alum water can be used for washing the mouth.
(viii) If teeth get sour then chew sesame.
(ix) Boil five cloves in water and wash.
(x) Gargle with self urine.

## Depression

*Symptoms* – This is mostly a psychological disease caused by the complications of modern life. A person feels ill without being ill virtually. If the doctor says that there is no disease then that doctor will be given up and another will be consulted. Due to negative thoughts the resistance power gets depleted. Insecurity, disappointment and despondency sets in. The patient does not like to talk or mingle with anyone. The person prefers to stay alone. Appetite is lost completely.

*Causes* – Continuous intake of stale food, tamasik food, suppressing defecation and urine, gastric trouble, inefficiency of adrenal glands, untimely meals, lack of nutrients, unbalanced food and other diseases and medicines.

*Treatment* – Juices, fruits, fresh vegetables and sprouted cereals should be included in the diet. Chillies, spices, fried food, sugar, maida and heavy foods should be given up. Soya bean and sesame milk is especially good. Soaked almonds should be eaten. Keep a weekly fast.

Mud pack, enema, hip bath, Sitz bath, spinal bath, dry rubbing of the body before bathing, hot foot bath and massage, etc.

Chakrasana, bhujangasana, shalabhasana, halasana, paschimottanasana, sarvangasana, etc. should be practised. Tribandhasna and gyan mudra should be adopted.

Anulom vilom, kapal bhati, bhastrika pranayama can be practised. Meditation is very important. In the morning take deep breaths while walking.

Give up negative thoughts and develop positive thinking. Laugh heartily.

This needs psychological treatment necessarily. Neither condemn nor criticise such a patient.

## Diabetes

Diabetes is characterised by an abnormally elevated level of blood glucose and excretion of excess glucose in the urine. This disease takes hold of the person gradually. For years the patient remains oblivious of the disease. The modern medical science considers it to be a disease of a life time. But in naturopathy it can be brought under control.

*Symptoms* – More glucose in the urine than normal. Urine is thick and sticky, the urge to urinate again and again, more hunger and thirst is experienced, skin gets dry, fatigue and weakness is experienced, healing of a wound is delayed, itching in the body, laziness, headache and irritability, etc.

*Causes* – Lack of physical work, excess of mental work, constant consumption of heavy, oily and sweet products, excessive obesity, indigestion, worries, agitation excessive consumption of liquor or intoxicating products, constipation, hereditary, wrong lifestyle, unbalanced food and mental tension.

*Warning* – Diabetics generally suffer from high blood pressure, heart diseases, gangrene, loss of eyesight, reducing hearing power, kidney ailments and paralysis, etc., therefore they should never be careless.

Diabetes is of two types:
(1) Insulin-Dependent Diabetes Mellitus (IDDM)
(2) Non-Insulin Dependent Diabetes mellitus (NIDDM

*Treatment* – Modern medical science has insulin as medicine for diabetes, but it is not the actual treatment of diabetes, it is only a means to keep it under control. To save oneself from the disease and be free from it, the best recourse is natural diet. Seasonal fruits (orange, apple, pear, papaya, watermelon, melon, guava, pineapple, etc.), salads (carrot, raddish, turnip, cucumber, long cucumber, spinach, mint, methi, coriander, cabbage, beans, capsicum, etc.), sprouts (moong, moth and gram, etc.), fruit juices and vegetable juices. If one is thirsty then drink lemon water or coconut water.

Fresh amla juice or dry amla powder with turmeric powder is very beneficial. In the season of blackberry (jamun) it must be eaten or half a spoon of blackberry seed powder should be taken with water in the evening. 15 gms of bitter gourd (karela) juice with 100 gm of water can be taken daily thrice a day for three months. Wheat grass juice helps in a great deal. One spoonful of methi seeds should be soaked in water and eaten and the water thereof should be consumed or make methi powder and take one spoonful daily. Less milk and more butter milk should be taken.

Soak 250 gms of ladyfinger cut into two pieces and soaked in water at night and in the morning drink that water and throw away the lady finger. Do this for a week.

Daily taking 5-10 bel leaves or sadabahar leaves, jamun leaves or margosa leaves work wonders in diabetes. Basil leaves are also beneficial. It reduces sugar.

Daily in the morning drink at least two glasses of water and eat two figs. Eat chapatti made of flour from the mixture of 25% wheat, 25% barley, 10% moong, 10% baajra, 10% phaphar (Kuttoo), 10% Gram, 5% Soyabean and 5% corn.

Sit bare bodied in sunshine, water from orange coloured bottle processed in sunrays should be drunk after meals.

On the abdomen mud pack, enema, hip bath, hot and cold fomentation on abdomen, Sitz bath is very beneficial.

Walk for four to five kilometers daily in fresh air and jog for a while. Try to do deep breathing in fresh air..

Shatkarmas (kunjal, jalneti, dhauti, etc.) are useful.

Suryabhedi, bhastrika, kapalbhati and nadishodhan, pranayama uddiyanbandh, mahamudra, breathing exercises, ardhamatsyendrasana, mayurasana, matsyasana, naukasana, halasana, paschimottanasana, bhujangasana, chakrasana, dhanurasana, mandookasana, koormasana, janushirshasana, urdhvahastottasana, padhastasana, katichakrasana, tribandhasana, garbhasana, bhoonmanasana, uttanapadasana, surya namaskar are beneficial. Practise agnisaar kriya.

*Harmful foods* – Sugar, ice cream, sweets, etc. ghee, butter, cold drinks, fried stuff, non-vegetarian food, liquor, sugar free tablets and stuffs made of maida.

*Note* – Do not stop taking insulin suddenly if you are used to it.

## Diarrhoea

*Symptoms* – Frequent loose or watery faeces is defecated.

*Causes* – Overeating or infected food, or infected water or defective digestion does not permit proper digestion of food. Digestive process takes out accumulated poisonous products in the form of loose motions. Thus it is a natural process of cleansing of the body which should not be suppressed by medicines. Otherwise it can assume the form of a chronic ailment.

*Treatment* – As per need fast for one or two days only on lemon water. When loose motions stop, then take a liquid diet like diluted butter milk, carrot juice, apple juice, pomegranate juice, coconut water, rice water, a little ground turmeric with water or butter milk. From juices one should come to a fruitarian diet and then come back to normal diet. Along with this lemon water enema or butter milk enema, mud pack on the abdomen and hip bath should also be taken.

## Dysentery

It is a serious disease of the bowels which causes the contents to be passed out of the body much more often and in a more liquid form than usual. It is caused by an infection which is spread by dirty water or food. In this along with the faeces there is bleeding and mucous also comes out. After defecating also there is discomfort, extreme pain in the belly, headache, loss of appetite, extreme thirst and weakness. Sometimes there is fever also which goes upto 104°F. There is laziness, unwillingness to work and mind feels dull.

*Causes* – Wrong lifestyle and improper food habits leads to accumulation of toxins and constipation cause formation of wounds in the colon. In those wounds the germs of this disease thrive and on the basis of these germs it is called amoebic dysentery or bacillary dysentery. Amoebic dysentery attacks slightly but if one is not careful then takes a long time to cure. Bacillary dysentery attacks heavily but gets cured fast.

*Treatment* – First clean the colon with enema of lukewarm water. The water of enema should slowly flow in. After taking enema have hot and cold fomentation on the abdomen and keep wet pack or mud pack on the abdomen. According to the condition of the ailing person the pack should be given repeatedly.

Hip bath is good. Once during the day hot foot bath should be given and after that whole body should be wiped with a towel.

As long as the disease is not cured, fast only on water or lemon water, etc. then as per need for a week remain on liquid diet, then fruits and salads and later on come back to normal diet. Butter milk must be taken.

Drink water of sky blue coloured bottle processed in sunrays and have complete rest.

## Ear diseases

*Symptoms* – Pain in the ear, swelling or redness in or around the ear. Boil or a liquid discharge from the ear, foul smell in the ear, impaired hearing or complete deafness.

*Causes* – Accumulation of a lot of wax in the ear, dryness in the ear, a food grain falling in the ear and then puffing up, repeated inflammation of the tonsils, teeth problem, sound pollution, injury in the ear, scratching the ear, water seeping into the ear, blood infection, indigestion, are the causes leading to trouble in the ear.

*Treatment* – If an insect goes in the ear, put drops of warm mustard oil in the ear. Insect will be killed and flow out with oil.

If there is humming in the ear then hot water enema should be taken to clean the stomach, as it is caused due to constipation or gas in the stomach.

If the ear is infected or inflamed then mustard oil heated up slightly with a pinch of salt in it should be dropped in the ear and fomentation near the ear should be done. Garlic could also be heated in mustard oil and that oil should be dropped in the ear thrice a day every morning, afternoon and evening, two drops at a time. For earache onion juice strained and warmed can be dropped in the ear, four drops at a time.

If there is a discharge from the ear or if it aches then the juice of soft margosa leaves and pure honey can be taken in equal quantities. This cures ear discharge, ear ache and deafness.

Drop of juice of peepal leaves or basil leaves cures deafness and ache in the ear. Keep cotton in the ear and put mud pack over it or give steam locally.

Two drops of cow's urine or self urine can be put in the ear. Fast for two to four days then take a fruitarian diet. Sprouted gram, fruits and vegetables should be consumed in ample quantities.

Take enema, do kunjal and jalneti, anulom vilom, bhastrika, bhramari pranayama. Laugh loudly. Surya namaskar, simhasana, dhanurasana, shalbhasana, bhujangasana can be done.

To save oneself from ear ailments every month put some drops of lukewarm mustard oil.

## Eczema

Effecting the skin, this is one of the most distressing ailment as compared to other skin troubles. This is not localised but has its connection with the entire system.

*Symptoms* — In this there is burning sensation, redness, itching and at night the intensity is more acute. Sometime there is secretion, the skin gets hard and perforates. Sometimes it gets blisters. Sometimes it is just dry eczema, in which the skin gets rough and thick and there is itching. In this disease, outwardly the condition may be different but internally the condition and cause are the same.

*Causes* — Wrong way of living and eating habits, which leads to accumulation of toxins, constipation, diseases like asthma suppressed by medicines, allergy, excretory organs are inactive, specially the skin.

*Treatment* — There is no permanent cure for it in medicine. But by naturopathy eczema can be cured forever.

Fast on vegetable soup, carrot and spinach juice, other liquid diet or live on water from three to ten days then for fifteen days live on fruit diet and for two weeks on a controlled diet. Repeat this cycle till such a time as it might take for the disease to be cured completely. Fruits, vegetables and salads are to be taken in ample quantities.

Drink two to three litres of water daily. Salt, sugar, tea, coffee, soft drinks, liquor etc. should not be used.

Boil margosa leaves and wash the skin with that water. Also take enema of this water. In morning and evening take hip bath for seven to fifteen minutes.

In the morning take air bath and sun bath. Apply mud pack locally, two or three times daily.

If the spot is aching too much then give steam or hot and cold fomentation.

Once or twice a week steam bath and wet sheet pack are beneficial. After bath massage with camphor mixed coconut oil.

Drink water and apply blue oil of green coloured bottle processed in sun rays.

To drink juice of margosa leaves with water on empty stomach is very efficacious in all skin ailments.

Practise kunjal, sutraneti and jalneti. Paschimottanasana, halasana, matsyasana, bhujangasana, dhanurasana, mandookasana, janushirshasana should be practised. Nari shodhan, bhastrika pranayama are beneficial.

## Epilepsy

*Symptoms* – Suddenly the body gets stretched and hand and feet get stiffened up and the patient faints and falls on the ground. Hands and feet get contortions and neck also gets twisted. Eyes pop out and eyelids become still. Froth comes out from the mouth and the jaws get stiffened up together and the tongue comes out. In this state there is fear of the tongue getting cut. The patient may defecate or urinate without his knowing. The body trembles. This fit can last for a few minutes to two-three hours or more than that. After the fit the patient gets sound sleep.

This disease begins in childhood and continues with full intensity in young age end thereafter gradually mellows down, sometimes it continues for a lifetime. As the disease gets intense, the mental condition of the patient deteriorates and the memory power gets weakened.

*Causes* – Due to wrong way of life and eating habits toxins get accumulated in the body and pressurise the mental chambers. Excessive consumption of tobacco or liquor, worms in the stomach and intestines, chronic constipation, menstrual complications among women, ailments of the nervous system, tumour in the brain, injury on the head, excessive physical or mental strain, mental tension, infections, fever etc. If parents are epileptic then the children also have a possibility of getting it.

*Treatment* – In the beginning for at least two months live only on fruits and vegetables and sprouted cereals and observe weekly fast only on fruits and vegetable juices.

At morning and evening take triphala with lukewarm water. Take soya bean milk and eat raw green leafy vegetables.

On the abdomen and forehead keep wet mud pack and enema should be taken. Daily hip bath, Sitz bath, cold water spinal bath should be taken and jalneti be practised.

Once a week wet sheet pack can be done. Drink a lot of water.

Drink water daily five to six times from sky blue bottle processed in sun rays, and use the same water for putting wet pack on the forehead which should be removed only on getting dry. Apply oil on the head from sky blue coloured bottle processed in the sun rays.

Sleep well as much as is desired. In this disease meditation is of great use. During a fit a handkerchief can be stuffed in the mouth, to prevent the person from cutting the tongue under his teeth.

At the time of fit, put nail of your thumb in the nail of the thumb of the patient and press it. This removes unconsciousness.

Sprinkling of water on the patient's face also brings him out of unconsciousness.

## Epistaxis

*Symptoms* – Bleeding from the nose.

*Causes* – Injury, scratching the nose, infection in the nose, high blood pressure, boils in the nose continuous chronic constipation, cleaning the nose with a jerk.

*Treatment* – Pour cold water on the head, make the patient smell wet mud. On the head and brain keep piece of cloth wet in cold water. Keep ice pieces in both the hands. Keep ice pack on the nose. Under the head a pillow can be placed, open all the buttons of the patient and make him breathe from the mouth. Fruitarian diet can be taken by the patient. If the nerve between the thumb and the index finger is pressed, it stops bleeding. Daily apply mustard oil in the nose.

## Fever

The normal temperature of the body is (98.6°F or 37°C) and when it increases beyond this point then it is supposed to be fever. This indicates that the body is burning up the toxins accumulated in the body and a cleansing of the working system is on, to make it reactive. But most of the people get afraid of this stage and resort to antibiotic medicines for treatment. This reduces resistance power of the body, and gives a chance to other diseases to thrive. Depending on the symptoms and infection there are different types of fevers.

1. **Influenza** – This is also called flu. It is an infectious disease. This affects the upper portion of the breathing system. During fever the patient feels cold and there is headache and muscular pain and inflammation in

the nose and throat. There is secretion from the nose and eyes. The body temperature remains 102°F for two to three days which sometimes rises upto 104°F. The influenza fever persists for four to five days.

2. **Pneumonia** — This is also an infectious disease. There is acute inflammation either in one lung or both the lungs. This disease begins with extreme exposure to cold. There is sharp pain in the chest and difficulty in breathing. Then cough starts coming out. There is headache and the body begins to tremble. The temperature can go up to 105°F and the pulse rate 150 per minute. This is caused due to various germs, viruses, fungus, etc.

   This can even cause pleurisy or any part of the lung can get damaged.

3. **Typhoid** — This is caused by a bacteria which reaches the intestines through food or water then enters the blood stream. After a long time the symptoms crop up. In the morning there is less fever but in the evening it increases and continues for many days. First the whole body experiences fatigue and then there is loss of appetite. The patient feels nausea and headache. Either there is constipation or loose motions. There is a thick layer of filth on the tongue and the front and sides of the tongue become red.

   Sometimes the patient feels extremely cold. Back pain, waist pain, ankle pain or sometimes the whole body pains. It causes enlargement of spleen and liver. The lower portion of the abdomen pains when pressed. Some patients even have bleeding from the intestines.

4. **Malaria** — This is also an infectious disease which is caused by various parasites. This is caused by biting of a female Anopheles mosquito. When a mosquito bites a malaria patient and then another, the parasites of this disease pass on to other. Thus a patient of malaria should be kept in a mosquito net. Malaria begins with a feeling of extreme cold, headache, legs starts paining

with high fever, which comes down with perspiration after sometime. This repeats daily or on alternate days depending on the type of parasites.

*Causes of all type of fevers* – Wrong lifestyle and poor eating habits cause increase of toxins in the body, which is the main cause of fever. This weakens the resistance power of the body.

*Treatment of all type of fevers* – Continue to fast till all the symptoms of fever are gone. Lemon water, coconut water, sour milk's water, lemon and honey water, boiled barley water or orange juice should be given. Sufficient quantity of water can be given. Drinking a lot of water is the best medicine for fever. When you feel cold then hot water, and when feeling hot cold water should be given. Vegetable juices can be taken. Green vegetable soup without salt in it should be consumed.

Methi seeds boiled in water, soaked black raisins water, basil boiled in water can be administered. Ginger juice and black pepper in honey can be given thrice a day. Boiled water of cinnamon (dalchini) with black pepper and honey is efficacious. Garlic is very useful in pneumonia.

After fasting start eating fruits. And later on normal diet which should include fruits, salads and sprouted cereals in sufficient quantity.

Warm water enema should be administered daily. On the abdomen mud pack, as per need hot or cold hip bath and Jalneti can be performed. If the fever is high then keep cold water pack on the forehead and belly. The body should be given sponge, wet sheet pack and hot foot bath. When the fever is not high then kunjal can be done.

If the person feels too cold then keep hot water bottle on the side and cover him with a blanket.

Dry friction is very beneficial. The patient should rest completely. Water from a blue bottle processed in sun rays should be taken after every two hours.

Practise shitali and shitkari pranayama and shavasana and meditation..

## Fissure/fistula

On the mouth of the anus the skin gets cracked, deep into the muscle there.

*Symptoms* – Pain around the anus, unbearable pain while passing stool, sometimes bleeding also occurs and itching around the anus.

*Causes* – The main cause of this disease is chronic constipation caused by wrong eating habits. Hard stool breaks the formation and membrane of the anus.

*Treatment* – The first thing is to put an end to constipation and stool should be regular and soft.

Thus remain on juices only for four to five days like sweet lemon, orange, pineapple, white pumpkin, bottle gourd, etc. and lemon water. Then for five days live on a fruitarian diet (Apple, papaya, guava, grapes, etc.) Thereafter adopt general balanced diet which includes chapatti of chaff mixed flour, unpeeled pulses, green vegetables, figs and dates, etc.

Sugar and sugar products, chillies, spices, fried products should not be consumed at all.

Drink water in sufficient quantity. Daily wash the anus with margosa water, hot water enema mud pack on anus and abdomen are also beneficial.

Drink water from a green bottle processed in sun rays. Exercise regularly, practise yogasanas, (uttanpadasana, suptpavanmuktasana, vajrasana, bhujangasana, shalbhasana, shavasana) and yogamudra, etc.

## Gas trouble

*Symptoms* – Indigestion causes gas formation in the stomach which passes out repeatedly from the anus or gets retained within, this causes gastric trouble in the body. The stomach inflates, there is restlessness, body also aches, there is lack of concentration in work, loss of appetite, nervous weakness, physical and mental imbalance.

*Causes* – Constipation, indigestion, improper food, not chewing the food properly, deficiency of any physical activity and relaxation, holding urine and stool for a long time, fear, unhappiness, worms, tension, unbalanced diet, etc.

*Treatment* – Fast on juices only for one or two days. Take lukewarm water with some honey, lemon and ginger squeezed into it. Butter milk is very beneficial. Then remain on a fruitarian diet with sufficient quantity of fruits, vegetables, sprouts and thereafter adopt normal food. Chapatti made of flour with chaff with some gram powder mixed in it should be eaten. Food can be chewed properly. Very hot or very cold food should not to be taken. A weekly fast is a must. Eat only twice a day. Sugar, tea, fried products, maida products, etc. should not be consumed. Sit in vajrasana after having meals. Daily eat ten black raisins and two figs soaked overnight. Take triphala powder with water every night. Coriander leaves should be chewed.

Small harad can be kept in the mouth and sucked. After meals breathe 8 times on your back, then 16 times lying on the right side and 32 times on the left side.

Use celery seeds, fenugreek seeds, aniseed, etc.

Hot and cold fomentation can be done on the abdomen and thereafter enema should be taken. Hip bath, wet sheet pack on the belly, mud pack, shankh prakashalana and breathing through the right nostril are helpful.

Suptpavanmuktasana, paschimottanasana, dhanurasana, shalbhasana, uttanpadasana, bhujangasana, halasana mayurasana and naukasana should be done. Lie on your back and do cycling. Uddiyan bandh and kapal bhati pranayama are very beneficial.

## Glaucoma

*Symptoms* – Due to too much liquid in the eyes the eye balls get pressurised and become hard. Eyebrows, forehead and other parts of the eye also feel the tension. On looking at light colour circles appear. If one is not alert it can also cause blindness.

*Causes* – Aqueous Humor is created in the eyes and it also gets out of the eyes. But due to obstruction caused by toxins, it stops coming out and the liquid in the eye increases which applies pressure on the eye balls. This is harmful for the optic nerves and can lead to blindness. Obstruction in the eyes is due to unbalanced food and living, use of medicines, smoking, tension,, diabetes, allergy, nervous system getting imbalanced, etc. and other diseases.

*Treatment* – Till acute symptoms are mellowed down, water, vitamin A,B, C dominated fruits and vegetables (lemon, amla, orange, pineapple, carrot, spinach, etc.) juices should be taken.

Mud pack on the abdomen, enema, hip bath, wet sheet pack, jalneti, hot and cold fomentation and mud pack on the eyes can be applied.

Daily chew five leaves of margosa. Till the effect is mellowed down for a week fruitarian diet can be taken and then normal food.

Heavy food stuff should be given up. Salt, chillies, spices and coffee should not be taken.

## Miscarriage

*Symptoms* – A lot of pain and bleeding from the uterus.

*Causes* – Congenital causes, imbalance of hormones, chronic constipation, excessive physical exertion, mental agitation, incompatible blood groups of husband and wife, high blood pressure, swelling in the kidneys, diabetes or any other disease.

*Treatment* – If there is slightest of bleeding from the vaginal path then the pregnant woman should immediately take bed rest. For two to three days she should lie on the bed. During the day for three to four hours, she should rest with her feet on a pillow instead of head on it. A pregnant woman should not lift weights. Morning and evening cold water wet sheet should be placed on the lower abdomen.

Balanced diet and sufficient quantity of fruits, milk, salads, sprouts and juicy food should be taken. Water chestnut (singhare) and black raisins are very good.

After the seventh month mostly uncooked foods should be taken.

Slight warm water enema, regular cold water hip bath, wet girdle pack can be used twice a day.

Imbalance of hormones gets rectified by yogasanas. For first two months sarvangasana, vajrasana, bhujangasana, shalbhasana, dhanurasana, paschimottanasana and konasana should be practised.

## Hair fall

Loss of hair at a very tender age has become a problem a problem for everyone these days.

*Causes* — Improper food and deficiency of vitamin B and natural salts and iodine, etc., tension, mental shock and other prolonged illnesses (typhoid, syphilis, cold, running nose, sinus, anaemia, cancer, etc.), not keeping the scalp clean, hereditary, deficient blood supply to the head, hormonal imbalance, excessive use of soaps, shampoos, etc. containing harmful chemicals in them, excessive use of hair dryer, ill effects of medicines, constipation, insufficient sleep and excessive mental work.

*Treatment* — Remove all the above noted causes. Make efforts to improve health generally. The food should be balanced and nutritious. For a week only fruitarian diet should be given. Cabbage, pineapple, amla can be used in the diet. Raw green vegetables, salads and seasonal fruits, sprouted cereals can be consumed in sufficient quantity. Chapatti made of flour with chaff, unpolished rice, fruits and vegetables should be included in your diet. Spinach and carrot juice is beneficial.

Always keep your scalp dry. Wash the head with curd. Massage the scalp with coconut milk, keep it for sometime and then wash your hair.

With your fingers massage the head daily before sleeping every night. Before a bath, for ten minutes rub the body.

Soak fenugreek seeds (methi) overnight and grind it in the morning into a paste and apply it on the hair.

Ground the leaves of beri and mix lemon juice in it. Apply this paste on the scalp which will help the growth of new hair. Application of fresh coriander juice and carrot juice into the roots of the hair stops hair fall.

On bald patches if onion juice is applied it leads to growth of hair. Grind carrot and apply the paste on the head and wash it after two hours.

For getting rid of baldness massage the head with coconut oil and lemon juice in it.

Daily massage the head with oil of blue bottle, processed in sun rays.

Washing the hairs by *reetha* and *sheekakai* is better for the health of the hairs.

After taking meals comb the hair and scratch the scalp with the comb. Daily two to three times for five minutes rub the nails of all the fingers against each other.

In open air breathe deeply and do exercises.

For a few days take mud pack on abdomen, enema, steam bath and hip bath.

Yognidra, vipareetkarni mudra, shavasana, sarvangasana, matsyasana and other topsy turvy asanas can be practised.

## Greying of hair

With ageing greying of hair is natural. But when untimely greying of hair occurs then it becomes a cause to worry, specially for women.

*Causes* — Mental tension, unbalanced food, deficiency of vitamin-B, iron, copper and iodine. Not cleaning the scalp properly, other diseases (sinus, chronic constipation, anaemia etc.) chemical based shampoos soaps and oils being used, hereditary and insufficient sleep, etc.

*Treatment* — Balanced diet with fruits, salads, sprout, green vegetables in sufficient quantity. Carrot, spinach and amla juice should be drunk. Eat black til and soya bean milk. Almonds and walnuts can be eaten. Ghee made of cow's milk be used. Daily a spoonful of triphala should be consumed.

At night amla and bhringraj can be soaked and in the morning head should be washed with its water or bathua leaves can be boiled and that water used for washing hair. Or the head could be washed with sour curd or lemon water. Washing hair with margosa leaves boiled in water is also useful.

Almond oil and amla juice can be mixed in equal quantities and the scalp massaged with it in the night.

At night ground basil and amla powder should be soaked in water and in the morning, the same water can be used to wash hair.

Amla powder mixed with lemon juice applied on hair makes them black soft and sturdy. Oil from sky blue bottle processed in the sun rays can be used for massaging. Remain free from mental tensions and worries. Yogasana, (sarvangasana, matsyasana shavasana) and yognidra can be practised. After meals scratch the head with the comb while combing hair.

Daily for five minutes rub all the finger nails of both the hands against each other two to three times a day.

## Magical hair oils

1. In an iron pot put one litre of coconut oil, 200 gms amla, 100 gms reetha and sheekakai powder, one big spoonful of henna and two spoons of ratnajot powder together and keep it in the sunshine for a week or boil it on slow flame. Then strain it and keep in a bottle with a lemon juice and camphor in it.

   *Benefit* — This blackens the hair, thickens them and makes them soft and long.

2. Half a kilogram of dry amla mixed with ¼kg mulathi powdered and soaked in water, eight times in quantity, at night. In the morning heat it on low flame till the water reduces to its half and then mix it well and strain it. This liquid be mixed in oil and heated up till such a time that the water evaporates. On getting cool mix some scent and colour as per your choice.
   *Benefit* – It cures, greying of hair and hair fall, continuous use blackens hair and makes them long and removes dryness on the head.
3. Take 250 gms of bottle gourd and grind it and strain it in a thin cloth, the remaining water can be kept aside. Then heat 250 gms of coconut oil on low flame and mix this water into it and let it boil. When all the water gets burnt then cool the oil and keep it in a bottle.
   *Benefit* – This strengthens the roots of the hair, cools the mind, and enhances memory power. Sometimes from the soles heat comes out, at such moment application of this oil gives relief.

## Halitosis (foul breath)

*Symptoms* – Bad smell in breath. Most of the people are completely unaware of this problem and the discomfort causes to others.

*Causes* – Bad teeth and gum conditions, chronic tonsilitis, chronic constipation, chronic gastritis, sinusitis, gastro-intestinal disorder, anaemia, smoking, chewing of tobacco etc.

*Treatment* – Remove the causes. Take juices for 1-2 days followed by uncooked food (fruits, vegetables, sprouts, etc.) for few days.

    Mud pack on abdomen, enema, kunjal.
    Do pranayama.
    Chew basil leaves or chew fresh mint leaves.
    Chew fresh coconut with basil leaves.
    Chew raisin and black pepper both together.
    Eat soaked fenugreek seeds.

Keeps the clove between the teeth.
Clean the mouth with neem (margosa) stick.
Do hot saline water gargles.

## Heart diseases

There are many diseases connected with the heart. Some of them are here under:

1. **Angina Pectoris** — In this fat gets accumulated under the internal lining intima of arteries causing more than 70% blockage, leading to improper supply of blood and oxygen to the heart. So the heart has to labour more and the result is this pain, which takes place for two to four minutes only. At this moment the patient is unable to walk or bend. This pain finds relief on taking rest or taking a sorbitate tablet.

2. **Coronary Thrombosis (Ac. Myocardial Infarction)** — Under the internal lining of the artery of the heart fat accumulates which causes blockage and also pressurises the walls of the artery leading to its cracking ultimately. As soon as it breaks due to certain chemical reactions, a thick clot of blood is formed and the blockage gets complete, i.e. 100%. It is extremely dangerous for the heart, since there is no blood supply, the muscles of heart are destroyed. It is also called heart attack.

3. **Arterio Sclerosis** — This is the disease of the artery walls which has its ill effects on the middle layer and later has its effect on the inner layers. Arteriosclerosis leads to loss of flexibility. Generally it occurs naturally but if it occurs at an early age and is too rapid then it becomes dangerous. It harms the coronary arteries and any part of body can get affected by it.

4 **Palpitation of Heart** — This leads to the heart beating rapidly. This disease is more common among women than in men. Weakness of the coronary muscles and nerves is the root cause of this. Very often during palpitation the hands get cold like ice.

5. **Enlargement of Heart**—When the quantity of toxins increases in the body then more pressure is put on the heart and to save this situation the heart gets enlarged. There are other reasons also for the enlargement of heart—blood pressure, weakness of heart valves blockage in the arteries of the heart, diabetes, alcohol, toxic substances, etc.
6. **Pericarditis**—When the outer membrane of the heart gets inflamed then there is mild pain and the pulse gets faster. Some times there is fever also. Sometimes there is accumulation of fluid in the membrane which makes the heart appear swollen. In this state breathing becomes difficult.
7. **Myocarditis**—The cardiac muscles get inflamed. Diabetes and pneumonia also cause this inflammation.
8. **Endocarditis**—This swelling is in the extreme interior of the heart.
9. **Valvular Disease**—Generally mitral valve gets affected and is called mitral stenosis, if hole enlarges it is called incompetence or both the problems can occur together. Aortic valve also gets affected similarly.
10. **Hypertrophy of the Heart Muscles**—When the cardiac muscle has to work excessively then they become thick. High B.P. is the main cause.
11. **Aneurysm**—The walls of arteries get weakened and balloon, sometimes it bursts. Then chances of survival are 20%.
12. **Fatty Degeneration**—Fatty patients have fat accumulation in their cardiac muscles also, like in the other parts. This leads to the destruction of the cells of cardiac muscle and in its place fat accumulates. Muscles with more fat become stiff. Consequently blood is not fully released. Along with this all the openings in the heart also becomes stiff which causes stenosis or regurgitation.. It leads to enlargement of heart.

13. **Irregular Heart beat**—In this the heart beat is not proper. Many causes of heart disease lead to discoordination in the heart beat.
14. **Tacky Cardiac**—Sometimes there is attack of rapidity in the pulse rate which can continue from few hours to eight days. During the attack the pulse rate is between 150 to 200 per minute.
15. **Slow Heart Beat**—Normally the pulse rate is 60-100, but sometimes the pulse rate falls. Healthy slow heart beat is an indication of good health. If the heart beat is less than 50 then it can be dangerous.
16. **Thrombosis**—Blood arteries have calcium, fat and cholesterol layers accumulated in them. If it gets accumulated in the arteries that carry blood to the brain then it could lead to paralysis. If the accumulation is in the arteries of the heart then it can lead to heart attack or angina.
17. **Rheumatic Heart Disease**—This is the result of rheumatic fever which affects the heart valves and joints in the body simultaneously and damages the heart valves. It can happen at any age but mostly it occurs between five to fifteen years of age. After fifty it does not occur.

*Symptoms of heart diseases*—Sudden excessive sweating, palpitation, heaviness in the chest, difficulty in breathing, feeling of suffocation, nausea, vomiting, vertigo or unconsciousness, burning sensation in the stomach, hand and feet getting cold, breathlessness caused by climbing up stairs.

If someone gets vertigo while getting up or lying down, and after a short while if it gets well then it should be treated as first indication of heart disease.

Sometimes it happens that the heart gets diseased but the symptoms are not clear.

Before the beginning of heart disease the patient feels difficulty in breathing. From this point of view it would not be wrong to say that asthma patients are basically heart patients also.

In a heart attack the pain in the heart is acute and generally the pain begins from the middle of the chest and spreads towards the left side. Sometimes it goes to the right hand shoulder and the lower jaw. This increases on walking or working too much. This ache continues for five to ten minutes or more, sometimes for hours together. There is associated sweating and breathing trouble.

## Check up and tests of heart disease

1. Physical Check up -Blood pressure and pulse rate is checked.
2. Blood Test— Serum Lipid profile, blood sugar rate is tested.
3. E.C.G. (Electro Cardiogram)—A change in the electrocardiogram indicates the existence of heart disease.
4. T.M.T.—This test is mainly done only when ECG shows no concrete result.
5. Echo Cardiogram—Generally this test is for the pumping power of the heart and the capacity of the valves.
6. Angiography—A long wire is used to put dye in the blocked artery to check the percentage of blockage.

## Confirmation tests of heart attack

(1) *E.C.G.* – In E.C.G. of a patient of heart attack very rapid changes are indicated. Elevated ST segment decide the heart attack.
(2) *Blood Enzyme Test* — Some muscles get damaged due to heart attack and from here some enzymes get into the blood stream. If these enzymes increase in the blood then that indicates heart attack. These enzymes are SGPT, CPK, CPKMB, LDH, SCOT.

## Causes of heart diseases

Excessive cholesterol, triglyceride, etc. in the blood, smoking and tobacco consumption, wrong way of living and food habits, meat, eggs, maida, sugar, salt, fried products, deficiency of roughage in food, excessive medication, tension, working beyond one's capacity, fatigue, anger, insufficient sleep, excessive sex, restlessness, worries, high blood pressure, diabetes, obesity, arthritis, fever, etc. are the causes of heart complications. Consumption of excess calcium tablets, deficiency of vitamin-D increases heart problems.

If the belly protrudes out more than the chest, there is possibility of heart disease. Sometimes it is hereditary also and sometimes it is due wrong lifestyle and improper diet also.

*Treatment of Heart Diseases* – One should guard against the causes of heart diseases. For heart patients fasting and food in little quantity is a boon.

Regular use of green leafy vegetables and sprouted food. Heart patient should take soya bean milk in place of animal milk.

Fast on coconut water, juices of green gourd, cucumber, spinach, carrot, beetroot, white pumpkin, etc. Fruits, salads should be consumed more. Pomegranate, amla, onion, garlic, sprouted alpha, lemon and honey water are very useful. Grapes and mango work like heart tonics.

Vitamin B controls cholesterol, that is why dough for chapatti should include chaff also. Sprouted food should be taken. Vitamin C converts cholesterol into bile salt, that is why lemon and amla are useful. Sesame (Til) milk compensates for deficiency of calcium.

Fenugreek seeds(methi) and black gram can be soaked at night in water and eaten along with its water. Bottle gourd juice with the leaves of basil and mint with pepper can be taken two to three times a day. Betel leaf, ginger, garlic, juice one spoonful mixed with one spoon of honey should be taken for 21 days continuously.

Lecithin which is available in green leafy vegetables in sufficient quantity prevents accumulation of fats in the arteries which is found in soyabean.

Mud pack on the belly, lemon water enema, twice chest pack, hip bath. After dry friction of the body cold water bath. During palpitation keep a thick water pack on the heart.

If the patient has cough then hot foot bath can be given. Sun bathing in the morning is efficacious. In the acuteness of ailment rest is the best medicine.

Arjun tree's peel can be soaked in water overnight and in the morning the water should be consumed after straining it. Heart ailments get cured from the root itself. The leaves of arjun tree are like jamun tree.

Wood of vijayshaar should be soaked in water and that water should be consumed in the morning. This wood can be used twice.

Cut peepal leaves from tip and bottom and make a soup which can be drunk thrice a day.

Walk for an hour in open air in the morning, yogasanas, (katichakrasana, vajrasana, padmasana, siddhasana, gomukhasana, tadasana, bhujangasana, konasana, naukasana, shavasana) breathing exercises should be practised. Practise heart mudra and yog nidra.

Keep away hurry, worry and curry.

Heavy food, chillies, spices, pickles, oily, fried products should be avoided.

## Hernia

Abnormal protrusion of any part out of its membrane is called hernia. It is of many types, and can be classified as per the part of the body affected.

1. **Hiatus Hernia**—Displacement of a portion of the stomach through the opening in the diaphragm through which the oesophagus passes is called hiatus hernia. This creates pain in the chest which moves to the left side and is sometimes mistaken for angina pain. It also gives pain under the throat. After meals the person feels

bloated and swallowing becomes difficult. It is very common. Most of the people above 60 suffer from it but the symptoms are not perceptible in many of them.
2. **Umbilical Hernia**—There is a protrusion of intestines near the navel. The navel is generally one or two centimetres below the centre of the body but when the intestine slips in the navel then it gets three centimetres above the centre, which looks very ugly.
3. **Femoral Hernia**—Part of intestines protrude out through femoral canal in front of the thigh joint and also effect the femoral artery which carries blood to the feet. It is common in women. It can be on any side or both the sides. It causes pain on coughing and near the thigh there is inflammation.
4. **Inguinal Hernia**—Protrusion through the inguinal canal alongside the spermatic cord in the male.
5. **Vaginal Hernia**—In the vaginal region intestines protrude out.
6. **Scrotal Hernia**—This creates swelling in the scrotum.

## Different states of Hernia

1. **Reducible Hernia**—When protruded hernia subsides then it is called reducible hernia.
2. **Irreducible Hernia**—When protruded hernia does not go back then it is called irreducible hernia.
3. **Strangulated Hernia**—When the protrusion has inflammation also then it is called strangulated hernia. There is cut of blood supply and the contents of hernia become gangrenous.

*Causes*—Chronic constipation, weakness, gas, suppressing the urinary and defecating urge, intoxication, tumour in the belly, due to obesity bulging of the belly, lifting weight, lack of exercise or hard work done by the body, applying pressure while defecating, wrong living and eating habits and overeating.

*Treatment* – When in acute condition fast on lemon water. Fast on juices weekly. Uncooked food (fruits, vegetables and sprouts) should be consumed in ample quantity.

Give up all food products creating constipation. Overeating should never be done. Fried food stuff and maida products must be given up completely.

Mud pack on the belly, enema, compress, hip bath and Sitz bath, dry friction and then bathing, hot foot bath. Drink water from blue bottle processed in sun rays. Almost 30 ml of this water should be drunk six times a day. The belly should be massaged with oil.

Paschimottanasana, yogmudrasana, garudasana, shalbhasana, sarvangasana halasana, matsyasana, urdhvasarvangasana, mandookasana, bhoonmanasana, koormasana, janushirshasana garbhasana and moolbandh are recommended.

One should practise tribandh and mahamudra. When suffering from hernia pain one should not indulge in physical exercises.

## High blood cholesterol

Excessive cholesterol is one of the main causes of heart trouble. This is a kind of fat in the form of very minute particles in blood. Cholesterol plays an important role in various activities of the body. This is necessary for creating the walls of tissues and assimilation of different hormones. It makes a covering for nerves and cells of the brain. It also creates bile juice for digestion. It makes fat to reach in different parts of the body and protects red blood cells. Mostly cholesterol is created in the liver, and some of it is received from food. Those who take a food which has too much cholesterol get high levels of cholesterol in their blood which is harmful for the heart.

This combined with protein is called lipoprotein. They are of two types. (1) Low density lipo protein, (2) High density lipo protein.

*Low Density Lipo Protein (LDL)* – This is a mixture of Tryglyceride (another name of oils) and protein. This is considered bad because it creates athroma in coronary arteries which consequently creates blockage in the artery and ultimately leads to heart attack.

*High Density Lipo Protein (HDL)* – This is considered to be good because it prevents creation of athroma.

If cholesterol is normal and the ratio of HDL is less or LDL is more, even then there is the possibility of blockage in the arteries.

*Causes* – Fried foods, animal milk and its products, heavy food consumed frequently, non-vegetarianism, eating eggs, junk food and fast food, etc. Alcoholism and smoking also increases cholesterol in the body. Mental tension also increases cholesterol, as tension increases the secretion of adrenal glands which affects the fat metabolism.

*Treatment* – It is necessary that LDL is reduced and all the food items which increase cholesterol should be given up as described above. Even the use of coconut or palm should be reduced.

Fibrous food, chapatti with chaff in the dough, unpeeled pulses, tomato, carrot, guava, green leafy vegetables, Cabbage, etc. should be taken. Vitamin B dominated food reduces LDL. Eat at least 50 grams of oat bran daily in any form. Carom seeds (*ajwain*) reduces cholesterol in the blood. Lecithin which is fatty food does not permit cholesterol to settle down in blood vessels and increases production of bile from the cholesterol hence reduces the cholesterol in the blood. Those who have high cholesterol must drink a lot of water. Coconut water is extremely efficacious. Coriander (*dhania*) water (water boiled with coriander in it) can be taken to remove excess cholesterol through urination.

Wheat grass juice, bitter gourd, isabgol reduces the cholesterol. Eat sprouted fenugreek seeds daily. Soak black gram overnight and drink that water in the morning. Chewing the black gram also benefits a lot.

Mud pack on the belly and hip bath are very useful. Steam bath is also good, but not for high blood pressure patients. Regular exercises and yogasanas reduce LDL and increase HDL.

## High blood pressure

High blood pressure is not a disease but a warning to set the system of the body right. High blood pressure is a curse of modern times which can lead to paralysis, failure of kidneys, defect in eyesight, extreme weakness and heart diseases, etc.

*Symptoms* – In the morning while walking there is pain behind the head and neck, restlessness, irritation, mental imbalance, headache, pain in the chest, perplexity, anger, poor digestive system, reddening of the eyes, palpitation, sleeplessness, bleeding from the nose, etc., and blood pressure measuring beyond normal.

*Causes* – Constipation, indigestion, increase of cholesterol in the blood, smoking, inefficiency of the kidneys, obesity, wrong food habits and way of living, acidic food products, salt, tea, coffee, sauce, fried spiced heavy food, etc. Working beyond one's capacity, lack of proper exercise and relaxation. During pregnancy toxaemia also causes high blood pressure.

*Treatment* – Remove the above stated causes. As far as possible live only on juices (cucumber juice, carrot juice, banana stem juice, beetroot juice, bathua and coriander juice, spinach juice, coconut water, lemon and honey water, bottle gourd juice, juice of the wheat grass) for a few days and thereafter for some days uncooked food (fruits, salads and sprouted).

Basil leaves and pepper should be taken together. In the morning basil leaves should be taken with honey.

In the morning take the juice of a lemon and one spoon of honey dissolved in water, it is very beneficial.

Drink water kept in a copper vessel overnight, use of triphla powder is beneficial. Two spoonful of fresh amla juice should be taken daily morning and evening. Daily drinking of three parts of carrot juice and one part of spinach juice cures all kinds of blood pressure, butter milk, water of coriander leaves, 25 ml of sweet margosa's juice is beneficial.

In high blood pressure six drops of garlic juice mixed in water should be taken four times a day. Raw garlic should be taken with honey or black raisins to cure high blood pressure. When the blood pressure gets normal use of garlic should be reduced gradually. Salt, ghee, pickle, chillies and spices and sweets should be avoided. Have weekly fast on juices. Vitamin C and potassium dominated food is especially beneficial.

Daily walk in the open air and deep breathing, cold water enema, mud pack and hot and cold fomentation on the belly, hot foot bath, spinal bath, hip bath, Sitz bath, chest pack, once a week wet sheet pack, rubbing of the body before and after bath. Jalneti, kunjal, shavasana are especially useful. Yognidra, gyanmudra should be practised. At the time of high blood pressure stop breathing from the right nostril and use the left one. Drink water before bath.

Yogasanas (shavasana, gomukhasana, ardhamatsyadrasana, vajrasana, padmasana, siddhasana, tadasana), pranayama (nadishodhan, sitkaari and shitali, should be practised without retention (kumbhak).

At the time of excessive blood pressure massage with ice over the head and spinal cord for five minutes.

Daily drink half a litre of water from a green bottle processed in sun rays. Massage with the oil of blue bottle processed in sunrays. Usually massage is done towards the heart, but in case of high blood pressure it is done in reverse direction.

Remove mental tensions and worries. High blood pressure patients are likely to get diabetes also.

## Hydrocele

Fluid gets collected in the scrotum and causes inflammation. Mostly scrotum on one side is stricken by the disease.

*Symptoms* – Without pain the size of the scrotum increases, sometimes they increase so much that walking becomes difficult. If there is pain and swelling, it indicates that infection has set in.

*Causes* – Accumulation of toxins in sex organs, wrong eating habits, other diseases suppressed with medicines, etc.

*Treatment* – Fast on juices for a week. For two weeks take uncooked food. In the morning daily take one glass of orange juice or pomegranate juice. Take raw salads with lemon juice in it.

Hip bath, Sitz bath, dry friction are very beneficial. Tub bath in hot saline water is also very useful. Fresh air and light exercises are quite necessary. Sun bathing is good.

## Hysteria

*Symptoms* – When a fit of hysteria takes place then hands and feet get stiffened up, the shape of the face gets distorted. Without any reason the affected starts yelling, grumbling and beating. Difficulty in breathing, pain in the chest and belly, feeling of something getting struck in the throat, paining on being merely touched by somebody, difficulty in looking at light.

In these fits a gas ball rises from the belly to the throat and the patient faints.

*Causes* – Mental or physical stroke, tension, worry, sadness, fear, constipation or any other diseases, menstrual disorder and grievances against the spouse.

*Treatment* – Loosen the clothes at the time of the fit and expose the body some fresh air. Rub the soles of feet and palms. At the time of unconsciousness, put the nail of your thumb in the nail of the thumb of the patient and poke it, to remove unconsciousness. Sprinkling of water on the face also removes unconsciousness. The patient should be made to smell asafoetida (heeng) and onion for bringing him back to consciousness.

For a few days try to be on juices and then on fruits and uncooked food and finally the patient should be brought back to balanced diet. Black Berry (Jamun) is very useful. The use of honey is beneficial.

Positive thinking should be developed. Necessary knowledge of copulating should be given to the patient. Practise dhyana and yognidra. Every day have bath in cold water and sun bath.

Practise padmasana, simhasana, vajrasana, tadasana, garbhasana, uttanpadasana, gorakshasana,

## Impotency

*Symptoms* – Weakness in erection of penis and premature ejaculaton is the first stage of impotency.

*Causes* – Overeating, excessive copulation, unnatural sex, masturbation, diseases of the digestive system (indigestion, constipation, acidity), diabetes, mental tension, fear of failure, feeling of insecurity, imbalance of endocrine glands, deficiency of vitamin E, psychological reasons, too much shyness, ignorance about copulation and other sexual diseases.

*Treatment* – To become strong, consumption of liquor, tobacco, cigarette, medicines, agitative products should be given up as they hamper life force and push the patient to more deterioration. They may give some excitement, but the end result is not good.

Begin with fasting remaining on a juicy diet and uncooked food for few days, come to a balanced and nutritious food later on. Carrot juice with honey, black raisins, dates, figs, coconut, soaked dry fruits can be eaten. Daily two almonds can be ground and mixed with honey and the mixture licked.. Daily for a week mix saffron (kesar) with milk and drink it up. Take wheat grass juice. Take mixed onion juice with honey.

Daily at night soak two spoonfuls of fenugreek (meethi) seeds and coriander powder and consume it with milk for a month. Amla powder with honey is recommended and milk and ghee should be consumed. Three grams of triphala powder, one gram of sesame oil, six gram honey should be given daily on an empty stomach. Daily put two to three dry dates in milk and boil, eat them and drink up the milk.

Basil seeds can be eaten with betel leaf and the root of basil chewed. Eat the overnight soaked black gram and the water can be drunk after mixing honey in it. Sesame milk is very good for male strength and formation of sperm.

The fruit of peepal tree should be dried in the shade and ground into fine powder and ten grams if it should be taken with hot milk daily. Daily 30 mg of black raisins should be consumed with milk. Daily take two spoonfuls of chestnut powder with milk for sperm formation. In winters bathua consumption increases formation of sperm and provides strength. Chestnut (Singhara) and aniseed (saunf) are beneficial. Raw turmeric juice, three spoons a day mixed with equal quantity of honey should be taken. 10-15 drops of garlic juice in a bowl of water be taken for a month.

Daily sprinkle water on the penis and scrotum. Give hot and cold fomentation to the penis. Castor oil should be massaged on the penis.

Remove constipation

Mud pack on the belly, enema, hot and cold hip bath, on the lower abdomen hot and cold fomentation, spinal bath, Sitz bath, can be tried..

Yogasana (sarvangasana, matsyasana, paschimottanasana, garudasana, shavasana, ardhmatsyendrasana, halasana, chakrasana, dhanurasana, suptvajrasana) and viparitkarni, yogmudra, ashwani mudra, pranayama, meditation and uddiyanbandh should be practised.

Agnisaar Kriya, Ashwini Kriya and Mool bandh are very useful and meaningful.

Six almonds soaked overnight with six black pepper and two grams fried ginger should be followed by milk. This should be done for 40 days for curing premature ejaculation. During this period do not have intercourse. Press the beginning of the wrist on both the hands. On the lower spinal cord and the penis, massage with oil from red bottle processed in the sunrays.

Do Mooladhar Chakra and Swadhisthan Chakra Power Promoting Exercises daily.

## Indigestion/dyspepsia

*Symptoms* – Loss of appetite, undigested food getting out as faeces, sweet and sour belches, nausea, disinterest in food, burning sensation in the throat and heart, gas formation, bad breath, feeling bloated, stomachache, vomit and accumulation of filth on the tongue.

*Causes* – Eating more than your appetite, eating rapidly, improper chewing, intake of too much heavy or oily food, stale or rotten food, not sleeping well, geeting down to work immediately after meals, fear, worries, jealousy, anger, tension drinking water along with food, tea, coffee, soft drinks, use of liquor, smoking, eating at irregular hours, consumption of incompatible food and lack of exercise.

*Treatment* – Remove the above stated causes. For one to three days fast on water, lemon water, coconut water, fruit juices of orange, pineapple, pomegranate, etc. and vegetable juices. Then for a few days fruit diet can be taken and then come back to normal food which includes fruits, vegetables, sprouts, etc, in ample quantity. Take tomato juice. Fenugreek seed soup should be taken. Take salad of cabbage.

Drink water half an hour before taking the meal.

Fried, roasted, spicy food, ,sweets and maida products should not be used. Whenever there is loss of appetite give up meals for one time or twice. Take meal only twice a day in routine.

Give up the habit of eating repeatedly, always eat slightly less than your appetite, eat saunf after meals. Pass urine immediately after meals and sit in vajrasana.

For increase in digestive power basil leaves or mint leaves can be ground and mixed in water to drink.

Use mud pack on the belly, enema, hip bath, kunjal and jalneti should be practised.

Yogasana (ardhamatsyendrasana, sarvagasana, uttanpadasana, suptpavanmuktasana, vajrasana, chakrasana, bhujangasana and shavasana ) should be done.

Yog mudra, kapalbhati, anulom-vilom, ujjai pranayama are helpful.

## Inflammation of nerves (neuritis)

In one nerve or more than one nerve inflammation takes place and efficiency of that nerve is affected.

*Symptoms* – Affected nerve has pain, pricking and burning sensation. In many patients the muscular portion around that nerve gets paralysed.

*Causes* – Wrong lifestyle and food habits, creates excessive acidity, unbalanced diet which causes deficiency of vitamins and minerals, injury and other infectious diseases.

*Treatment* – According to the condition of the disease, a few days fast in which carrot juice, beetroot juice, apple juice, pineapple juice, orange juice should be taken. Consume a balanced diet having fruits, vegetables and sprouts.

Tea, coffee, maida, refined, sugar, tinned food products should not be taken. Soya milk can be taken with honey. Bath with saline water specially on the affected area. Enema, spinal bath, hip bath, Sitz bath, yogasana, pranayama, dhyan should be practised.

## Insomnia

Insomnia is a disease of the civilised society. On an average an adult human being requires six hours of sleep. It is during sleep only that the tensed muscles and nerves get rest, and renovation of the cells takes place.

Sound sleep without any obstruction is necessary for a good health. Improper sleep can affect your health, lead

## Natural Treatment of Various Diseases

to lack of concentration, tired eyes, fatigue, emotional and mental stress and other diseases, etc.

*Causes* – Mental tension, worries, mental work beyond capacity or lack of physical work, anger, constipation, eating too much at night, eating late at night, excessive consumption of tea and coffee, sleeping on an empty stomach, smoking, gastric trouble, anaemia, taking a lot of medicines for treating certain diseases, etc.

*Treatment* – First of all avoid the causes of insomnia. For a few days try to remain only on the juices (orange, sweet lemon, cucumber, etc.) then seasonal fruits, then uncooked food (fruits, vegetables, sprouts, etc.) and then come back to a normal balanced diet.

Take bottle gourd with curd. Take milk, curd and butter milk. Take pepper, honey and with fennel seeds in curd. Drink lemon honey with water. Chew a bit of harad and suck its juice. Spicy and fried foods be given up.

Taking long deep breath, walk bare foot on grass. Regular exercises and running must be practised.

Enema, mud pack, jalneti, hip bath, Sitz bath, spinal bath, weekly wet sheet pack. Before going to sleep hot foot bath should be taken. While sleeping soles should be massaged with mustard oil.

Oil from blue bottle processed in sun rays can be applied on the head.

Surya namaskar, vajrasana, makarasana, sarvang-asana, matsyasana, uttanpadasana, paschimottanasana, halasana, bhujangasana and supt pavanmuktasana should be practised.

Shitali, Sitkari, Nadishodhan Pranayama, meditation should be practised.

## Intestinal worms

Worms generally thrive in children, but sometimes they are also found in adults.

1. *Thread Worms* – They are thread like in shape, white coloured a quarter of an inch to half inch long. They sometimes cause loose motions or constipation.
2. *Round Worms* – They are like earthworms and their length is a few inches. They cause nausea, vomits, loss of weight, fever, irritability, etc.
3. *Hook Worms* – They enter the body through the skin. They are very minute and are found in filthy water. Hook worms can cause anaemia.
4. *Tape Worms* – They are five to ten metres long and affect the brain also. They enter the body through half cooked meat.
5. *Giardias* – These are a kind of bacteria unseen by eyes. They cause weakness in the legs.

*Symptoms* – Indigestion, stomachache, paleness, loss of appetite, loose motions, itchy nose, clattering of teeth at night, swelling in the anus, irritability, sleeplessness, bad breath, dark circles around the eyes, urge to eat again and again, getting nightmares, nausea, vomits, loss of weight, fever, weakness in the legs.

*Causes* – Eating mud, eating without washing the hands, poking by a finger in the nose then putting the finger in the mouth, eating things fallen on the ground, sucking of thumb, continuous constipation and use of infected water.

*Treatment* – Remove the above said causes. As required, fast for first three days on lemon water. As per need fast may be on juices (carrot, raw pumpkin, coconut water and pomegranate, etc.) Thereafter as per requirement for a few days eat fruits, salads, etc. and then come down to normal food. A child should not be given milk but juices mixed with water.

Raw vegetables and ripe fruits which children can chew and eat must be prescribed. Butter milk is beneficial.

For tapeworm fast for a longer duration under the supervision of a naturopath.

Hot and cold fomentaton on the belly should be done. Mix honey and lemon in water and administer it in enema. Margosa leaves' water or asafoetida water can also be used for enema.

Mud pack, hip bath and shankh prakshlana are very effective. Nauli, uddiyan bandh, mayurasana, naukasana are beneficial.

## Some other home remedies

1. If one spoonful of mint juice is given in the morning and evening, it destroys worms.
2. Two parts of curd and one part of honey should be mixed and licked by the patient.
3. Three spoonfuls of pomegranate juice destroys worms in children.
4. Spinach leaves should be grounded with aniseed and mixed with water. Drink this as it helps remove worms.
5. Small children should be given heated up onion juice a spoonful in the morning and one in the evening to kill the worms.
6. Margosa leaves should be ground and mixed with water to drink.
7. A child who cannot take margosa water, he may be given a capsule filled with margosa leaves paste.
8. The juice of bel tree leaves destroys worms if one spoonful of it is taken in the morning and evening.
9. Fresh amla juice can be taken one spoonful in the morning and evening.
10. Bottle gourd (ghiya) seeds should be soaked and peeled and ground to mix in water. Drinking this worms are killed and even tape worms are removed from the body.
11. A spoonful of raw papaya juice with a spoonful of honey mixed in three to four spoons of hot water should be consumed to destroy round worm.

## Jaundice

*Symptoms* – Eyes, skin, urine, nails become pale. Stomach gets upset, constipation, loss of appetite, nausea, laziness, headache, sleeplessness, bitter taste in the mouth, pain in the liver and enlargement of liver, dark coloured urine, clay-coloured stool.

*Causes* – Blockage in the bile duct prevents bile to go to the intestines, instead it gets mixed up with the blood. Too much medication, for other reasons red blood cells get reduced in quantity, disease of the liver, too much copulation, gall bladder has stone formation or tumour, malaria, typhoid, pneumonia, heart disease, improper living, excessive eating, excessive use of salt and excessive intoxification, immaturity of the liver, which happens in a large number of new born infants. (This is usually normal, goes away on its own and results in no problems).

*Treatment* – As far as possible try to consume only lemon water and juices of orange, sweet lemon, grapes, apple, sugarcane, etc. If fresh grapes are not available then water of soaked raisins should be given.

Thereafter fruits and salads especially those rich in iron should be consumed. Bitter gourd juice mixed with water can also be taken. Spinach juice and figs are also very beneficial.

Radish juice mixed with lemon juice is good to drink. This should be taken twice a day.

Water from green bottle processed in sunrays can be taken. Enema, mud pack, cold hip bath, Sitz bath, hot and cold fomentation and wet sheet pack on the liver should be done.

Nadi shodhan pranayama, anulom-vilom pranayama, vipritkarni, yogasana, (uttanpadasana, bhujangasana, shavasana) are recommended.

## Kidney diseases

Kidneys in the body are extremely important as they take away waste matter from the blood to produce urine.

Some of the kidney problems are given as under:
1. Nephritis — Kidneys get inflamed which increases blood urea, serum critinine and blood pressure.
2. Nephroisis — Inefficiency of renal tubules or they get damaged. This causes swelling in the body and albumin increases in the blood.
3. Pynophritis — In this there is pus formation and swelling in the kidneys.
4. Chronic Renal Failure — This destroys the capacity to work. With high blood pressure level of blood urea, serum critinine, sodium and potassium level increases to dangerous proportions. In medical science to filter the blood temporarily, dialysis is done.

*Symptoms of kidney diseases* — Inflammation on feet and face and near the eyes, fever with cold, pain in lower back, pain or difficulty in urination, giddiness, restlessness, fatigue, albumin in urine, urea increases in blood, colour of urine becomes dark.

*Causes* — Increase of toxins in the body, overeating and erroneous food habits. Use of salt, sugar, spices, liquor and other agitative food stuffs. Constipation, other suppressed diseases, too much medication, deficiency of vitamins and minerals in food are some other causes of kidney diseases.

*Treatment* — Fasting is useful to take out toxins from the body and thus as per requirement fast for a few days on juices, (carrot, bottle gourd, cabbage juice, etc.). Raw potato and watermelon juice is very effective. After that for a few weeks take, mainly lemon, orange, papaya, banana, etc. Intake of food products rich in protein should be reduced. Water of soaked black raisins should be consumed.

Till the patient has not fully recovered salt should not be used.

Mud pack on abdomen and back, dry friction, hot water enema, hot hip bath, hot foot bath, sunbath, wet sheet pack, hot and cold fomentation on the lower portion of the back and wet pack should be done.

Complete rest is advised. Drink water from green bottle processed in sun rays.

Meditation and nadi shodhan pranayama should be practised.

If doing acupressure treatment press the portion below ankles with your thumb. Press the relative pressure points of lower part of vertebral column, kidneys, gall bladder and adrenal glands.

## Leucoderma

This is not a disease but unhealthiness of skin. Due to the deficiency of melanin pigment the skin becomes white. This does not spread with contact and is not hereditary either. It does not have physical pain, burning sensation or itching, etc. Only patches are there which appear ugly and cause mental tension and inferiority complex in the patient.

White patches are not incurable, therefore there need not be any feeling of inferiority or disappointment. If there are only a few patches then they can be treated easily and can be prevented from increasing, otherwise it takes a few months to some years to cure them.

*Symptoms* – On the skin of any part of the body a small spot initially from yellow colour becomes white and spreads to different parts of the body in the form of patches.

*Causes* – Consumption of unmatched food items, worms in the intestines, dysentry, constipation, diseases of the digestive system, reaction of skin diseases and ill effects of medicines consumed to suppress skin diseases. Strong antibiotics and strong medicinal reactions in typhoid, etc. Putting bindi on forehead of poor quality, ill effects of cosmetics like bleachers, synthetic clothes worn excessively, intoxication, adulterated food, consumption of excessive salt, and spices, hormonal imbalance, deep grief and mental shock, suppressing natural calls like vomit or stool or urination, asthma, eczema, diabetes, liver ailments, boils, injuries or burns.

*Treatment* – Initially try to take only the juices of fruits and vegetables. Thereafter for a year or two live on uncooked food (fruits, vegetables, sprouted cereals) and fortnightly fast on juices.

Carrot, beetroot, soaked or sprouted black gram, figs, dates, basil leaves, triphala mixed with little turmeric, margosa leaves are especially useful.

Drink water which has been kept overnight in a copper vessel. Avoid tea, coffee, sugar, salt, chillies spices, tinned food, intoxicating products, meat, egg, etc.

The most important is the cleaning of digestive system. For that mud pack on the belly, enema, hip bath, kunjal, steam bath should be taken daily, continuously for a few days. Then gradually reduce it. Lemon juice water, enema or neem (Margosa) leaves is very helpful.

Take wheat grass juice daily in the morning and evening.

A small spoonful of *baavachi* powder should be taken with water every morning and evening, which is very useful.

Massage with oil from green bottle and drink water from green bottle both processed in sunrays. Take sunbath positively.

Application of basil juice on the spots removes them over a period of time.

Massage with your own urine which is one week old for 5-10 minutes continuously in sunrays. This can remove the patches from the root itself.

## Leucorrhoea

*Symptoms* – Vagina secretes white or yellow or other mixed coloured fluid, which may cause itching in the vagina or around it. It can happen at any age, and almost all women are affected by it some time or the other. Sometimes secretion is negligible and women neglect it, but sometimes it is more. In some cases the secretion is odourless and in some the smell is horrible. Pain in hands, feet, waist, head, etc., burning sensation in urination, heaviness in the lower abdomen, constipation, weakness and restlessness, non-concentration in work excessive urination, loss of appetite, while walking heaviness in the loins, etc. The symptoms of this disease aggravate during menstrual period. This problems destroys beauty and health. If it is chronic then dark circles come around the eyes.

*Causes* – Too much toxins in the body, improper diet and wrong lifestyle, constipation, worries, lack of physical activity, deficiency of vitamins and minerals in the food, consumption of tea, coffee, sugar, salt, fried, roasted and spicy food products. Spinal problem, too much weight or being under weight, problems of endocrine glands, non-hygeinic condition of the vagina. Intercourse during menstrual bleeding, too much sex or dissatisfaction in sexual relations, masturbation, other diseases and excessive medication and irregular menstrual cycle.

*Treatment* – Fast on warm lemon water and juices (white pumpkin, coconut water, cabbage, etc). For one week take uncooked food (fruits, vegetables, sprouted food, etc.). Calcium and iron dominant food should be consumed. Fresh amla juice and black gram soup should be taken. Drink lemon water a number of times during the day. Abstain from taking sour things.

50 gms finger cut into long pieces should be boiled in 250ml water and strained. This should be drunk regularly for a few days. Basil juice be taken with honey mixed in it. Basil leaves juice mixed with rice starch can be taken regularly. The juice of doob grass or wheat grass can be taken daily.

Early morning for three days on empty stomach drink soaked rice water, it helps a lot. Drinking fresh boiled rice water from 3 to 7 days continuously is very beneficial.

Peepal tree fruit taken with milk cures chronic leucorrhoea.

Lukewarm water of margosa leaves or water of alum should be poured in the vagina (by vaginal douche).Take the vaginal douche and enema of Arjun tree peels. A soft cloth folded and soaked in cold water should be placed in the vaginal passage.

Mud pack, enema, hot and cold hip bath in the morning and in the evening, Sitz bath, sunbath, dry friction of the body. During menstrual period stop treatment and take rest. Worries, fears, mental tensions should be given up. At night for an hour wet pack on the waist should be kept.

Drink water from a green bottle processed in the sun rays. Nadi shodhan, ujjai, bhastrika pranayama, and moolbandh and uddiyanbandh can be practised.

Paschimottanasana, sarvangasana, halasana, padmasana, bhujangasana, shalbhasana should be practised. Acupressure can be done on the sides of both the wrists and below the ankle of both feet. It is very useful.

## Liver diseases

The main liver ailments are swelling of the liver (hepatitis), jaundice, cirrhosis of the liver, etc.

*Swelling of the Liver* — This is caused due to infection or accumulation of toxins. This is an acute disease which affects the efficiency of the liver and assumes dangerous proportion. It is called jaundice or cirrhosis of the liver.

*Symptoms* — Weakness, nausea, fever, headache, loss of appetite, pain and swelling in the liver. Some people get jaundice also. Jaundice has been described earlier also.

*Cirrhosis of the Liver* — Due to virus, toxins or lack of nutrients the cells of liver degenerate.

*Symptoms* — Repeated gastric problems or indigestion and sometimes vomiting or nausea. Sometimes pain in abdomen and loss of weight.

In the advanced stage of the disease foul breath is emitted, the skin gets pale, blood vessels of the abdomen get swollen.

*Causes of Liver diseases* — Mostly these are caused by alcoholism, tea, coffee, other exciting products, unnatural and fibre less food, much fatty and chemicalised food and malnutrition. Enlargement of spleen or any other disease or excess consumption of medicines like quinine, etc. are also the causes.

*Treatment of Liver Diseases* – If the liver is given rest then it has the capacity to heal itself. Fasting gives extreme relief to the liver.

According to need fast for a few days on coconut water, lemon water and water from a green bottle processed in sun rays.

The fast should be concluded with juice consumption. This includes amla, orange, sweet lemon, carrot, green vegetables, etc. alternatively. Then juice of fruits, fruits with pulp, salads, sprouted food and then a balanced diet should be adopted. Avoid cooked food for as long as possible.

Daily drink two to four glasses of water and then go for a walk, that helps in liver ailment. Do mud pack on abdomen, enema, abdomen compress, wet sheet pack, hip bath etc.

## Low blood pressure (hypotension)

The process of arteries throwing off blood in the system weakens. Exceedingly low blood pressure means that blood circulation is being slow, consequently the brain and different parts of the body do not get sufficient nutrition and the quantity of blood also goes down in the body.

*Symptoms* – Laziness, lack of concentration in any work, fatigue, headache, loss of memory, vertigo and depression.

*Causes* – Unbalanced food, deficiency of proteins vitamin B and C. Due to bleeding also blood pressure falls. In the state of anaemia, cholera, acute vomiting, typhoid, after getting burnt paucity of liquid in the body, excessive mental work, menstrual complications, problems of endocrine glands, mentally emotional and constipation, the blood pressure goes down. Low blood pressure is more common among women as compared to men.

*Treatment* – Medication is meaningless and also harmful in it. Sufficient water, juices, fruits, vegetables, sprouted pulses, soup, milk, curd, honey, soaked raisins, atta with chaff, mint water and juice of beetroot are very useful. On an empty stomach fresh leaves of basil should be chewed with honey.

Lukewarm water enema, mud pack on the belly, massage of the spine, wet sheet pack, weekly steam bath are helpful.

Before bathing for 10-15 minutes dry friction can be done.

## Low blood sugar (hypoglycaemia)

If the sugar content gets low in blood then it can affect the brain dangerously.

*Symptoms* – Between two meals peevish urge to eat sweets is the first sign.

When blood sugar level falls much below normal, symptoms such as nervousness, irritability, fatigue, depression, disturbed vision and headache appear. Other symptoms are sweating, trembling, absentmindedness, dizziness, palpitation of heart and some sexual disturbances.

*Causes* – Excess use of maida and sweets, mental tension, low blood pressure, disturbed function of liver and endocrine glands, wrong level of insulin in a diabetic.

*Treatment* – Remove the above said causes. Mint water, grapes juice, sweet lemon juice, sweet fruit juice, vegetable juice are specially beneficial.

Seasonal sweet fruits, vitamin B, C and E dominated food stuff be taken. Patients of low blood sugar should take meals at small intervals.

Refined food, coffee, alcohol, soft drinks should be avoided.

## Measles

This is an infectious disease affecting children. It spreads speedily from one child to another. That is why other children should not be allowed to come in contact with the diseased child.

*Symptoms* – Sneezing, running nose, reddening of eyes, dry terrible cough, fever upto 104°F. On third day of fever small red boil like pimples appear on the face and chest which remain there for four to five days. As they start disappearing cough and fever also subside. In measles sometimes there is pnuemonia.

*Causes* – Wrong lifestyle and unhealthy diet, unhealthy atmosphere, dirty clothes, dirty bed, sleeping in closed room, etc which leads to low resistance to infection.

*Treatment* – Give only liquid diet, mainly orange juice, lemon water, then fruits and then normal food.

Heavy food, roasted, fried, salt, chillies, spices, sweets, etc should not be given. On the abdomen wet mud pack, hot water enema, wet sheet on the chest, margosa leaves boiled in water for sponge and bath.

Mulethi powder with honey should be given.

Grinded clove with honey should be administered. Take a small quantity of turmeric with honey. Half to one gram brinjal seeds can be taken. Keep the doors, windows open with slight sunshine coming in.

The patient's body can be kept warm. Put hot water bottle under the soles of the feet to keep the body warm. The patient should take full rest. After the fever is over and other symptoms subside, rest should be given for another 24 hours.

## Weak memory

*Symptoms* – Forgetfulness, slight headache, inability to tolerate noise, lack of concentration.

*Causes* – Low level of intelligence, low blood circulation in the brain, getting embroiled in own problems, excessive mental pressure, some injury or disease.

*Treatment* – Stop taking tea, coffee, sugar, maida, liquor, soft drinks, etc. Roasted and fried food, chillies and spices should be given up.

Take a balanced diet which includes fresh fruits, vegetables, sprouts, etc. sufficiently. Take cow's milk or sesame (til) milk. Grapes and apple are very useful. Four or five walnuts and two figs should be eaten. Soaked almonds can be chewed well. Black raisins can be eaten after soaking them.

Basil, almonds, black pepper can be grinded and mixed with honey for eating. Basil juice with honey should be consumed every day. In the morning five basil leaves should be taken with water.

Almond oil can be put in the nose. Jalneti, tub bath, hip bath, Sitz bath should be taken. Shavasana, yognidra, dhyan be practised. Vajrasana, paschimottanasana and nadishodhan and bhastrika pranayama should be done. Gyan mudra is very effective.

## Meningitis

*Symptoms* – High fever, stiffness in the neck and back, the patient lies with his knees folded towards the chin and the eyes turned away from light. There are rashes on the skin, constipation and vomiting. Patient becomes drowsy, confused and may be unconscious.

*Causes* – This is an infectious disease caused by bacteria or virus. This infection is transmitted through the ailments of the throat, lungs, ear, nose, etc. Tuberculosis also causes this in the brain. An injury on the head or scalp also causes this ailment.

*Treatment* – For a few days the patient is kept on complete rest, and given only orange juice. This will increase energy and urination to take toxins out of the body which leads to increase in resistance power.

The use of garlic is very useful, drink lemon and honey water. Margosa leaves juice should be mixed in water to drink.

When the fever gets normal and the tongue is clean then juicy fruits should be taken for the next five days.

Hot water enema can be given. If fever is 102°F then keep a wet sheet on the forehead. If the fever does not go down then use wet sheet pack. Hot and cold fomentation should be done on the spinal cord.

Lie in a tub full of saline water for 20 to 25 minutes.

## Menopause

Around the age of 40 to 50 years menstrual bleeding stops naturally which is called menopause. Menopause happens in three following ways—
1. If the body is healthy, then without any trouble the menstrual bleeding comes to an end and the woman does not even feel it.
2. The menstrual bleeding reduces gradually before a final close.
3. The menstrual cycle becomes irregular and the difference between two cycles goes on increasing.

If menstrual bleeding does not occur for six months then it may be deemed that menopause has taken place. In case after six months once again menstrual bleeding takes place then it is post menopausal bleeding and in this condition a lady doctor should be consulted without delay for proper treatment and diagnosis.

During menopause the body experiences some changes which frighten and upset women. They are all natural symptoms of menopause. In medical terminology these symptoms can be called menopausal syndromes.

*Symptoms(Menopasual syndrome)* – Hot flushes, sweating, inadequate sleep, depression, palpitation, feeling of pin pricks on hands and feet. Headache, ringing sounds in the ear, irritability, pain in joints, pain in the waist, endocrine glands also get affected and voice becomes harsh, growth of moustache and beard, obesity, dry skin, falling of hair, fatigue, weakening of the brain and lack of mental concentration.

Some women suspect that menopause means beginning of old age and end of their beauty or sexual life getting upset. But all these apprehensions are wrong.

*Treatment* – If the woman is taking proper diet and leads the right kind of a life and has been following a proper daily routine then even after menopause her health and beauty is maintained. On the contrary sometimes it becomes better and attractive than before.

During menopause a woman's physical, mental and emotional state is very delicate. Thus all the members of the family must be sympathetic and cooperative specially the husband. Due to carelessness at this time, there could be a disease connected with the uterus or the woman can be come psychotic. If the symptoms of menopause are excessive, it indicates that there is too much toxins. She should strive for complete natural health.

She should eat food dominated by vitamin C, D, E and calcium which includes fruits, vegetables, sprout, coconut powder and dryfruits in ample quantities. Even fruit juice should be taken adequately. Beet root juice is very useful, it should be taken in small quantity.

Sesame (Til) milk is very useful. Heavy foods, maida, sugar, chillies spices, etc. should not be taken. A spoonful of carrot seeds should be boiled in a glass of cow's milk for 10 minutes and be consumed daily as medicine.

Constipation should not be allowed. If necessary apply mud pack on the abdomen and also enema.

Daily morning walk, jogging, swimming, horse riding, cycling, etc. postpones menopause. Yogasana, pranayama, dhyan, yognidra, etc. are helpful in this period.

## Menstrual disorder

*Symptoms* – At the age of 11 to 14 menstrual bleeding from the vagina begins and continues till the age of 45 to 50 years and then stops. This bleeding continues from three to five days. Generally if there is a gap of 28 days then it should be considered normal. If sometimes early or sometimes late then it is irregular. In the beginning for a year or two if it is irregular, then need not worry. During pregnancy and breast feeding menstrual beeding stops. Following are the main complications of menstrual cycle :

1. Amenorrhoea – If menstrual bleeding does not start till the age of 16 then it is called amenorrhoea. If once the menstrual bleeding begins and then after a period of time it stops then it is called secondary amenorrhoea.
2. Dysmenorrhoea – Extreme pain in the lower abdomen one or two days before monthly menstrual bleeding is dysmenorrhoea.
3. Metrorrhagia – Irregular menstrual cycle.
4. Poly Menorrhoea – Regular menstrual cycle with a gap of less than 21 days is Poly Menorrhoea.
5. Menorrhagia – Regular menstrual cycle getting prolonged due to bleeding for many days.
6. Hyper Menorrhoea – During regular menstrual cycle excessive bleeding is there.
7. Hypomenorrhoe – During irregular menstrual cycle in normal days very little bleeding is there.
8. Meno Metrorrhagia – Irregular menstrual cycle and excessive bleeding for more days than the normal duration.
9. Post Menopausal Bleeding – After menopause recurrance of bleeding.
10. Break Through Bleeding – Bleeding between two menstrual cycles. If it is sometimes caused due to eating pills for contraception.
11. Pre-menstrual syndrome – This is found in at least 40% of the fertile women. The symptoms are – headache before menstrual bleeding, nausea, anger, fatigue, stomach ache, swelling on hands and feet, tension, pain in the waist.

*Causes of menstrual disorders* – Wrong way of living and diet, not observing abstention during menses, constipation, lack of physical activity, dissatisfied and restless mind, polluted atmosphere, nervous weakness, hormonal complication, complications of the sexual organs, mental tension and other diseases.

*Treatment of menstrual disorders* – As per requirement fast for few days on juices. Coconut water, barley water, coriander water, buttermilk should be taken in sufficient quantity. Pomegranate, cabbage juice and grapes are very good. Beetroot juice should be taken 70-80 ml twice or thrice a day. Raw bitter gourd juice is recommended. For five days live on uncooked food (Fruits, vegetables, sprouted pulses, coconut powder, etc.) and then come back to normal diet with adequate quantity of fruits, vegetables and sprouted daals and pulses.

Boiled vegetables with a little salt and black pepper be taken. Avoid chillies and spices, roasted fried and heavy food, tea, coffee, maida products, sugar, cake and tinned products.

Reduce the use of salt. Take amla juice with honey on an empty stomach. At night soak ten raisins and five almonds and eat them up with milk in the morning.

Fenugreek seeds should be soaked for four hours and boiled in that water till the water is reduced to ¼ of its quantity and strain it and drink with honey in it. One spoonful of basil juice, equal quantity of honey, a small quantity of black pepper should be mixed in it and taken twice a day for two months.

Dry the fruit of peepal tree and strain it in a cloth and eat regularly. Boil coriander seeds and drink that water regularly. Similarly, ginger boiled in water also helps. Boil *bathua* to drink. The powder of the root of basil should be taken with betel leaf. One spoonful of sesame well ground should be eaten with hot water. Triphala powder can be taken with turmeric powder.

Relaxing adequately is necessary. Deep breathing while going for a morning walk is important.

Negative thinking, should be given up and positive attitude adopted.

Bhujangasana, shalbhasana, vajrasana, paschimottanasana, konasana, ardhamatsyendrasana, shavasana, and yognidra should be practised. Moolbandh is very useful. Mud pack, enema, hip bath, dry friction of the body can be done. Wet girdle pack should be done twice a day on an empty stomach. Application of red oil on the waist is beneficial.

*Note* – During bleeding mud pack, wet girdle pack, yogasana, etc. should not be done.

## Migraine (hemicrania)

*Symptoms* – On one side of the head there is extreme pain. With this nausea, vomiting, irritability and disturbance in vision also occurs. Generally attack of migraine comes at regular intervals.

*Causes* – Chronic constipation, running nose, cold, physical complications, unbalanced diet and living, lack of work and relaxation, mental and physical tension, medication, menstrual complications, sight problem, liver complication or weakness, etc. and other diseases.

*Treatment* – Fast on juices (carrot juice, beet root juice, cucumber juice, cabbage juice, coconut water, etc.). Thereafter uncooked food (fruits, salads, sprout) should be taken and then normal diet.

Coriander, chaulai, methi, bathua, figs, amla, lemon, pomegranate, guava, apple, etc. should be taken essentially.

Wrong eating habits and eating late in the night be should given up. Tinned, stale, spicy and sweet products should not be taken.

Daily for a few days take juice of basil leaves with honey every morning and evening. Juice of doob grass can also be taken. Juice of tender leaves of Peepal be sucked. Tie up cabbage leaf on the forehead.

Take steam inhalation by nostril. Change the breath (swar). For a month do jalneti daily. Kunjal, spinal bath, Sitz bath, hot foot bath should be done. Dhyan, shavasana, yognidra, yogasana and pranayama can be practised regularly.

## Mucus

*Symptoms* – Defecating faeces with mucus in it, reluctance and loss of appetite, lack of courage, laziness, disinterest in work, feeling depressed, etc.

*Causes* – Weak digestion which causes digestive juices to become slicky and get out of the body with faeces.

*Treatment* – Fast for a few days on juices (coconut water, white pumpkin juice, cucumber juice, lemon water, orange juice, pineapple juice, and butter milk, etc.) Thereafter remain on a fruitarian diet. Then fruits, salads, sprouted food stuff can be taken for a few days and finally come back to a normal diet including uncooked food.

During this period mud pack on the abdomen and enema be done along with keeping a weekly fast. This ailment takes a lot of time to get cured. Therefore, there is no need to worry.

Hot water with curd churned very well with slight salt should be used for enema. This takes out the mucus stuck in the intestines.

## Multiple sclerosis

This is a chronic and ever aggravating nervous disorder. This destroys myelin which provides covering for the nerves, consequently the communication process of nerves gets disturbed and the affected portion slows down or stops functioning. This is more common among women.

*Symptoms* – The symptoms of this disease are different among different patients. Initially the symptoms are prominent and then disappear for weeks, months or even years. This can attack any time again or never in life.

In the beginning excessive fatigue, imbalance and lack of coordination is experienced, numbness and weakness of limbs, loss of sexual sensation, eye problems occur, speech gets defective and loss of urinary bladder control. The patient may have one or more symptoms depending on the location and extent of damage to the nerve tissues.

*Causes* – Accumulation of toxins due to unbalanced diet and living, acute diseases, mental tension, etc., patients with in the past two years may have experienced some mental stress.

*Treatment* – For four to five days fast on juices of fruits and vegetables. During this time take hot water enema. Thereafter take uncooked food (fruits, vegetables, sprouts etc.)

Take all seasonal fruits and vegetables, they are beneficial. Carrot, cabbage, cucumber, radish, beetroot and tomato are specially good.

Vitamin B and E are very important. They are available in ample quantities in sprouts. Take mud pack on abdomen, enema, steam bath, spinal bath. Do not let the patient get tired. Stay away from mental worries. Yogasana, shavasana and yognidra should be practised.

## Mumps

This is an infectious disease caused mainly in the salivary glands and gonads. This generally occurs till 15 years of age. Once if it occurs then it rarely repeats.

*Symptoms* – First inflammation takes place around one ear on the lower side and extends up to the jaw with a lot of pain. Then the second side also shows the same symptom. Chewing and swallowing becomes difficult. If this disease attacks elders then it is more problematic. Ovaries of women and testicles of men also get inflamed. It also affects the reproductivity of many patients.

*Causes* – It is an infectious disease which is caused due to accumulation of toxins in the body.

*Treatment* – As long as there is fever rest completely. For a few days take fruits and vegetable juice, thereafter take salads and fruits.

# Natural Treatment of Various Diseases

Saline gargles, hot water enema, hot and cold fomentation are recommended.

*Local treatments* —

Grind harad and paste over the inflamed portion. On peepal leaves apply ghee and heat them and tie upon the swollen area, that provides relief.

Ground ginger should be put on the inflamed portion.

Margosa leaves should be ground and mixed with turmeric for application on the inflamed portion. Mud pack can be used on the affected portion.

## Muscle cramps

*Symptoms* — Stiffness in muscles can happen in any part of the body but it is generally in the legs.

*Causes* — It is generally due to inability to absorb vitamin B, D, natural salts, calcium, potassium and magnesium. Other causes are mental tension, irritability, psychological and hormonal.

*Treatment* — Balanced diet which should include fruits, salads, sprouts, etc in ample quantities should be taken.

Fenugreek seeds, kalaunji and sesame are very useful. Drink honey and lemon water.

Massage the affected part with mustard oil or coconut oil mixed with camphor.

The food should be calcium and magnesium dominated. Green leafy vegetables, milk, buttermilk (*mathha*), *khubani*, sesame, etc. should be taken.

Do not eat sour fruits, Amla juice be taken daily,

Sesame (til) milk is very useful, Massage and apply hot and cold fomentation.

## Nervous weakness (neurasthenia)

This is a disease of the modern civilisation.

*Symptoms* – Sleeplessness, indigestion, irregularities related to sex, fear, anger, worries, jealousy, tension, unable to concentrate on any work, distrust, uncertainty, loss of interest in work, doubt, weakness in body, loss of courage, tendency to commit suicide, loving to be alone and not finding peace anywhere.

*Causes* – Excessive mental and physical work, mental tension, depression, use of intoxicating products, unbalanced diet and living, too much of sex and deficiency of metal in the body.

*Treatment* – Such a patient needs a lot of sympathy. Talk sweetly with him. Permit the patient to sleep as much as he does, never wake up in the midst of sleep.

Remind the patient of the success achieved in the past, the good deeds done in the past, the places visited by him and good remembrances, his wishes be given importance and should not argue with the patient.

Involve the patient in games, laughter and jokes for entertainment. According to his needs he should be given rest. Food should be as per patient's choice. No pressure is to be put on him.

Carrot and cucumber juice, coconut water, juice of doob grass, black raisins should be soaked overnight and eaten in the morning and its water drunk.

Drink water immediately after getting up in the morning.

Make chapatti with chaff.

Sprouted gram, moong, groundnut and seasonal fresh fruits and raw salad should be taken.

Curd is very good.

Give up sweets and heavy food.

Drink water from blue bottle processed in sun rays.

Enema, mud pack, hip bath, Sitz bath, weekly wet sheet pack, hot and cold fomentation of the spinal cord should be done, A wet towel can be kept on the head.

Morning walk is efficacious. Uttanpadasana, sarvangasana, pavanmuktasana, chakrasana, ardhamatsyendrasana, shavasana, yog nidra and dhyan should be practised.

## Obesity

*Symptoms* – Accumulation of fat in the body is obesity. It is not a disease itself but opens doors for many other diseases like diabetes, blood pressure, heart disease, ulcer, paralysis, skin trouble, sleeplessness, arthritis, asthma, sterility, impotency, etc.

*Causes* – Overeating, laziness and too much sleeping, lack of exercise and a habit of keeping seated, excessive consumption of fatty food, maida, sweets, salty, roasted and fried products, liquor, smoking, tea, coffee, betel, tobacco, etc. Tension, hereditary, disorder of endocrine glands and excessive medication.

*Treatment* – Gradually reduce food consumption, live on juices then as per requirment live on uncooked food.

Later get back to normal diet including chapatti with chaff, boiled vegetables, butter milk without butter should be taken. In the morning on an empty stomach drink lukewarm lemon water.

Chew food to make it fine as liquid in the mouth. Ghee, sweets, roasted and fried food stuff should be kept away. Must urinate after eating food. At night take triphala. Drink 10-12 glasses of water daily.

Daily take one glass of water with basil juice. Apply mud pack on the abdomen, hot and cold fomentation on the abdomen, enema, hip bath, kunjal, steam bath, abdomen compress, weekly wet sheet pack, shankh prakshalana, sun bathing, hot foot bath dry friction of the body are helpful, Tub bath should be taken with hot saline water.

Water from orange bottle processed in sun rays should be taken. In the morning walk breething deeply and for two minutes laugh loudly.

Do cycling exercise by both legs and hands in morning and evening. Do sun mudra. Pashimottanasana, suptpavanmuktasana, bhujangasana, shalbhasana, katichakrasana, and vajrasana be done. Uddiyan-bandh and moolbandh should be practised.

Breathing exercises are very important. Practice agnisaar kriya and kapalbhati pranayama.

## Oedema (dropsy)

*Symptoms* – Swelling on any part of the body like hands, feet, face, chest, abdomen or on many parts.

*Causes* – Accumulation of toxins in the body. This is mostly in case of heart and kidney ailments and shows over the face and below the eyes and is generally more in the morning. Liver ailments and hormones can also be the cause. Sometimes in the pre menstrual phase and pregnancy also there is swelling. Imbalance of the thyroid also causes this ailment. If it is due to allergy then there is swelling along with itching.

*Treatment* – Upto four or five days as per need take juice diet ( juices of orange, pomegranate, sweet lemon, carrot, green gourd, white pumpkin and coconut water etc.) then green vegetable soup and a fruitarian diet should be taken. Use of pineapple is efficacious. In the morning chew garlic and take bitter gourd juice.

Salt, chillies, spices, deep fried and fried food stuff and heavy food should not be taken.

Margosa leaves are very useful. They should be chewed and ground to be taken with water.

Water from green bottle processed in sunrays should be taken. Enema, mud pack on the abdomen can be used. Slight sun bathing is necessary.

## Osteoporosis

The bones can get brittle at any age but mostly after the age of fifty it is common, that too among women, it begins with menopause.

*Symptoms* – Pain in feet, bending of the back, hip bone becomes thin, the capacity to turn around reduces stiffness in the waist muscles, breaking of bones at the slightest of jerk.

*Causes* – Unbalanced diet, deficiency of calcium and vitamin D, smoking, liquor alcohol, hormonal imbalance after menopause, non absorption of calcium in the body. Lack of physical exercise, alcohol, smoking, excessive use of tea, coffee, soft drink, sugar, etc. Steroids, diuretic, painkillers and medicines used for blood pressure.

*Treatment* – From 4-5 days fast on fruits and vegetable juices (like orange, lemon, pineapple, papaya, green vegetables, cabbage, radish leaves, beetroot, etc).

Thereafter have a balanced diet of fruits, vegetables, coconut powder and sprouted.

Take milk of sesame. Dry fruits be taken. Do not overeat but chew well. Heavy food, roasted and fried, sweets, sugar, maida, etc be kept away.

Mud pack on abdomen and enema should be administered.

Regular exercises are recommended. Sunbath and drinking water from white bottle processed in sun rays.

## Paralysis

Whenever any blood vessel has obstruction in the brain and whichever part does not get blood becomes inactive and the parts controlled by that part of the brain also do not work as they do not get directions from the brain. Left part of the brain controls right part of the body and right part of the brain controls left part of the body (except the eyes). This is a nervous disorder and is connected with the spinal cord.

### *Different types of paralysis:*

1. **Hemiplegia** – This affects one half of the body either right or left.
2. **Paraplegia** – This affects both lower limbs.
3. **Monoplegia** – This damages only one leg and one arm.
4. **Quadriplegia or Diplegia** – This affects all the four limbs.
5. **Myelitis** – Inflammation of spinal cord could be due to viral infection, tuberculosis, syphilis etc.
6. **Bulbar Paralysis or Aphasia** – When nerves responsible for speech get paralysed and the tongue gets stiffened causing difficulty in speech.

7. **Facial Paralysis** – A part of the face gets stiffened and twisted. One corner the mouth is pulled low and the cheek on one side gets loose. Unknowingly saliva drops out of the mouth and the patient can not spit out straight.
8. **Vocal Cords Paralysis** – In the throat there is the vocal cord and when it gets paralysed then human being stops speaking altogether or partially.
9. **Lead Paralysis** – On the edges of jaws a blue line appears which is a special symptom to diagnose the ailment. Mostly the right hand and when the disease is acute then both the hands get affected, the wrist muscles become weak and retroverted. The muscles of arms and back get diseased.

*Symptoms of Paralysis* – One or more parts of the body stop functioning. Its attack occurs all of a sudden but actually the disease begins much before it. Paralysis on the left side of the body is more dangerous as it can stop the heart beat and fear of death is there.

If the patient of paralysis is able to feel pinch then he can be cured of his ailment with the ordinary treatment

## Symptoms before the attack of Paralysis

1. Any part of the body has vibrations and itching.
2. The side which is going to paralyse, the nostril of that side specially itches.
3. The part which is going to be affected, its nerves become weak and the part feels non existent.
4. The mind is not enthusiastic, there is disinterest in doing any work, and the capacity to indulge in sex lowers.

## Symptoms of curable Paralysis

1. If the disease has struck recently and its attack is ordinary.
2. If the patient is of a lower age and the life force in him is still substantial.

# Natural Treatment of Various Diseases

3. There is no other complication apart from paralysis.
4. The digestion is good.
5. If after attack the affected part appears normal in colour and shape and its size does not reduce or expand as compared to the position before the attack.

## Symptoms of uncurable Paralysis

1. Pregnant, post natal stage, child and old who are very weak.
2. The colour of the affected part has changed completely or has become very thin or small.
3. If the disease is caused due to breaking of the muscle completely.
4. If the patient is unable to feel the needle's prick or pinch.
5. If the patient is lacking intelligence and his activity is also hampered.
6. If there is continuous flowing from the mouth, nose and eyes.
7. If the patient is unable to swallow water and the eyes are transfixed.
8. If the power to see, hear and touch is no longer there.
9. If the patient has other disease also.

*Causes* — Wrong way of living and improper diet, any sudden happening, extreme happiness or sorrow, too much indulgence, excessive mental work, deficiency of elements, harmful injury of the brain and the spine, experiencing headache excessively, accumulation of poisonous elements in the body, various diseases of the spine and brain, high blood pressure, chronic heart disease, arthritis, epilepsy, etc. keeping awake at night, excessive medication, excessive intoxication, reading writing too much, strain and mental tension etc.

*Treatment* — Daily give lemon water enema, and make the patient sweat daily. Steam bath, hot wet sheet pack, sun bathing, etc. are helpful. If the patient is very weak or suffers from high brood pressure then too much heat need not be given. Hot and cold fomentation on the spine, wet sheet be put on the abdomen and spinal cord, on the belly mud pack should be applied, hip bath and gyan mudra should be practised. Water from yellow bottle processed in the sun rays can be given, half a cup four times a day. Affected portion should be given red light and hot and cold fomentation.

From three to ten days only juices should be taken (lemon water, coconut water, fruits and vegetable's juice, amla juice with honey.).

To get rid of paralysis juice of apple, pears and grapes should be mixed in equal quantity, it is very efficacious. The juice of wheat grass is very beneficial. Thereafter for a few weeks uncooked food be taken (fruits, vegetable and sprouted). Daily eat soaked fig. Sufficient quantity of water should be consumed. Paralysis patient unless is well need not take cold water and not even bathe in cold water. The place of living should be kept warm. Dry friction or massage should helps, but massage should be done slowly.

Complete mental and physical relaxation is necessary. This is why dhyan and yognidra have a special place.

In this disease, physical exercises contribute a lot. Sometimes the nerves which are pressed, regain their shape with exercise and become active.

## Parkinson's disease

*Symptoms* – Parkinson's disease does not occur all of a sudden. This is an old ailment of the brain which gradually affects the patient that is why the disease is diagnosed after a long time. Its main symptom is trembling in hands and feet. Some times this symptom is reduced slowly and then it subsides. In many patients the symptom of trembling are not perceptible but they become unable to write and the hand writing is not legible, the letters get zig zag. The grip of the hand weakens, causing difficulty in holding anything. Sometimes even the jaw muscles, tongue muscles

# Natural Treatment of Various Diseases

and muscles of the eyes experience trembling. As the disease grows the muscles become stiff and solid. The patient's walk becomes irregular and beyond his control. While walking he could fall. Saliva drops out of the patient's mouth, and he loses balance of the body. His voice gets low, wobbly, with a tremor, the person begins to stammer and speech is not clear. The capacity to think reduces, the patient prefers to sit quiet. Normally a patient of Parkinson's disease suffers from constipation, sweats more, experiences difficulty in urination and turning the neck. Mentally the thinking is rigid, destructive, negative and irritable.

*Causes* – Negative thinking, mental tension, brain injury consumption of sleeping pills or medicines for depression.

Those who indulge in consumption of tobacco, smoking, fast foods, liquor, intoxicating medicines, etc, among them this disease is prominent. Continuous deficiency of vitamin E is also a cause of it.

*Treatment* – For four to five days live on lemon water, coconut water, juices of fruits and vegetables. Thereafter for eight to ten days live on uncooked food (fruits, vegetables and sprouted etc.).

The milk of soya bean and sesame or goat's milk should be used. Green leafy vegetables can be consumed in the form of salads. Vitamin E dominated food is specially useful. Do not take tea, coffee, intoxicating stuff, salt, sugar, tinned food, etc. Practise meditation and light yogasanas. Morning walk in open air with deep prolonged breathing is very good. Have positive thoughts and try to be happy.

## Piles

*Symptoms* – Just at the mouth of the anus, there is swelling either outside or inside. It can also bleed. After passing stool a burning sensation is experienced. On the mouth of the anus itching creates difficulty in sitting properly. It can be of two types, one causing bleeding and the other without bleeding.

*Causes* – Its main cause is constipation. To hold the urge of defecation, washing arms with hot water after defecating, applying pressure while defecating, spicy food, heavy and stimulating food, tension, intake of medicines, staying awake at night and less use of fruits and vegetables.

*Treatment* – For two days fast on liquid diet, then for two weeks remain on uncooked food, weekly fast, in the morning and at night eat two soaked figs and drink the water there of and take triphala powder.

Two spoonful of black til chewed along with cold water regularly, can cure the most chronic piles. Jaggery mixed with bel powder should be consumed. Tea, coffee, chillies spices are prohibited. Drink water of green bottle processed in sunlight.

Avoid prolonged sitting or standing positions.

Drink at least 8-10 glasses of water every day.

Apply mustard oil in the anus (Ganesh Kriya) daily at night, on abdomen apply mud pack, enema, on the anus keep mud ball. In case the inflammation has increased or there is bleeding then mud pack should be cooled in ice before application. The moles be given hot fomentation and then mud pack be applied, in a few days the moles will get dried and disappear. In the morning have hip bath and evening have Sitz bath and apply moolbandh necessarily.

Nadishodhan, kapalbhati pranayama, ashwni mudra, supt pavanmuktasana, bhujangasana, shalbhasana, suptvajrasana, dhanurasana, shavasana and after a while sarvangasana, matsyasana, halasana, chakrasana are useful.

For instant relief apply vaseline mixed with equal quantity of camphor.

Do Mooladhar Chakra and Swadhisthan Chakra power Promoting Exercise daily.

## Pimples (acne)

*Symptoms* – At youngest age small pimples develop on the face and leave black spots behind. Sometimes people squeeze

## Natural Treatment of Various Diseases

them. If pimples increase then even a beautiful face also appears ugly.

*Causes* – When the toxins do not get an outlet through urine and faeces, sweat, breath, then they find a new way to come out and appear through the skin of the face in the form of pimples. The main cause for this is constipation, lack of cleanliness of the skin, heavy and acidic diet (sweets, salt, maida, tea, roasted, fried, chillies, spices, tea and coffee, etc.) Masturbation, too much studies and laziness are also its causes which degenerate digestion.

*Treatment* – Cleaning up the stomach is the best treatment for pimples, for this for a week apply mud pack on the abdomen daily. Margosa leaves water or ordinary water can be used for enema and have hip bath.

- Live on liquid diet for one or two days (juices of fruits and vegetables, coconut water, etc.). For a week have only uncooked food (fruits, raw vegetable and sprouted cereals etc.).
- For 10 days drink wheat grass juice daily on an empty stomach.
- During the day juices of green leafy vegetables (mint, coriander, spinach, etc.)or chewing them is good. If available drink spinach and carrot mixed juice or tomato juice positively. Drink lemon water.
- Turmeric mixed with honey can be licked. Drink water from green bottle processed in sunrays. At night before sleeping keep wet pack on the face. Take air bath and sunbath.
- Exercise of the cheeks should be practised.
- Go for morning walk with deep prolonged breath.

### Local treatment

1. Hot and cold fomentation twice a day on the face where pimples have cropped up.
2. For a week margosa, mint, basil leaves should be ground and mixed with multani mud for application on the face.

This pack can be kept for 15-20 minutes before washing the face finally.
3. For a week give steam of water boiled with margosa leaves on the face, for 5-7 minutes daily.
4. For a few days basil leave juice and lemon juice be mixed together in equal quantity for application on the face. This removes black circles and spots.
5. Do not use soap.
6. For a week in a spoonful of curd two drops of honey should be mixed and applied on the face daily.

*Note* – After getting cured, keep all causes leading to pimples away, start eating normal balanced diet.

## Pleurisy

The pleural membrane which covers and protects both the lungs gets inflamed.

*Symptoms* – There is sharp and stabbing pain in any part of the chest. Most of the people feel cold. The chest becomes heavy and there is fever. Later in some patients the fluid comes out of the membrane and fills the chest.

*Causes* – Catching cold followed by congestion and swelling of the pleural membrane. This disease may be a complication of pneumonia or pneumonia may be a complication of pleurisy.

*Treatment* – Its only cure is fasting, only water and orange juice should be given, the fast can continue for a week.

After the acute symptoms have subsided, the patient may adopt a milk diet (soyabean milk or sesame milk).

During this period daily hot water enema should be administered, wet sheet pack, sponging of the body with luke warm water, hot chest compression daily twice or thrice.

Sun bath and dry friction is important. When the temperature gets normal and there is good appetite then one may conclude that the condition has improved and the problem is over.

## Prostate disorder

Prostate gland is a male gland. This is on the mouth of the urinary bladder and the upper part of the urinary track is surrounded by it on all sides.

It is reddish brown and measures about 3.5 cm in length. and 2.5 cm in width comparable to the shape and size of a large chestnut.

From this gland a sticky, white, thick secretion takes place, when the male gets excited and the sperm reaches the prostate then this secretion keep them alive and plays an important role in ejecting them out. When this gland gets enlarged then obstruction in the work of the urinary bladder and urinary track occurs.

*Symptoms* – The flow of urine gets thin, urination is obstructed and is in small quantity. At night a number of times one gets up for passing urine. At one time the whole quantity of urine is not ejected out. The flow of urine is obstructed and some time only drops fall out. The patient loses control over urine and stool. By putting a finger in the anus enlarged prostate can be examined, due to enlargement of the prostate gland headache, irritability, restlessness, fatigue, laziness and weakness occur.

*Causes* – Wrong way of living and diet, mental tension, worries, anger, use of intoxicating products, constipation and suppressing the pressure of urine or stool, etc.

Sitting at one place continuously, affects the pelvic region which can lead to inflammation of the prostate.

*Treatment* – Remove the above stated causes. Fast on juices for a day or two and then for eight to ten days take uncooked food containing fruits and vegetables. Drink sufficient water. Lemon water, coriander water, raw coconut water is specially good, juices of cucumber, water melon, cabbage, white pumpkin, carrot and pineapple, etc. are also good.

Heavy and exciting food stuff like ghee, sweets, fried stuff should not be taken. Do not permit constipation.

Take soup of *kulthi* and spinach in equal quantity. Two figs soaked overnight should be eaten and the water thereof drunk.

On the abdomen mud pack should be applied, enema given and Ganesh Kriya done. Hot and cold hip bath or hot and cold fomentation between anus and scrotum.

After food one must urinate.

Take hot foot bath before sleeping. Compress on all sides of abdomen and carry it above the genitals towards back, use it at the time of sleeping.

If there is difficulty in ejecting urine then drink water from sky blue bottle processed in the sun rays.

Soak a yellow harad in water and when it swells up chew it up after taking out the seed and drink that water. Small harad should be kept in the mouth and sucked.

Siddhasana, sarvangasana and vajrasana should be done.

Nadishodhan, kapal bhati, bhastrika pranayama should be done.

Ashwini kriya or mool bandh and mahabandh are useful.

## Psoriasis

This disease does not cure soon. It is not infectious. It can not damage any part of the body. It only destroys beauty. If it did not have devastating proportions and itching, it could be lived with easily.

*Symptoms* – Red or brown perforations appear under a transparent white cover. Sometimes they upsurge only as much as the tip of a pin. It begins on elbows, knees, calves, hips behind the ears and scalp. Sometimes the disease is for name's sake and sometimes it spreads throughout the body. Sometimes the patient has no idea of the disease. Many patients have psoriasis on their head which is mistaken for dandruff and ignored. But when it crosses the limit of hair and spreads ever the forehead then it causes worry. Sometimes it comes all of a sudden and subsides. Itching is not a symptom of psoriasis but when it itches it is extremely painful. Depression, worries, mental tension increase the complication of itching.

Psoriasis can cause many ailments like flowing nose, cold, tonsillitis, digestive disorders, etc. If it is five to seven years old then arthritis also takes place.

*Causes* – sensitiveness, nervous weakness, erratic endocrine glands, digestive disorder, inharmonious food, unbalanced food, uncontrolled life, failures in life, difficulties, worries and allergy, etc. In the family history the possibility of the disease could be there.

Skin cells normally have an age of 30 days. Old cells die and fall and new ones replace them, this process goes on continuously without our knowing. When this process gets distorted then some of the old cells continue to accumulate and new ones also come up. There is an ascent on the skin. Those cells which are without blood circulation are dead. Their cover like transparent layers keep on shedding.

*Treatment* – For seven days fast on juices (carrot, beetroot, cucumber, white pumpkin, cabbage, bottle gourd, grapes juice etc. and coconut water etc.). Then for a few weeks uncooked food (fruits, raw vegetables, sprouts etc.) should be taken. Thereafter normal balanced diet should be adopted including fruits, salads in more quantity.

Animal milk and its products, meat, egg, tea, coffee, liquor, cola, sugar, maida, roasted and fried products, tinned products, radish and onions, etc. should not be taken.

Water from green bottle processed in sunrays should be used for drinking, and oil from green should bottle be applied.

Milk of sesame, coconut or soya bean is good. Amla is useful. Vitamin E dominated, sprouted wheat be eaten. Bajra and jwar chapatti is good.

In the morning breathe in open air, early morning sun bathing, margosa leave water bath, weekly saline water tub bath is recommended. Daily enema specially during fasting. Walk bare foot on grass.

## Pyorrhoea

*Symptoms* – On pressing gums pus oozes out. While brushing bleeding takes place. If not treated then mouth gives foul smell. Bleeding with pus start. This bleeding impairs when reaching the stomach and affects the heart, brain, kidney, liver, lungs, etc. It may lead to loss of supporting bone of teeth and ultimately to tooth loss.

*Causes* – lack of dental hygiene, excess use of white flour and sugar, use of medicines, deficiency of vitamin B and C and other diseases.

*Treatment* – Keep fasting on juices for 2-3 days. Take uncooked food (fruits, vegetables, sprouts, etc.) for one week. Take plenty of food containing vitamin B and C, such as orange, amla, lemon, sprouts food. Eat cabbage by chewing. Have mud pack on abdomen, enema, hip bath, steam bath, sun bath daily for detoxification of the whole body.

Mix few drops of mustard oil in equal quantities of turmeric powder and salt and rub it on the gums with your fingers.

Massaging the gums with lemon juice also helps. Neem (*margosa*) stick is beneficial for brushing the teeth.

Chew ten neem (margosa) leaves daily. While urinating or evacuation of bowels, press the jaws tight. Gargle with saline lukewarm water. After brushing massage the gums with fingers.

## Rickets

Rickets is an disease of infancy and early childhood in which the bones are softened and deformed, caused due to deficiency and malnutrition common among poor children.

*Symptoms* – Restlessness, fretful and pale, toneless muscles, unnatural postures, excessive sweating of the head, loose motions, diarrhoea and anaemia. The bones get moulded easily. Due to softness of the ribs and vertebral column the chest gets deformed. It takes time for a baby to be able to get up, learn to get up, sit, stand and walk.

*Causes* – This is caused due to deficiency of vitamin D, which is essential for absorbing calcium, phosphorous. Malnutrition is another main cause.

*Treatment* – The child should get mother's feed for a year, then cow's milk or goat's milk diluted with water should be given. Breast feeding mother should get calcium and vitamin D dominated food. Sesame milk is very useful.

Bathing in the air and sunshine is necessary. Massage the spinal cord. Keep wet pack on the lower abdomen.

## Scurvy

*Symptoms* – Bleeding from the gums, black and blue spots on the body specially on the feet. Pain in walking, swelling on exterior organs and anaemia is also possible.

*Causes* – This is caused due to deficiency of vitamin C. It is also due to tension, because tension consumes vitamin C substantially.

*Treatment* – Food plays an important role in its treatment. Balanced diet containing fruits, green leafy vegetables, coconut powder, milk, butter milk in sufficient quantity is recommended. Vitamin C dominant foods like, lemon, amla, orange, pineapple, guava, tomato, mango, green vegetables and sprouted cereals, etc. should be consumed. Lemon and honey water can be taken twice a day. Juice of amla or amla powder with honey can be taken thrice a day.

## Sciatica

*Symptoms* – In the sciatica nerve from the lower portion of the back upto the foot there is unbearable pain. The patient cannot straighten his leg and cannot stand also. There is vertigo. Sometimes the pain is low, sometimes it is acute. Fever also comes up.

*Causes* – Accumulation of toxins around the sciatica nerve which press the nerve, disc problem, arthritis in the lower part of the vertebral column (backbone). For a long time one side posture while standing or sitting, unbalanced diet, keeping awake at night, working more than one's capacity, irregular way of life diet and intercourse, injury in the lower portion of the spine for any reason.

*Treatment* – Fast on hot water and lemon water, then juices (white pumpkin is most useful), uncooked food (fruits, salads, dates, sprouted cereals). Use jayaphal. Garlic piece can be swallowed with water. Fruit juices should be taken thrice a day and amla juice mixed with honey can be taken.

Mud pack, enema, hip bath, Sitz bath, leg pack, as per need hot and cold hip bath or hot and cold fomentation on lower part of spine, hot foot bath, sun bathing, oil massage, spinal bath, weekly wet sheet pack.

Sleep on a wooden slab or the floor. Take complete rest. Massage with oil from red bottle processed in sun rays and drink water from orange coloured bottle.

Grind basil leaves and mix water to drink. Haarsingaar leaves can be boiled and the water should be taken on an empty stomach daily.

Yogasana, garudasana, vajrasana, gomukhasana, yognidra, nadishodhan pranayama, supt pavanmuktasana, bhujangasana, shalbhasana, shavasana and uttanpadasana can be practised. In the morning and evening clap for two minutes daily with both the feet.

## Sinusitis

*Symptoms* – It is an inflammation of the mucous membrane lining the paranasal sinuses in the nose, which makes the voice hoarse, difference in taste and smell, causes headache, frequent cold, sometimes even fever, growth of flash inside the nose, secretion flowing through the nose, blockage in breathing and pain in the sinus portion.

*Causes* – Improper diet and way of living, constipation, eating, consuming cold products, mental, physical and emotional tension, allergy to certain food products and dust, imbalance of endocrine glands, disease of the liver, animal milk and milk products in excessive use. Any disease of the nose, mouth, gums and throat can cause sinusitis. Sinusitis causes ailments of the eyes, ears, meningitis, boils in the lungs, inflammation in the breathing passage, swelling in the vocal cords, etc.

*Treatment* — Fast on lemon water and juices for few days. Cucumber juice, carrot juice, beetroot juice are very useful. Apart from banana, try to have more of uncooked food. Then have normal diet. Heavy, fatty, roasted, fried food, chillies spices should be kept away. Foods with vitamin A and C domination can be consumed. Eat onion and garlic. Take salads. Instead of animal milk take sesame or coconut milk. White sugar and salt are the greatest enemies.

Apply mud pack on abdomen, enema, jalneti, sutra neti, hot foot bath, hot and cold fomentation of the nose, daily take steam on the face twice, dry friction can be done. Sleep as much as required, rest and fresh air is necessary.

Four drops of almond oil or mustard oil can be put in the nose. Anulom-vilom, suryabhedi, pranayama, viparitkarni, bhujangasana, yogmudra, shavasana are good.

Put pressure on the tips of the fingers and thumb.

## Skin diseases

*Symptoms* — Skin diseases are of many types like dermititis, boils, ringworms, scabies, etc. Their causes and treatment are almost similar.

*Causes* — Problem in the liver and digestive process, chronic constipation, accumulation of toxins due to erroneous diet and living, wearing synthetic or wet clothes, mental tension or worries, lack of hygiene and infections, etc.

*Treatment* — Depending on the condition fast from one to seven days on juices (spinach, cucumber, carrot, cabbage white pumpkin juice, etc. and coconut water). Then as per requirement take uncooked food (fruits, salads, sprouted) for a few days. Sugar refined products, tea, coffee should not be taken. Bitter gourd (karela) juice with lemon juice can be taken. Soak fenugreek seeds in water for 12 hours and drink its water daily in the morning and evening. Daily eat basil leaves and figs.

On an empty stomach drink neem (*margosa*) leaves water. Margosa leaves can be boiled in water and one should bathe in that water and administer enema with it.

Do kunjal and shankhprakshalana. Paschimottanasana, sarvangasana, matsyasana, suryanamaskar and yogmudra can be practised. Jalandhar and uddiyan bandh, nadishodhan, bhastrika, sheetali, kapalbhati pranayama be done. Coconut oil with camphor mixed in it be massaged over ring worms and scabies. Mint juice can be applied on it. Hot and cold fomentation can be done and wet mud pack applied.

Water from green bottle processed in sunrays should be drunk and oil processed in green bottle can be applied mixed with lemon juice. Coconut oil with lemon juice should be applied over the diseased portion.

Over moles raw potato slices or raw onion can be rubbed for two weeks a number of times daily. Do not take salt at all. On a boil heated up betel leave with castor oil can be tied overnight. The boil will burst and the pus will flow out. Apply turmeric on the boil. Washing a boil with saline water reduces pain. Application of ice over a boil reduces pain and swelling, hot fomentation and application of mud thereafter provides relief in pain.

## Stammering and lisping

*Symptoms* — While talking unable to pronounce certain letters is lisping. Sometimes there is little stammering which disappears gradually.

*Causes* — Defect in the control of the muscles and the nerves involved in speech causes obstruction in pronunciation repeatedly. The speed coordination of the tongue and lips required for proper speech is with difficulty and simultaneously creates sound in vocal cords which leads to lisping. This difficulty occurs individually in a few words only.

*Treatment* – Chewing amla cures stammering and lisping among children.

Ten almonds, ten peppers can be ground together mixed with misri for licking daily which cures stammering and lisping.

Amla powder can be mixed with ghee made of cows milk and licked daily for curing lisping and stammering. A dry date boiled in milk can be eaten and that milk also can be drunk. Do not take any thing for two hours thereafter. This will clear the sound. Honey and pepper be mixed for licking daily.

Roasted alum be kept in the mouth daily before sleeping. After a month lisping and stammering will get cured.

After food keep cardamom and clove in the mouth. Clean the tongue daily. Do not permit constipation to take place. From the mind the element of fear should be taken out and mind should be strengthened. Drink water kept in a shankh overnight, it brings success. Eat seasonal fruits as much as possible.

Enema, kunjal, sutraneti and jalneti be practised. Simhasana, dhanurasana, halasana, mandookasana, matsyasana, suptvajrasana, janushirshasana he practised and khechri mudra be performed.

## Sterility

*Symptoms* – Inability to conceive is sterility.

*Causes* – Reproductive organs are defective by birth or due to some accident, the body has some other diseases, irregular menstruation, worries, tensions and fear.

*Treatment* – Two things are very important. First the nerves of the vagina should be healthy, for that right diet and proper rest without tension is essential. Secondly, the vaginal secretion should be alkaline, therefore the diet of the woman should be alkaline so ample quantity of uncooked food and soaked dry fruits should be taken.

Fasting for detoxification is necessary, therefore, fasting for one or two days at regular intervals is recommended. Instead of milk take more curd. In the morning take one spoonful of honey with lemon juice in lukewarm water.

Salt, chillies, spices deep fried and fried products, sugar, tea, coffee, maida, etc. should not be taken. Do not permit constipation to take place.

Food with predominance of vitamin C and E should be consumed. Thus lemon, orange, amla, sprouted wheat, etc. are necessary. In winters daily chew 5-6 leaves of garlic and drink milk over it.

Soup of jamun leaves should be taken with honey. The roots of Banyan tree can be dried in shade and ground into a powder. After the menstruation is over it should be taken for three days continuously at night with milk. Repeat this process till conception takes place.

During menstruation chew basil seeds. Six grams of aniseed (saunf) powder should be consumed with ghee for three months. It enables the woman to conceive.

Mud pack on the lower abdomen, hip bath wet girdle pack and hot water enema should be taken.

Alum in a cotton pack soaked in water be kept in the vagina at night before sleeping. In the morning the cotton will have a milky layer. Till this milky layer does not stop appearing repeat the process. When it stops it may be understood that sterility is over.

Maintain a gap of at least six months in intercourse, it will provide rest to the reproductive organs.

Sarvangasana, matsyasana, ardhmatsyendrasana, paschimottanasana, salbhasana are recommended.

Do Mooladhar Chakra and Swadhisthan Chakra Power Promoting Exercise daily.

## Checking reproductive capacity

Take two pots with wheat or gram sown in the mud in them. In one of them the woman should urinate and in the other the male should urinate. After three to four days the seeds will sprout. The pot in which the seeds do not sprout means the person does not have reproductive capacity and the pot in which seeds sprout, the person urinated in has reproductive capacity.

## Stone

Actually stone is accumulation of particles of toxins. It can be formed at different places in the body. It can be small, big, and of many different shapes.

*Stone of Gall Bladder* – This is more common among women as compared to men.

*Symptoms* – In the initial stages the symptoms of reluctance and indigestion occur. Heaviness after meals, acute pain in the gall bladder is the main symptom of this disease. Along with it generally there is trembling, fever, uneasiness, nausea and vomiting.

*Causes* – Overeating, excess of fat in the food, medication, excessive spices, sleeplessness, alcoholism, constipation, lack of hard work, meat and egg consumption, and menstrual disorders.

## Stone of the kidney and urinary tract

*Symptoms* – In the frontal abdomen suddenly a very severe pain occurs, sometimes there is nausea and also vomiting. Difficulty is experienced in urination, due to pain sometimes fever occurs. There is trembling and weakness. Sometimes there could be blood in urine. Because of obstruction in the urinary tract the flow of urine splits. Sometimes the stone remains in the urinary organs for a considerable time and does not create any problem.

*Causes* – Suppressing the urge to defecate or urinate, drinking water, excessive salt, chillies, spices, pickle, sugar, maida products, roasted, fried products, too much medication, tobacco, gutka, deficiency of vitamin A, B and C, arthritis, too much physical and mental strain and worries, etc.

*Treatment of Stones* – As long as it is acute, drink hot lemon water and fast. Thereafter from three to seven days live on white pumpkin juice, banana stem juice mixed in coconut water, cabbage juice, water melon juice, orange juice and bottle gourd juice, etc. For six weeks try to be on fruits. Grapes, apple, pear, pineapple, amla etc. be used.

Ripe jamun, methi, bathua, chaulai, coriander and mint leaves are very useful. Spinach juice mixed with honey be consumed. Its 20 gram juice be taken three to four times a day. Soup of green vegetables be taken.

Protein dominated food stuff and fat containing products like milk, cream, cheese, ghee etc. should not be taken. Non-vegetarian food is prohibited.

Five grams of papaya root, well washed and ground with water and strained in a thin cloth should be taken for three weeks on an empty stomach, the stone in the gall bladder will dissolve and flow out.

For all types of stones 50 grams of kulthi pulse should be washed and soaked in water in the evening and its water can be drunk in the morning after churning it. Eat figs with basil leaves. Daily eat 2-4 leaves of khatumba.

For six months take basil leaves' juice with honey. Its regular intake prohibits formation of stone in the future. Spinach and tomato are held responsible for stone formation but if they are consumed in raw form, stone is never formed.

Wet mud pack on the abdomen, enema, hot and cold fomentation on the abdomen, hip bath, steam bath, wet sheet pack, hot foot bath, Sitz bath, dry friction, massage of the spinal cord is very useful. Drink water from white bottle processed in sunrays which will provide vitamin D to the body and absorb calcium.

Yogmudrasana, halasana, dhanurasana bhujangasana, shalbhasana, paschimottanasana, sarvangasana and pranayama are very important.

For immediate treatment as long as pain is not subsided sit in hot water in the tub. When the water gets cool replenish it with hot water.

If it is not possible to sit in hot water in a tub then take a towel wet in hot water and keep it on the abdomen and keep changing it on short intervals.

## Thalassemia

In thalassemia the body cannot make enough haemoglobin leading to sever anaemia. Approximate every month repeated blood transfusion is required otherwise death occurs.

*Symptoms* – Paleness, retarded growth, enlargement of liver spleen and heart, very less percentage of haemoglobin, body and mind becomes weak. These are called thalassaemia major patient.

Other patients are called thalassemia trait minor or carrier. They carry one defective (thalassemia) gene but are not affected by it and live normal and healthy life like others. They do not know that they are carriers unless they have a special blood test (HbA2/Hb electrophoresis).

*Causes* – It is a hereditary disease. Since if both husband and wife are thalassemia trait (minor) then in each pregnancy there is a 25% chances of having a Thalassemia major (diseased) child, 50% chances of having a Thalassemia trait child (healthy and normal but carrier like parents) and 25% chance of having a normal child (not even a carrier).

If out of both one partner is Thalassemia trait then child will not be thalassemia major. There are 50% chances that child will be Thalassemia trait and 50% chances child will be normal.

*Treatment* – Durability of the Red Blood Corpuscles (RBC) of Thalassemia patients is about 20 to 25 days whereas the longevity of the RBC of the normal healthy person is about 120 days. With repeated safe blood transfusion every 2-4 weeks one can live a near normal life.

Other treatment is bone marrow transplantation. Enormous cost, high risk and lack of matched donor restrict its viability.

Iron can not be adequately assimilated in the body of the Thalassemia. Hence such excess of iron needs to washed out from the body.

So food must be completely uncooked (fruits, vegetables, sprouts, etc.) Eat the blood building ripe fruit of banyan tree. Fruits with plenty of vitamin-C (lemon, orange, grapes, guava, pine apple, amla, etc.) help in absorption of iron. Drinking fresh cow's urine or self urine is also found very helpful. Scientific massage and sunbath are very helpful.

Daily wheat grass juice must be consumed. Patient must walk barefoot upon the earth or grass.

Sun processed water in orange or yellow bottle will be tonic to them. Mud pack on abdomen, enema, Sitz bath, wet sheet pack, etc. are very necessary. Daily clapping is very useful.

Do cheeks power promoting exercise and dhanurasana, chakrasana, urdhvasarvangasana, sarpasana, matsyasana, halasana, padmasana, yog mudrasana. Do laughing and meditation. Avoid meat, eggs, spices, salt, sugar, milk.

## Thinness

*Symptoms* — If the weight is less than normal as per the age then it is thinness. Such people get tired very fast and their resistance power is low. Such people are prone to get tuberculosis, breathing trouble, pneumonia, heart trouble, kidney ailments, typhoid and cancer. Pregnant women have the problem of malnutrition

*Causes* — Digestive disorders and improper absorption of food, malnutrition, mental and emotional stress, worries, hormonal imbalance, defective metabolism, excessive or very little exercise, tape worms etc. in the intestines, chronic loose motions or constipation, diabetes, tuberculosis, sleeplessness, liver ailments and other ailments.

*Treatment* – Eating excessively to increase weight is useless as this can increase thinness. First of all, digestion is to be set right. For this fast for few days as per need, then come to natural food (fruits, salads, sprouted pulses, etc.) including milk, banana, soaked dates, ripe mango, raisins, etc. in ample quantity. Thereafter eat balanced food including fruits, salads in ample quantity, but do not eat more than the appetite.

Daily take 100 gms of green leaves (spinach, cabbage, bathua, coriander, mint, radish leaves etc.) necessarily. Juice of doob grass, and cocounut water be consumed. Use honey.

Regularly 50 gms spinach juice and 100 gms carrot juice and 50 gms. of beet root juice be mixed to drink for removing weakness.

Enema, hip bath, sufficient exercise daily, yogmudrasana, sarvangasana, halasana, matsyasana, pranayama and mahabandh are useful.

Practice meditation, it removes tension and inner strength increases.

## Throat diseases

*Symptoms* – Obstruction in the throat, heaviness, difficulty in breathing, fever, headache, fatigue, hoarseness.

*Causes* – Polluted air and water, eating sour stale and cold products, complication in the thyroid and parathyroid glands, excessive talking, irritating products, chillies, spices drinking water immediately after oily food consumption.

*Treatment* – As per need fast for one or two days on juices. Take pineapple, papaya, apple, figs, mulberry (*shehtoot*), fenugreek and garlic, etc.

Grapes improve the quality of sound.

In case of throat scraping lick basil leaves' juice slowly and ginger juice mixed with honey.

If the voice is hoarse and there is swelling in the throat then fresh lemon juice mixed with water can be used for gargles. In throat diseases hot mud pack can be tied around the neck and have a fast and do enema.

If there is pain in swallowing then gargle with water from blue bottle processed in sunrays. Hot and cold fomentation of the throat can be done.

If the throat aches on talking too much then lick basil juice mixed in honey. If the throat gets hoarse due to delivering a speech then boil dry figs and gargle with this water.

Take triphala powder and drink milk over it.

Massage the mid point of thumb and index finger. Simhasana and suryanamaskar are useful.

## Thyroid diseases

Thyroid is an endocrine gland which controls the metabolic activities of the body.

They affect most thyroid ailments are most common among women. During puberty, pregnancy, menopause or physical tension.

The following are thyroid ailments

1. **Goitre** — One or more nodules of thyroid get swollen up. This inflammation appears on the throat. Sometimes this swelling may not appear on the throat but can be felt on the skin.

   *Symptoms* – Concentration power weakens, depression, feels like weeping, petulency, loss of mental balance and loss of weight.

   Gradually obstruction is created in the internal organs which over a period of time leads to toxicity in the body.

2. **Hyper Thyroidism** — Thyroid gland produces more hormones.

   *Symptoms* – Loss of weight, restlessness, weakness inability to bear heat, excessive sweating, trembling of fingers, palpitation of heart, urination takes places a number of times, fatigue, memory becomes weak, high blood pressure, excessive appetite, complications in menstruation, falling of hair, etc.

3. **Hypothyroidism** — Thyroid gland produces less hormones.

*Symptoms* — Increase in weight, inability to bear cold, constipation, dryness of hair, aching waist, joints get stiff, pulse rate goes down, swelling on the face, etc.

Blood test for thyroid diseases — Both the hormones tri-iodothyronine and tetra-iodohyronine are produced by thyroid gland, their quantity in the blood decides whether the hormones are excessive along with other symptoms, then thyroid is enlarged and the patient has hyper thyroidism. If with other symptoms the quantity of hormones is less then thyroid gland is contracted and it is hypothyroidism.

*Causes of thyroid diseases* — Deficiency of iodine in food. It is seen among those people who eat only cooked food, and do not eat natural food. Natural food provides necessary iodine content which gets destroyed when cooked. Mental and emotional tension, hereditary, erroneous diet and way of living.

*Treatment of thyroid deseases* — For first five days only juices (coconut water, cabbage, carrot, beetroot, pineapple, orange, apple, grapes juice, etc.) should be taken. Thereafter for three days fruits and sesame (til) milk be consumed, then adopt normal diet which should include green leafy vegetables, fruits, salads, sprouted etc. in ample quantity.

At least for a year, half of the food should consist of fruits, salads and sprouted. Lotus seeds, makhana, water chestnut (Singhara) are useful.

Maida, sugar, roasted and fried products, tea, coffee, liquor, tinned product etc. are very harmful and should not be consumed at all.

In a cup full of spinach juice one spoon of honey be added and ¼th spoon of cumin seed (jeera) powder be mixed and taken every night before sleeping.

In a glass of water soak two spoons of dry coriander and in the morning mash it and boil, till the quantity is reduced to one fourth, and drink daily on an empty stomach. Daily gargle with saline water.

Mud pack, enema, hip bath etc. will detoxify the body. On the throat apply wet sheet pack and mud pack.

Do not permit to get tired. Relax completely and sleep as much as is necessary. Remain away from physical emotional and mental tension.

To keep the endocrine glands healthy yogasana and pranayama are very important. Shavasana, yognidra, suptpavanmuktasana, matsyasana, suptavjrasana and neck exercises must be done.

Do ujjayi and bhramari pranayama and jalandhar bandh be practised.

## Tonsillitis

Tonsils are two small lymphoid organs one on each side of the throat. They protect the throat against germs and also work like a barometer indicating infection elsewhere in the body by becoming sore and swollen.

*Symptoms* – the tonsils are seen to be inflamed and red. Other symptoms are sore throat, fever, headache. The tongue gets a white covering. The breath smells foul. When the disease starts the body feels very cold and then fever occurs. The body aches and throat pains.

*Causes* – This is not a disease of the throat, but a sign of stomach ailment. Indigestion, accumulation of waste in the intestines, pressure of undigestable food on the stomach, blood impurities, exposure to cold and eating ice cold products.

*Treatment* – Getting tonsils operated leads to loss of memory, impotency, epilepsy fits, obesity, women's hips expand and menstrual disorder. It should be treated with naturopathy alone.

Keep the patient on fruits and vegetables if the child is being breastfed, the mother should be kept on fruits and vegetables. For one day it is preferable to remain on juices. The mother should apply lemon juice with her fingers on the tonsils and if the child is grown up then he should take gargles with lemon juice water.

Carrot, beetroot, cucumber juice, lemon, orange, pineapple, radish and spinach juice are beneficial. Eat black raisins and figs. Honey and ginger juice mixed together should be consumed .

Milk, curd, sweets, roasted and fried products chillies spices should not be taken.

Drink water by sipping it gradually. Do saline and turmeric water gargle.

Gargle with coriander juice or with water of boiled margosa leaves. Gargle with the soup of amaltas. Clove and basil leaves soup be taken and its steam can be given to the throat.Triphala powder be taken with hot water at night.

Drink water four times a day from sky blue bottle processed in sunrays. Hot and cold fomentation of the throat helps a lot. Tie a wet pack on the throat at night. Massage the points between toe and fingers of the feet and thumb and fingers of the hand for two minutes each. Hot foot bath, wet sheet pack, hip bath, steam bath are good.

For cleaning up of the stomach take mud pack on the abdomen and enema.

## Tuberculosis

This can happen in lungs, bones, intestines or glands, etc or any other part of the body.This is an infectious disease.

*Symptoms* – Cough, fever, fatigue, reduction of weight gradually, loss of appetite and blood with cough.

*Causes* – Resistance power gets low in the body and toxins get increase. The main reason behind it is working more than one's capacity, suppressing the urge to urinate or defecate, excessive loss of semen, staying at a wet place, lack of sunlight, working environment full of dust particles and infections in the air, lack of light and sunshine, deficiencies in food stuff.

Due to these 60 mycobacterium tuberculosis.

*Treatment* – Coconut water and white pumpkin juice.

Soup of fresh spinach leaves and two spoonful of fenugreek seeds mixed with honey should be eaten twice or thrice a day. This loosens the cough sticking inside. Saltless fruits, salads and sprouted food can be taken.

Dates, grapes, pomegranate, guava, green vegetable soup, almonds, black raisins, melon seeds, sesame milk, lemon water, garlic, onions are very useful. Amla juice with honey is recommended. Basil leaves and neem leaves must be consumed. Keep clove in the mouth.

Keep the patient in open air. The shade of margosa or peepal tree is specially beneficial. Take long deep breath.

Margosa water enema, hip bath, kunjal, chest pack, jalneti should be taken. Try to sit in the sun also for sometime. Keep away from mental tensions.

Anulom vilom pranayama, gomukhasana, matsyasana, uttanmandookasana, katichakrasana, tadasana, naukasana, makarasana, dhanurasana, etc. can be practised.

## Ulcer

*Symptoms* – Sour belching, sometimes bitter taste in the mouth, burning sensation in the chest and throat, stomachache, constipation, sometimes bleeding with faeces, irritability, sleeplessness, mental weakness, pain and vomiting sensation simultaneously and sometimes bleeding along with vomits. After taking meals the burning sensation lessons or wears off.

*Causes* – Excessive use of salt, chillies, spices, stale roasted and fried food, tea, coffee and sugar in excessive use, maida products, excessively oily products, smoking, liquor and other intoxicating products. Mental tension, anger, fear, keeping awake at night, laziness, chronic constipation, overeating, eating food that is too hot or too cold.

*Treatment* – Remove the above stated causes. Cabbage salad and its juice cures the ulcer completely. Firstly be on white pumpkin juice, beetroot juice, cucumber juice, spinach juice, amla juice with honey. Then take uncooked food (fruits like papaya, cheekoo, custard apple (*shareefa*), mango, dates, ripe banana, melon, etc and fresh raw vegetables). Do not eat very sour fruits. *Khubani* must be taken. Eat at regular intervals after a gap of two hours in small quantities and then go back to normal diet gradually. Cold coconut milk should be taken. Drink cold water. Fenugreek leaves soup is good. Apply mud pack on abdomen, enema, hip bath, kunjal, wet pack on the abdomen, once a week wet sheet pack. Daily walk, physical and mental rest.

Paschimottanasana, sarvangasana, halasana, bhoonmanasana, janushirshasana, vajrasana, mandookasana, padhastasana, shavasana etc.

Local treatment of tongue and mouth ulcer – Mouthwash with coriander juice or alum powder mixed with water.

Hot and cold mouth wash for a minute or so alternately helps a lot.

Wash the mouth with lemon water.

Boil water with fresh tomato juice and when it cools down wash the mouth with it.

Cumin seeds and black cardamom should be ground in equal quantities and take a spoonful of it twice or thrice a day.

If the patient is a smoker, alcoholic, tobacco addict and panmasala user, then all these be given up.

Give up mental tension and relax.

## Urinary tract infection

*Symptoms* – Urinating repeatedly at night, while urination experiencing pain or burning sensation, urine containing pus or blood, fever, backache, vomiting, etc. Since it is an ailment of the urinary tract it also affects the vagina.

*Causes* – Suppressing the urge to urinate, enlargement of the prostate gland, stone, kidney ailment, injury, lack of hygiene of the reproductive organs, diabetes, drinking less water.

*Treatment* – For two to three days fast and take juice in ample quantity to remove infection.

Cucumber juice is very useful. Radish leaves juice, spinach juice and coconut water should be mixed in equal quantity for consumption.

Raw coconut water, barley water, green coriander water, sour milk water, butter milk should be consumed in maximum quantity and drink sufficient amount of water.

For a few days take uncooked food and do not take salt. Black sesame and one spoonful honey should be mixed together and consumed thrice a day. Basil leaves can be taken. Mud pack on lower abdomen, enema, bath before going to sleep, fifteen to twenty minutes of hip bath is recommended.

On the infected part wet pack can be easily kept in the underwear before going to sleep at night. Wear a dry underwear over it, and then the night suit.

Walk in open air with deep breathing.

After meals urination is necessary, this averts urinary complications.

## Uterus diseases

### Prolapse of the Uterus

*Symptoms* – Uneasiness in the abdomen and lower portion of the waist, a feeling of something pressurising downward, excessive menstrual bleeding, very little vaginal secretions urinating frequently and difficulty in intercourse.

*Causes* – Overeating, gas, chronic constipation, wearing tight clothes, weak internal muscles, lack of exercises, other diseases and negligences at the time of delivery.

## Inflammation of the Uterus

*Symptoms* – Slight fever, headache, loss of appetite, pain in the lower part of waist and abdomen and itching in the vagina.

*Causes* – Exposure to cold during menstruation, excessive intercourse, uterus getting displaced, too much medication, erroneous diet and way of living.

*Treatment* – Live only on juices for four to five days, then on uncooked and finally on balanced food.

Salt, chillies spices, roasted and fried products, sweets, etc. should be abstained from.

Mud pack on the abdomen, enema, hot and cold hip bath, should be done. Put salt in the tub and sit for fifteen to twenty minutes. Daily lie with feet lifted up about one foot above the bed. Complete rest and shavasana is recommended. Practise Ashwani Mudra.

Practise mooladhar chakra and swadhisthan chakra and power promoting exercises daily.

## Varicose veins

*Symptoms* – Veins carrying blood to the heart get thickened and can be seen protruding anywhere in the body but commonly they are seen in the legs. They cause pain in the legs, fatigue. There is heaviness, limbs swell up, at night there are cramps in the legs. The colour of the skin changes and skin disease occurs in the lower parts.

*Causes* – The veins carrying blood towards the heart have valves so that the blood flow is only in one direction. Constipation, defective food habits, lack of exercise, standing for a long time, tight clothes, obesity, pregnancy, etc. cause blockage in the flow of blood in these veins leading to enlargement of these veins and so their valves stop working. Consequently blood collects in these veins and gets accumulated, leading to swelling and other complications

This is more common among women.

*Treatment* — Coconut water, barley water, green coriander water, cucumber juice, carrot cabbage spinach juices, etc. should be taken while fasting. Green vegetable soup is good. Then for a few days consume fruits, salads, sprout in ample quantity. Vitamin C and E dominated food should be taken. Then take slightly boiled vegetables.

Salt, chillies-spices, roasted and fried, sweets, maida products should not be taken.

Hot water enema, hip bath, application of mud on the feet is recommended. Reduce weight if overweight. Walk in the water.

Stiffness, and pain be treated with hot and cold foot bath.

Twice in a week sit in saline water tub for 15-20 minutes. Standing in deep waters also helps. Sleep with feet lifted upward. Elastic girdle should not be worn for too long.

Yogmudrasana, viparitkarni, sarvangasana, shirshasana, suryanamaskar, suptpavanmuktasana, uttanpadasana should be done.

## Venereal diseases

Mainly there are two diseases, syphilis and gonorrhoea.
1. **Symptoms Syphilis** — In the first stage within a week of the infection a small boil appears on the top of the penis or at the opening of the vagina and pus formation takes place. In the second stage sex organs get inflamed. In the other parts of the body red patches occur on the skin, swelling, perforations and boils occur. In the third stage the skin, the joints, heart and nervous system get affected and the patient becomes blind and deaf.

    *Causes* — This is an infectious disease which is caused by indulging in sex or kissing a patient of this disease. Touching things used by such patient also causes this disease.

2. **Gonorrhoea Symptoms** — Itching in the urethra. Pain and burning sensation while urinating. Along with

urine excretion of white or pale substance or pus. Swelling of the testes.

Among women first there is pale secretion from the vagina, pain occurs while urinating and the muscles at the mouth of the vagina swell up, this inflammation reaches the uterus. If the woman is pregnant it can lead to an abortion or the foetus can also get infected.

First this disease remains restricted to the penis or vagina, later it affects other parts of the body.

*Causes* – Almost same as Syphilis.

*Note* – Syphilis has wounds on the outer side of the body and gonorrhoea has internal wounds.

**Treatment of venereal diseases** – The patient should stay away from copulation and keep his clothes, etc. away from others and should not feed his used food or water to others. First the patient's blood is to be purified and for taking out the infected waste products, fast is necessary which can be of seven to fourteen days duration. In this only juices should be taken and ample amount of water drunk. Watermelon, cucumber, carrot, beetroot, spinach, white pumpkin, green vegetables juice and coconut water is very useful. After that for somedays fruit diet then uncooked food (fruits, salads, sprouted pulses or daals, etc.) should be taken.

The juice of wheat grass is efficacious 25gms leaves of amaranth (*chaulai*) should be taken twice or thrice a day. Juice of amla with a little turmeric and honey should be taken. For clearing the bowels enema can be taken. Wash the wounds with boiled water of margosa. Apply mud pack daily on the swelling, ulcer and boils. Hot hip bath and wet sheet pack are recommended.

# Vomiting

*Symptoms* – The food does not go to the intestines from the stomach, but coming out from the mouth is vomiting.

*Causes* – Eating more than required or eating poisonous food leads to accumulation of toxins, the stomach does not accept any thing and throw the food through the mouth.

*Treatment* – Never suppress vomiting by any treatment, on the contrary it should be helped to come out easily. Drink water even though it is thrown off. Kunjal can be done. All the toxins will come out of the system along with water.

As long as there is vomiting drink ordinary water or lemon water and nothing else. When vomiting stops and the condition of the stomach is improved then begin with juices and then fruitarian diet and come back to normal food. Do not take heavy food stuff which is difficult to digest.

If even after evacuation of the bowels the urge to vomit is there, then for twenty minutes keep cold wet pack on the abdomen.

On the abdomen mud pack should be used and enema given for cleansing the body.

## Child diseases

A newly born child's health depends on the mother's way of life and diet. Only treating the child and leaving the ailing mother alone would keep the child unhealthy. A breast fed child should be treated for his ailment and also the mother along with him should be treated necessarily. The mother should be given only fruits, vegetables and milk and enema be given to clean the bowels. The mother should triphala, basil and margosa leaves to purify the blood.

**Throwing up milk** – Normally children throw up milk. The main reason for this is drinking more milk than required. The child should be given water or if possible a spoonful of orange juice should be mixed in it before feeding him.

**Teething problems** – Boil two spoonfulls of saunf in a cup of water and then strain the water and give it to the child one spoonful four times a day. It will not cause much trouble in teething and the child will not weep too much.

Apply fresh amla juice on the gums which makes the process of teething easy. 100 gms pineapple juice with a little lemon juice should be given daily. Basil leaves juice mixed with honey can be applied on the gums and given to the child to lick.

In case there is constipation then grapes juice be given. In case there is loose motion then pomegranate juice be given. If there is fever then water of cow's milk turned sour should be given. In case of vomiting pomegranate juice be given.

**Bronchopneumonia**—Pure milk, fruit juices, mud pack on the belly and enema given. If the ribs are contracting and causing commotion then apply mud pack after every three hours. Ghee and carom seed (*ajwain*) should be heated up and with that the chest massaged.

**Enlargement of the infant's liver**—If the mother would eat maida, ghee and sugar excessively then the breast fed child's liver will get enlarged. The mother should have milk, fruits and vegetables mostly and drink lemon water. Going for a walk and light exercises are good.

**Stomachache and mucus**—Coriander and dry ginger should be boiled and that concentrated water given to drink. Grind asafoetida (*heeng*) with water and apply it on the navel. On the abdomen hot and cold fomentation and mud pack should be applied. One gram *ajwain* powder mixed with lukewarm water should be given twice or thrice a day.

**Sucking Thumb**—The mother should take calcium dominated diet.

**Eating mud**—In the early stage of childhood children develop a habit of eating mud which causes complications in their stomach. If the stomach aches, give two cloves ground or boiled to the child.

**Vomiting**—Amla and black raisins be ground and strained, and honey should be mixed to aniseed. This should be given half to one spoonful thrice or four times a day.

Coriander, aniseed (*saunf*), cardamum, cumin and mint be taken in equal quantity and soaked in water. After a while be crushed and strained. This water should be given with lemon juice repeatedly during the day or roasted cardamom powder mixed with honey be given twice or thrice a day. In 5-10 ml. lemon juice mix a bit of salt and water be given twice or thrice a day. Lemon juice and pomegranate juice should be mixed and given or honey may be added to it.

Starch from boiled rice is also useful. The child should be given milk in proportion to his appetite. Excessive feeding makes the child vomit.

**Constipation**—Erroneous diet of the mother, giving thick milk to the child causes constipation.

Stop giving milk, give juice of fruits and vegetables. If the child can eat fruits then give pulp of fruits. Mud pack and enema should be administered. Harad powder with rock salt can be given thrice a day or three to four grams of isabgol powder be given with milk at night before sleeping.

**Loose Motions**—Aniseed powder mixed with bel powder cures green, yellow and red loose motions among children.

Five to ten grams of pomegranate peel powder mixed with honey be licked twice or thrice a day. The pulp of bel should be given twice or thrice a day or one fourth of jayaphal powder should be given with lukewarm water twice or thrice a day.

**Cough in Chest**—Mix one part betal leaves juice, one part ginger juice and two part honey and half spoon be given to the child.

**Blisters in the Mouth**—In love of the child the mother feeds milk excessively which is not digested well and gets fermented. When the complication gets acute then there are blisters. Thus it becomes necessary to clean the stomach. Harad should be ground in water or rose water for the child to drink. Keep mud pack and make the child drink water repeatedly. Juices of orange, sweet lemon can be given. Sour milk's can water be given with honey.

# Natural Treatment of Various Diseases

**Bed wetting**—Do not give sweets. Take out seeds of black raisin and instead put pepper there and feed two to three of them early in the morning. Dates, dry dates can also be fed. At night give one spoonful of honey. Mix one spoonful honey in one cup of water and give for four to five days. Grind black sesame and make powder of it and give this before drinking milk.

Give walnut and raisins. Rice, banana, milk and butter milk should be avoided. Mud pack on the lower abdomen, hot and cold fomentation on the spine for eight to ten minutes. Massage of the spine in sunshine is important. Water from green bottle processed in sunrays should be taken thrice or four times.

**Cold and cough**—One or two grams of fried turmeric powder should be taken with honey thrice or four times daily.

Black pepper, dried ginger and peepal should be taken in equal quantities (one or two grams of powder) and mixed with honey twice or thrice a day.

Garlic can be boiled in water and crushed and mixed with five to ten gram misri and given twice or thrice a day.

On the stomach hot and cold fomentation can be given daily at an interval of two to three hours and wet sheet pack be kept on the abdomen three or four times a day.

## Miscellaneous diseases

(1) **Cracking heels**—In lukewarm water put two spoonful of salt and keep both the heels in it for a short while. Then rub the soles with a cloth to dry, change the water and repeat this process. This will take out dirt from the soles and heels then apply mustard oil and wear cotton socks.

After bathing or while sleeping apply mustard oil on the navel and rub twenty to twenty five times.

Pour two drops of honey in a spoon of curd and apply on the cracking heels and wash after ten minutes.

(2) **Corns** — Put the feet in hot saline water twice a day. Tie raw potato on the corns for two to three days. For three to four days continuously tie banana peel on the corns.

Apply juice of unripe papaya thrice a day. Apply white juice of unripe fig.

(3) **Sunburn** — Apply juice of raw potato on affected skin. Mix turmeric powder in the milk and rub on the skin. Apply coconut water. Use cucumber or water melon juice.

Applying hot paste of wheat flour mixed with turmeric powder and mustard oil packed in the cloth on the effective part is very useful.

(4) **Stomachache** — Fast on lemon water. Rest completely. Then take coconut water, juices, vegetable soup. Hot water enema, hot and cold fomentation, mud pack on the abdomen and wet sheet pack.

For immediate treatment mix salt with ajwain and consume it with lukewarm water. If the stomachache is chronic then hip bath, steam bath, hot foot bath, etc. can be done.

(5) **Hiccups** — Drink one glass of water or one spoonful of honey.

Small cardamum be taken with basil leaves. Chew two to three cloves with water.

(6) **For increasing height** — Soyabean milk, sesame milk, green leafy vegetables, fruits, salads must be consumed more.

Do tadasana, supt pawanmuktasana, uddiyanbandh, nadi Shodhan pranayama.

(7) **Early ageing** — Boil ten grams of chaff of wheat in one cup of water and strain and add two almonds ground in it and mix milk and misri in it. Continuous intake of this drink averts ageing.

One bowl of gram and three spoons of fenugreek seeds should be soaked together, and strained. In that water mix lemon juice and honey and use this regularly.

Small harad can be kept in the mouth to suck. Take one spoon trifla with water at night daily.

To avoid tiredness and sadness of old age, music is a good source.

(8) **Louses in hair**—Amla powder can be strained and mixed with lemon juice and applied in the roots of the hair. Garlic juice can be mixed with lemon juice for application on the head.

Custard apple (Sharifa) seeds can be ground with water to make a paste. This should be applied on the head at night and washed in the morning. Be repeating it two three days louses will be gone. Take care that this does not get into the eyes.

(9) **Wart (Mole) on face**—Grind black pepper and alum in form of a paste and apply on the mole.

(10) **Nausea during journey**—Keep a clove in the mouth and suck.

(11) **To avert epidemic infections**—Drink basil and margosa leave's juice morning and evening.

## Nature cure in sudden accidents

**Getting burnt**—Immediately on getting burnt soak the affected portion in water. If it cannot be soaked then pour cold water continuously on the spot or keep cold wet pack till the burning sensation is not gone. This averts appearance of blisters.

**Getting cut with a sharp edge**—If any part of the body gets cut with a kinfe, sharp weapon or blade then on that portion tie cold water pack or pour water. Cold water stops bleeding immediately and also heals a cut wound rather fast.

**Venomous bite**—Wasp, honey bee, scorpion or in case of any other venomous bite the affected part of the body should be soaked in water. After a while pain and burning sensation will be okay. Water extracts the heat of the venom.

**Sprain** – On slipping down or falling into a ditch the heel of the foot gets twisted and the ligament of the joint gets ruptured which causes inflammation and pain. This condition is called sprain. Similarly the wrist joint some times gets sprained.

On the spot where it has sprained, a ice cold wet cushion should be kept and that spot bandaged. In winters use hot water. Eat vitamin C dominated food products.

# In Ayurveda causes, symptoms and Natural Treatment of Diseases

According to Ayurveda diseases are caused due to three defects –
1. Vata (Gas), 2. Pitta (Acid), 3. Kapha (Cough)

*Note* – There could be one defect, mixture of two which is most common and all the three defects could be there (Tridosh)

| | Vata (Gas) | Pitta (Acid) | Kapha (Cough) |
|---|---|---|---|
| **Causes** | Erroneous diet (maida, fine flour, besan, excessive intake of pulses, heavy food, non vegetarian food, use of ice etc.) laziness in life, lack of sunbath and exercises. Leading to weakness of digestion and constipation causing formation of filthy gas, which strikes where ever in the body it pains and this pain is the cause of gas defect. | The root cause of acidity is also erroneous diet, sugar, salt, chillies spices, intoxicating products, heavy foodstuff and only cooked food, etc. 80% of the food should be alkaline stuff (fruits, vegetables etc. uncooked food) and 20% acidic, cooked food, etc. But actually it is reverse which increases acidity and the defect of acidity crops up. | Ghee, oil, butter or fatty products require a lot of hard work and exercise to digest them. Due to lack of these the fats do not digest completely. When fat intake is more than the digestive capacity then the defect of cough appears. Eating curd or taking milk at night increases cough defects. |

| Symptoms | Vata (Gas) | Pitta (Acid) | Kapha (Cough) |
|---|---|---|---|
| 1. Body formation | Body is dry, cut with scratches and is thin, unable to bear cold, organs are hard. | Body delicate, fragile and unable to bear heat. | Body bulky, oily, beautiful and shapely. Discomfort in winter. |
| 2. Complexion | Mostly dark | Pale | Fair |
| 3. Skin | Dry, rough and cold. Lips and feet crack, veins protrude. | Skin Pale, soft, full of boils and moles. Palms, tongue, lips, ears, etc. are red. | Skin is oily and soft. |
| 4. Sweat | Little in quantity without any odour. | Excessive, hot and with foul odour. | Normal and cool. |
| 5. Hair | Dry, stiff, small and scanty. | Greying and falling of hair at an early age. | Heavy, black, curly and oily hair. |
| 6. Eyes | Dull and with darkness and sunk in hollows. | Red or pale | White or soft. |
| 7. Mouth | Dry mouth. | Throat feels dry. | Excessive cough in the mouth. |

|  | Vata (Gas) | Pitta (Acid) | Kapha (Cough) |
| --- | --- | --- | --- |
| 8. Appetite | Sometimes less appetite sometimes more some times digestion is all right, sometimes there is constipation. | Appetite is more and digestion is good. | Less appetite. After eating a little feels full. |
| 9. Thirst | Sometimes less, sometimes more. | Excessive. | Less |
| 10. Tongue | Dirty, rough or dry and cracked. | Red and a little black, blister on the tongue. | With a white and sticky covering, wet and white. |
| 11. The taste in the mouth | Tasteless or bad | Bitter or sometimes sour. | Sweet and sometimes saliva flows out. |
| 12. Voice | Cracking and heavy, excessive talking. | Clear/good orator. | Sweet to talk. |
| 13. Nails | Dry and rough. | Red nails. | Oily nails. |
| 14. Faeces | Little, hard, broken and full of froth. | More loose, pale, with burning sensation prone to loose motions. | Solid, oily and with mucus. |

|    | Vata (Gas) | Pitta (Acid) | Kapha (Cough) |
|---|---|---|---|
| 15. Urine | Slightly yellow. | Excessively yellow and blue and sometimes red. | White and with froth, thick and greasy. |
| 16. Walk | Fast | Ordinary | Slow |
| 17. Sleep | Sleep less, more yawning, while sleeping chattering of teeth. | Very little sleep. | Excessive sleep and laziness in the body. |
| 18. Dreams | Flying in the air. | Sees a fire, gold, electricity, stars, sun moon etc. bright things. | Seeing river, pond, lake and the sea. |
| 19. Pulse | Zigzag, fast and irregular. | Jumpy, agitated, and heavy. | Slow, weak and soft. |
| 20. Interests | Cold and cool things do not appeal. Desire to have hot things. Like sweet, sour and salty products. | Heat and hot things do not appeal. Cold things, ice, spicy, bitter and sweet products appeal. | Dislike for cold and incurs discomfort. Sunlight and air appeals. Hot food, oily, bitter, spicy products attract. |
| 21. Nature | Dry-rough, prone to anger instable intellect, fearful worried, in a hurry, | Irritable and hot tempered, prone to anger, easily getting angry and easily getting | Peaceful, courageous soft natured stable minded, tolerant of pain and fatigue |

|  | Vata (Gas) | Pitta (Acid) | Kapha (Cough) |
|---|---|---|---|
|  | indecisive, never takes work seriously, courageous, mobile, able to understand a subject fast and easily forgetful. | and is easily appeased. Takes logical decisions, helpful to friends, but with a few friends, good orator, strong will power, sharp memory power, dominating, inventor and courageous. | lazy, lover of comfort, romantic and emotional, subdued, content, likes discipline and kind hearted. |
| 22. Propensity of Ailments | Gas in the stomach, ache in the legs, joints pain, sciatica, paralysis, numbing of body parts, flutter, shivering, pulsate, tilting, trembling, strain in the nerves, convulsions, sudden pain in any part of the body, deafness and fever. | Burning sensation in the body, chest and stomach etc. Has sour belches, rashes on the skin (allergy), anaemia skin diseases (itching, boils rashes etc.) cancer, leprosy enlargement of liver and spleen, heart troubles, diabetes kidney ailments and weakness, etc. | Breathing ailments (cough, asthma etc.) cough coming out repeatedly, cold, running nose and tuberculosis, inflating of body and increase in obesity. |//
| **Nature Cure** 1. Food | Fibrous food (uncooked) fruits salads, leafy vegetables | When there is no appetite take only fruit juices and | Oily, heavy food stuff, fried products and iced products |

|  | Vata (Gas) | Pitta (Acid) | Kapha (Cough) |
|---|---|---|---|
|  | to be used more frequently black raisins, figs, berries ginger, basil, carrot, soyabean, aniseed, small cardamom, etc. Garlic and Butter can be used. | vegetable juices, when there is less appetite, only fruits and salads. Take uncooked food till health is regained. Carrot juice is specially beneficial. Sour, spicy, salty and sweets should not be eaten. Pomegranate, black raisins, figs, jamun, doob juice, water chestnut, aniseed be used. Garlic and black raisins can be consumed. | be given up, should not take milk or curd. Take milk of soyabean. Fresh amla juice be taken, if not available eat dry amla by sucking it in the mouth. Black raisins, figs, raw spinach and guava be taken Ginger, basil leaves, figs, soyabean carrots be used. Garlic+Honey be used. |
| 2. Fast | Fast on vegetable juice. | Vegetable and fruit juices should be taken separately while fasting. | Green vegetable soup should be taken while fasting. |
| 3. Sunrays Treatment | Green colour | Sky blue, purple and blue colour | Yellow, orange and red colour |

|   | Vata (Gas) | Pitta (Acid) | Kapha (Cough) |
|---|---|---|---|
| 4. Shat karma | Kunjal, dhauti shankhprakshalana. | Kunjal (prohibited in last stages) dhauti (dipped in milk) shankh prakshalana (prohibited in ulcer patients). | Kunjal, dhauti, jalneti, kapalbhati, shankh prakshalana (in the last stages of tuberculosis it is prohibited) |
| 5. Yogasana | Paschimottanasana, halasana, bhujangasana, dhanurasana, vajrasana, mayurasana, mandookasana, suptpavanmukt asana, koormasana, suptvajrasana, uttanmandookasana, uttankoormasana, janushirshasana, padhastasana, chakrasana. | Paschimottanasana, halasana janushirshasana. (Keeping feet on the thighs), ardhamatsyendr-asana, koormasana, vajrasana, mandookasana, padhastasana, garbhasana, uttanpadasana, sarvangasana. | Breathing exercises and gomukhasana. Matsyasana, uttanmandookasana, uttankoormasana, suptvajrasana, bhujangasana, dhanurasana, naukasana, katichakrasana, tadasana, chakrasana, shalbhasana, makarasana. |
| 6. Pranayama | Bhastrika | Shitali, shitkari ujjayi (without retention). | Suryabhedi, bhastrika (without retention). |
| 7. Mudra | Mahamudra, viparitkarni, uddiyanbandh. | Mahamudra (without retention). | Uddiyanbandh and mahamudra. |

# Ramanama and natural treatment

Rama, Allah and God are convertible terms. There is only one omnipotent and omnipresent God. He is named variously and we remember Him by the name which is most familiar to us.

Mere physical treatment of man's ailments is not enough. The patient's mind and soul requires to be treated also. When these will be healthy, the body will itself become free from diseases. To achieve this goal nothing is efficacious as Ramanama, or a devout faith in, and reliance on, the Great Physician. In the armoury of the naturopath, Ramanama is the most potent weapon. The spread of Ramanama and pure living are the best and cheapest preventives of disease.

Ramadhun recited by millions of mankind with true beat of time, is different in kind from and infinitely superior to the display of military strength.

If Ramanama is recited from the heart, it charms away every evil thought and evil thought gone, no corresponding action is possible. The outward helps are all useless if the mind is weak. The *Gita* truly says that mind makes the man and can also ruin him. The mind is everything and it can make a Heaven of Hell or a Hell of Heaven.

Ramanama cannot come from the heart unless one has cultivated the virtues of truth, honesty and purity with in and with out. To take Ramanama from the heart means deriving help from an incomparable power. This power is capable of removing all pain.

Most important of all, do not lose self confidence. When your passions threaten to get the better of you, go down on your knees and cry out to God for help. Ramanama helps infallibly. A person who is filled with the presence of God and has thus attained the state of dispassion, can surmount handicaps occurring in the way of long life. When a man comes to that complete living faith in the unseen power and has become free from passion, the body undergoes internal transformation. This does not come about by mere wish. It needs constant vigilance and practice.

Man should seek out and be content to confine the means of cure to the five elements of which the body is composed, i.e., earth, water, akash, sun and air. On course, Ramanama must be the invariable accompaniment. If inspite of this, death supervenes, we may not mind. On the contrary it should be welcomed. Science has not so far discovered any recipe for making the body immortal. Immortality is an attribute of the soul. That is certainly imperishable, but it is man's duty to try to express its purity. If we accept this reasoning it will automatically limit the means permissible under Nature Cure. And man is thereby saved from all the paraphernalia of big hospitals and eminent doctors, etc.

# Books by Dr. Brij Bhushan Goel

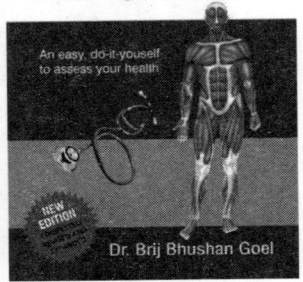

## Secrets of GOOD PARENTING
Everything you need to know about the challenges of parenting
Parenting techniques that help raise well-balanced children
Dr. Brij Bhushan Goel

## Secrets of GOOD LIVING
Simple tips to make your daily life joyful and productive
Your guide to Health and Success
Dr. Brij Bhushan Goel

## Secrets of NATUROPATHY & YOGA
A whole new approach to natural remedies and treatments
Good health and rejuvenation the natural way
Dr. Brij Bhushan Goel

## Secrets of DIAGNOSIS
How to listen to body signals to avoid being a patient
An easy, do-it-yourself to assess your health
Dr. Brij Bhushan Goel

## Secrets of NATURAL DIET
How to reap optimum health benefits through uncooked food
Discover the hidden qualities of a raw food diet
Dr. Brij Bhushan Goel

For catalogue write to:
**Sterling Publishers (P) Ltd.**
A-59, Okhla Industrial Area,
Phase-II, New Delhi-110020.
Tel: 26387070, 26386209;
Fax: 91-11-26383788
E-mail: mail@sterlingpublishers.com
www.sterlingpublishers.com